STUDY GUIDE

MACROECONOMICS
Explore & Apply

STUDY GUIDE

MACROECONOMICS
Explore & Apply

Ronald M. Ayers
Robert A. Collinge

Upper Saddle River, New Jersey 07458

Executive Editor: Rod Banister
Project Manager: Marie McHale
Manager, Print Production: Christy Mahon
Production Editor & Buyer: Wanda Rockwell

Copyright © 2004 by Pearson Education, Inc., Upper Saddle River, New Jersey, 07458.
Pearson Prentice Hall. All rights reserved. Printed in the United States of America. This publication is protected by Copyright and permission should be obtained from the publisher prior to any prohibited reproduction, storage in a retrieval system, or transmission in any form or by any means, electronic, mechanical, photocopying, recording, or likewise. For information regarding permission(s), write to: Rights and Permissions Department.

Pearson Prentice Hall™ is a trademark of Pearson Education, Inc.

10 9 8 7 6 5 4 3
ISBN 0-13-016423-2

TABLE OF CONTENTS

PREFACE i

PART 1: A JOURNEY THROUGH THE ECONOMY
1. The Economic Perspective 3
2. Production and Trade 31
3. Demand and Supply 61
4. The Power of Prices 95

PART 2: MONITORING THE MACROECONOMY
5. Measuring National Output 129
6. Unemployment 155
7. Inflation 177

PART 3: AGGREGATE SUPPLY AND AGGREGATE DEMAND
8. A Framework for Macroeconomic Analysis 205
9. Short-Run Instability 233
10. Aggregate Expenditures 265

PART 4: INCENTIVES FOR PRODUCTIVITY
11. Fiscal Policy in Action 301
12. Economic Growth 329

PART 5: MONEY IN THE MACROECONOMY
13. Money, Banking, and the Federal Reserve 359
14. Monetary Policy and Price Stability 387

PART 6: THE GLOBAL ECONOMY
15. Into the International Marketplace 415
16. Policy Toward Trade 443
17. Economic Development 473

Preface

Using the *Study Guide* for *Macroeconomics: Explore & Apply*

Congratulations on your purchase of the *Study Guide* for *Macroeconomics: Explore & Apply*. Each chapter in the *Study Guide* corresponds to a chapter in your textbook. To make the *Study Guide* as easy to use as possible, each chapter is laid out with the following arrangement:

1. **Chapter Review.** Detailed bullet points condense each chapter according to each major heading. Chapter reviews provide convenient summaries, but are not intended to substitute for a careful reading of the text.

2. **StudyChecks.** Up to 10 questions and problems per chapter are integrated throughout the Chapter Review. This material helps you get the most out of your reading. Some of the exercises require you to draw a graph or work out a numerical calculation.

3. **Fill in the Blanks.** By completing the sentences, you will be able to test your mastery of the chapter. Once the blanks have been filled in, this section of the study guide also provides a second, brief chapter review.

4. **True/False/Explain.** Twenty-five statements are presented per chapter, including five for the chapter's Explore & Apply section. To get the most out of this feature of the *Study Guide*, you should explain each false statement in the space provided.

5. **Multiple Choice.** Twenty-five multiple choice questions per chapter, including five for each Explore & Apply section, allow you to test and deepen your understanding of the chapter content.

6. **Grasping the Graphs.** Major graphs from the textbook are repeated without some of their descriptive labels. You are to fill in these or other applicable labeling in the space provided.

PREFACE

7. **Answers.** Answers are provided at the end of each chapter for all items in that chapter. We suggest that you first work through the material on your own, and then refer to the answers to check your work. If you do not understand the reason for an answer, you may wish to reread the relevant section of the chapter.

Do not hesitate to write in answers, make notes, and otherwise personalize *your Study Guide*. Getting actively involved in this way deepens and broadens learning. Although no study guide can guarantee you perfect understanding or a perfect score on an exam, working through these materials will enhance your grasp of economic principles and your ability to apply them.

Part 1

A Journey Through the Economy

Chapter 1

THE ECONOMIC PERSPECTIVE

CHAPTER REVIEW

- **Economics** studies the allocation of limited resources in response to unlimited wants.

1.1 Scarce Resources, Unlimited Wants

- Economics is about choice. We are forced to choose because of **scarcity**, which means that society does not have enough resources to produce all the goods and services we want to consume. Securing the most value from limited resources is the objective of economic choice.

- We commonly make choices at **the margin,** meaning incrementally—in small steps. Decision making at the margin is about the choice of a little more of this and a little less of that. It's about weighing and balancing the benefits and costs of alternatives.

- It is not a scarcity of money that is at the root of economics. Scarce resources lead to scarce goods, whether or not money is involved.

- Resource allocation refers to the uses to which resources are put. How resources are used depends partly upon *technology*, which refers to the techniques of production. When new technologies are created, among the results can be new ways of doing things, new product choices, and new uses for resources. When society makes choices about what will be produced it is also choosing its allocation of resources.

1.2 Surveying the Economic Landscape

- **Microeconomics** studies the individual parts of the economy. It looks at the choices of individuals in their roles as consumers and as workers. It also includes the choices of businesses—*firms*—which are the companies that produce goods and services as their outputs. Microeconomics also studies the industries within which firms operate, where an *industry* is composed of firms producing similar outputs.

- Microeconomics revolves around the interaction of consumers and producers in markets. Markets can take physical, electronic, or other forms. The common characteristic of all markets is that they make possible the voluntary exchange of resources, goods, and services. Market prices serve as the signals that guide the allocation of resources. Participants in the economy make choices based upon the *incentives* provided by the prices they face, meaning that these prices motivate their actions.

- **Macroeconomics** looks at the big picture. It concentrates on the analysis of economic *aggregates*, total values that describe the economy as a whole.

- The most important aggregate is *gross domestic product (GDP)*, which measures the market value of a country's aggregate output – the market value of the goods and services that a country produces in one year.

- Macroeconomics was first considered a separate field of study following the 1936 publication of *The General Theory of Employment, Interest, and Money* by British economist John Maynard Keynes [1883-1946].

1.3 Three Basic Questions: What, How, and for Whom

- Every economy must answer three basic economic questions:
    1. **What?** What goods and services will be produced and offered for sale and in what quantities?
    2. **How?** How will goods and services be produced? There are numerous production techniques available. Some methods of production use simple hand tools and much labor. Other production methods employ machines or computers in combination with labor.
    3. **For whom?** Who will consume the goods and services that are produced?

- When it comes to deciding what, how, and for whom, society must choose among three kinds of *economic systems*. Government might make the decisions. If so, the economy is termed **command and control.**

- Alternatively, government might stay out of the picture and allow economic choices to be made entirely in the marketplace. In that case, the economy is characterized by laissez-faire free markets, also termed laissez-faire capitalism. Laissez faire means "let it be." **Free markets** are characterized by freedom of choice in both production and consumption. Free markets are associated with capitalism, in which resources are privately owned.

- In practice, all countries have **mixed economies,** meaning that they choose a combination of markets and government. Different countries choose different combinations, with some leaning toward command and control, and others toward laissez faire. The exact mix is influenced by custom, tradition, religion, political ideology, and other factors.

- **There are two primary economic objectives to guide countries in choosing how much government to mix with free markets. The first objective is** *equity*, **which refers to fairness.**

- **The second economic objective is *efficiency*, sometimes called economic efficiency, which means that resources are used in ways that provide the most value**—that maximize the size of the economic pie. Efficiency means that no one can be made better off without someone else becoming worse off. Efficiency has both a technological and allocative component, defined as follows.

- **Technological efficiency** implies getting the greatest quantity of output for the resources that are being used. Conversely, for any given output, technological efficiency requires that a least-cost production technique must be chosen.

- **Allocative efficiency** involves choosing the most valuable mix of outputs to produce.

- **There is frequently a tradeoff between efficiency and equity**, meaning that more equity may result in less efficiency, referred to as more *inefficiency*. Likewise, less equity may result in greater efficiency.

StudyCheck 1

Define the three types of efficiency. Define equity. Why do goals of efficiency and equity often conflict?

- Government *central planning* sets production plans for most goods, which are produced by government-owned state enterprises. The result of command-and-control methods is often inefficiency, in which resources are squandered on the production of the wrong goods and services or wasted through use of the wrong production techniques.

- Centrally planned economies must also match production to consumption. If production fails to match their plans, then the government may be forced to ration goods and services. Government *rationing* occurs when consumers are permitted to buy only limited amounts of the goods they want.

- In the *Wealth of Nations*, published in 1776, Scottish philosopher-economist Adam Smith described how the **invisible hand** of the marketplace leads the economy to produce an efficient variety of goods and services, with efficient production methods as well. Guided by this invisible hand, producers acting in their own self-interests provide consumers with greater value than even the most well-intentioned of governments. An essential ingredient of the invisible hand is *competition*, which pits rival firms against one another in a contest to win the favor of consumers.

- All participants in a market economy, including consumers, businesses, investors, and workers, make choices on the basis of information conveyed by market prices. The collection of prices in product and resource markets is termed the *price system*. **Prices provide information about scarcity. It is the price system that allocates resources in a market economy to their highest-valued uses.**

- Guided by market prices, free-market choices lead the economy toward allocative efficiency. The preferences of consumers dictate answers to the "what" question. Competition provides the incentive for firms to choose least-cost production techniques, thus answering the "how" question. The "for whom" question is answered when people offer their labor and other resources in the marketplace—their incomes reflect the value of these resources to others.

> **StudyCheck 2**
> What is the primary advantage of capitalism over central planning? What is a possible disadvantage?

- Sorting out when government intervention is helpful and just how it might best be done is probably the most challenging task facing a nation and one that different countries answer in different ways. The result is that all economies combine government action and the marketplace. Some economies, such as that of Cuba, lie toward the command-and-control end of the spectrum. Others place greater reliance upon the marketplace, but still retain a role for government.

- The following table summarizes the key differences between laissez faire, command and control, and mixed economies

A Brief Comparison of Basic Economic Systems

	Laissez Faire	**Mixed Economy**	**Command and Control**
Key Characteristics	Limited role for government implies a small government with few powers. Low taxes. Private property.	Significant role for government. Taxes take a significant portion of national output. Most production of goods and services occurs in the private sector, but many regulations and some government production.	Government ownership of property and government directives control the production of goods and services.
Organizing Principle	Invisible hand guides free markets.	Mix of free markets and command and control. Emphasis upon markets relative to government varies from country to country.	Central planning of the economy by government.
Daily Life	Large degree of personal freedom. Most goods and services provided by the private sector, including such essentials as food and education. Market prices and market wages.	Moderate limits on personal freedom because of government regulation and taxation. A few essential goods, education for example, provided by government, while others, such as food, provided by the private sector. Market prices, with the possibility of some government price controls. Minimum wage laws and a small degree of other government control of wages.	Severe limits on personal freedom due to government control of the economy. Most goods provided by government. Prices set by government rather than the market. Government-set wages.
Countries Where Applied	None, although the U.S., Australia, and some other countries value laissez faire in principle.	All countries, including China, Russia, and other countries in transition away from command-and-control.	None entirely. Cuba and North Korea come the closest.

1.4 Economic Analysis

- The practice of economics involves analysis and problem solving. Sometimes these problems force us to think in terms of value judgments; sometimes they are factual. Care must be taken to avoid faulty reasoning that leads to false conclusions. An example is the *fallacy of composition*. This error in reasoning occurs when it is assumed that what is true at the micro level must also be true at the macro level. In other words, the fallacy of composition involves the observation of a truth about some individual component of the economy accompanied by the assumption that this truth will also apply to the economy at large.

- **Normative** statements have to do with behavioral norms, which are judgments as to what is good or bad. Examples of normative statements often include "ought" or "should" in them. They imply that something deserves to happen, such as: "The federal government ought to balance its budget."

- **Positive** statements have to do with fact. They may involve current, historical, or even future fact. Positive statements concern what is, was, or will be. The accuracy of positive statements can be checked against facts, although verifying predictions about the future will have to wait until that future arrives.

- Both positive and normative economics rely upon theory, which is organized thought aimed at answering specific questions. Theories can be tested by logic and, for positive economic theories, by data. Theories are first tested for their internal logic. Does a theory make sense? Sometimes the testing stops there. When feasible, theories are tested by collecting facts to see whether the facts are consistent with the theory. Testing of theories allows us to judge their value, so that the results become more than mere opinion or idle speculation.

- Economics, like other academic fields such as physics, psychology, and political science, makes extensive use of models. A **model** is a simplification of reality that emphasizes features essential to answering the questions we ask of it. A roadmap is a familiar model.

- Economic models remove unneeded detail, keeping only features that are essential. Keep in mind a guiding principle when producing a model. This principle is termed *Occam's razor*, formulated by the 14th century English philosopher William of Occam. Occam argued that reasoning is improved by focusing one's thinking on the most essential elements of an issue. He suggested using a figurative razor to cut away the unnecessary elements from analysis. Occam's razor increases the likelihood that modeling will lead to correct conclusions when the principle is applied correctly.

- To keep models simple, economists make *assumptions*, meaning that they act as though certain things are true without proving them to in fact be true. One common assumption is termed *ceteris paribus*, which is Latin for holding all else constant. The assumption of *ceteris paribus* allows us to look at one thing at a time.

2.5 From Mao to Now—Market Incentives Take Hold in China

- Like the former Soviet Union and other communist countries, the People's Republic of China was guided by the philosophy of the controversial 19th-century theorist, Karl Marx. Marx had a simple maxim: "From each according to his ability, to each according to his need." This idea was used to justify a strong central government that would allocate resources according to the communist idea of equity. That idea focused on equal outcomes rather than equal opportunities. Equality would be achieved by government ownership of resources and government central planning of the economy.

- Marxist governments expounded a philosophy of *egalitarianism,* in which everyone would get identical access to everything from soap to medical care. Unfortunately for an economy, egalitarianism provides little incentive for people to be productive.

- With central planners attempting to direct the what, how, and for whom of production, bad choices were made and resources were squandered. Everyone had a job, but productivity and purchasing power lagged badly behind the West. China, already the most populous nation on earth, faced a population explosion that promised to lead to mass starvation and unrest unless the economy could be made to perform. Thus, the turn to the market.

- The advantage of a market economy is that the marketplace rewards those producers best able to offer goods and services of value to others. The better a person is at providing things of value to others, the more will be that person's income. A problem arises that, through no fault of their own, people do not all have the same potential.

- Enter government, with its power to tax. Specifically, government redistributes wealth by imposing taxes that take wealth from those who can afford to give and that give to those in need. Taken to an extreme, this redistribution of wealth would eliminate incentives for individuals to behave more productively and lead to stagnation. Therefore, in taxing, government must weigh the trade-off between equity and incentives for efficiency. In the case of China this has meant the willingness to keep taxes relatively low and tolerate inequality in income and wealth.

APPENDIX: Working with Graphs and Data

- Economists draw graphs in order to clarify thoughts and show economic relationships in a way that can be more easily understood than with words alone. Graphs that present factual information are often drawn as line graphs, bar charts, and pie charts, all of which are seen in this book.

- Other graphs represent economic models and contain lines that are referred to as curves. The horizontal line is commonly called the X axis and the vertical line the Y axis, with the specific labels of the axes varying from graph to graph, depending on what the graph is modeling.

- Each axis of the graph of a model is labeled with the name of a variable, where a variable refers to the name of anything that can change. Within the axes, a relationship between two variables is shown by a curve—a line. Some graphs will have more than one curve in them. Other graphs will only show one curve.

- Curves that slope upward to the right show a *direct relationship,* also termed a *positive relationship,* between the variables. Curves that slope downward to the right show an *inverse relationship,* also termed a *negative relationship.*

- The slope of a curve is measured by the amount of change in the variable on the vertical axis divided by the amount of change in the variable on the horizontal axis. Slope is sometimes referred to as the "rise over the run." Straight lines are linear and always have a constant slope. This means that if you know the slope between any two points on the line, you know the slope everywhere on the line. The slope of a nonlinear curve changes from one point to the next on the curve.

StudyCheck 3

3. Graph the following data points. Show the slope of the resulting line.

Data Point	City	Coat Sales	Average January Temperature
F	Tropical City	100 units	50 degrees
G	North Town	200 units	40 degrees
H	Snowbound	300 units	30 degrees
I	Cold City	400 units	20 degrees
J	Arctica	500 units	10 degrees

StudyCheck 4

4. If Harry smokes a cigar, 20 people leave the room. If Harry smokes two cigars, 25 people leave the room. Graph this relationship, making sure to label the axes of your graph. Is the relationship positive or negative?

- Merely glancing at a curve is often revealing. When the curve slopes upward to the right, you know that it has a positive slope and thus shows a direct relationship between the variables on the axes. Likewise, when the curve slopes downward to the right, it has a negative slope that portrays an inverse relationship between the variables.

- The slope of a curve provides information at the margin.

- A change in the relationship between two variables is indicated by a shift in a curve. The student should also be aware that **there is a difference between a shift in a curve and a movement along a curve.**

- Some graphs show two different relationships between the variables on the axes. Each relationship will be illustrated by its own curve. An example of this possibility occurs when two curves intersect—cross each other. When two curves intersect, the intersection point will sometimes be of particular interest. **At the intersection point the values of each variable will be identical for both relationships—both curves.**

- *Time-series data* show the values of a variable as time passes. Economists utilize time-series data when changes in the value of a variable over time are the focus of interest. *Cross-sectional data* are fixed at a moment in time, but vary in some other way. In other words, cross-sectional data change because of some cause that is unrelated to the passage of time.

StudyCheck 5

Give an example of time-series data and an example of cross-sectional data.

- Economic research utilizes data in order to identify problems and issues, and to provide evidence about the causes of economic phenomena. Much of the numerical data economists use is collected by various levels of government. Important nongovernmental sources of data include industry trade associations, the United Nations, the Organization for European Community Development (OECD), the International Monetary Fund (IMF), Standard and Poor's, Moody's, and Robert Morris Associates.

FILL IN THE BLANKS

1. _____ studies the allocation of _____ resources in response to unlimited wants. We are forced to choose because of _____, which means that society does not have enough resources to produce all the goods and services we want to consume. We commonly make choices at the _____, meaning incrementally—in small steps.

2. Resource _____ refers to the uses to which resources are put. How resources are used depends partly upon _____, which refers to the techniques of production

14 CHAPTER 1

3. _____ studies the individual parts of the economy. It looks at the choices of individuals in their roles as consumers and as workers. It also includes the choices of businesses—_____—which are the companies that produce goods and services as their outputs. It also studies the industries within which firms operate, where an *industry* is composed of firms producing similar outputs.

4. _____ looks at the big picture. It concentrates on the analysis of economic *aggregates*, total values that describe the economy as a whole. The most important aggregate is _____ _____ _____ (GDP), which measures the market value of a country's aggregate output – the market value of the goods and services that a country produces in one year.

5. Every economy must answer three basic economic questions: (1) _____?(2) _____? (3) _____ _____?

6. When it comes to deciding on answers to the three basic questions, society must choose among three kinds of *economic systems*. Government might make the decisions. If so, the economy is termed _____ and _____.

7. If government stays out of the picture and allow economic choices to be made entirely in the marketplace, the economy is characterized by _____-_____ free markets.

8. In practice, all countries have _____ economies, meaning that they choose a combination of markets and government.

9. There are two primary economic objectives to guide countries in choosing how much government to mix with free markets. The first objective is _____, which refers to fairness. The second economic objective is economic _____, which means that resources are used in ways that provide the most value—that maximize the size of the economic pie. This means that no one can be made better off without someone else becoming worse off.

10. _____ _____ implies getting the greatest quantity of output for the resources that are being used. For any given output, this requires that a least-cost production technique must be chosen.

11. _____ _____ involves choosing the most valuable mix of outputs to produce.

12. There is frequently a _____ between efficiency and equity, meaning that more equity may result in less efficiency, referred to as more *inefficiency*. Likewise, less equity may result in greater efficiency.

13. Government _____ _____ sets production plans for most goods, which are produced by government-owned state enterprises. Government _____ occurs when consumers are permitted to buy only limited amounts of the goods they want.

14. In the *Wealth of Nations*, published in 1776, Scottish philosopher-economist _____ _____ described how the _____ _____ of the marketplace leads the economy to produce an efficient variety of goods and services, with efficient production methods as well. An essential ingredient is _____, which pits rival firms against one another in a contest to win the favor of consumers.

15. The use of prices to help answer the three basic questions all economies must answer characterizes the _____ system.

16. The _____ _____ _____ is error in reasoning that occurs when it is assumed that what is true at the micro level must also be true at the macro level.

17. _____ statements have to do with behavioral norms, which are judgments as to what is good or bad. Examples often include "ought" or "should" in them.

18. _____ statements have to do with fact. They may involve current, historical, or even future fact.

19. _____ is organized thought aimed at answering specific questions. A _____ is a simplification of reality that emphasizes features essential to answering the questions we ask of it.

20. The 14th century English philosopher William of Occam argued that reasoning is improved by focusing one's thinking on the most essential elements of an issue, a principle termed _____ _____.

21. To keep models simple, economists make _____, meaning that they act as though certain things are true without proving them to in fact be true.

22. One common assumption is termed _____ _____, which is Latin for holding all else constant.

23. Marxist governments expounded a philosophy of _____, in which everyone would get identical access to everything from soap to medical care.

24. Government redistributes wealth by imposing _____ that take wealth from those who can afford to give and that give to those in need. Taken to an extreme, this redistribution of wealth would eliminate incentives for individuals to behave more productively and lead to

stagnation. Therefore, in taxing, government must weigh the _____ between equity and incentives for efficiency.

APPENDIX

25. Some graphs represent economic models and contain lines that are referred to as _____. The horizontal line is commonly called the X axis and the vertical line the Y axis, with the specific labels of the axes varying from graph to graph, depending on what the graph is modeling. Each axis of the graph of a model is labeled with the name of a _____, referring to the name of anything that can change.

26. Curves that slope upward to the right show a _____ relationship, also termed a positive relationship, between the variables. Curves that slope downward to the right show an _____ relationship, also termed a negative relationship.

27. The _____ of a curve is measured by the amount of change in the variable on the vertical axis divided by the amount of change in the variable on the horizontal axis, sometimes referred to as the "rise over the run."

28. A change in the relationship between two variables is indicated by a _____ in a curve.

29. At the intersection point of two curves the values of each variable will be _____ for both relationships—both curves.

30. _____-_____ data show the values of a variable as time passes. _____-_____ data are fixed at a moment in time, but vary in some other way.

TRUE/FALSE/EXPLAIN
If false, explain why in the space provided.

1. Without scarcity, there would be no need for economics.

2. The essence of scarcity is a lack of money.

3. Making choices at the margin is about a little more of this and a little less of that.

4. The right to private property is an essential ingredient of a free market economy.

5. Allocative efficiency refers to selecting the most valuable combination of goods and services to produce.

6. The invisible hand of the marketplace refers to the framework of laws and regulations within which firms must operate.

7. A prediction that the unemployment rate will reach twenty percent in the year 2020 is an example of positive economics.

8. The best economic models include as much real-world detail as possible.

9. Goods and services are the same as resources.

10. Consumer decisions about what to buy will affect the allocation of resources.

11. Microeconomics is about the big public policy issues.

12. An industry is a group of firms producing a similar output.

13. Industry studies are an example of macroeconomic analysis.

18 CHAPTER 1

14. Allocative efficiency requires the use of a least-cost production technique.

15. Economic efficiency encompasses both allocated the efficiency and technological efficiency.

16. Equity means fairness.

17. In the last couple of centuries, there has been little relationship between political and economic ideas.

18. The fallacy of confusion is an error in reasoning which involves assuming that what is true for a part of the economy must also be true for the whole economy.

19. The following is a normative statement: "Movies today are too violent."

20. Economic models built on the principle of Occam's razor will include as many details of the real world as possible.

E&A 21. China has turned to market incentives to help its economy grow.

22. Like the former Soviet Union and other communist countries, the People's Republic of China was guided by the philosophy of the controversial 19th-century theorist, Karl Marx.

23. Lack of incentives for productivity is a major failing of egalitarianism.

24. The ideas of Karl Marx were used by China and the former Soviet Union to justify a strong central government.

25. A philosophy of egalitarianism has guided Western economies to success relative to China and the former Soviet Union.

APPENDIX

26. If two variables have a direct relationship to each other, an increase in one variable is associated with a decrease in the other.

27. A curve with a negative slope shows a direct relationship between variables.

28. When there is a change in the relationship between variables, we can illustrate the change by a shift in a curve.

29. An example of cross-sectional data is the current inflation rates in the countries of Europe.

30. An example of time-series data would be the average unemployment rate in 1995 in the ten largest cities in the United States.

MULTIPLE CHOICE
Circle the letter preceding the one best answer.

1. Most generally, economics is about
    a. money.
    b. profit.
    c. control.
    d. choice.

2. Making decisions of the margin means to make them
   a. logically.
   b. in the marketplace.
   c. all at once.
   d. incrementally.

3. The more redistributional is the tax system,
   a. the more productive economy is likely to be.
   b. the less productive the economy is likely to be.
   c. the more laissez-faire the economy is likely to be.
   d. the more efficient the economy is likely to be.

4. Of the following, which is the most likely to involve microeconomics?
   a. A study of the airline industry.
   b. A study of inflation.
   c. A study of economic growth.
   d. A study of a country's employment.

5. Keynesian economic theory is most closely associated with
   a. microeconomics.
   b. macroeconomics.
   c. efficiency.
   d. equity.

6. The three fundamental economic questions are
   a. who, what, where?
   b. how when, why?
   c. will, won't, whether?
   d. what, how, for whom?

7. The two primary economic goals are
   a. equity and efficiency.
   b. capitalism and communism.
   c. efficiency and equality.
   d. free markets and command and control.

8. Which of the following is NOT a type of efficiency?
   a. Allocative efficiency.
   b. Technological efficiency.
   c. Economic efficiency.
   d. Equity efficiency.

9. Which of the following is an example of technological efficiency?
   a. Choosing the best combination of goods and services to produce.
   b. Getting the most toothpicks from the inputs devoted to toothpick making.
   c. Ensuring that everyone has enough money to buy the necessities of life.
   d. Ensuring that everyone has equal opportunities in life.

10. Which of the following is an example of allocative efficiency?
    a. Choosing the best combination of goods and services to produce.
    b. Getting the most toothpicks from the inputs devoted to toothpick making.
    c. Ensuring that everyone has enough money to buy the necessities of life.
    d. Ensuring that everyone has equal opportunities in life.

11. Information about the scarcity of one resource relative to another is most likely to be provided by
    a. government.
    b. prices.
    c. market failures.
    d. normative economic statements.

12. In a capitalist economy, economic activities are coordinated by
    a. tradition.
    b. prices.
    c. government.
    d. business firms.

13. In laissez-faire free markets, the government is responsible for
    a. income redistribution.
    b. policies to improve efficiency.
    c. determining what prices will be charged for goods and services.
    d. nothing.

14. The proper functioning of the invisible hand requires
    a. monopoly.
    b. a fair distribution of income.
    c. competition.
    d. government ownership of large industries.

15. *The Wealth of Nations*, published in 1776, was written by
    a. John Maynard Keynes.
    b. Sir Isaac Arnold.
    c. Karl Marx.
    d. Adam Smith.

16. Which of the following illustrates the fallacy of composition?
    a. If I can sell my product for a higher price, I am better off. Thus, my customers are better off.
    b. If I can sell my product for a higher price, I am better off. Thus, if prices of all products rise, all sellers are better off.
    c. If I can sell my product for a higher price, I am better off. Thus, my customers are worse off.
    d. If customers want my product so much that I can sell it for a higher price, it must be the higher price that attracts the customers.

17. Trying to determine the effect of mad-cow disease upon the sales of beef and poultry would involve
    a. positive macroeconomics.
    b. positive microeconomics.
    c. normative macroeconomics.
    d. normative microeconomics.

18. "I expect that Congress will continue to run a budgetary deficit for the foreseeable future." This statement is an example of
    a. positive macroeconomics.
    b. positive microeconomics.
    c. normative macroeconomics.
    d. normative microeconomics.

19. To the extent that they explain the questions we ask of them, the best models are the
    a. simplest.
    b. most complex.
    c. most descriptive.
    d. most mathematical.

20. The principal of eliminating unnecessary details and models is called
    a. the fallacy of composition.
    b. normative analysis.
    c. positive analysis.
    d. Occam's razor.

21. If output is divided equally among all citizens, a country is following a policy of
    a. egalitarianism.
    b. equal rights.
    c. equity.
    d. laissez faire.

22. The primary economic problem of communism has been
    a. the lack of personal incentive to be productive.
    b. that people in a communist society are unselfish.
    c. that following the philosophy of Karl Marx would be inequitable.
    d. that workers exploit capitalists.

23. When Mao led the country, the People's Republic of China was guided by the philosophy of Karl Marx, with
    a. reliance upon free markets to achieve the goal of equality.
    b. central planning combined with private ownership of resources as the country strived for equality.
    c. central planning combined with government ownership of resources as the country strived for equality.
    d. no emphasis upon equality, and no consistent economic system to guide the country.

24. China's transition to a mixed economy since 1978
    a. does not allow privately-owned companies.
    b. imposed price controls on all goods and services.
    c. resulted in collective farms replacing individual farms.
    d. included the establishment of a stock market.

25. In China today, millionaires
    a. find their wealth taxed away by China's high tax rates.
    b. do not exist since there is not sufficient wealth to allow anyone to become a millionaire.
    c. are allowed to exist.
    d. must hide their wealth since accumulating more than $3,000 is a crime.

APPENDIX

26. In economics, the concept of a curve would include
    a. a downward sloping straight line.
    b. an upward sloping straight line.
    c. a curving line.
    d. all of the above.

27. Direct relationships between variables are illustrated graphically by curves that
    a. slope upward to the right.
    b. slope downward to the right.
    c. are horizontal.
    d. are vertical.

24 CHAPTER 1

28. A decreasingly positive slope is shown in Multiple Choice Figure 1 as curve
   a. A.
   b. B.
   c. C.
   d. D.

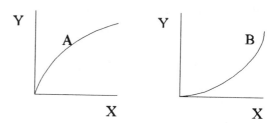

29. A increasingly negative slope is shown in Multiple Choice Figure 1 as curve
   a. A.
   b. B.
   c. C.
   d. D.

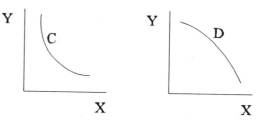

Multiple Choice Figure 1

30. If you wished to study differences in the economy between the administrations of Presidents Carter, Reagan, Bush, Clinton, and GW Bush, you would most likely seek out
   a. cross-sectional data.
   b. cross-time data.
   c. time-series data.
   d. time-out data.

GRASPING THE GRAPHS
Fill in each box with a concept that applies.

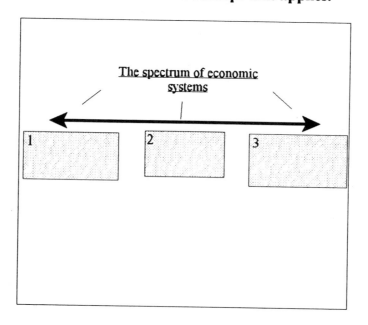

APPENDIX
In the following graph, use the information in the table to identify points.

Hypothetical Data on Yearly Rainfall and Umbrella Sales

Data Point	Community	Yearly Rainfall	Umbrella Sales
A	Center City	30 inches	100 units
B	Moose Haven	40 inches	200 units
C	Blountville	50 inches	300 units
D	Houckton	60 inches	400 units
E	Echo Ridge	70 inches	500 units

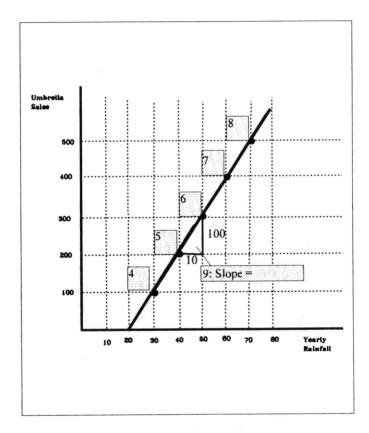

26 CHAPTER 1

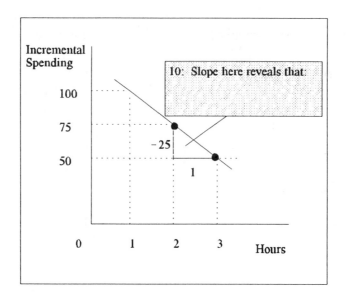

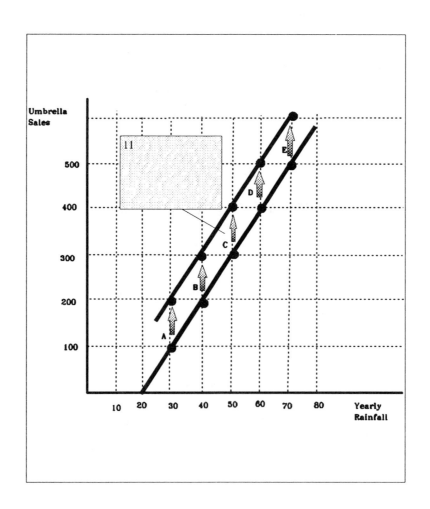

THE ECONOMIC PERSPECTIVE 27

**For additional practice in grasping this chapter's graphs,
visit http://www.prenhall.com/ayers and try *Smart Graph* 1,
along with *Active Graphs* 1, 2, 3, 4, and 5.**

ANSWERS

STUDYCHECKS

1. Economic efficiency is a situation where you cannot make anyone better off without making someone else worse off. It involves getting the most value from available resources. Technological efficiency is to get the most output from given inputs or, conversely, to use the fewest inputs for a given output. Allocative efficiency is to produce the most valuable combination of outputs. Equity is fairness. Equity may call for the redistribution of income, which in turn reduces people's incentives to be productive.

2. Capitalism provides incentives for productivity, and thus "bakes a bigger pie." However, it can slice that pie more unequally than under a Marxist egalitarian philosophy. Capitalism is thus sometimes perceived as inequitable.

3. See StudyCheck 3 Figure.

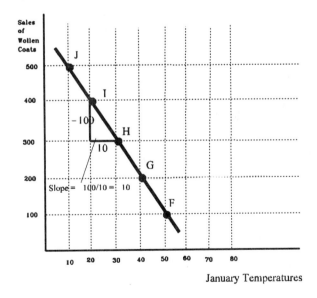

StudyCheck 3 Figure

28 CHAPTER 1

4. The relationship is positive. See StudyCheck 4 Figure.

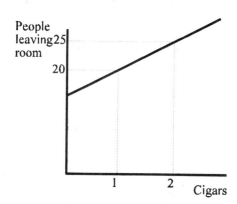

StudyCheck 4 Figure

5. An example of time-series data is any data that varies over time. Examples are many, including yearly values for GDP, the unemployment rate, and interest rates. Cross-sectional data varies, but in some way other than time. Examples are many, including the value of GDP in a particular year for different countries, and the unemployment rate in a particular year for different countries.

FILL IN THE BLANKS

1. Economics, limited, scarcity, margin
2. allocation, technology
3. Microeconomics, firms
4. Macroeconomics, gross domestic product
5. What, How, For whom
6. command and control
7. laissez-faire
8. mixed
9. equity, efficiency
10. Technological efficiency
11. Allocative efficiency
12. tradeoff
13. central planning, rationing
14. Adam Smith, invisible hand, competition
15. price
16. fallacy of composition
17. Normative
18. Positive

19. Theory, model
20. Occam's razor
21. assumptions
22. ceteris paribus
23. egalitarianism
24. taxes, tradeoff
25. curve, variable
26. direct, inverse
27. slope
28. shift
29. equal
30. Time-series, Cross-sectional

TRUE/FALSE/EXPLAIN

1. True.
2. False, scarcity exists even if there is no money.
3. True.
4. True.
5. True.
6. False, the invisible hand of the marketplace refers to the forces of competition that lead to be efficiency.
7. True.
8. Defaults, the best economic models include only as much detail as necessary to answer the questions that they are to be asked.
9. Defaults, resources are used to produce goods and services.
10. True.
11. False, macroeconomics is about the big public policy issues, wild microeconomics concerns the details of the economy.
12. True.
13. False, industry studies are an example of microeconomic analysis.
14. False, that would be technological efficiency.
15. True.
16. True.
17. False, politics and economics have been so entwined that the field of economics used to be known as political economy.
18. False, that would be the fallacy of composition.
19. True.
20. False, Occam's razor requires models to be a simple as possible.
21. True.
22. True.

30 CHAPTER 1

23. True.
24. True.
25. False, the attempt to achieve egalitarianism in Communist countries resulted in poor economic incentives and economies that were unsuccessful relative to the market economies of the West.
26. False, a direct relationship means that an increase in one variable would increase the other variable.
27. False, a curve with a negative slope shows an inverse relationship between variables.
28. True.
29. True.
30. False, time-series data refers to data across a span of time, such as number of years.

MULTIPLE CHOICE

1.	d	9.	b	17.	b	25.	c
2.	d	10.	a	18.	a	26.	d
3.	b	11.	b	19.	a	27.	a
4.	a	12.	b	20.	d	28.	a
5.	b	13.	d	21.	a	29.	d
6.	d	14.	c	22.	a	30.	c
7.	a	15.	d	23.	c		
8.	d	16.	b	24.	d		

GRASPING THE GRAPHS
Examples of correct answers

1. laissez-faire free markets
2. mixed economy
3. command and control
4. A
5. B
6. C
7. D
8. E
9. 100/10 = 10
10. The added revenue from staying open another hour is $25 less than for the previous hour.
11. The curve has shifted upward, implying more umbrella sales at each level of rainfall.

**Visit the Collinge/Ayers Companion Website at http://www.prenhall.com/collinge
for further activities and exercises for this chapter.**

Chapter 2

PRODUCTION AND TRADE

CHAPTER REVIEW

2.1 Scarcity and Choice

- Scarcity means we have to make choices. **Opportunity costs** represent the value of forgone alternatives. The opportunity cost of an action is the value of the single most highly valued alternative choice that has been forgone. The money you pay for an item could have alternatively been spent on something else. The value of the best alternative use of that money is an opportunity cost, but not usually the only opportunity cost. The value of forgone alternative uses of time or other non-monetary resources must also be included.

- *Resources* are combined to produce outputs of goods and services. *Inputs* is another name for resources, which are usually divided into the categories of land, labor, capital, and entrepreneurship. We refer to the ability of a resource to produce output as that resource's *productivity*.

- **Land** refers to all natural resources in their natural states. **Labor** refers to people's capacity to work. It ignores the increased labor productivity from acquired skills and the development of peoples' abilities, which constitute **human capital.** Human capital is a special case of an economy's third resource, capital. **Capital** is anything that is produced in order to increase productivity in the future. Along with human capital, there is also *physical capital*, which includes buildings, machinery, and other equipment. Caution: The definition of capital used in economics differs from that used in finance. Financial capital refers to financial instruments, such as stocks, bonds, and money.

- **Entrepreneurship** is taking personal initiative to combine resources in productive ways. Entrepreneurs take risks, but have the potential to become the economy's movers and shakers. Countries tap the creative potential of entrepreneurship in order to improve the value they get from other resources.

- The possibilities for combining an economy's resources depend upon technology. **Technology** refers to possible techniques of production. Technological advances both improve the selection of goods and services and the manner in which we can produce them.

2.2 Production Possibilities

- The **production possibilities frontier** illustrates scarcity and choice by assuming that only two goods can be produced. It is termed a *frontier* because it represents the limits of output possibilities, given current resources and technology.

- Castaway Island is inhabited exclusively by a castaway named Hank. His options are to catch fish or harvest coconuts. He values both of these foods in his diet and can spend up to eight hours a day to obtain them. The amounts he can obtain are shown in the table below.

Data Point	Fish Caught per Day	Coconuts Collected per Day
A	5	0
B	4	10
C	3	16
D	2	19
E	1	21
F	0	22

- The more fish Hank catches, the fewer coconuts he can collect. The inverse relationship between fish and coconuts illustrates the opportunity cost of Hank using his limited resource, time.

- The opportunity cost of more fish is the number of coconuts forgone. As Hank increases his catch from zero fish (row F in the table) to a maximum of five fish (row A), we see the number of coconuts he collects drop at an increasing rate. In other words, the opportunity cost of the first fish is only one coconut. The opportunity cost of two fish is giving up three coconuts. Then opportunity costs really jump. The opportunity cost of four fish is 12 coconuts, which is quadruple the opportunity cost of two fish. Five fish carry an opportunity cost of 22 coconuts, meaning that Hank must give up all coconuts if he wants to catch five fish. The table below shows these opportunity costs. The final column shows *marginal opportunity cost*, which is the additional opportunity cost from catching one more fish.

Data Point	Fish caught per day	Opportunity Cost (number of coconuts forgone)	Marginal Opportunity Cost (change in number of coconuts forgone)
F	0	0	undefined
E	1	1	1
D	2	3	2
C	3	6	3
B	4	12	6
A	5	22	10

- The numbers for marginal opportunity cost illustrate a principle known as the **law of increasing cost**, which states that as an economy adds to its production of any one good, the marginal opportunity cost of that good will rise. The reason is that resources are often specialized, being more suitable to producing one output than another output. So to increase the output of a good, the most appropriate resources are used first, followed by resources that are increasingly less appropriate for producing that good.

- Because marginal opportunity cost increases as output increases, the production possibilities frontier is bowed outward, meaning that its slope becomes increasingly negative. In contrast, if marginal opportunity cost were constant, the production possibilities frontier would be a straight line with a constant downward slope. In producing any good X, an economy first uses resources that are best suited to producing X. If the economy keeps adding to the production of good X, it uses resources that are increasingly less well suited to X, but increasingly better suited to some other good, Y. The result is that the production of good Y drops at an increasingly rapid rate as X production increases. The production possibilities frontier bows outward because resources are not equally suited to the production of different goods.

- All points within or along the production possibilities frontier are feasible combinations of two goods. For the economy to reach that frontier, it must use all of its resources. It must also use these resources efficiently in the technological sense of getting the most output for given inputs. Otherwise, the economy would be inefficient and at a point inside the frontier. In short, **any point along the production possibilities frontier is a technologically efficient combination of outputs.**

- Points inside the frontier are inefficient and points outside the frontier are currently unattainable.

> **StudyCheck 1**
> Draw a production possibilities frontier, labeling the points that are technologically efficient. Also show which combinations of outputs are possible and which ones are currently impossible. Make sure that you label the axes of your graph.

- Allocative efficiency implies a specific point on the production possibilities frontier that is the most valuable combination of outputs. In general, **there will be only one point on the production possibilities frontier that is allocatively efficient**, and we cannot know what it is by sight. However, the invisible hand of the market economy will tend to lead the economy to that point on the production possibilities frontier that is the allocatively efficient combination of outputs.

- Production possibilities will depend on how much of each resource the economy has and on the technology that is available to make use of those resources. As resources increase or technology improves, production possibilities grow and the economy's entire production possibilities frontier shifts outward. **When the production possibilities frontier shifts outward, the economy experiences *economic growth*.** Economic growth occurs when the economy uses expanded production possibilities to produce an output of greater value.

- In the event of natural disasters, the exhaustion of natural resources, or anything else that causes an economy's resource base to shrink, the country's production possibilities will also shrink, which would lead to negative economic growth.

- It takes capital to make use of technological change and increase labor productivity. Since capital represents output that is produced now for the purpose of increasing productivity later, the creation of capital comes at the expense of current consumption.

- When an economy is devoting nearly all of its resources to producing goods for current consumption, the result is that the amount of capital it possesses decreases over time, because of equipment wearing out, buildings falling into disrepair, and other forms of *depreciation*. With its economy producing too little new capital to offset depreciation of existing capital, the production possibilities frontier shifts inward. If the country trades off some current consumption for significantly more production of capital, depreciation can be more than offset. The result is that the production possibilities frontier shifts out over time.

- Technological change can increase productivity across a broad range of industries, as with the better information flows made possible by modern computers and telecommunications. Oftentimes, however, technological change is specific to an industry. In the case of general growth, productivity in both the pretzel and pumpkin industries increases. In the case of specialized growth, productivity increases in only one industry. **Specialized growth thus pivots the production possibilities frontier in the direction of more output in the industry affected by the technological change.**

StudyCheck 2

Using a production possibilities frontier, show how the Internet has expanded economic growth. Briefly note on your graph why this growth occurred.

36 CHAPTER 2

> **StudyCheck 3**
> Draw two production possibilities frontiers, labeling the axes with the goods pretzels and pumpkins. On one of your graphs, show the effects of a general increase in the economy's resources. On the other graph, show the effects of only technological change in the pretzel industry. Label the first graph general growth and the second graph specialized growth.

- To summarize, the production possibilities frontier shows how much of one good can be produced for any feasible amount of another good. If an economy is on its frontier, the opportunity cost of producing more of one good is less of the other good. The production possibilities frontier is bowed outward, consistent with the law of increasing cost. Every point along the production possibilities frontier is technologically efficient. Points inside the frontier imply some unemployed or misallocated resources and are thus inefficient. Points outside the frontier are unattainable with current resources and technology. Economies grow by acquiring resources or better technology, which shifts the frontier outward. If the economy acquires resources that are specialized in the production of a certain good, the production possibilities frontier pivots outward in the direction of more of that good.

2.3 The Circular Flow of Economic Activity

- **Money** is a medium of exchange, meaning that it facilitates the exchange of goods and services. Without money, people would be forced to exchange goods directly, a situation known as **barter**. Barter would be very difficult in a complicated economy.

- Many things have served as money through the years. In prisoner-of-war camps in World War II, cigarettes served as money. Traditionally, gold, silver, and other scarce metals have been considered money, since they are inherently scarce and relatively easy to transport in the form of coins. Paper is even easier to transport, which is why it is the most common form of money in use today. However, for paper or anything else to be used as money, its quantity must be limited, which is why counterfeiting is illegal. Government must also be careful about printing too much currency if it wishes its currency to retain value as money.

- The **circular flow** of economic activity is a model that depicts how markets use the medium of money to determine what goods and services are produced and who gets to buy them. The **output market** is where businesses sell goods and services to consumers.

- The **input market** illustrates that households supply the resources of land, labor, capital, and entrepreneurship. All of these resources are ultimately owned by people, who make up households. The sale of resources to business provides the income that households use to buy products. Since people own businesses, business profits also belong to households. For this reason, the circular flow of inputs and outputs is maintained by a counterflow of dollars. Through taxation, regulation, and production, government influences the mix of goods that is produced and the manner in which resources are used. The circular flow model could be expanded to include foreign commerce, banking, or other economic details, but would become difficult to interpret.

StudyCheck 4

Draw and explain the meaning of the circular flow model of economic activity.

38 CHAPTER 2

2.4 Expanding Consumption Possibilities through Trade

- For their own self-interest, economies engage in trade with other economies. This is true for national economies, regional economies, local economies, and even personal economies.

- People specialize in their jobs according to their interests and opportunities. They then use the income they earn in order to purchase goods and services. Note that this is a two-part decision. First people decide what to produce; then they decide what to consume. The economies of countries engaged in international trade operate the same way.

- In order to gain from trade, an economy must *specialize* according to its **comparative advantage. An economy has a comparative advantage in producing a good if it can produce that good at a lower opportunity cost than could other economies.** This means the economy chooses to produce those things it does well relative to other things it could be doing.

- Contrary to popular belief, trade is not based on **absolute advantage,** which refers to the ability to produce something with fewer resources than could others. **To gain from trade, specialize according to comparative advantage, whether or not you have any absolute advantage.**

- Countries gain from trade whether or not they have an absolute advantage in anything. The country can start off rich or poor and still gain from trade. While a country is constrained to produce along or inside its production possibilities frontier, it can exchange some of its own output for the output of other countries.

- Goods and services a country sells to other countries are termed **exports.** Exports are traded for **imports,** which are goods and services a country buys from other countries. **Through trade, a country can consume a combination of goods and services that lies outside its production possibilities frontier, meaning that the country's consumption possibilities will exceed its production possibilities.**

- International trade is more important to small countries than to large countries. This is because, the larger is the country, the more opportunities there are to specialize internally.

- If a country has a comparative advantage in producing certain goods, it can produce those goods cheaply relative to the other goods that it could produce. Those goods in which it has a comparative advantage will be the goods it can offer at the best prices in the international marketplace. Thus, without any economic research, economies engaging in international trade naturally tend to export those goods for which they have a comparative advantage and import the rest.

- Consider a model involving two countries, Japan and England, that can each produce only computer memory chips and oil. Assume that all computer memory chips are interchangeable and that oil is also identical. The productivity of workers is shown in the table below. Note that in this example Japan's workers are more productive at both producing oil and manufacturing computer chips, meaning that Japan has an absolute advantage in both computer chips and oil production.

Productivity per Worker in Japan and England

Country	Computer Memory Chips	Barrels of Oil
Japan	10 units per day	4 per day
England	5 units per day	3 per day

- The key to computing comparative advantage is to measure opportunity costs, shown in the table below.

Computing Opportunity Cost and Comparative Advantage

Product Location	Opportunity Cost (C is computer chips and B is barrels of oil)	Opportunity Cost per Unit
Computer chips in Japan	10C for 4B	2/5 barrel of oil (.4B)*
Computer chips in England	5C for 3B	3/5 barrel of oil (.6B)
Oil in Japan	4B for 10C	5/2 computer chips (2.5C)
Oil in England	3B for 5C	5/3 computer chips (1.67C)**

*Lower opportunity cost per unit of computer chips implies comparative advantage in Japan.
**Lower opportunity cost per unit of barrels of oil implies comparative advantage in England.

- In Japan, we see that making a computer chip requires giving up the ability to make 2/5 or .4 barrels of oil, while in England the computer chip costs 3/5 or .6 barrels of oil. Since Japan has a lower opportunity cost of producing the computer chips, it is said to have a comparative advantage in computer chips. Verify for yourself that England has a comparative advantage in oil.

40 CHAPTER 2

StudyCheck 5

Suppose that there are two countries, Tryhard and Trynot. In Tryhard, each hour of labor can produce either 8 units of good X or 8 units of good Y. In Trynot, each hour of labor can produce either 2 units of good X or 4 units of good Y. Compute the opportunity cost of: a) X in Tryhard; b) Y in Tryhard; c) X in Trynot; d) Y in Trynot. If these countries trade only goods X and Y, which country will produce X? Which will produce Y? Explain.

 ## 2.5 Guns and Butter—Victory from a Strong Economy

- When the United States decided to strengthen its armed forces in the 1980s, the Soviet Union struggled so hard to keep pace that it impoverished its own people and lost its will to exist. The Soviet Union was formally dissolved in 1991 without a shot being fired, breaking up into several different countries, including Russia.

- Now, as we seek to surmount the unfolding terrorist threats of the 21st century, the lessons of America's 20th century success can help guide our way. How has the United States has been able to maintain prosperity during peacetime and yet still have the wherewithal to be victorious in wartime? The secret has been the vibrancy of a strong U.S. economy, meaning that the United States has been able to maintain production possibilities that exceed those of its adversaries.

- Let guns represent military output and butter represent output for civilian consumption. Because of its strong economy, the United States could increase its production of guns to exceed that of the Soviet Union and still have more butter for its civilians. When the Soviets tried to match U.S. spending on guns in the 1980s, their production of butter fell so low that the Soviet people were forced to endure severe hardships.

- To maintain a strong economy, a country must use its existing resources and technology efficiently. Moving from an inefficient economy to an efficient economy allows the production of both more guns and more butter. The economy must use the right people and the right capital to produce the right goods in the right way. By producing more in the present, the economy also has more ability to put aside some current consumption of guns and butter in favor of investing in new capital and better technology that will allow production possibilities to grow over time. In other words, the more efficient an economy is in the present, the more ability it will have to expand its production possibilities for the future.

StudyCheck 6

Labeling the axes as guns and butter, show on a production possibility frontier how an economy can move from being inefficient to being efficient and the changes in output that this could lead to. Show also that the economy can produce more output over time by being efficient.

- The United States has been able to use its production possibilities with relative efficiency and achieve significant economic growth over time by relying in large measure upon the marketplace to allocate resources. The lure of profit in the market economy has motivated people and companies to look for the most valuable products to produce, keep costs as low as possible, and invest in new capital that expands the country's production possibilities frontier. These actions constitute the invisible hand of the marketplace that motivates individuals out for their own self-interest to best serve the needs of others.

- While there are exceptions in which either markets or government policies have failed to achieve efficiency, it is its reliance upon a market economy that has generally allowed the United States to prosper relative to its adversaries with more centralized economies.

- The 20th century has not always brought victory to the U.S. or other prosperous countries. As the U.S. learned in Cuba and Vietnam, citizens of impoverished countries can be stubborn adversaries when their patriotic zeal is aroused. Why not peace, with its promise of prosperity?

- Whether the world in the 21st century sees economic victory or the impoverishment of warfare might hinge in part upon attitudes. Are people of impoverished nations inspired to recreate for themselves the success of the U.S. and other developed countries? Or is that prosperity seen as out of reach and the source of resentment and ongoing conflict?

FILL IN THE BLANKS

1. _____ _____ represent the value of forgone alternatives.

2. _____ are combined to produce outputs of goods and services. They are usually divided into the categories of land, labor, capital, and entrepreneurship. We refer to the ability to produce output as _____.

3. _____ refers to all natural resources in their natural states. _____ refers to people's capacity to work. It ignores the increased labor productivity from acquired skills and the development of peoples' abilities, which constitute _____ _____. _____ is anything that is produced in order to increase productivity in the future. Along with human capital, there is also _____ capital, which includes buildings, machinery, and other equipment. _____ is taking personal initiative to combine resources in productive ways.

4. _____ refers to possible techniques of production. Technological advances both improve the selection of goods and services and the manner in which we can produce them.

5. The _____ _____ _____ illustrates scarcity and choice by assuming that only two goods can be produced. It represents the limits of output possibilities, given current resources and technology.

6. Castaway Island is inhabited exclusively by a castaway named Hank. His options are to catch fish or harvest coconuts. He values both of these foods in his diet and can spend up to eight hours a day to obtain them. The amounts he can obtain are shown in the table below.

PRODUCTION AND TRADE   43

Data Point	Fish Caught per Day	Coconuts Collected per Day
A	5	0
B	4	10
C	3	16
D	2	19
E	1	21
F	0	22

The opportunity cost of the first fish is _____ coconut. The opportunity cost of two fish is giving up _____ coconuts. The opportunity cost of four fish is _____ coconuts.

7. Marginal opportunity cost is the additional opportunity cost from catching one more fish. The marginal opportunity cost of the first fish is _____ coconut. The marginal opportunity cost of the second fish is _____ coconuts. The marginal opportunity cost of the fourth fish is _____ coconuts.

8. The law of _____ _____ states that as an economy adds to its production of any one good, the marginal opportunity cost of that good will rise.

9. Because marginal opportunity cost increases as output increases, the production possibilities frontier is _____ _____, meaning that its slope becomes increasingly negative. In contrast, if marginal opportunity cost were constant, the production possibilities frontier would be a _____ line with a constant downward slope.

10. All points within or along the production possibilities frontier are _____ combinations of two goods. For the economy to reach that frontier, it must use all of its resources. It must also use these resources _____ in the technological sense of getting the most output for given inputs. Otherwise, the economy would be inefficient and at a point _____ the frontier. Points _____ the frontier are currently unattainable.

11. _____ efficiency implies a specific point on the production possibilities frontier that is the most valuable combination of outputs.

12. As resources increase or technology improves, production possibilities grow and the economy's entire production possibilities frontier shifts _____. When the production possibilities frontier shifts outward, the economy experiences economic _____.

13. When an economy is devoting nearly all of its resources to producing goods for current consumption, the result is that the amount of capital it possesses decreases over time, because of equipment wearing out, buildings falling into disrepair, and other forms of _____. With its economy producing too little new capital, the production possibilities frontier shifts _____.

14. In the case of _____ growth, productivity in a variety of industries increases, and the production possibilities frontier shifts outward along both axes. In the case of _____ growth, productivity increases in only one industry, which pivots the production possibilities frontier in the direction of more output in one industry.

15. _____ is a medium of exchange, meaning that it facilitates the exchange of goods and services. Without money, people would be forced to exchange goods directly, a situation known as _____.

16. The _____ _____ of economic activity is a model that depicts how markets use the medium of money to determine what goods and services are produced and who gets to buy them. The _____ market is where businesses sell goods and services to consumers. The _____ market illustrates that households supply the resources of land, labor, capital, and entrepreneurship.

17. In order to gain from trade, an economy must specialize according to its _____ advantage. An economy has a _____ advantage in producing a good if it can produce that good at a lower opportunity cost than could other economies. This means the economy chooses to produce those things it does well relative to other things it could be doing. Trade is not based on _____ advantage, which refers to the ability to produce something with fewer resources than could others.

18. Goods and services a country sells to other countries are termed _____. _____ are goods and services a country buys from other countries. Through trade, a country can consume a combination of goods and services that lies _____ its production possibilities frontier, meaning that the country's consumption possibilities will exceed its production possibilities.

19. International trade is more important to _____ countries than to _____ countries.

20. Consider a model involving two countries, Japan and England, that can each produce only computer memory chips and oil. Assume that all computer memory chips are interchangeable and that oil is also identical. The productivity of workers is shown in the table below. Note that in this example Japan's workers are more productive at both producing oil and manufacturing computer chips, meaning that Japan has an _____ advantage in both computer chips and oil production. The country with a comparative advantage in computer

memory chip production is _____, while the country with the comparative advantage in oil production is _____.

Productivity per Worker in Japan and England

Country	Computer Memory Chips	Barrels of Oil
Japan	10 units per day	4 per day
England	5 units per day	3 per day

E&A 21. To maintain a strong economy, a country must use its existing _____ and _____ efficiently.

22. Moving from an _____ economy to an _____ economy allows the production of both more guns and more butter.

23. The lure of _____ in the market economy has motivated people and companies to look for the most valuable products to produce, keep costs as low as possible, and invest in new capital that expands the country's production possibilities frontier.

24. These actions constitute the _____ _____ of the marketplace that motivates individuals out for their own self-interest to best serve the needs of others.

25. People of impoverished countries might be _____ to emulate the success of developed countries, or this success might alternatively become a source of _____ and _____.

TRUE/FALSE/EXPLAIN
If false, explain why in the space provided.

1. The opportunity cost of a city park to the city that owns it is best measured by the budget required to police and maintain that park.

2. If you start your own business, you are an entrepreneur.

3. A bowed-out production possibility frontier shows that the incremental opportunity cost of each additional unit of either good will be lower than it was for the preceding unit.

4. Human capital is created when a person acquires knowledge and skills that can increase his or her earnings.

5. Technological change in the widget industry will pivot the production possibility frontier in the direction of more widgets.

6. Other things equal, if a country produces more capital goods, its production possibility frontier will shift out over time.

7. There is only one point on the production possibility frontier that is technologically efficient.

8. The circular flow diagram shows the flow of resources, and the flow of goods and services, while ignoring money.

9. In the circular flow model of economic activity, resources are assumed to be owned by businesses.

10. A country that trades with other countries can consume outside its production possibility frontier.

11. To gain from trade, a country must be able to do something better or with fewer resources than the other country.

12. When we make economic decisions, our goal is always to maximize the opportunity cost of our actions.

13. The countries of Superior and Wannabee produce nothing but fish and movies. The residents of Superior are far better suited to both activities than are the residents of Wannabee. This means that Superior has a comparative advantage in both goods.

14. Relative to most countries, the United States has a comparative advantage in goods that are produced with a high proportion of capital, including human capital.

15. If a country has an unproductive labor force and few other resources, it is better off not trading with other countries.

16. It is impossible for a country to have a comparative advantage in all goods.

17. A country gains by protecting its high-paying jobs.

18. The marketplace identifies the goods for which individuals and countries have comparative advantages.

19. If it takes 12 units of labor to produce gizmos, and 24 units of labor to produce gadgets, the opportunity cost of a gizmo is two gadgets.

20. If workers in country A can produce 10 widgets or 10 gizmos per day, while workers in country B can produce 5 widgets or 1 gizmo per day, the two countries can both gain from trade if country B specializes in the production of widgets.

21. The Soviet Union was dissolved in 1991 after a violent revolution in which hundreds of thousands of people died.

22. A vibrant U.S. economy in the 20th century meant the United States could maintain production possibilities in excess of the production possibilities of its adversaries.

23. The more efficient an economy is in the present, the more ability it will have to expand its production possibilities for the future.

24. Former Soviet Premier Mikhail Gorbachev has in recent years ridiculed the ways of the Soviet Union.

25. As the United States learned in Cuba and Vietnam, it is weapons and not patriotic zeal that matters in wartime.

MULTIPLE CHOICE
Circle the letter preceding the one best answer.

1. Human capital refers to
   a. money.
   b. money, but not if it's owned by businesses.
   c. work effort.
   d. acquired skills and abilities.

2. Water flowing down a river represents the resource of
   a. land.
   b. technology.
   c. capital.
   d. entrepreneurship.

3. Suppose that the Capitalist Computer Corporation is about to finish a new office building in downtown Richville. When completed, this building will house all Capitalist operations and still have five vacant floors. In order to retain maximum flexibility for future operations, Capitalist Computers has decided to not lease out this extra space. The opportunity cost of this decision is
   a. the cost of building those five floors.
   b. the cost of maintaining those five floors while they are vacant.
   c. the total payments Capitalist Computers could have received by leasing out those five floors.
   d. zero, because the space remains vacant.

4. Of the following, the opportunity cost of attending class on any given day is most likely to be
   a. tuition.
   b. the cost of books.
   c. the pleasure of sleeping late.
   d. a higher grade on the test.

5. The relationship between marginal opportunity cost and total opportunity cost is:
   a. Marginal opportunity cost is the sum of all the total opportunity costs.
   b. Total opportunity cost is the sum of all the marginal opportunity costs.
   c. Marginal opportunity cost equals total opportunity cost divided by output.
   d. Total opportunity cost equals marginal opportunity cost divided by output.

6. Marginal opportunity cost is the _____ of the production possibilities frontier.
   a. height
   b. width
   c. direction
   d. slope

7. The outwardly bowed shape of the production possibilities frontier can be explained by
   a. specialization of resources.
   b. consumer preferences.
   c. the circular flow diagram.
   d. absolute advantage.

50 CHAPTER 2

8. In Multiple Choice Figure 2-1,
   a. point D is more technologically efficient than point C.
   b. point C is more technologically efficient than point D.
   c. both points C and point D are equally technologically efficient.
   d. neither points C nor D are technologically efficient.

9. In Multiple Choice Figure 2-1, the marginal opportunity cost of increasing fish production from two to three would be
   a. 3 coconuts forgone.
   b. 16 coconuts forgone.
   c. 6 coconuts forgone.
   d. 2 fish forgone.

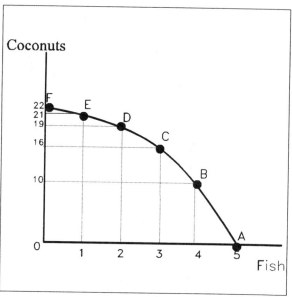

Multiple Choice Figure 2-1

10. Multiple Choice Figure 2-2 shows _____ economic growth.
    a. general
    b. specialized
    c. positive
    d. negative

11. An economy that invests heavily in capital goods in one year will find that, in following years,
    a. its production possibility frontier has shifted out.
    b. it is consuming a more equitable combination of goods.
    c. it is consuming a more efficient combination of goods.
    d. it cannot produce as many capital goods.

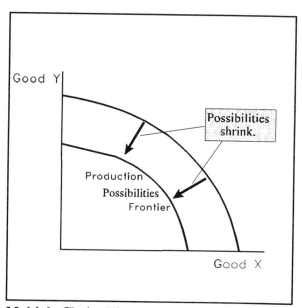

Multiple Choice Figure 2-2

12. Exchanging goods for goods is known as
    a. stock trading.
    b. bond trading.
    c. barter.
    d. debasement.

13. In a circular-flow graph, spending by business equals
    a. total profits.
    b. income to households.
    c. spending on services, but not on goods.
    d. the increase in inventories.

14. As a general economic rule, economic well-being in a country is _____ by allowing imports, and _____ by allowing exports.
    a. increased; increased
    b. decreased; increased
    c. increased; decreased
    d. decreased; decreased

15. When two countries trade with each other,
    a. both countries' production possibility frontiers shift outward.
    b. they move from one point to another on their respective production possibility frontiers
    c. they both move to points outside their respective production possibility frontiers.
    d. they both move to points inside their respective production possibility frontiers.

16. International trade tends to be most important to
    a. small, specialized countries.
    b. large, diversified countries.
    c. primitive economies.
    d. communist countries.

17. A country that agrees to trade with another country where workers are paid a considerably lower real wage is likely to see its standard of living
    a. rise, but exports fall.
    b. and exports both fall.
    c. and exports both rise.
    d. fall, but exports rise.

18. When the United States trades with Mexico and other countries that have an abundance of relatively unskilled labor, the effect on the U.S. labor market is to reduce
    a. demand for relatively unskilled labor.
    b. wages for both skilled and unskilled labor.
    c. employment in all U.S. industries engaged in international trade.
    d. exports in an amount equal to the increasing imports.

52 CHAPTER 2

19. Suppose one acre of land is able to produce 5,000 bushels of rice or 6,000 bushels of wheat in Louisiana. In Arkansas, one acre of land can produce 3,000 bushels of rice or 4,000 bushels of wheat. Arkansas has a comparative advantage over Louisiana in
   a. only wheat.
   b. only rice.
   c. both wheat and rice.
   d. neither wheat nor rice.

20. Suppose that M.J. and Rodney are stranded on a tropical island containing streams teeming with delicious fish. There is nothing to do but fish, cook, or relax. It takes Rodney two hours to catch a fish and three hours to cook a fish. M.J. can catch a fish in one hour, and also cook a fish in an hour. Both M.J. and Rodney are indifferent as to whether they'll spend their time fishing or cooking. It is likely that
   a. Rodney will do most of the fishing and M.J. most of the cooking.
   b. M.J. will do most of the fishing and Rodney most of the cooking.
   c. M.J. will do most of both the fishing and cooking.
   d. Rodney will do most of both the fishing and cooking.

E&A 21. The 20th century has often been called America's century. Of the following, the most likely explanation is
   a. the economic and military dominance of the United States and the 20th century.
   b. the opportunities opened up to the United States in the 20th-century by the Louisiana purchase.
   c. the opportunities opened up to the United States in the 20th-century by technological change.
   d. that America claimed ownership of most of the world's resources in that century.

22. Of the following, the most likely reason for the Soviet Union's demise is that
   a. it was unable to match the United States militarily in the 1980s.
   b. it might have been able to match the United States militarily in the 1980s, but its citizens would have been left with a very low standard of living.
   c. its citizens came to believe that democracy was a better form of government and refused to work until it was established in the Soviet Union.
   d. access to the Internet caused disenchantment among Soviet youth with the Soviet system.

23. An economy is better able to grow if it is efficient then if it is inefficient because
   a. efficiency allows more production from the economies resources.
   b. efficiency reduces discontent among workers.
   c. efficiency is equitable.
   d. greater efficiency is the same thing as economic growth.

24. The United States economy has been relatively efficient over time in large part due to its reliance upon
    a. a strong military.
    b. a market economy.
    c. a pattern of continuous warfare.
    d. impoverishment of other nations.

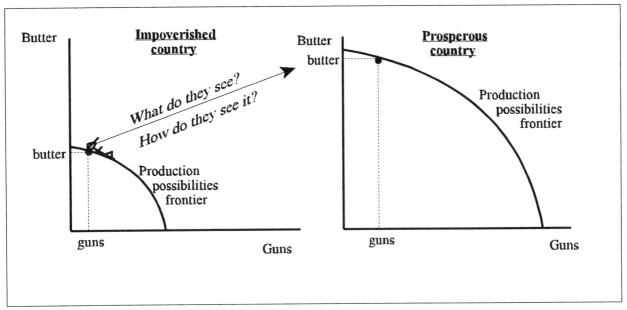

Multiple Choice Figure 2-3

25. The questions shown in the left side of Multiple Choice Figure 2-3 refer to
    a. how prosperous countries are viewed by residents of impoverished countries.
    b. how impoverished countries are viewed by residents of prosperous countries.
    c. whether residents of impoverished countries believe that prosperous countries have truly achieved technological efficiency.
    d. whether impoverished countries can achieve the equity that is clearly visible in prosperous countries.

GRASPING THE GRAPHS
Fill in each box with a concept that applies.

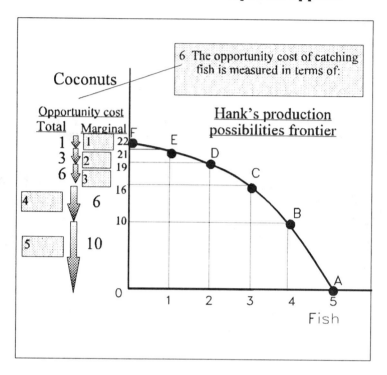

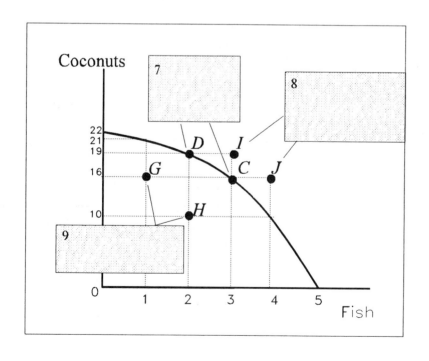

PRODUCTION AND TRADE 55

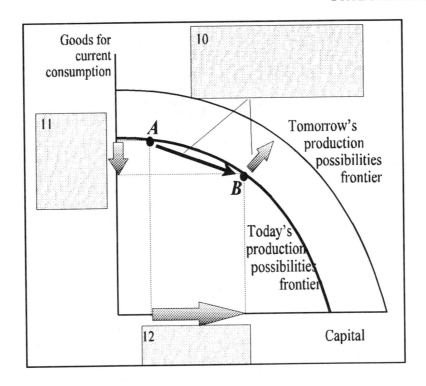

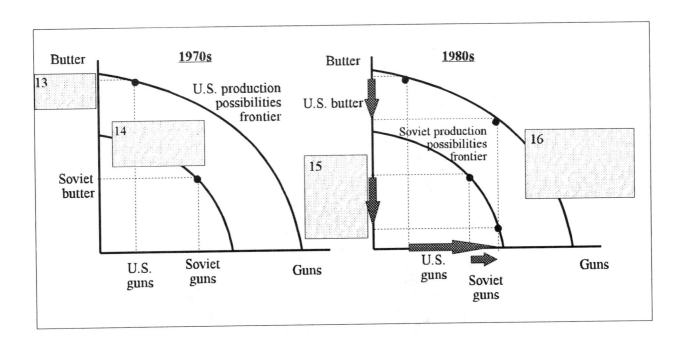

For additional practice in grasping this chapter's graphs, visit
http://www.prenhall.com/ayers and try *Smart Graphs* 2 and 3,
along with *Active Graphs* 6, 7, and 8.

ANSWERS

STUDYCHECKS

1. See StudyCheck 1 figure.

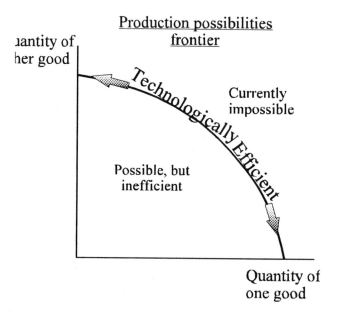

StudyCheck 1 Figure

2. See StudyCheck 2 Figure.

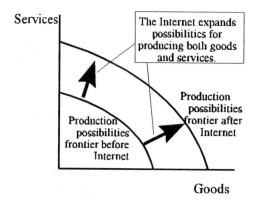

StudyCheck 2 Figure

3. See StudyCheck 3 Figure.

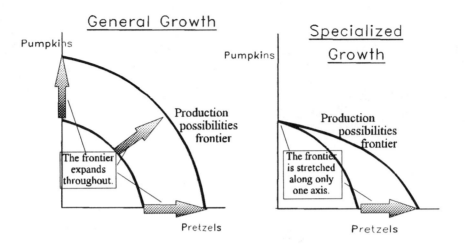

StudyCheck 3 Figure

4. The circular flow model shows that the sale of resources in the input market provides households with the income to make purchases in the output market. In the aggregate, these flows must be equal in dollar terms. The model is illustrated in StudyCheck 4 Figure.

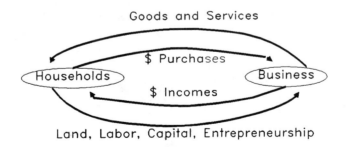

StudyCheck 4 Figure

58 CHAPTER 2

5. The opportunity cost of:
   - X in Tryhard = 1Y;
   - Y in Tryhard = 1X;
   - X in Trynot = 2Y;
   - Y in Trynot = ½X.

   Countries specialize according to which has the lowest opportunity cost of each good. That means that Tryhard will produce X and Trynot will produce Y.

6. See StudyCheck 6 Figure.

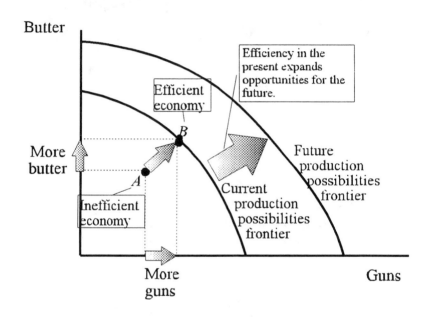

StudyCheck 6 Figure

FILL IN THE BLANKS

1. Opportunity costs
2. Resources, productivity
3. Land, labor, human capital, capital, physical, entrepreneurship
4. Technology
5. production possibilities frontier
6. one, three, twelve
7. one, two, six
8. increasing costs
9. bowed outward, straight
10. efficient, efficiently, inside, outside

11. Allocative
12. outward, growth
13. depreciation, inward
14. general, specialized
15. Money, barter
16. circular flow, output, input
17. comparative, comparative, absolute
18. exports, Imports, outside
19. smaller, larger
20. absolute, Japan, England
21. resources, technology
22. inefficient, efficient
23. profit
24. invisible hand
25. inspired, resentment, conflict

TRUE/FALSE/EXPLAIN

1. False, the opportunity cost is the value that the land, time, and money involved in maintaining the park would have had their next best alternative uses.
2. True.
3. False, the opportunity cost will be higher because the bowed-out shape implies an increasing incremental tradeoff.
4. True.
5. True.
6. True.
7. False, all points are technologically efficient.
8. False, money is an integral part of the circular flow of inputs and outputs.
9. False, resources are assumed to be owned by households.
10. True.
11. False, even though the country might not have an absolute advantage in anything, it can still gain by trading according to its comparative advantage.
12. False, we would seek to minimize opportunity costs.
13. False, although Superior would have an absolute advantage in both goods, it would have a comparative advantage only in one of them.
14. True.
15. False, the country would gain by specializing according to its comparative advantage and trading with other countries.
16. True.
17. False, although workers in those jobs would gain, the country as a whole would lose because its consumption possibilities would diminish.
18. True.

60 CHAPTER 2

19. True.
20. True.
21. False, although the Soviet Union was dissolved in 1991, it was dissolved peacefully.
22. True.
23. True.
24. True.
25. False, patriotic zeal has proved very important in warfare in Cuba, Vietnam, and elsewhere.

MULTIPLE CHOICE

1. d
2. a
3. c
4. c
5. b
6. d
7. a
8. c
9. a
10. d
11. a
12. c
13. b
14. a
15. c
16. a
17. c
18. a
19. a
20. a
21. a
22. b
23. a
24. b
25. a

GRASPING THE GRAPHS
Examples of correct answers

1. 1
2. 2
3. 3
4. 12
5. 22
6. Coconuts forgone
7. Either would be possible and efficient.
8. Neither is possible.
9. Both are possible, but neither is efficient.
10. By choosing less current consumption and more capital, the production possibilities frontier grows faster over time.
11. Current consumption forgone today
12. Increase in capital produced today
13. U.S. butter in the 1970s
14. Soviet production possibilities frontier in the 1970s
15. Decrease in Soviet butter production from the 1970s to the 1980s
16. U.S. production possibilities frontier in the 1980s

**Visit the Ayers/Collinge companion Website at http://www.prenhall.com/ayers
for further activities and exercises for this chapter.**

Chapter 3

DEMAND AND SUPPLY

CHAPTER REVIEW

- *Competition* provides consumers with alternatives. The competition by producers to satisfy consumer wants underlies markets, which are characterized by demand and supply. Market economies rely upon competition, and thus upon demand and supply, to answer the three basic economic questions: What? How? For whom?

3.1 Demand

- Demand relates the quantity of a good that consumers would purchase at each of various possible prices, over some period of time, ceteris paribus. Demand is a relationship, not a single quantity. The terms demand, demand schedule, and demand curve all refer to the same thing. For a given price, demand tells us a specific quantity that consumers would actually purchase. This quantity is termed the **quantity demanded**.

- Demand must be defined for a set period of time. Moreover, anything else that might influence the quantity demanded must be held constant. This is termed the *ceteris paribus* condition. It means that we only look at one relationship at a time, where *ceteris paribus* is the Latin for holding all else equal.

- Demand is an inverse relationship between price and quantity demanded. As price rises, quantity demanded falls. As price falls, quantity demanded rises. This relationship is termed the **law of demand**.

- Anything that causes the demand curve to shift is termed a *shift factor*. **An *increase in demand* occurs when demand shifts to the right. A *decrease in demand* occurs when demand shifts to the left.** Note that a change in the price of the good neither increases nor decreases demand—demand does not shift. Rather, **a price change would change the quantity demanded, which involves *moving along the demand curve*, but would not change the demand curve itself.** A lower price results in a movement down the demand curve, while a higher price causes a movement up the demand curve.

- Some things are more likely to shift demand than are others. As mentioned, consumer income is a likely shift factor. **For *normal goods*, an increase in income shifts demand to the right.** However, there are many goods that people buy less of as their incomes rise. These are termed **inferior goods. An increase in income shifts the demand for inferior goods to the left.**

- Changes in the prices of substitutes and complements also shift demand. A **substitute** is something that takes the place of something else. Different brands of coffee are substitutes. So are coffee and tea. A **complement** is a good that goes with another good, such as ketchup on hot dogs or cream in coffee. **Demand varies directly with a change in the price of a substitute. Demand varies inversely to a change in the price of a complement.**

- **Changes in tastes and preferences will also shift demand.** Over time, as some items become more popular, their demand curves shift out. Other items see their popularity fade and their demand curves shift in. Producers often use advertising in an attempt to influence tastes and preferences toward their particular brand of product.

- Changes in population, in expectations about future prices, or in many other factors can cause demand to shift. **Demand will increase or decrease to the extent that population increases or decreases. A change in consumer expectations about future prices will shift demand in the present.** For example, if you expect prices to fall in the future, you might put off your purchases now, in effect shifting your current demand curve to the left. You would be treating future purchases as a substitute for current purchases. For some products, other factors could be significant, such as conjectures about future technologies that might make products with current technologies obsolete.

StudyCheck 1

List several reasons that demand might decrease, as in part (a) of the following figure. List several reasons that demand might increase, as in part (b) of the following figure.

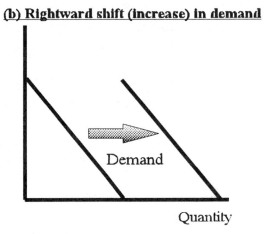

3.2 Supply

- **Supply** relates the quantity of a good that will be offered for sale at each of various possible prices, over some period of time, ceteris paribus. This quantity is termed the **quantity supplied.** Note that supply and quantity supplied are not synonyms. Supply refers to the entire set of data that relates price and quantity and is thus also called a *supply schedule* or *supply curve*. Quantity supplied is the quantity associated with a single point on that schedule. As price changes, quantity supplied changes, but supply does not.

- In contrast to the downward-sloping demand curve, the supply curve nearly always slopes upward to the right. This direct relationship between price and quantity supplied is known as the **law of supply**. As price rises, the quantity offered for sale by producers increases. The reason is that a higher price means higher revenue per unit sold, which will in turn cover the cost of producing some additional units.

- An *increase in supply* occurs when the entire supply curve shifts to the right, with more quantity supplied at each particular price. Likewise, a *decrease in supply* occurs when the entire supply curve shifts to the left, showing less quantity supplied at any particular price. A change in price does not shift supply, but rather causes a *movement along supply*.

- Supply's most important shift factors differ from those for demand. When it comes to supply, changes in expectations as to future prices are still important, but it is the expectations by producers, and not by consumers, that matter. The other important supply shift factors are different from the demand shift factors. In addition to producer expectations as to future prices, important shift factors include: 1) the number of firms; 2) prices of inputs; 3) technological change; 4) restrictions in production; 5) prices of substitutes in production; and 6) prices of jointly produced goods.

- **Today's supply curve shifts in the opposite direction from changes in expected future prices.** Supply shifts directly with the change in the number of firms producing a good.

- If the price of labor or other input prices fall, firms see their expenses drop, and are willing to produce more at any given price. Hence, a decline in input prices increases supply, meaning that supply shifts to the right. Were input prices to increase, supply would decrease, meaning that it would shift to the left. In that case, fewer units are offered for sale at any given price. In general, **supply will shift in the opposite direction from changes in input prices.**

StudyCheck 2

List several reasons that supply might decrease, as in part (a) of the following figure. List several reasons that supply might increase, as in part (b) of the following figure.

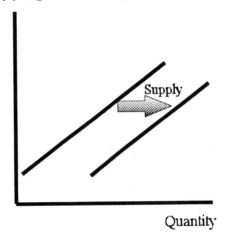

- Firms adopt technological change in order to produce more output per unit of input. This has the same effect as a decrease in input prices. **Technological change in the production of any good shifts its supply to the right.**

- Firms sometimes face restrictions in how they are allowed to do business. **Production restrictions decrease supply.**

- **Supply varies inversely to the price of a substitute in production.** Be aware that substitutes in production are not the same as the substitutes in consumption that shift demand.

- Some products are produced jointly, such as beef and leather. An increase in the popularity and price of beef would lead to a movement up the supply curve for beef. The greater quantity supplied of beef means that more cattle are raised for slaughter, which has the effect of shifting the supply of leather to the right. In brief, more leather would be offered for sale at each price of leather, in response to people consuming more steak and hamburger. Thus, **supply varies directly with the prices of products that are jointly produced.**

3.3 Equilibrium—Demand Meets Supply and the Market Clears

- **Demand can be one individual's or the market's as a whole. Likewise, supply can be from one firm or all firms in the market.**

- Market demand is the sum of all the individuals' demands in that market. Summing individuals' demands is straightforward if you remember to add quantities, not prices. For each price, the quantity demanded in the marketplace is the sum of the quantities demanded by all consumers. On the graph of demand, **market demand is the horizontal summation of individuals' demand curves.**

StudyCheck 3

Draw a single graph indicating somebody's demand curve for tacos. Calling this person Larry, label the demand curve "Larry's demand." Be sure to label the axes of your graph, too. On the same graph, draw market demand, given that there are a total of three people willing to buy tacos and that each has a demand curve identical to Larry's.

StudyCheck 4

Graph the supply and demand for MARGARINE. Label price and quantity. Suppose that the price of BUTTER increases. Make appropriate changes in the margarine market.

- Market supply depicts the total quantity offered for sale in the market at each price. To obtain market supply, merely add the quantities offered for sale by all sellers at each price. Graphically, **market supply is the horizontal summation of each seller's supply curve.**

- **There is only one price that *clears the market*, meaning that the quantity supplied equals the quantity demanded.** The market-clearing price and the resulting quantity traded comprise what is known as the **market equilibrium,** meaning that there is no tendency for either price or quantity to change, *ceteris paribus*. Market equilibrium is determined by the intersection of supply and demand.

- At any price above the equilibrium price, there would be a **surplus,** representing the excess of quantity supplied over quantity demanded. In any market in which a surplus occurs, some sellers would cut their prices slightly in order to be the ones that make the sales. Other suppliers would then be without customers, and would consequently lower their own prices enough to capture customers from their competitors. This leapfrogging process would continue until the quantity demanded and supplied are equal, which occurs at the equilibrium price.

- A price that is below the equilibrium price results in a **shortage,** equal to the amount by which quantity demanded exceeds quantity supplied. Whenever there is a shortage in any market, buyers compete against each other for the limited quantities of the goods that are offered for sale at that price. For sellers, shortages provide an opportunity both to raise prices and to increase sales, a doubly appealing prospect. Price would thus rise to its equilibrium value, the point at which the shortage disappears. Thus, without any guidance, the invisible hand of the market eliminates either surpluses or shortages and leads to the market-clearing equilibrium.

- Suppose either supply or demand were to change. For example, suppose an increase in consumer income or a decrease in the price of a complement shifts demand to the right. One of the most common mistakes students make is to think this shift in demand would also shift supply. It would not, because demand is not a shift factor for supply. Rather, the rightward shift in demand leads to a movement up the supply curve and results in a new, higher equilibrium price and quantity. More generally, **a change in supply would cause a movement along demand. Similarly, a change in demand would cause a movement along supply.**

- The market equilibrium will change whenever supply or demand shift. Taken one curve at a time, there are only four shifts possible: 1) An increase in supply, which shifts supply to the right. 2) A decrease in supply, which shifts supply to the left. 3) An increase in demand, which shifts demand to the right. 4) A decrease in demand, which shifts demand to the left.

- The table describes the effects of a shift in demand or a shift in supply:

The Four Basic Cases of Shifting Demand and Supply

Case	Demand	Supply	Equilibrium Price	Equilibrium Quantity
1	No change	Shifts right	Falls	Rises
2	No change	Shifts left	Rises	Falls
3	Shifts right	No change	Rises	Rises
4	Shifts left	No change	Falls	Falls

StudyCheck 5

Using a graph, show the effect on the market equilibrium price and quantity of a decrease in the number of firms supplying a good. Label all curves, the initial price (P1), the final price (P2), the initial quantity (Q1), the final quantity (Q2), and the axes of the graph.

- To understand the effects on price and quantity when there are simultaneous shifts in supply and demand, combine two shifts from the table above. The table shows the outcome of simultaneous shifts:

The Four Cases of Simultaneous Shifts in Demand and Supply

Case	Demand	Supply	Equilibrium price	Equilibrium quantity
5 (cases 1 and 3)	Shift right	Shifts right	Direction uncertain	Rises
6 (cases 2 and 4)	Shifts left	Shifts left	Direction uncertain	Falls
7 (cases 2 and 3)	Shifts right	Shifts left	Rises	Direction uncertain
8 (cases 1 and 4)	Shifts left	Shifts right	Falls	Direction uncertain

- Notice that in the case of simultaneous shifts, the change in either equilibrium price or quantity is listed as uncertain to indicate that the direction in which the equilibrium price or quantity will move cannot be known without additional information. The direction in which either price or quantity changes will be uncertain when the shifts in demand and supply pull the equilibrium in opposite directions.

StudyCheck 6

Show how a simultaneous increase in both demand and supply can lead to any of the following three outcomes: (a) no change in price; (b) a decrease in price; or (c) an increase in price. Use three separate graphs to show these three cases. In each case, note that the equilibrium quantity increases.

StudyCheck 7

Suppose demand and supply both shift to the left. Using three separate graphs, show how these shifts could lead to a higher price, a lower price, or no change in price, but always lead to a lower quantity.

StudyCheck 8

Using a graph, show the effects on equilibrium price and quantity of a large increase in supply combined with a small increase in demand.

E&A 3.4 **Demanding Better Schools, Supplying Better Schools**

- Consistent with the law of demand, the lower the price of a college education, *ceteris paribus*, the greater the number of students who will apply and the more education they will choose. To promote higher education, government offers tax deductions, subsidies, and financial aid that in effect lowers its price.

- High school seniors seriously consider a varied assortment of colleges. In lower grades, however, there is a powerful financial incentive to choose only the government-provided local public school. The reason is that taxpayer financing makes those schools free to the student.

- Inefficient schools are insulated from competitive pressures to reform because even the best private schools find it hard to compete with "free" and it would take moving to a new school district to enroll in a different public school.

- If there were no free public schools, the invisible hand of the market would cause schools to become efficient at responding to the demands of parents. Schools that are most efficient at providing value would gain students, while others would lose them. However, because family incomes differ, the outcome would lead to unequal opportunities for schooling.

- Limited competition is provided by *charter schools*, a form of public school. Much more competition can be achieved through *vouchers*, which provide money that recipients can spend, but restrict that spending to a certain category of goods. *School vouchers* provide parents with money that can only be spent on schooling their children. With vouchers, the money is received by the school of each parent's choosing rather than being spent directly by the government-run public school.

- School vouchers were first proposed in 1955 by Nobel-prize-winning economist Milton Friedman. Today, voucher programs of one sort or another are underway in Ohio, Florida, Texas, and elsewhere.

- Vouchers lower the price of private schooling to parents, thus increasing their quantity demanded. Private schools are willing to offer greater quantities supplied at lower prices because of the supplemental payment they receive from vouchers, a rightward shift in supply when parents are provided vouchers. The result is a lower price and more children enrolled in private schools. In the market for the substitute government-run public schools, which offer unlimited enrollments at a price of "free" to the parents, the result is a decrease in demand and enrollments. With vouchers, the location, design, and operation of schools is driven by market demand.

- Opponents of vouchers fear that the competition for voucher money would cause schools to shortchange educational objectives and promote popular, but not very worthwhile, activities. Voucher critics want to see schooling remain in the hands of educational professionals whose motives they perceive as more focused on learning and less on money. Just like inefficient companies in other sectors of the free market, inefficient public schools would whither and die. So, too, would inefficient private schools. The process might be hard on the students.

- Perhaps more experiments with vouchers will clarify the issues. By promoting competition, vouchers offer the promise of improved schools. Will parents demand well for their children or should that choice be left to educational professionals?

StudyCheck 9
Explain the workings of, and motivation for, a system of school vouchers.

FILL IN THE BLANKS

1. _____ by producers to satisfy consumer wants underlies markets. The what, how, and for whom questions are answered in a market economy by _____ and _____.

2. _____ relates the quantity of a good that consumers would purchase at each of various possible prices, over some period of time, ceteris paribus. For a given price, demand tells us a specific quantity that consumers would actually purchase. This quantity is termed the _____ _____.

74   CHAPTER 3

3. Anything besides price that might influence demand must be held constant, termed the _____ _____ condition, meaning that we only look at one relationship at a time, holding all else equal.

4. The law of demand is an _____ relationship between price and quantity demanded. As price rises, quantity demanded _____. As price falls, quantity demanded _____.

5. Anything that causes the demand curve to shift is termed a shift factor. An increase in demand occurs when demand shifts _____. A decrease in demand occurs when demand shifts _____.

6. The most important shift factors for demand are _____, _____, _____, the prices of _____ or _____, and _____ about future prices.

7. Note that a change in the price of the good neither increases nor decreases demand—demand does not shift. Rather, a price change would change the _____ _____, which involves moving along the demand curve, but would not change the demand curve itself. A lower price results in a movement _____ the demand curve, while a higher price causes a movement _____ the demand curve.

8. For _____ goods, an increase in income shifts demand to the right. However, there are many goods that people buy less of as their incomes rise. These are termed _____ goods, and an increase in income shifts the demand for them to the _____. A _____ is something that takes the place of something else. A _____ is a good that goes with another good. Demand varies directly with a change in the price of a substitute. Demand varies inversely to a change in the price of a complement.

9. Changes in tastes and preferences will also shift demand. Over time, as some items become more popular, their demand curves shift to the _____. Other items see their popularity fade and their demand curves shift to the _____. Demand will increase or decrease to the extent that population increases or decreases. A change in consumer expectations about future prices will shift demand in the present. If you expect prices to fall in the future, you might put off your purchases now, in effect shifting your current demand curve to the _____. You would be treating future purchases as a substitute for current purchases.

10. _____ relates the quantity of a good that will be offered for sale at each of various possible prices, over some period of time, ceteris paribus. This quantity is termed the _____ _____.

11. The direct relationship between price and quantity supplied is known as the _____ _____. As price rises, the quantity offered for sale by producers _____. An

increase in supply occurs when the entire supply curve shifts to the _____, while a decrease in supply occurs when the entire supply curve shifts to the _____. A change in price does not shift supply, but rather causes a _____ _____ _____.

12. In addition to producer expectations as to future prices, important shift factors for supply include the number of _____, the prices of _____ , _____ improvements, restrictions in production, _____ of substitutes in production; and _____ of jointly produced goods.

13. Today's supply curve shifts in the _____ direction from changes in expected future prices. Supply will shift in the _____ direction from changes in input prices. Technological improvements in the production of any good shifts its supply to the _____. Production restrictions _____ supply. Supply varies _____ to the price of a substitute in production. Supply varies _____ with the prices of products that are jointly produced.

14. Market demand is the _____ of all the individuals' demands in that market. Market supply depicts the total quantity offered for sale in the market at each price. To obtain market supply, _____ the quantities offered for sale by all sellers at each price.

15. The market-clearing price and the resulting quantity traded comprise what is known as the market _____, meaning that there is no tendency for either price or quantity to change, *ceteris paribus*.

16. Market equilibrium is determined by the intersection of _____ and _____. At any price above the equilibrium price, there would be a _____, representing the excess of quantity supplied over quantity demanded. price that is below the equilibrium price results in a _____ equal to the amount by which quantity demanded exceeds quantity supplied.

17. Suppose either supply or demand were to change. For example, suppose an increase in consumer income or a decrease in the price of a complement shifts demand to the right. One of the most common mistakes students make is to think this shift in demand would also shift supply. It would not, because demand is not a shift factor for supply. Rather, the rightward shift in demand leads to a movement up the supply curve and results in a new, higher equilibrium price and quantity. More generally, a change in supply would cause a _____ along demand. Similarly, a change in demand would cause a _____ along supply.

18. The market equilibrium will change whenever supply or demand shift. Taken one curve at a time, there are only four shifts possible: 1) An _____ in supply, which shifts supply

76 CHAPTER 3

to the right. 2) A _____ in supply, which shifts supply to the left. 3) An _____ in demand, which shifts demand to the right. 4) A _____ in demand, which shifts demand to the left.

19. The table describes the effects of a shift in demand or a shift in supply:

The Four Basic Cases of Shifting Demand and Supply

Case	Demand	Supply	Equilibrium Price	Equilibrium Quantity
1	No change	Shifts right	_____	_____
2	No change	Shifts left	_____	_____
3	Shifts right	No change	_____	_____
4	Shifts left	No change	_____	_____

20. To understand the effects on price and quantity when there are simultaneous shifts in supply and demand, combine two shifts from the table above. The table shows the outcome of simultaneous shifts:

The Four Cases of Simultaneous Shifts in Demand and Supply

Case	Demand	Supply	Equilibrium price	Equilibrium quantity
5 (cases 1 and 3)	Shift right	Shifts right	_____	Rises
6 (cases 2 and 4)	Shifts left	Shifts left	_____	Falls
7 (cases 2 and 3)	Shifts right	Shifts left	_____	Direction uncertain
8 (cases 1 and 4)	Shifts left	Shifts right	_____	Direction uncertain

E&A 21. In lower grades, there is a powerful financial incentive to choose only the government-provided local public school. The reason is that taxpayer financing makes those schools _____ to the student. _____ schools are insulated from competitive pressures to reform because even the best private schools find it hard to compete with "free" and it would take moving to a new school district to enroll in a different public school.

22. If there were no free public schools, the invisible hand of the market would cause schools to become _____ at responding to the demands of parents. Schools that are most efficient at providing value would gain students, while others would lose them.

23. Limited competition is provided by _____ schools, a form of public school. Much more competition can be achieved through school _____, which provide parents with money that they must spend on schooling their children.

24. Vouchers lower the _____ of private schooling to parents, thus increasing their quantity demanded. Private schools are willing to offer greater quantities supplied at lower prices because of the supplemental payment they receive from vouchers, a _____ shift in supply when parents are provided vouchers. The result is a lower price and more children enrolled in private schools. In the market for the substitute government-run public schools,

which offer unlimited enrollments at a price of "free" to the parents, the result is a _____ in demand and enrollments.

25. With vouchers, the location, design, and operation of schools is driven by market _____.

TRUE/FALSE/EXPLAIN
If false, explain why in the space provided.

1. A decrease in price shifts demand to the right.

2. A decrease in income decreases demand for a normal good.

3. Technological change has the effect of shifting supply to the left.

4. Market demand is the horizontal summation of all buyers' demands.

5. An increase in supply increases demand.

6. If demand shifts to the right and supply shifts to the left, we know that price will rise.

7. If demand shifts to the right and supply shifts to the left, we know that quantity will not change.

8. An increase in price will result in a decrease in demand.

9. Demand shifts to the right if the good in question is normal and income increases.

10. If the wage rate falls, the supply of a good will shift to the left.

11. If the actual price exceeds the market equilibrium price, there will be a shortage.

12. If the price of spaghetti increases, demand for meatballs would decrease.

13. If the price of spaghetti increases, the supply of meatballs would increase.

14. Both government regulations and restrictive union work rules tend to shift supply to the left.

15. If the market price is below the equilibrium price, the equilibrium price will fall.

16. Whenever demand shifts, supply also shifts.

17. Demand in the present shifts to the left when consumers hear news that the market price is likely to rise in the future.

18. Supply in the present shifts to the left when producers hear news that the market price is likely to rise in the future.

19. When additional producers enter the market, the market supply shifts upward.

20. Generic paper towels would be an example of an inferior good.

E&A 21. Charter schools are public schools that are established by the parents and certified by the state.

22. School vouchers would reduce competition among schools.

23. Because you get what you pay for, the quality of education depends only upon how much money is spent, not upon whether schools are run by government or the private sector.

24. Vouchers are proposed as a way for parents to shop for schools.

25. Government usually spends about the same amount of your tax money on your children whether or not you send them to a religious school.

MULTIPLE CHOICE
Circle the letter preceding the one best answer.

1. Which of the following is a statement of the law of demand?
    a. As the price of a good falls, demand rises, *ceteris paribus*.
    b. As the price of a good rises, demand rises, *ceteris paribus*.
    c. As the price of a good falls, the quantity demanded rises, *ceteris paribus*.
    d. As the price of a good falls, the quantity demanded falls, *ceteris paribus*.

80 CHAPTER 3

2. A decrease in the price of french fries would cause
   a. the demand for hamburgers to shift to the right.
   b. a movement up the demand curve for hamburgers.
   c. the demand for hamburgers to shift to the left.
   d. a movement down the demand curve for hamburgers.

3. If a good is inferior and income goes up,
   a. supply of that good will shift to the right.
   b. supply of that good will shift to the left.
   c. demand for that good will shift to the right.
   d. demand for that good will shift to the left.

4. The market demand curve for a good is the
   a. horizontal summation of each individual's demand curve.
   b. horizontal summation of each individual's demand curve minus market supply.
   c. vertical summation of each individual's demand curve.
   d. vertical summation of each individual's demand curve minus market supply.

5. In Multiple Choice Figure 1, the quantity demanded by Jill at a price of $2 is given by the length of arrow
   a. A.
   b. B.
   c. C.
   d. D.

6. In Multiple Choice Figure 1, the quantity demanded by Jack at a price of $3 is given by the length of arrow
   a. A.
   b. B.
   c. C.
   d. D.

7. In Multiple Choice Figure 1, adding together the lengths of arrows C and D tells the market
   a. supply.
   b. quantity demanded at a price of $2.
   c. price.
   d. quantity supplied at a price of $2.

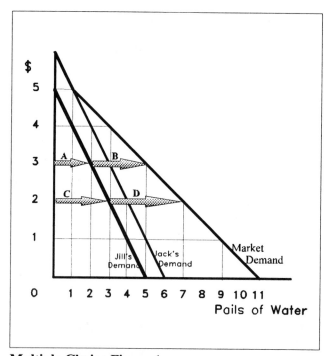

Multiple Choice Figure 1

8. A decrease in the popularity of blue denim would
   a. shift the supply of blue denim to the right.
   b. shift the supply of blue denim to the left.
   c. cause a movement up the blue denim supply curve.
   d. cause a movement down the blue denim supply curve.

9. Ceteris paribus, an increase in the demand for Pepsi would
   a. increase the supply of Pepsi.
   b. increase the demand for Coke.
   c. decrease the supply of Coke.
   d. increase the quantity of Pepsi supplied.

10. And increase in supply is the same as
    a. a rightward shift in the supply curve.
    b. an upward shift in the supply curve.
    c. a downward shift in the supply curve.
    d. a leftward shift in the supply curve.

11. If wage rates go down,
    a. supply shifts to the right.
    b. supply shifts to the left.
    c. demand shifts to the right.
    d. demand shifts to the left.

12. If government regulations increase costs,
    a. supply shifts to the right.
    b. supply shifts to the left.
    c. demand shifts to the right.
    d. demand shifts to the left.

13. Beef and hides represent
    a. substitutes in consumption.
    b. substitutes in production.
    c. complements in consumption.
    d. complements in production.

82 CHAPTER 3

14. In Multiple Choice Figure 2, the arrow labeled A is the
   a. surplus if the price is $4.
   b. shortage if the price is $4.
   c. quantity supplied at a price of $4.
   d. quantity demanded at a price of $4.

15. In Multiple Choice Figure 2, the arrow labeled B is the
   a. surplus if the price is $2.
   b. shortage of the price is $2.
   c. quantity supplied at a price of $2.
   d. quantity demanded at a price of $2.

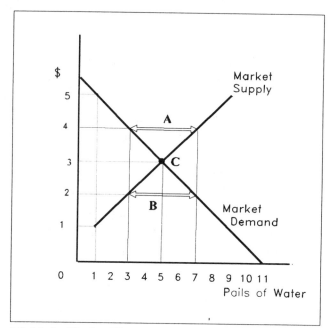

Multiple Choice Figure 2

16. In Multiple Choice Figure 2, point C represents the
   a. surplus at a price of $3.
   b. shortage at a price of $3.
   c. surplus at a price of $2.
   d. market equilibrium.

17. If the market price is above its equilibrium value, the market price will
   a. decrease, because some producers will not sell as much as they would like to at that price and proceed to cut their prices, which causes other producers to do the same.
   b. decrease, because a price that is above the equilibrium price would be illegal according to the law of demand.
   c. remain the same, because the concept of a market equilibrium refers to a tendency for prices to increase, and there is no reason for price to increase if it is already above its equilibrium value.
   d. increase, because a price that is above the market equilibrium tends to rise.

18. If demand shifts to the right, and supply does not shift, the equilibrium
   a. price and quantity will both rise.
   b. price and quantity will both fall.
   c. price will rise and quantity will fall.
   d. price will fall and quantity will rise.

19. If the demand and supply of a product both increase, then
    a. both price and quantity must rise.
    b. price rises, but quantity remains constant.
    c. quantity rises, but the change in price cannot be predicted without more information.
    d. price falls, but the change in quantity cannot be predicted without more information.

20. Which of the following COULD NOT explain an increase in both price and quantity?
    a. Supply and demand both shift right.
    b. Supply remains unchanged, and demand shifts right.
    c. Supply shifts right, and demand shifts left.
    d. Supply shifts left, and demand shifts right.

21. In government-run public schools, a child's school is usually determined by
    a. where that child lives.
    b. a lottery system.
    c. which parents are willing to pay the most.
    d. competitive testing of skills and abilities.

22. A charter school is a
    a. school that would not exist except for school vouchers.
    b. public school that is established by parents.
    c. private school with a religious affiliation.
    d. private school with no religious affiliation.

23. _____ specify an amount that the holder can spend, but restrict that spending to a certain category of goods.
    a. Mandates
    b. Taxes
    c. Vouchers
    d. Price supports

24. The primary purpose of school vouchers is to
    a. allow parents to express their religious preferences in terms of their children's education.
    b. standardize educational opportunities for all children.
    c. get around the Supreme Court ruling that charter schools are unconstitutional.
    d. promote efficiency through competition among schools.

25. A major objection to school vouchers is that
    a. they are inefficient.
    b. parents are not formally trained in how to best educate their children.
    c. it would greatly increase the influence of teachers' unions.
    d. they would cost much more than government-run public schools.

GRASPING THE GRAPHS
Fill in each box with a concept that applies.

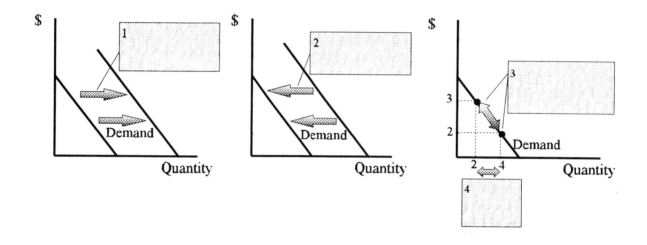

DEMAND AND SUPPLY 85

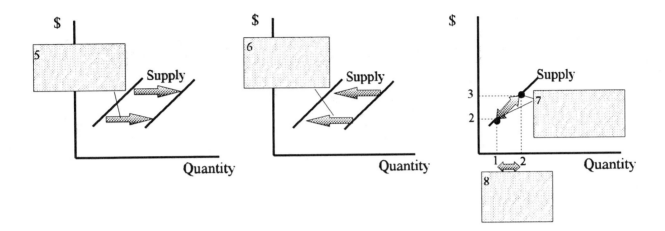

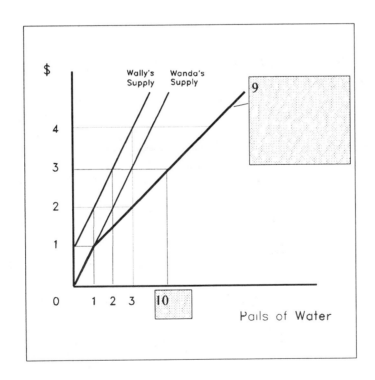

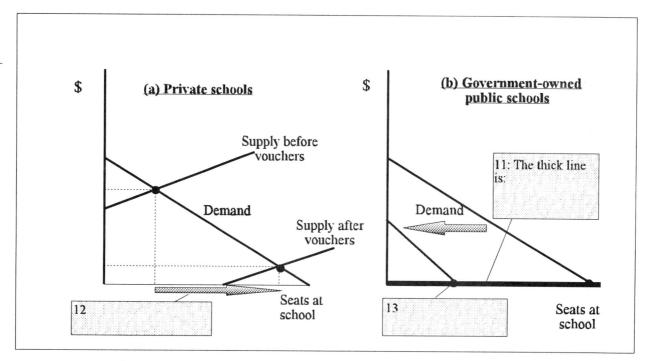

For additional practice in grasping this chapter's graphs, visit
http://www.prenhall.com/ayers and try *Smart Graphs* 4, 5, 6, 7, and 8,
along with *Active Graphs* 10, 11, 12, and 13.

ANSWERS

STUDYCHECKS

1.

Demand decreases (shifts to the left) when:	Demand increases (shifts to the right) when:
The price of a substitute decreases.	The price of a substitute increases.
The price of a complement increases.	The price of a complement decreases.
The good is normal and income decreases.	The good is normal and income increases.
The good is inferior and income increases.	The good is inferior and income decreases.
Population decreases.	Population increases.
Consumers expect price to decrease in the future.	Consumers expect price to increase in the future.
Tastes and preferences turn against the product.	Tastes and preferences turn in favor of the product.

2.

Supply decreases (shifts to the left) when	Supply increases (shifts to the right) when
The number of sellers decreases.	The number of sellers increases.
The price of labor or any other input rises.	The price of labor or any other input falls.
Producers expect prices to rise in the future.	Producers expect prices to decline in the future.
Government, labor union, or other restrictions on production practices increase cost.	Technological change lowers cost.
The price of a substitute in production rises.	The price of a substitute in production falls.
The price of a jointly produced product falls.	The price of a jointly produced product rises.

3. See StudyCheck 3 Figure.

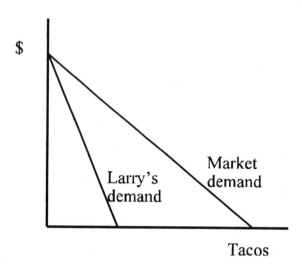

StudyCheck 3 Figure

4. See StudyCheck 4 Figure.

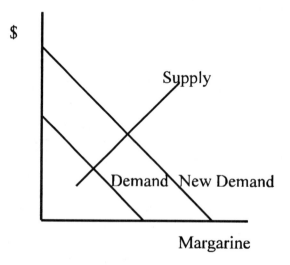

StudyCheck 4 Figure

5. See StudyCheck 5 Figure.

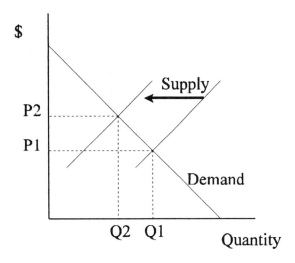

StudyCheck 5 Figure

6. See StudyCheck 6 Figure.

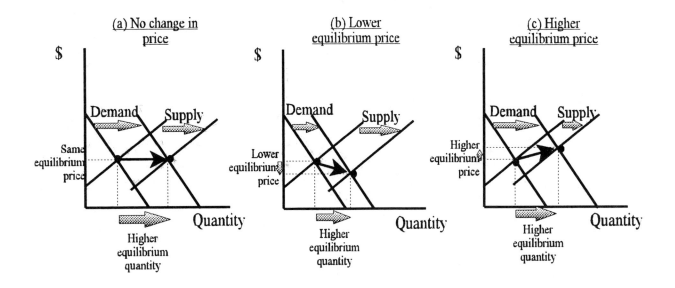

StudyCheck 6 Figure

7. See StudyCheck 7 Figure.

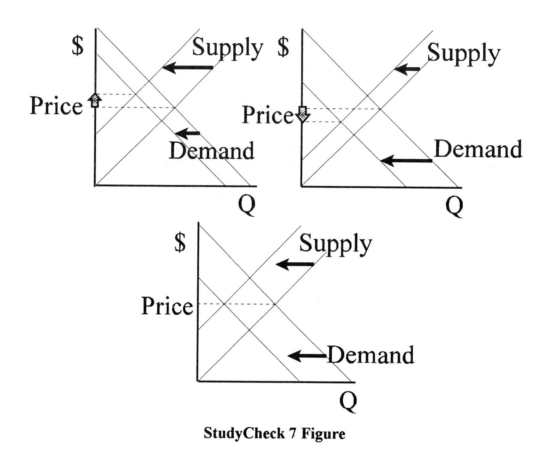

StudyCheck 7 Figure

8. See StudyCheck 8 Figure.

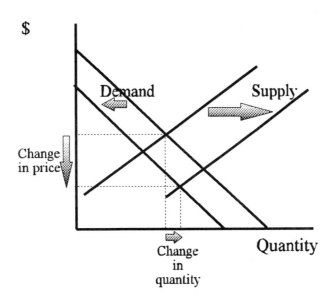

StudyCheck 8 Figure

9. A school voucher system gives parents vouchers that represent money, but only if spent on schooling for their children. Numerous details would be specified, such as whether the vouchers would apply to parochial schools. The motivation is to introduce competition into the market for children's education. Voucher proponents argue that competition would lead to efficiency, as schools seek to attract parents' voucher spending by offering the most valuable education for the money. Opponents claim that parents will not choose as well as professionally trained educators.

FILL IN THE BLANKS

1. Competition, demand, supply
2. Demand, quantity demanded
3. ceteris paribus
4. inverse, falls, rises
5. to the right, to the left
6. incomes, population, tastes and preferences, substitutes, complements, expectations
7. quantity demanded, down, up
8. normal, inferior, left, substitute, complement

9. right, left, left
10. supply, quantity supplied
11. law of supply, rises, right, left, movement along supply
12. firms, inputs, technological, prices, prices
13. opposite, opposite, right, decrease, inversely, directly
14. sum, add
15. equilibrium
16. supply, demand, surplus, shortage
17. movement, movement
18. increase, decrease, increase, decrease
19. Case 1: falls, rises; Case 2: rises, falls; Case 3: rises, rises; Case 4: falls, falls
20. Case 5: direction unknown; Case 6: direction unknown; Case 7: rises; Case 8: falls
21. free, Inefficient
22. efficient
23. charter, vouchers
24. price, rightward, decrease
25. demand

TRUE/FALSE/EXPLAIN

1. False, there is a movement down the demand curve, but the demand curve itself does not shift.
2. True.
3. False, supply would shift to the right.
4. True.
5. False, an increase in supply would increase the quantity demanded because it would cause the equilibrium price to the lower.
6. True.
7. False, without further information, we do not know if the equilibrium quantity will rise, fall, or remain unchanged.
8. False, it is the quantity demanded that would decrease.
9. True.
10. False, supply would shift to the right.
11. False, there would be a surplus.
12. True.
13. False, spaghetti and meatballs are not substitutes in production, and so the price of one has no effect on the supply of the other.
14. True.
15. False, the market price would tend to rise to the market equilibrium but the equilibrium price itself would not change.

16. False, a shift in demand does not shift supply.
17. False, consumers would demand more in the present if they expect price to go up in the future.
18. True.
19. False, supply shifts to the right.
20. True.
21. True.
22. False, vouchers would increase competition among schools.
23. False, the efficiency with which money is spent can vary among schools.
24. True.
25. False, government usually spends tax money only on schools that are provided by the government and that do not teach religion.

MULTIPLE CHOICE

1.	c	8.	d	15.	b	22.	b
2.	a	9.	d	16.	d	23.	c
3.	d	10.	a	17.	a	24.	d
4.	a	11.	a	18.	a	25.	b
5.	c	12.	b	19.	c		
6.	b	13.	d	20.	c		
7.	b	14.	a	21.	a		

GRASPING THE GRAPHS
Examples of correct answers

1. Increase in demand
2. Decrease in demand
3. Movement along demand
4. Change in the quantity demanded
5. Increase in supply
6. Decrease in supply
7. Movement along supply
8. Change in the quantity supplied
9. Market supply, which is the horizontal summation of Wally's supply and Wanda's supply
10. 5

11. Supply by the government
12. Equilibrium quantity after vouchers
13. Increased private-school enrollment

Visit the Ayers/Collinge companion Website at <http://www.prenhall.com/ayers> for further activities and exercises for this chapter.

Chapter 4

THE POWER OF PRICES

CHAPTER REVIEW

- The marketplace depends on **price signals**, meaning that the market price sends a message to consumers and producers. The price signals to consumers how much of a good they will wish to buy, and signals to producers how much of a good they will wish to sell.

4.1 Price Signals for Efficient Choice

- Consumers buy something because they expect that they will be better off by doing so. Likewise when producers sell something. So when a consumer buys a good that a producer sells, both parties are better off. The mutual gains from such market exchanges lead the economy to greater efficiency.

- The demand curve depicts the quantity that would be purchased at each of various prices, *ceteris paribus*. Another way of looking at it is that the demand curve shows the maximum price the consumer would pay for each quantity that might be purchased. This maximum price is the consumer's **marginal benefit**—the incremental value of each additional item consumed.

StudyCheck 1
Using a graph, illustrate the concept of marginal benefit.

- Consider Dwight, who is shopping for blue jeans. The table below shows how demand translates into marginal benefit and total benefit. Dwight's *total benefit* from his blue-jean purchases is the sum of his marginal benefit from each pair. So, if he buys 3 pair, the blue jeans would bring Dwight $45 worth of total benefit, where $45 = $20 + $15 + $10.

Dwight's Demand and Benefits from Blue Jeans

(a) Dwight's Demand for Blue Jeans		(b) Dwight's Benefits from Buying Blue Jeans		
Price	Quantity	Quantity	Marginal Benefit	Total Benefit
$20	1	1	$20	$20
$15	2	2	$15	$35
$10	3	3	$10	$45

- Since Dwight must pay for the blue jeans he buys, the value to him of his blue-jean purchases equals the total benefit from the blue jeans minus what he pays. This value is termed **consumer surplus**, which is difference between the total benefit and total cost to the consumer. Graphically, it is the demand curve minus price.

- The table below computes consumer surplus for three different prices of blue jeans. As you can see in that table, **consumer surplus varies inversely with price.** The greater the price the less is consumer surplus and the lower the price the greater is consumer surplus.

Dwight's Consumer Surplus from Blue Jeans

Price	Quantity Bought	Total Benefit	Total Paid	Consumer Surplus
$20	1	$20	$20	$0
$15	2	$35	$30	$5
$10	3	$45	$30	$15

- A supply curve shows the quantity that would be offered for sale at each of various prices, *ceteris paribus*. The supply curve also depicts the minimum price that the producers of a good would be willing to accept for each quantity offered. That minimum price is the producer's *marginal cost*, which is the incremental cost of producing each additional item offered for sale.

THE POWER OF PRICES 97

StudyCheck 2

Using a graph, illustrate the concept of marginal cost.

- Consider Buddy, who sells blue jeans. The table below shows how supply translates into marginal cost and total cost. Buddy's *total cost* of blue-jeans sold is the sum of his marginal cost from selling each pair. So, if he sells 3 pair of blue jeans, he would incur total costs of $22.50, where $22.50 = $5 +$7.50 + $10.

Buddy's Supply and Costs of Blue Jeans

(a) Buddy's Supply of Blue Jeans		(b) Buddy's Costs of Producing Blue Jeans		
Price	Quantity	Quantity	Marginal Cost	Total Cost
$5	1	1	$5	$5
$7.50	2	2	$7.50	$12.50
$10	3	3	$10	$22.50

- The value Buddy receives from the sale of his product equals total revenue minus total cost. This value is termed **producer surplus**, which is the excess of revenue to producers over their costs of production. Graphically, it is the market price minus the supply curve. If the price of blue jeans is $10 in our example, then Buddy would sell three pair for a total revenue of $30, where total revenue is computed by multiplying price by quantity. Subtracting the total cost of $22.50 from the $30 would leave him with a producer surplus of $7.50.

- The table below computes producer surplus for three different prices of blue jeans. As seen in that table, **producer surplus varies directly with price.**

    Buddy's Producer Surplus from Blue Jeans

Price	Quantity Sold	Total Cost	Total Revenue	Producer Surplus
$5	1	$5	$5	$0
$7.50	2	$12.50	$15	$2.50
$10	3	$22.50	$30	$7.50

- **Markets are efficient to the extent that they maximize *social surplus*, which is the sum of consumer and producer surplus.** Social surplus is the difference between how much a good is worth and how much it costs to produce. It is the total value the economy gains by having the good produced and consumed. In the blue jeans example, the social surplus at a price of $10 would be $22.50, which equals $15 in consumer surplus for Dwight plus $7.50 in producer surplus for Buddy.

- Any time marginal benefit exceeds marginal cost, social surplus would increase if more of the good were to be produced and sold. That is just what the marketplace does. Producers keep on selling until their marginal cost just equals the market price. Likewise, consumers keep on buying until their marginal benefit equals the market price. This means that marginal benefit equals marginal cost at the market equilibrium price and that social surplus is maximized. Any more output would add more cost than benefit.

- Thus, the *rule of efficiency* states that **the efficient output occurs when society's marginal benefit equals marginal cost.** The marketplace achieves an efficient output through price adjustments. At the market equilibrium price, marginal benefit equals marginal cost and social surplus is maximized. The intersection of demand and supply establishes the efficient quantity. Since demand represents marginal benefit and supply represents marginal cost, the rule of efficiency is satisfied.

- The triangular area of forgone social surplus caused by inefficient pricing is called a **deadweight loss**. The size of the deadweight loss will decrease when the price is closer to the market price, but increase when the price moves farther away from its equilibrium value. Prices that differ from their equilibrium values will not persist because those prices will adjust toward equilibrium. The deadweight loss will in this way eventually disappear.

- Some necessities that have a great deal of intrinsic worth are priced lower than luxuries we could easily do without. For example, people pay much more for a diamond than for a glass of water, which seems paradoxical. The paradox disappears when we realize that price merely tells the value of a good at the margin. The last bit of water is not worth much when water is plentiful. It is the scarcity of diamonds that keeps that price high. To understand the total value of a good, though, we must look beyond price to consumer surplus. The consumer surplus from water purchases is vastly greater than the consumer surplus from diamond purchases.

- Questions of efficiency often arise in the context of international trade. If a country chooses not to engage in international trade, the market prices of its goods and services would reflect only the supply and demand within that country. Those prices are called *domestic* prices. Opening an economy to international trade will change market prices in a country by bringing into its markets a world of new consumers and producers. Countries that trade buy goods and services from other countries—their *imports*. They also sell goods and services to other countries—their *exports*. Whether a country imports a good or exports a good will depend upon whether the good's world equilibrium market price is below or above what the country's price would otherwise have been—its domestic price.

- In other words, **the result of trade is that the price in the domestic market will come to equal the world market price.** If the domestic price rises to meet a higher world price, then the country exports the good. If a lower world price causes the domestic price to drop, then the country imports the good, meaning that it is purchased from producers in other countries. In either case, there are some people within the country who gain and others who lose.

- Allowing imports increases social surplus. Although the lower price will cause producer surplus to shrink, the increase in consumer surplus more than compensates for that loss. Because the gains to consumers more than offset the losses to producers, efficiency calls for allowing imports.

- Allowing exports increases social surplus. Although the higher price will cause consumer surplus to shrink, the increase in producer surplus more than compensates. Because the gains to producers more than offset the losses to consumers, efficiency calls for allowing exports.

- In short, consumers come out winners from imports, but producers lose. Producers come out the winners from exports, but consumers lose. In each case, though, the gains exceed the losses. So, whether it be from imports or from exports, the country as a whole comes out the winner.

100   CHAPTER 4

> **StudyCheck 3**
> Using two graphs, show how a country gains from allowing exports. On your first graph, show the social surplus without trade. On your second graph, show how allowing exports increases this surplus.

4.2 Price Ceilings—Holding Prices Down

- A **price ceiling**, is a law that establishes a maximum price that can be legally charged for a good. With rising populations in competition for scarce land, major cities sometimes choose rent controls as a way to insulate tenants from higher housing costs. **Rent controls** hold the monthly price of rental housing to below its equilibrium level. Price tries to rise, but bumps up against the rent control ceiling. For these rent controls to be meaningful, the ceiling price must be set below the market equilibrium price. The result is a housing shortage, in which less housing is offered for lease, while more housing is demanded.

- One effect of rent controls is to transfer wealth from current landlords to current tenants. Such **transfer payments** in which one party's loss is another's gain are not themselves inefficient since they merely redistribute social surplus. However, when transfer payments are caused by government price controls, there are multiple sources of inefficiency, in which social surplus shrinks. The first inefficiency is the deadweight loss triangle associated with a less-than-efficient overall quantity.

- A second source of inefficiency comes from misallocating apartments that are leased. Since any tenant would be constrained to pay the same rent and there are more potential tenants than available apartments, the landlord would find it easy to discriminate, whether on the basis of income, occupation, or anything else the landlord thinks is important.

- A third inefficiency involves **search costs**, which are the costs of finding an apartment. Since landlords have plenty of prospective tenants for rent-controlled apartments, they do not need to advertise. So some enterprising would-be tenants have taken up such tactics as reading the obituaries or, to get the jump, listening to police radios and checking out emergency rooms. In the absence of rent controls, there would be little or no need for such wasteful behavior.

- **The inefficiencies of rent controls are likely to get worse over time** as demand grows with an increasing population while rent-controlled apartments are allowed to deteriorate.

- While rent controls have problems, there are also problems associated with removing them. The immediate effect of abolishing rent controls is that rents jump to their market equilibrium value.

- There are alternatives to rent controls. One alternative is to identify the needy and assign them housing vouchers. **Housing vouchers** are government grants that the recipient can spend only on housing.

- Local governments have often attempted to protect consumers against **price gouging**, which is the disparaging term for hiking up prices in response to temporary surges in demand. The idea is to promote equity. The cost is in terms of efficiency, though, because high prices in times of emergency prevent shortages and allocate sought-after goods to those who value them the most.

- Profitably high prices also motivate rapid restocking, which means that prices do not stay high for long. Local governments also often have laws against *ticket scalping*—the practice of buying tickets at the price set by concert promoters and then reselling at whatever the market will bear. Scalping is a form of *arbitrage*, which means buying low and selling high. Arbitrage directs goods to their highest-valued uses, thus efficiently allocating seats at concerts, ball games, and other events. As for equity, however, opinions differ.

StudyCheck 4

Using supply and demand analysis, indicate graphically the effects on price, quantity demanded, and quantity supplied resulting from imposition of rent-control legislation which lowers rents below their free-market equilibrium level. Be sure to label: 1) the axes of your graph; 2) supply (S); 3) demand (D); 4) price before rent control (Pb); 5) price after rent control (Pa); 6) quantity demanded after rent control (Qd); 7) quantity supplied after rent control (Qs).

StudyCheck 5

Explain the economic grounds upon which laws against price gouging have been justified. What is the primary economic objection?

4.3 Price Floors—Propping Prices Up

- Although consumers are better off when prices are low, producers prefer them high. Both groups often turn to government for help. If politics dictates propping up prices, government can establish a **price floor**, also termed a **price support**, which sets a minimum price that producers are guaranteed to receive. One way to implement a price floor is for government to agree to buy at that floor price. This approach can cause surpluses to pile up at taxpayer expense. Such is the case of agricultural price supports. Note that the term *surplus* in this context refers to a quantity of output, specifically the excess of what is produced over what is consumed, not to the term social surplus that is also used in this chapter.

- Although only two percent of the United States labor force currently derives a living from agriculture, the political influence of agriculture has been strong enough to maintain agricultural price supports in the U.S. since the 1920s. These price supports have been justified on two counts. One is that they sustain the lifestyle of the family farm, an American tradition. However, the reality is that family farming has continued to decline, and a disproportionate amount of price support payments have gone to large farms and corporations. The second justification is that they ensure a plentiful supply of food for American consumers. This line of reasoning does not withstand the logic of economic analysis.

- The effects of an agricultural price support, holding price above its equilibrium value, are more farm output produced, but less consumed. The result is a surplus. Such agricultural surpluses have averaged many billion dollars' worth of foodstuffs annually in the United States.

- The effect of agricultural price supports is to transfer money from both taxpayers and consumers to those in the agriculture industry. Maintaining a high price redistributes social surplus from consumers to producers. There is a deadweight loss associated with both increased production and decreased consumption.

- Additional deadweight loss can be expected to occur because government must buy and dispose of the surplus quantity, which is nearly impossible to do in an efficient manner. Government cannot merely sell the surplus to the highest bidder, because it must prevent the surplus commodities it buys from being distributed to people who would otherwise purchase that product in the marketplace. To do otherwise would merely mean more of a surplus that government would be forced to buy, because those who received from government would buy less from farmers.

- One option is to give the surplus quantity away in a relatively unpalatable form, such as by turning excess milk into powdered milk. Another option is to export the surplus in a manner that does not compete with other agricultural exports. For example, foreign aid to impoverished countries might work, to the extent that the aid does not supplant other food imports from the donor country.

- The **minimum wage** is a requirement that employers pay no less than a specified wage rate. The higher wage means that more people are willing to work. The higher wage for low-skilled labor also means that fewer jobs are offered. Fast food restaurants, car washes, and other businesses "make do" with fewer people, but train and work them harder. They also may replace some labor with capital, such as automated dishwashers and car-washing equipment. The result is that, along with higher wages comes a surplus of labor—or a shortage of jobs, depending upon how you look at it. Because higher wages are offset by fewer jobs, there is no guarantee that minimum wage laws actually increase the total amount firms spend to employ low-skilled workers.

- As was the case with rent controls, minimum wage requirements facilitate discrimination. With numerous applicants for each job opening, employers can pick and choose as they wish. It would be quite difficult to prove if they choose to discriminate on an illegal basis. While the pay is higher, the jobs and extra pay go to those applicants who need help the least.

- There are alternatives to the minimum wage that target the problem of low wages without controlling price. One alternative is to subsidize the earnings of low-income workers. Such a subsidy is already embedded in the U.S. personal income tax—the earned income tax credit. The drawback is that earnings subsidies come at a high budgetary cost, because they reduce government tax collections or involve actual cash payments.

- Subsidies to education also serve as an alternative to the minimum wage. Such subsidies include free public schooling or government financial assistance to students attending private schools, subsidized student loans for college students, and subsidized tuition at public universities. The more widely available are educational opportunities, the more skills the workforce will acquire. The result is that the supply of low-skilled labor shifts to the left. The leftward shift in supply increases the equilibrium wage for low-skilled labor, which is the purpose of minimum wage laws.

StudyCheck 6

Consider the market for unskilled labor, where a minimum wage prevents the price from reaching an equilibrium. Depict this on a graph, labeling: 1) the axes of the graph; 2) Supply (S); 3) Demand (D); 4) wage (W) in the presence of the minimum wage law; 5) the amount of any surplus or shortage (label either surplus or shortage); 6) the quantity of labor actually employed (LE).

StudyCheck 7

Show the manner in which subsidies to education can increase wages for low-skilled labor.

4.4 Around the World—Black Markets as a Safety Valve

- Price controls are practiced throughout the world. Price support programs have been common in agriculture.

- Any time government tries to hold prices above or below market equilibrium, it provides profit opportunities to those willing to take advantage of them. **Black market** activity is said to occur when goods are bought and sold illegally.

E&A ## 4.5 The Price of Power

- It was the winter of 2001 when inadequate electricity supplies prompted rolling blackouts in California that cut off electricity to 670,000 households and businesses for two hours at a time.

- In order to increase the efficiency with which electricity was generated and distributed at the wholesale level, California lawmakers deregulated the wholesale electricity market. Deregulation caused the state's wholesale electricity providers to compete for customers. Competition reduces costs through weeding out inefficiencies. *Ceteris paribus*, greater efficiencies in wholesale electricity production and distribution causes the wholesale electricity supply to shift to the right and the price of electricity in the wholesale market to fall. Utilities pay less for the electricity they distribute and these savings are passed along to the utilities' residential and business customers. So California lawmakers felt comfortable promising California voters that their electricity rates would not go up, at least not very much, and might even go down.

- In the real world many things can change at once. In particular, world crude oil prices skyrocketed, more than doubling soon after California's deregulation of wholesale electricity took effect. The prices of natural gas, coal, and other substitutes for crude oil likewise increased. Since oil and other fuels are significant inputs into the production of electricity, rising fuel prices shifted the supply of electricity at the wholesale level significantly to the left. That leftward shift more than offset any rightward shift caused by deregulation. The decrease in the supply of wholesale electricity caused the wholesale price of electricity to rise sharply.

- Left to itself, the marketplace will not allow a shortage for long. The price of electricity at the retail level will rise in response to a shortage. In turn, consumers will consume less electricity, and producers will provide more until an equilibrium is reached. But, because of the lawmaker's promise that consumer electricity prices would be held in check, rates were held down to less than the market equilibrium price. The result in the retail electricity market was a shortage.

- There was no incentive for the utilities to provide additional electricity because the controlled price they were allowed to charge their customers was less than what they were paying for the electricity they bought on the wholesale market. Losses among the California utilities climbed to $13 billion (as reported by SoCal Edison and Pacific Gas & Electric) and they were teetering on the brink of bankruptcy before the state fashioned a plan to keep the power on. Under the terms of that plan, California borrowed $10 billion to tide the utilities through, with California taxpayers responsible for repaying this added debt.

- The restructuring of the electricity industry toward more competition is not just a California event. About half of the states are currently active in this effort, with electricity deregulation moving from the planning stage to reality in state after state. The experience of California, one of the first to deregulate, will be remembered and analyzed for what can be learned. The most vivid memory is sure to be of the electricity shortages caused by the price ceiling.

StudyCheck 8

Using separate graphs, show the effects of deregulation and energy price increases on the equilibrium in California's wholesale electricity market. Explain how this market analysis could have helped California lawmakers avoid the electricity shortages the state experienced in 2001.

FILL IN THE BLANKS

1. The marketplace depends on price _____, meaning that the market price sends a message to consumers and producers. Consumers buy something because they expect that they will be better off by doing so. Likewise when producers sell something. So when a consumer buys a good that a producer sells, both parties are better off. The mutual gains from such market exchanges lead the economy to greater _____.

2. The demand curve depicts the _____ that would be purchased at each of various prices, *ceteris paribus*. Another way of looking at it is that the demand curve shows the _____ price the consumer would pay for each quantity that might be purchased, the consumer's _____ _____—the incremental value of each additional item consumed.

3. Consider Dwight, who is shopping for blue jeans. The table below shows how demand translates into marginal benefit and total benefit. Dwight's total benefit from his blue-jean purchases is the sum of his _____ benefit from each pair. So, if he buys 3 pair, the blue jeans would bring Dwight $_____ worth of total benefit.

Dwight's Demand and Benefits from Blue Jeans

(a) Dwight's Demand for Blue Jeans		(b) Dwight's Benefits from Buying Blue Jeans		
Price	Quantity	Quantity	Marginal Benefit	Total Benefit
$20	1	1	$20	$20
$15	2	2	$15	$35
$10	3	3	$10	$

4. Since Dwight must pay for the blue jeans he buys, the value to him of his blue-jean purchases equals the total benefit from the blue jeans minus what he pays. This value is termed _____ _____, which is difference between the total benefit and total cost to the consumer. Graphically, it is the demand curve minus _____.

5. The table below computes consumer surplus for three different prices of blue jeans. As you can see in that table, consumer surplus varies inversely with price. The greater the price the less is consumer surplus and the lower the price the greater is consumer surplus. Dwight's consumer surplus from 3 pairs of blue jeans equals $_____.

Dwight's Consumer Surplus from Blue Jeans

Price	Quantity Bought	Total Benefit	Total Paid	Consumer Surplus
$20	1	$20	$20	$0
$15	2	$35	$30	$5
$10	3	$45	$30	$

6. A supply curve shows the _____ that would be offered for sale at each of various prices, *ceteris paribus*. The supply curve also depicts the _____ price that the producers of a good would be willing to accept for each quantity offered, which is the producer's _____ cost, which is the incremental cost of producing each additional item offered for sale.

7. Consider Buddy, who sells blue jeans. The table below shows how supply translates into marginal cost and total cost. Buddy's total cost of blue-jeans sold is the sum of his _____ cost from selling each pair. So, if he sells 3 pair of blue jeans, he would incur total costs of $_____.

Buddy's Supply and Costs of Blue Jeans

(a) Buddy's Supply of Blue Jeans		(b) Buddy's Costs of Producing Blue Jeans		
Price	Quantity	Quantity	Marginal Cost	Total Cost
$5	1	1	$5	$5
$7.50	2	2	$7.50	$12.50
$10	3	3	$10	$

8. The value Buddy receives from the sale of his product equals total revenue minus total cost. This value is termed _____ _____, which is the excess of revenue to producers over their costs of production. Graphically, it is the market price minus the _____ _____.

9. The table below computes producer surplus for three different prices of blue jeans. As seen in that table, producer surplus varies directly with price. If the price of blue jeans is $10 in our example, then Buddy would sell three pair for a total revenue of $30, where total revenue is computed by multiplying price by quantity. The producer surplus is $_____.

Buddy's Producer Surplus from Blue Jeans

Price	Quantity Sold	Total Cost	Total Revenue	Producer Surplus
$5	1	$5	$5	$0
$7.50	2	$12.50	$15	$2.50
$10	3	$22.50	$30	$

10. Markets are efficient to the extent that they maximize _____ _____, which is the sum of consumer and producer surplus.

11. The rule of efficiency states that the efficient output occurs when society's _____ _____ equals _____ _____. The intersection of _____ and _____ establishes the efficient quantity. The triangular area of forgone social surplus caused by inefficient pricing is called a _____ _____.

110   CHAPTER 4

12. That people pay much more for a diamond than for a glass of water refers to the _____ of diamonds and water. The explanation for this behavior is that the _____ _____ from water purchases is vastly greater than that from diamond purchases.

13. The market prices of goods and services that reflect only the supply and demand within a country are called _____ prices. Opening an economy to international trade will change market prices in a country by bringing into its markets a world of new consumers and producers. Countries that trade buy goods and services from other countries—their _____. They also sell goods and services to other countries—their _____. Whether a country imports a good or exports a good will depend upon whether the good's world equilibrium market price is _____ or _____ what the country's price would otherwise have been. In other words, the result of trade is that the price in the domestic market will come to _____ the world market price. If the domestic price rises to meet a higher world price, then the country _____ the good. If a lower world price causes the domestic price to drop, then the country _____ the good, meaning that it is purchased from producers in other countries.

14. Allowing imports increases _____ surplus. Although the lower price will cause _____ surplus to shrink, the increase in _____ surplus more than compensates for that loss.

15. Allowing exports increases _____ surplus. Although the higher price will cause _____ surplus to shrink, the increase in _____ surplus more than compensates.

16. A _____ _____ is a law that establishes a maximum price that can be legally charged for a good. _____ _____ hold the monthly price of rental housing to below its equilibrium level.

17. One effect of rent controls is to transfer wealth from current landlords to current tenants. Such _____ _____ in which one party's loss is another's gain are not themselves inefficient since they merely redistribute social surplus. However, when transfer payments are caused by government price controls, there are multiple sources of inefficiency, in which social surplus shrinks. One inefficiency is the _____ _____ triangle associated with a less-than-efficient overall quantity. Another inefficiency involves _____ costs, which are the costs of finding an apartment. There are alternatives to rent controls. One alternative is to identify the needy and assign them _____ _____, government grants that the recipient can spend only on housing.

18. Local governments have often attempted to protect consumers against _____ _____, which is the disparaging term for hiking up prices in response to temporary

surges in demand. Ticket scalping is a form of _____, which means buying low and selling high.

19. If politics dictates propping up prices, government can establish a price _____, also termed a price _____, which sets a minimum price that producers are guaranteed to receive. The effect of holding price above its equilibrium value is a _____.

20. The _____ _____ is a requirement that employers pay no less than a specified wage rate. The result is that, along with higher wages comes a _____ of labor.

21. Any time government tries to hold prices above or below market equilibrium, it provides profit opportunities to those willing to take advantage of them. _____ _____ activity is said to occur when goods are bought and sold illegally.

22. In order to increase the efficiency with which electricity was generated and distributed at the wholesale level, California lawmakers _____ the wholesale electricity market.

23. Deregulation caused the state's wholesale electricity providers to compete for customers. Competition reduces costs through weeding out inefficiencies. *Ceteris paribus*, greater efficiencies in wholesale electricity production and distribution causes the wholesale electricity supply to shift to the _____ and the price of electricity in the wholesale market to _____.

24. World crude oil prices subsequently skyrocketed, more than doubling soon after California's deregulation of wholesale electricity took effect. The prices of natural gas, coal, and other substitutes for crude oil likewise increased. Since oil and other fuels are significant inputs into the production of electricity, rising fuel prices shifted the supply of electricity at the wholesale level significantly to the _____, offsetting any rightward shift caused by deregulation, causing the wholesale price of electricity to _____.

25. Because of the lawmaker's promise that consumer electricity prices would be held in check, rates were held down to less than the market equilibrium price. The result in the retail electricity market was a _____.

TRUE/FALSE/EXPLAIN
If false, explain why in the space provided.

1. For an economy to be efficient, it must maximize value, as measured by consumer and producer surplus.

2. Consumer surplus is measured as the difference between demand and market price.

3. If Jack purchases a pail of water for $5 that he was willing to pay $7 for, then Jack's consumer surplus for the pail of water is $7.

4. The paradox of diamonds and water illustrates that it is consumer surplus that truly measures the total value consumers receive from the things they buy.

5. The presence of a price ceiling means that some consumers who value a good quite highly may be unable to buy it.

6. For a price ceiling to be effective, it must be above the market equilibrium price.

7. Rent controls are usually in the short-term interest of renters.

8. Rent controls make discrimination less costly and harder to prove.

9. Under a housing voucher plan, it makes good sense to read the obituaries in order to identify which apartments are likely to come up for rent.

10. Rent controls make it difficult to renovate run-down neighborhoods.

11. While ticket scalping is likely to be efficient, it is commonly considered to be inequitable.

12. So-called price gouging in response to natural disasters can be an efficient way to allocate scarce goods.

13. When a surge in demand causes the price of a good to rise dramatically, economists say that a shortage exists.

14. A price support increases the market equilibrium quantity.

15. Despite being difficult to sell politically, economic analysis suggests that agricultural price supports are an efficient way to provide an income to farmers.

16. Because agricultural price supports promote production, they allow consumers to buy more food.

17. The best way to get rid of surpluses which are accumulated under price support programs is for government to auction off those surpluses in the free market.

18. Minimum wage laws make it easier for employers to discriminate.

CHAPTER 4

19. Minimum wage laws are likely to prevent those with the poorest work skills from finding a job.

20. Minimum wage laws reduce employment.

E&A 21. California experienced electricity blackouts, but never for essential services such as street lights.

22. Nature was mostly to blame for the electricity blackouts that occurred in California.

23. The idea of deregulating electricity is to introduce competition that reduces costs by increasing efficiency.

24. Left to itself, the marketplace will not allow a shortage too last long.

25. As a result of controlling the price of electricity, the state of California was forced to borrow millions of dollars in order to assist electric companies.

MULTIPLE CHOICE
Circle the letter preceding the one best answer.

1. Markets are efficient to the extent that they maximize
    a. social surplus.
    b. equity.
    c. marginal benefit.
    d. producer surplus.

2. The difference between a consumer's maximum willingness to pay and the price he or she actually pays is termed
   a. equilibrium.
   b. social benefit.
   c. consumer surplus.
   d. opportunity cost.

3. Suppose Chip's demand for bags of potato chips is:

Price	Quantity demanded
$5	0
$4	1
$3	2
$2	3
$1	4
$0	5

   What is Chip's consumer surplus if the price per bag is $1?
   a. $16.
   b. $12.
   c. $6.
   d. $4.

4. Suppose that Jack is willing to pay up to $10 for the first pail of water, $8 for the second, $6 for the third, and $4 for the fourth. If the price of pails of water is $5 each, Jack will buy ____ pails of water and receive a total of ____ worth of consumer surplus.
   a. 3; $9
   b. 4; $9
   c. 4; $13
   d. 3; $12

5. Suppose that the market supply curve offers a quantity of 1 at $1, 2 at $2, 3 at $3, and 4 at $4. If the market price is $4, producer surplus is:
   a. $2.
   b. $4.
   c. $6.
   d. $8.

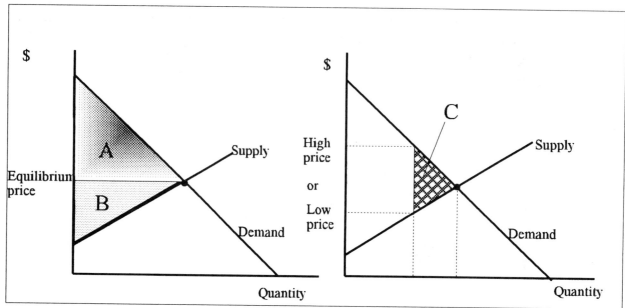

Multiple Choice Figure 1

6. In Multiple Choice Figure 1, consumer surplus is shown by
   a. area A.
   b. area B.
   c. area C.
   d. area A + B.

7. In Multiple Choice Figure 1, producer surplus is shown by
   a. area A.
   b. area B.
   c. area C.
   d. area A + B.

8. In Multiple Choice Figure 1, social surplus is shown by
   a. area A.
   b. area B.
   c. area C.
   d. area A + B.

9. In Multiple Choice Figure 1, deadweight loss is shown by
   a. area A.
   b. area B.
   c. area C.
   d. area A + B.

10. The rule of efficiency requires that
    a. producer surplus equal consumer surplus.
    b. market prices be fair.
    c. marginal social benefit equal marginal social cost.
    d. people buy low and sell high.

11. The competitive marketplace maximizes
    a. consumer surplus, but not producer surplus.
    b. producer surplus, but not consumer surplus.
    c. the sum of consumer and producer surplus.
    d. the ratio of consumer surplus to producer surplus.

12. An effective price ceiling will result in
    a. an equilibrium quantity.
    b. a shortage.
    c. a surplus.
    d. an efficient allocation of resources.

13. Which of the following is LEAST likely to occur under rent controls?
    a. Landlords will discriminate illegally.
    b. Tenants will find it difficult to move.
    c. The quality of apartments will go down.
    d. The quantity of apartments rented will increase.

14. Once rent controls have been in effect for many years, they are usually difficult to remove. The most likely reason is that
    a. tenants would face huge increases in their rents.
    b. rent controls have had time to prove that they are efficient.
    c. landlords develop a vested interest in keeping the controls in place.
    d. removal of rent controls would violate landlords' property rights.

15. A market-based alternative to rent controls that could ensure affordable housing is
    a. housing price supports.
    b. housing vouchers.
    c. urban renewal.
    d. anti-gouging laws.

16. In Multiple Choice Figure 2, the deadweight loss from reduced consumption is given by
    a. area A.
    b. arrow B.
    c. area C.
    d. arrow D.

17. In Multiple Choice Figure 2, arrow D represents the
    a. deadweight loss from reduced consumption in response to agricultural price supports.
    b. increase in output caused by agricultural price supports.
    c. shortage caused by agricultural price supports.
    d. surplus caused by agricultural price supports.

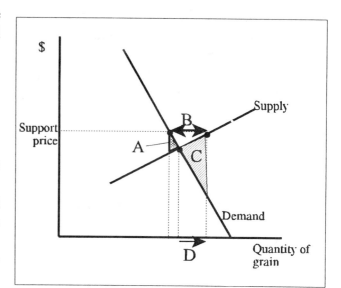

Multiple Choice Figure 2

18. A substantial increase in the minimum wage is likely to be good for
    a. employers, because it would ensure a higher quality workforce.
    b. the most needy - those with the least desirable education and work habits.
    c. new entrants into the labor force seeking to gain experience.
    d. the most employable of the workers currently holding minimum wage jobs.

19. In Multiple Choice Figure 3,
    a. both Dave and Tony are sure to get jobs.
    b. neither Dave nor Tony are likely to get jobs.
    c. although Dave is willing to work for less than Tony, Tony might nonetheless get the job.
    d. although Tony is willing to work for less than Dave, Dave might nonetheless get the job.

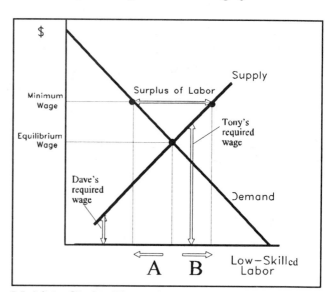

Multiple Choice Figure 3

20. In Multiple Choice Figure 3, arrow A might be labeled _____ and arrow B labeled _____.
    a. decrease in job applicants; increase in job applicants.
    b. decrease in jobs; increase in job applicants.
    c. surplus; shortage.
    d. shortage; surplus.

21. The fundamental reason for electricity shortages in California in 2001 was
    a. price controls for wholesale electricity, along with deregulation of retail electricity prices.
    b. deregulated wholesale electricity prices along with price controls for retail electricity.
    c. deregulation of both the wholesale and retail electricity prices.
    d. price controls in the electricity market at both the wholesale and retail levels.

22. Multiple Choice Figure 4 shows the effect of controlling the retail price of electricity when wholesale prices increase. In this figure, the quantity demanded will be given by
    a. point A.
    b. point B.
    c. point C.
    d. arrow D.

23. In Multiple Choice Figure 4, the arrow labeled D shows
    a. a surplus.
    b. a shortage.
    c. the quantity demanded.
    d. the quantity supplied.

24. The shift in supply shown in Multiple Choice Figure 4 was most likely caused by
    a. price controls.
    b. increased demand.
    c. increased competition.
    d. higher oil prices.

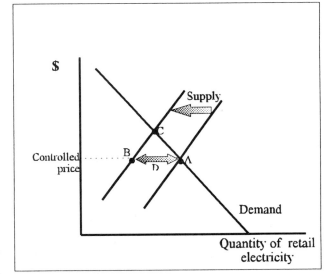

Multiple Choice Figure 4

25. Deregulation of wholesale electricity markets has occurred or is in the process of occurring
    a. nowhere in the world but in California.
    b. in Russia, Cuba, and California, but nowhere else.
    c. in numerous states.
    d. in all fifty states and most countries.

120 CHAPTER 4

GRASPING THE GRAPHS
Fill in each box with a concept that applies.

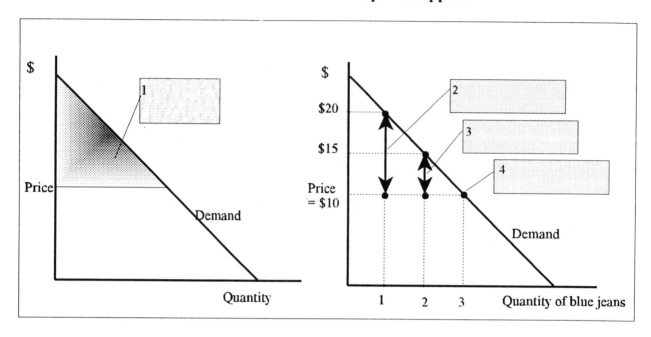

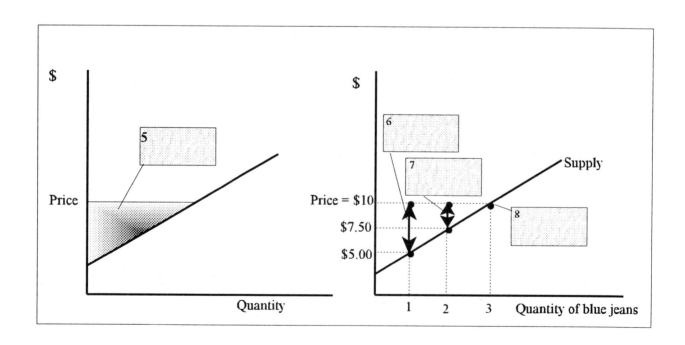

THE POWER OF PRICES 121

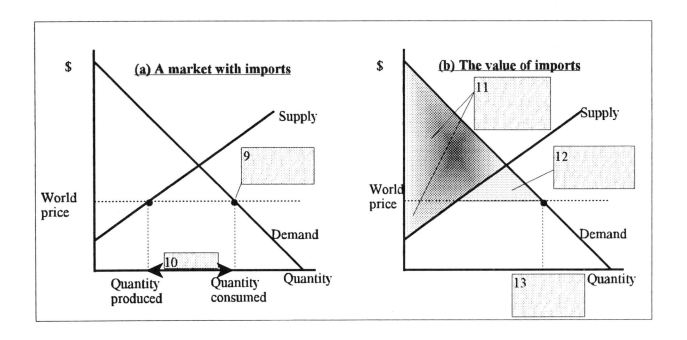

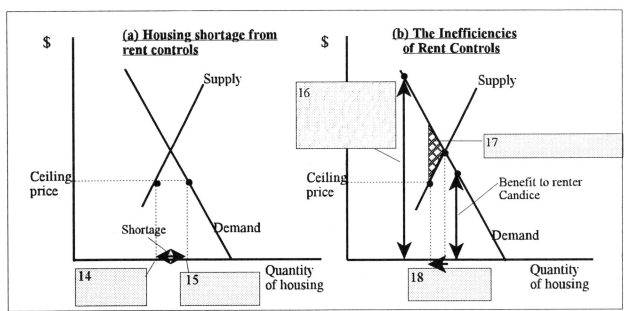

For additional practice in grasping this chapter's graphs, visit
http://www.prenhall.com/ayers and try *Smart Graph* 9, along with
Active Graphs 14, 15, 16, 17, 18, 19, and 20.

ANSWERS

STUDYCHECKS

1. See StudyCheck 1 Figure.

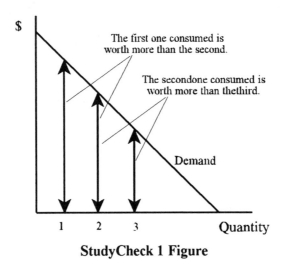

StudyCheck 1 Figure

2. See StudyCheck 2 Figure.

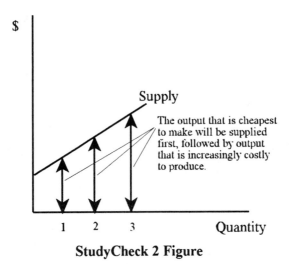

StudyCheck 2 Figure

3. Exports result from a world price that exceeds what the country's equilibrium price would be without trade. In StudyCheck 3 Figure, the higher world price causes the country's consumption to fall and production to rise, with the difference being the amount exported, as shown in (a). The value of social surplus increases by the triangular area shown in (b). However, the gains go disproportionately to producers. Consumer surplus is less because of the higher price.

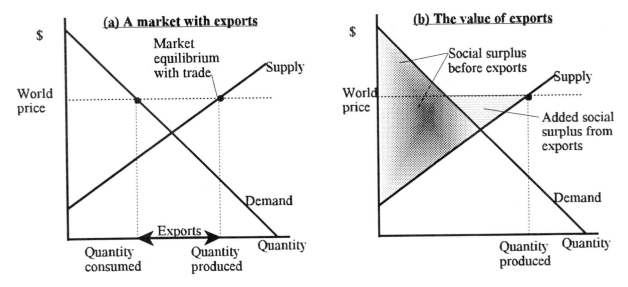

StudyCheck 3 Figure

4. See StudyCheck 4 Figure.

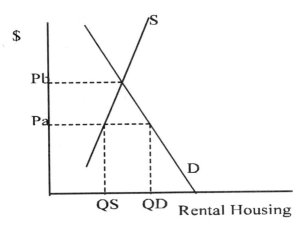

StudyCheck 4 Figure

124   CHAPTER 4

5. The justification is the perception of equity—windfall profits might seem unfair. The objection is that restricting price is inefficient.

6. See StudyCheck 6 Figure.

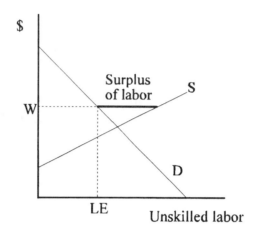

StudyCheck 6 Figure

7. See StudyCheck 7 Figure.

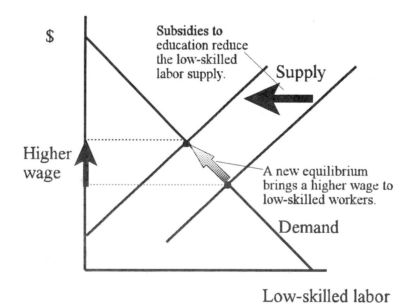

StudyCheck 7 Figure

8. See StudyCheck 8 Figure. Increased competition after deregulation was expected to shift supply to the right and lower electricity prices, as shown in (a). However, soaring prices of

crude oil, coal, and natural gas—inputs into the production of electricity—more than offset the effects of deregulation. The result was that electricity supply in fact shifted to the left, causing price to increase as shown in (b). Had California lawmakers recognized this analysis, they might have avoided price ceilings that would not allow electricity retailers to pass along increases in wholesale costs that deregulation could not prevent.

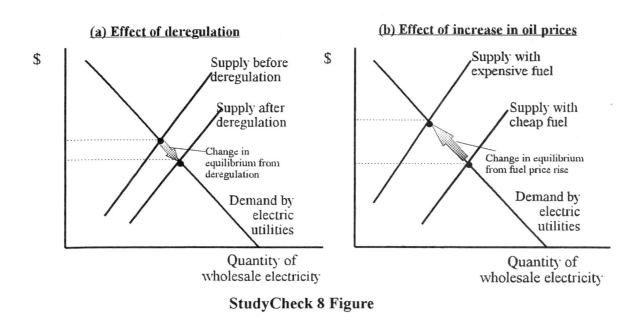

StudyCheck 8 Figure

FILL IN THE BLANKS

1. signals, efficiency
2. quantity, maximum, marginal benefit
3. marginal, $45
4. consumer surplus, price
5. $15
6. quantity, minimum, marginal
7. marginal, $22.50
8. producer surplus, supply curve,
9. $7.50
10. social surplus
11. marginal benefit, marginal cost, demand, supply, deadweight loss
12. paradox, consumer surplus
13. domestic, imports, exports, less that, greater than, equal, exports, imports
14. social, producer, consumer
15. social, consumer, producer
16. price ceiling, Rent control

126 CHAPTER 4

17. transfer payments, deadweight loss, search, housing vouchers
18. price gouging, arbitrage
19. floor, support, surplus
20. minimum wage, surplus
21. black market
22. deregulated
23. right, fall
24. left, rise
25. shortage

TRUE/FALSE/EXPLAIN

1. True.
2. True.
3. False, consumer surplus is $2.
4. True.
5. True.
6. False, a price ceiling will have no effect unless it is below the market equilibrium price.
7. True.
8. True.
9. False, housing vouchers give renters greater purchasing power, but do not cause shortages and so do not require prospective renters to make extraordinary efforts to be the first to see an apartment.
10. True.
11. True.
12. True.
13. False, a surge in demand would cause the price to rise as far as necessary to equate the quantity demanded and the quantity supplied.
14. False, a price support keeps price above the market equilibrium price, but does not change the value of either the market equilibrium price or quantity.
15. False, agricultural price supports are an easy sell politically, but are shown to be inefficient by economic analysis.
16. False, consumers buy as much food as they want to without the existence of price supports, which increase the price such that consumers would want to buy less.
17. False, those surpluses cannot be auctioned off in the free market, as any of the surplus quantity sold would merely displace the sales of farmers who would then line up to sell their output to the government.
18. True.
19. True.
20. True.
21. False, even street lights in San Francisco were disrupted.

22. False, the shortages resulted from a combination of deregulated wholesale electricity markets and price controls on retail electricity.
23. True.
24. True.
25. True.

MULTIPLE CHOICE

1.	a	8.	d	15.	b	22.	a
2.	c	9.	c	16.	a	23.	b
3.	c	10.	c	17.	b	24.	d
4.	a	11.	c	18.	d	25.	c
5.	c	12.	b	19.	c		
6.	a	13.	d	20.	b		
7.	b	14.	a	21.	b		

GRASPING THE GRAPHS
Examples of correct answers

1. consumer surplus
2. $10 consumer surplus for first pair
3. $5 consumer surplus for second pair
4. no consumer surplus for third pair
5. producer surplus
6. $5 producer surplus for first pair
7. $2.50 producer surplus for second pair
8. no producer surplus for third pair
9. quantity demanded
10. imports
11. social surplus
12. increase in social surplus from imports
13. quantity consumed
14. quantity supplied
15. quantity demanded
16. This person values housing highly, but may not get any.
17. deadweight loss
18. fewer units rented

Visit the Ayers/Collinge companion Website at http://www.prenhall.com/ayers for further activities and exercises for this chapter.

Part 2

MONITORING THE MACROECONOMY

Chapter 5

MEASURING NATIONAL OUTPUT

CHAPTER REVIEW

5.1 Macroeconomic Goals

- **Economic growth, full employment, and low inflation are three goals of macro policy.** Since these goals may at times conflict with each other, there is sometimes disagreement among policymakers over which goal should receive first priority in the design of government policies.

- Economic growth occurs when the economy's total output of goods and services increases. Higher living standards are a by-product of economic growth. In effect, growth enlarges the economic pie, allowing many people bigger slices.

- An economy grows because of increases in available resources and improvements in technology. Economists believe that the economy can sustain a long-term growth rate of 2.5 percent per year. Some optimists argue that a sustained growth rate of as much as 5 percent is possible.

- Doubling times, such as that for aggregate output, can be estimated using the *rule of seventy-two*. Whatever the continuously compounding percentage growth rate of a variable is, dividing that number into 72 will reveal the approximate doubling time. For example, a 5 percent growth rate means that output doubles about every 14.4 years, because 72/5 equals 14.4.

- In practice, economic growth does not occur in a smooth fashion. The economy surges and stumbles at periodic intervals. These ups and downs in the growth of output sometimes put the economy above, and other times below, its long-run sustainable growth rate.

- High employment is a major goal of public policy. When economic growth falls short, unemployment is usually the result.

- *Inflation* is a sustained rise in the general price level. Inflation is usually expressed in terms of the *inflation rate*, the annual percentage increase in the general level of prices. Policymakers in government seek to preserve the value of money by keeping the inflation rate low.

5.2 Measuring National Output

- The value of goods and services produced is the single most important measure of the nation's output. According to the circular flow of income, the value of national output must be identical to the value of national income. This equality occurs because every dollar that buyers spend on output represents income to the sellers of that output as depicted in the circular flow model.

- One way to measure output is to classify the goods and services produced according to who is purchasing the output. To this end, purchases are classified by dividing the economy into four sectors, each identified with a different type of purchaser. These sectors are: households, businesses, government, and the foreign sector. Each unit of output is eventually purchased by one of these sectors. The output is valued at *market value,* which is measured by market prices.

- Output is measured by tallying the market value of *final goods and services*—those which are sold to their final owners. The most widely reported measure of the economy's output is **gross domestic product (GDP),** the market value of the final goods and services produced in the economy within some time period, usually 1 quarter or 1 year. Spending on *intermediate goods*—goods used to make other goods—is not included in GDP so as to avoid double counting, the counting of the same output twice.

- In order to track spending in different parts of the economy, GDP is measured as the sum of spending on output by households, businesses, government, and the rest of world. Looking at GDP as the sum of consumption spending, investment, government purchases, and spending related to foreign commerce on GDP is termed the *expenditure approach*. Another approach, the *incomes approach*, measures GDP as the sum of wages, rent, interest, and profit.

StudyCheck 1

Using the incomes method, list the four major components of GDP.

- Purchasing by households comprises **consumption spending**. Household spending makes up the majority of spending in the U.S. economy, generally close to 70 percent of total spending. This spending may be on services or on consumer durable or nondurable goods. Nondurables are goods that are consumed quickly, by definition in 1 year or less. Durables are goods that have an expected life span of more than 1 year.

- **Investment**—spending now in order to increase output or productivity later—is the most variable component of GDP over time. The GDP statistics record only three measurable types: (1) Purchases by firms of **capital,** such as new factories and machines; (2) Consumers' purchases of **new housing,** a form of consumer capital; (3) The market value of the **change in business inventories** of unsold goods.

- **Gross investment** is the total amount of investment that takes place. Gross investment by private sector firms, *gross private domestic investment*, is the measure of investment used to compute GDP. It usually amounts to between 15 and 18 percent of GDP. Private sector investment is counted in gross investment, since government investment is counted in government's contribution to GDP. Gross investment includes U.S. investment spending by foreign citizens as well as U.S. citizens.

- **Net investment** is gross investment minus depreciation. A positive value for net investment measures the increase in the economy's productive capacity. A negative value for net investment means that depreciation exceeded the total amount of investment. When the focus is on net investment, **net domestic product (NDP)** is a more appropriate measure than GDP. NDP equals GDP minus depreciation.

- Governments at the federal, state, and local levels accounted for about 18 percent of the total purchasing of goods and services in the U.S. economy in 2001. Although estimates are imprecise, perhaps one-tenth of government purchasing could be classified as investment.

- Government *transfer payments,* such as Social Security and unemployment benefits, are received by individuals who do not provide goods and services in return. **Government purchases and investment should be distinguished from government transfer payments. The latter are not included in the computation of GDP.** To the extent that transfer payments are used by the households that receive them to buy goods and services, they are counted as consumption spending.

- Exports minus imports defines *net exports*. It is the value of net exports that goes into GDP. A negative value for net exports means that spending on imports is greater than spending on exports; a positive figure means that spending on imports is less than spending on exports. The value of net exports varies from year to year, but has been negative for many years.

132 CHAPTER 5

5.3 Gross Domestic Product—A Closer Look

- The four kinds of spending that when added together sum to GDP are: Consumption spending, gross investment, government purchases and net exports. As an equation, we have:
  GDP = consumption spending + gross investment + government purchases + net exports

- *Per capita GDP* is GDP per person. The total U.S. GDP of $10.1 trillion in 2001 is more easily placed into perspective when divided by the population that year of about 285 million persons. Performing the indicated division we see that per capita GDP for 2001 was about $35,400.

- **GDP may be viewed as the sum of values added in the economy.** Each firm takes inputs of materials and intermediate goods and increases their value through the firm's production process. **Value added** equals the revenue from the sale of output minus the cost of purchased inputs.

- Observe he computation of value added in the production of a single jar of dill pickles. A seed company produces cucumber seeds that are sold to a farmer. Suppose it takes 30 cents worth of seeds to grow the cucumbers in a jar of dill pickles. Assuming the seed company buys no intermediate goods, this initial step generates 30 cents of value added by the seed company. The farmer who purchases the 30 cents worth of seeds subsequently sells the resulting cucumber crop to the pickle maker for $1.00. The farmer has added value equal to 70 cents. The pickle maker sells the pickles to a supermarket for $1.50 and in so doing contributes another 50 cents in value added. When the supermarket sells the pickles to shoppers for $$2.25 a jar, an additional 75 cents is contributed toward value added:
  Increase in GDP from production of a jar of pickles
  =
  $0.30 + $0.70 + $0.50 + $0.75 = $2.25

- Until 1992, the chief measure of the economy's output was *gross national product (GNP)*. GNP differs from GDP in that **the value added to production by resources located outside the United States, but owned by U.S. citizens, is counted in GNP.** Unlike GDP, **GNP excludes value added within the United States by foreign-owned resources. Typically, U.S. GDP and GNP differ by less than 1 percent**, so that either can be used to evaluate the performance of the economy.

- Market transactions that go unreported make up the **underground economy**. Some of these goods and services are illegal. The underground economy includes other goods and services that, while not illegal, are not reported to government so that their producers can avoid paying taxes. The existence of an underground economy means that GDP understates the economy's true output.

- GDP does not include the value of *household production*, which is the production of goods and services for use within the household.

- GDP is an imperfect measure of welfare. One reason is that *intangibles,* such as feelings of peace, freedom, and opportunity, cannot be measured easily. Other things increase GDP, but do not actually indicate that the economy is better off. An example is increases in military spending.

- It would be useful to have a single *measure of economic welfare* that could take into account the effects of intangibles on our overall standard of living. Efforts have failed to lead to a widely accepted alternative to GDP itself.

- Increases in the measured value of a nation's output, its GDP, may occur for two reasons: (1) Because of an increase in physical output; (2) As a consequence of price increases in the form of inflation. An increase in GDP due solely to price increases does not increase economic welfare since there is no increase in physical output to make people better off.

- In reality, when GDP rises there is usually a mix of both an increase in physical output plus price changes. Removing the effects of price changes from the value of GDP allows us to identify the increase in physical output.

- **Nominal GDP** is the value of GDP expressed in current dollar terms. The nominal value may be thought of as "what you see is what you get," because the nominal value is not adjusted for the rise in the nominal value that accompanies inflation. By contrast, **real GDP** adjusts for inflation the nominal value of GDP. Real GDP expresses GDP in terms of a constant value of money—dollars with the same purchasing power.

- The *GDP chain-type price index*, also called the *GDP chained price index*, is an index of prices that measures price changes over time. An increase in the value of the GDP chained index with the passage of time indicates that the general level of prices has increased. The GDP chained price index is used to compute real GDP, as follows:
    Real GDP = (nominal GDP/GDP chained price index) × 100

5.4 The Business Cycle—The Ups and Downs in Economic Activity

- The term **business cycle** refers to the expansions and contractions in economic activity that take place over time. Figure 5-5 shows the stages of a business cycle as a smooth curve. The low point in economic activity is called the *trough.* Following the trough is the *expansion* stage. When the expansion is ready to end, the economy reaches its *peak,* and then falls into *recession.* An especially severe recession is termed a *depression.* Subsequently, another trough will mark the point where the process begins repeating itself.

- The economic fluctuations represented by the business cycle are an example of *short-run* features in the economy. The business cycle occurs around an upward *trend* in real GDP. Economic trends describe persistent features in the economy. Thus, trends describe the *long-run* features of the economy.

- In the real world, the ups and downs in the economy do not occur in such a smooth fashion. Expansions typically last much longer and are much stronger than recessions. Thus the business cycle occurs within the context of a rising trend in real GDP.

- Who decides when the economy leaves one stage of the business cycle and enters the next stage? An independent organization, the National Bureau of Economic Research (NBER), is entrusted with the dating of business cycle turning points. In many instances, the NBER will not announce the onset of a recession until it has observed the indicators for months. There are also often delays in dating the beginning of expansions.

- Many economic variables move either up or down at the same time each year. These seasonal effects make it difficult to disentangle actual growth in economic variables from changes in them due to seasonal volatility. That is why most published economic data are seasonally adjusted, using statistical models. Seasonal adjustments to data help reveal the underlying trends.

- There are hundreds of economic indicators capable of illuminating various aspects of the economy. Some of these indicators, called **leading indicators,** will usually change direction before the economy does. Examples include the index of building permits, housing starts, and manufacturers' new orders for durable goods. These data series and several others are combined to form a composite index of leading indicators, which receives much attention from the media.

- Other indicators, the *lagging indicators,* usually change direction only after the economy has already done so. The unemployment rate and expenditures on new plants and equipment are examples.

- Many indicators change direction about the same time the economy changes direction. These are called *coincident indicators.* Examples include the index of industrial production and the prime interest rate charged by banks.

> **StudyCheck 2**
> Distinguish between a leading, coincident, and lagging indicator. Provide one example of each.

5.5 Assessing Economic Performance—Dare We Predict the Future?

- The federal budget deficit is associated with a shortfall of federal revenues below expenses. Until the surpluses of 1999 and 2000, the federal government incurred a budget deficit every year between 1960 and 1998. In response to citizen outrage over the deficits, Congress revised its budgetary practices. The result has been to give economic statistics a more central role than ever before.

- In 1985, in an attempt to lead the federal budget into balance, Congress passed the Gramm-Rudman-Hollings Act. This legislation set specific deficit-reduction targets. Each time targets were not met, the act called for across-the-board budget cuts that would bring spending into line with those targets. According to the Gramm-Rudman targets, the federal deficit was to be eliminated by 1991.

- In 1991 the federal budget deficit was $267 billion dollars, higher than it had ever been before. What happened? Well before 1991, Congress had modified and then abandoned the Gramm-Rudman-Hollings approach. The across-the-board budget axe was not used. It fell victim to special interests, especially the interests of Social Security recipients. Too much spending was exempted from cuts.

- Congress has instead instituted a different set of budgetary procedures to add some integrity to the budget process. Specifically, in the Budget Enforcement Act of 1990, Congress legislated that policy changes should not increase the budget deficit. Thus, policy changes that would add to the budget deficit must be balanced by other changes that would offset that effect. Doing so sounds reasonable, but brings back that basic statistical problem—measuring the effects on government revenues and expenses of alternative public policies.

- Is government able to forecast the effects of policy changes? In 1990 Congress imposed a surcharge on luxuries, including among other things, new yachts and other luxury boats. Immediately after the so-called luxury tax took effect, orders for new yachts all but disappeared. Although the tax rate was higher, government revenue from boat sales was much lower. Overall the luxury tax did bring in more money, but the amount was about $13 million by 1993, rather than the $76 million over that period that was designated in the Congressional budget.

- Although the revenue effect of the luxury tax could have been predicted with much greater accuracy, the Budget Enforcement Act did not allow Congress to do so in its budgetary calculations. Thus, the luxury tax surcharge was assumed to bring in $76 million dollars of extra revenue, which then allowed Congress to pass an additional $76 million of new spending programs.

- This traditional manner of computing the effects of federal actions is known as *static scoring*. Static scoring assumes no general change in behavior as a result of government policy changes. Hence, the effect of the luxury tax on the demand for luxury goods was ignored.

- The alternative is called *dynamic scoring*, which does allow for consideration of all behavioral changes caused by changes in government policy.

- Static scoring has been a budgetary mainstay because it provides an obvious baseline estimate, the baseline being the status quo. Analysts may know that behavior will change, but are unlikely to agree on exactly what forms the changes will take or how significant will be their effects. Because of such disagreement, dynamic scoring must inevitably lead to controversy.

- Everyone in the budget process knows that static scoring gives wrong answers. If the government were to follow a dynamic scoring standard, who could tell what questionable assumptions would lie buried beneath the surface?

- The issue of static versus dynamic scoring underscores the old adage that politics makes strange bedfellows. Conservatives seeking to cut taxes find themselves allied with liberals seeking to expand government spending on social programs. Both support dynamic scoring. On the other side are conservatives and liberals who fear political manipulation of the budget process. Whatever the immediate outcome of this tug-of-war, the issue will remain with us.

StudyCheck 3

Distinguish between static scoring and dynamic scoring. What is the main advantage and disadvantage of dynamic scoring relative to static scoring?

APPENDIX: The National Income and Product Accounts

- The Bureau of Economic Analysis (BEA), an arm of the U.S. Department of Commerce, is responsible for the preparation of the final reports detailing the national income and product statistics. These reports are prepared using data obtained from other government agencies. Individual tax returns, obtained from the Internal Revenue Service, are an important source of data. Survey data are also extensively employed.

- Users of BEA data are familiar with the notion of preliminary and revised data. Preliminary data are estimates that are subject to change. Revised data incorporate changes in data made necessary as more complete information becomes available with the passage of time. Data may be revised several times before the BEA is satisfied with its accuracy. The process of revision can occasionally drag on for years.

- Most data are available at quarterly or annual intervals, although some data is available monthly. The monthly Commerce Department publication, the *Survey of Current Business*, is the primary source of national income and product data. BEA-developed data can also be found in other government publications, including the annual *Economic Report of the President*.

- In calculating GDP it is useful to recognize that every dollar of production creates an equivalent dollar of spending. **Since every dollar of spending generates a dollar of income for someone, the value of production and income is also equal.** Goods and services are produced and sold, with the dollars spent by purchasers being collected by businesses. These dollars go toward the payment of incomes—wages to workers, for example.

138 CHAPTER 5

- The equality of production and income means that GDP can be calculated in two ways. The **expenditures approach** sums spending on consumption, investment, government purchases, and the value of net exports. On the right side of the table, the **incomes approach** sums various income items plus other charges against GDP.

- By making adjustments to GDP, other measures of aggregate economic activity can be calculated, as follows:
    - *Gross national product (GNP):* GNP = GDP + income received by U.S. firms and workers outside the United States − income received by foreign firms and workers within the United States
    - *Net national product (NNP):* NNP = GNP − capital consumption
    - *National income (NI):* NI = NNP − indirect business taxes − business transfer payments − statistical discrepancy + subsidies less surplus of government firms
    - *Personal income (PI):* PI = NI − corporate profits − net interest − social security taxes − wage accruals less disbursements + government transfer payments to persons + personal interest income + personal dividend income + business transfer payments to persons
    - *Disposable personal income (DPI):* DPI = PI − personal tax and non-tax payments

---

StudyCheck 4

Explain how GDP and GNP differ.

FILL IN THE BLANKS

1. _____ _____, _____ _____, and _____ _____ are three goals of macro policy.

2. Economic _____ occurs when the economy's total output of goods and services increases.

3. An economy grows because of increases in available resources and improvements in technology. Economists believe that the economy can sustain a long-term growth rate of _____ percent per year. Some optimists argue that a sustained growth rate of as much as _____ percent is possible.

4. Doubling times, such as that for aggregate output, can be estimated using the _____ __ _____-_____. A 5 percent growth rate means that output doubles about every _____ years.

5. _____ is a sustained rise in the general price level. The annual percentage increase in the general level of prices is called the _____ _____.

6. One way to measure output is to classify the goods and services produced according to who is purchasing the output. To this end, purchases are classified by dividing the economy into four sectors, each identified with a different type of purchaser. These sectors are: _____, _____, _____, and the _____ sector. Each unit of output is eventually purchased by one of these sectors. The output is valued at _____ value.

7. Output is measured by tallying the market value of _____ goods and services—those which are sold to their final owners. The most widely reported measure of the economy's output is _____ _____ _____, the market value of the final goods and services produced in the economy within some time period, usually 1 quarter or 1 year. Spending on _____ goods—goods used to make other goods—is not included in GDP so as to avoid double counting, the counting of the same output twice.

8. Looking at GDP as the sum of consumption spending, investment, government purchases, and spending related to foreign commerce on GDP is termed the _____ approach. Another approach, the _____ approach, measures GDP as the sum of wages, rent, interest, and profit.

9. Purchasing by households comprises _____ spending. _____—spending now in order to increase output or productivity later—is the most variable component of GDP over time. The GDP statistics record only three measurable types: (1) Purchases by firms of _____, such as new factories and machines; (2) Consumers' purchases of _____ _____, a form of consumer capital; (3) The market value of the change in _____ _____ of unsold goods. _____ investment is the total amount of investment that takes place. _____ investment is gross investment minus depreciation.

10. Government _____ _____, such as Social Security and unemployment benefits, are received by individuals who do not provide goods and services in return.

11. Exports minus imports defines _____ _____, which goes into GDP. A negative value means that spending on _____ is greater than spending on _____.

12. _____ _____ GDP is GDP per person.

13. Each firm takes inputs of materials and intermediate goods and increases their value through the firm's production process. _____ _____ equals the revenue from the sale of output minus the cost of purchased inputs.

14. Until 1992, the chief measure of the economy's output was _____ _____ _____. This measure differs from GDP in that the value added to production by resources located outside the United States, but owned by U.S. citizens, is counted. Unlike GDP, this measure excludes value added within the United States by _____-_____ resources.

15. Market transactions that go unreported make up the _____ economy. GDP does not include the value of _____ production, which is the production of goods and services within the home. GDP is an imperfect measure of welfare. One reason is that _____ cannot be measured easily. It would be useful to have a single measure of economic _____ that could take into account the effects of intangibles on our overall standard of living. Efforts have failed to lead to a widely accepted alternative to GDP itself.

16. _____ GDP is the value of GDP expressed in current dollar terms. The nominal value may be thought of as "what you see is what you get," because the nominal value is not adjusted for the rise in the nominal value that accompanies inflation. By contrast, _____ GDP adjusts for inflation the nominal value of GDP, expressing GDP in terms of a constant value of money—dollars with the same purchasing power.

17. The *GDP chain-type price index*, also called the *GDP chained price index*, is an index of prices that measures price changes over time. An increase in the value of the GDP chained index with the passage of time indicates that the general level of prices has increased. The GDP chained price index is used to compute real GDP, as follows:
    Real GDP = (_____ _____ ÷ GDP chained price index) × 100

18. The term _____ _____ refers to the expansions and contractions in economic activity that take place over time. Figure 5-5 shows the stages of a business cycle as a smooth curve. The low point in economic activity is called the _____. Following this stage is the _____ stage. When that stage is ready to end, the economy reaches its peak, and then falls into _____.

19. There are hundreds of economic indicators capable of illuminating various aspects of the economy. Some of these indicators, called _____ indicators, will usually change direction before the economy does. Other indicators, the _____ indicators, usually change direction only after the economy has already done so. Many indicators change direction about the same time the economy changes direction. These are called _____ indicators.

20. The federal budget _____ is associated with a shortfall of federal revenues below expenses.

21. In 1985, in an attempt to lead the federal budget into balance, Congress passed the _____-_____-_____ Act. This legislation set specific deficit-reduction targets. Each time targets were not met, the act called for across-the-board budget cuts that would bring spending into line with those targets.

22. The _____ _____ Act of 1990, Congress legislated that policy changes should not increase the budget deficit. Thus, policy changes that would add to the budget deficit must be balanced by other changes that would offset that effect.

23. This traditional manner of computing the effects of federal actions is known as _____ _____. This method assumes no general change in behavior as a result of government policy changes. The alternative is called _____ _____, which does allow for consideration of all behavioral changes caused by changes in government policy.

APPENDIX

24. _____ data are estimates that are subject to change. _____ data incorporate changes in data made necessary as more complete information becomes available with the passage of time.

25. The equality of production and income means that GDP can be calculated in two ways. The _____ approach sums spending on consumption, investment, government purchases, and the value of net exports. The _____ approach sums various income items plus other charges against GDP.

26. By making adjustments to GDP, other measures of aggregate economic activity can be calculated, as follows:
    - _____ _____ _____ (GNP): GNP = GDP + income received by U.S. firms and workers outside the United States – income received by foreign firms and workers within the United States
    - _____ _____ _____ (NNP): NNP = GNP – capital consumption

142 CHAPTER 5

- _____ _____ (NI): NI = NNP − indirect business taxes − business transfer payments − statistical discrepancy + subsidies less surplus of government firms
- _____ _____ (PI): PI = NI − corporate profits − net interest − social security taxes − wage accruals less disbursements + government transfer payments to persons + personal interest income + personal dividend income + business transfer payments to persons
- _____ _____ _____ (DPI): DPI = PI − personal tax and non-tax payments

---

TRUE/FALSE/EXPLAIN
If false, explain why in the space provided.

1. One of the three primary macroeconomic goals is low employment.

2. The rule of seventy-two is used to compute the amount of time it takes a variable to increase seventy-two times.

3. When the U.S. government measures the value of gross domestic product, it includes the value of intermediate goods.

4. Consumption spending makes up about half of total spending.

5. Investment includes consumer spending on durable goods.

6. The value of new houses and the value of existing houses that are sold are included in the value of GDP.

7. Generally, gross investment would be less than net investment.

8. Government purchases include the value of transfer payments.

9. Net exports equal imports minus exports.

10. Net exports has had a negative value for many years.

11. The cash income earned from illegal activities is not included in GDP.

12. *Per capita* GDP is GDP per person.

13. The difference between GDP and GNP is typically very small in percentage terms.

14. The market value of a product can be viewed as the sum of its values added at each stage of production.

15. The output of goods and services by the underground economy is included in GDP.

16. Real GDP is obtained by dividing nominal GDP by the GDP price index and then multiplying by 100.

17. The turning point at the bottom of the business cycle is called the recession.

144 CHAPTER 5

18. When real GDP is viewed over many years, the trend shows a slight decline.

19. Recessions occur frequently and typically last for long periods of time.

20. The unemployment rate is a leading indicator of economic activity.

21. A federal budget deficit is the outcome when the federal government's expenses are greater than its revenues.

22. Under static scoring a tariff cut is automatically scored as a revenue loser.

23. In static scoring the status quo is assumed.

24. Dynamic scoring allows for consideration of behavioral changes caused by modifications to government policies.

25. Most political conservatives support static scoring and most political liberals support dynamic scoring.

APPENDIX
26. To revise data means to adjust it for the effects of inflation.

27. The only valid method to calculate GDP is to add up consumption, investment, government purchases, and net exports.

28. The difference between GDP and GNP is that GDP includes net exports while GNP does not.

29. U.S. gross national product (GNP) is arrived at by taking GDP and then adding income received by U.S. firms and workers outside the United States and then subtracting income received by foreign firms and workers within the United States.

30. Among the items subtracted from national income to arrive at personal income is the Social Security tax.

MULTIPLE CHOICE
Circle the letter preceding the one best answer.

1. Three macroeconomic goals are
   a. economic growth, low employment, and low inflation.
   b. economic growth, high employment, and high inflation.
   c. a managed economy, low unemployment, and zero inflation.
   d. low prices, many job openings, and low taxes.

2. Gross domestic product is
   a. a country's total output of final products, measured in physical units.
   b. the true value of a country's output, irrespective of market prices.
   c. the sum of the market values of all intermediate goods and final outputs.
   d. the sum of the market values of all final outputs, only.

3. Intermediate goods and services are
   a. purchased by final users.
   b. goods that are not sold in the year in which they are produced.
   c. used to make final goods and services.
   d. valued at market prices and counted in the computation of GDP.

4. Consumption spending accounts for about _____ percent of GDP.
   a. 30
   b. 50
   c. 70
   d. 90

5. As measured in GDP, investment includes all of the following EXCEPT
   a. purchasing stocks and bonds.
   b. accumulating inventory of products.
   c. consumers' purchases of new housing.
   d. new factories.

6. Gross domestic product exceeds net domestic product by the amount of
   a. private sector investment.
   b. private and government investment.
   c. depreciation of the economy's stock of capital.
   d. indirect business taxes.

7. Net exports equal
   a. exports + imports.
   b. exports − imports.
   c. exports/imports.
   d. exports × imports

8. Gross domestic product is equal to consumption spending plus government
   a. transfer payments, plus investment, plus exports, minus imports.
   b. purchases of goods and services, plus investment, plus exports, minus imports.
   c. transfer payments, plus government purchases of goods and services, plus investment, plus exports, minus imports.
   d. transfer payments, minus government purchases of goods and services, plus investment, plus exports, minus imports.

9. GDP may be viewed as the sum of _____ in the economy.
   a. all the money
   b. total spending on intermediate and final goods and services
   c. values added
   d. consumer spending

10. Jeff picks wild mushrooms growing in the woods, which he then dries and packages to send to Wild Foods Market. He is paid one dollar for each package of mushrooms, which the store sells for $2. Each package of mushrooms sold contributes $____ to GDP, which breaks down into $____ of value added by Jeff and $____ of value added by Wild Foods Market.
    a. $2, $0, $2
    b. $2, $2, $0
    c. $2, $1, $2
    d. $2, $1, $1

11. If exports are $10, imports are $15, net investment is $20, depreciation is $5, transfer payments are $8, government purchases are $25, and consumption spending is $75, what is the value of GDP?
    a. $168
    b. $120
    c. $125
    d. $100

12. If all married couples were to divorce and pay for household services performed,
    a. it would make no difference to the GDP accounts, since the government is not interested in private affairs of households.
    b. welfare of the average person would increase, because there would be more incomes.
    c. personal income would be unaffected, but the income distribution would change.
    d. GDP would increase.

13. The underground economy in the United States
    a. is insignificant.
    b. measures the potential output forgone due to the existence of discouraged workers.
    c. causes measured GDP to understate actual the economy's actual output .
    d. was in existence primarily in the years prior to the Civil War, and was associated with the movement of slaves by abolitionists.

14. Intangibles
    a. are things that cannot be easily measured.
    b. have value, and so are included at market value in the computation of GDP.
    c. have no value, and so can be ignored in evaluating economic welfare.
    d. are exported but not imported.

15. Typically, nominal GDP rises faster than real GDP because of
    a. deflation.
    b. disinflation.
    c. inflation.
    d. errors in the price index used in calculating real GDP.

16. Real GDP is measured in dollars of _____ purchasing power, while nominal GDP is measured in _____ dollars.
    a. constant, current
    b. current, constant
    c. zero, constant
    d. constant, zero

17. Suppose nominal GDP equals $100, while the GDP price index equals 125. Real GDP equals
    a. $225.
    b. $120.
    c. $100.
    d. $80.

18. In measuring the business cycle, we primarily look at the behavior of
    a. nominal GDP.
    b. real GDP.
    c. the unemployment rate.
    d. an index of business cycle indicators.

19. The stage of the business cycle that follows a recession and precedes an expansion is called
    a. peak.
    b. trough.
    c. recession.
    d. U-turn.

20. A coincident indicator
    a. does not exist.
    b. changes direction before the economy.
    c. changes direction after the economy.
    d. changes direction about the same time as the economy.

21. Between 1960 and 1997, the federal budget
    a. was in balance every year.
    b. experienced a deficit every year.
    c. showed a surplus every year.
    d. bounced between surpluses and deficits.

22. Following the passage of the Gramm-Rudman-Hollings legislation in 1985, by 1991 the
    a. federal budget was in balance.
    b. federal budget showed a small surplus.
    c. federal budget showed a large surplus.
    d. deficit was higher than it had been before.

23. The traditional technique the federal government uses to compute the effects of its actions is termed
    a. dynamic scoring.
    b. static scoring.
    c. equilibrium scoring.
    d. hogwash.

24. Suppose Congress is considering a proposal to cut tax rates in the hope that the lower rates will stimulate economic growth, thereby expanding the tax base in the future and leading to higher tax revenues over time. If Congress uses static scoring, it must
    a. assume that tax revenues will fall.
    b. assume that tax revenues will rise.
    c. assume no change in tax revenues.
    d. analyze how the tax cut will affect the macroeconomy.

25. The debate over President George W. Bush's tax cuts led to the Congressional Joint Committee on Taxation to declare that
    a. static scoring should be used in budget studies.
    b. dynamic scoring should be used in budget studies.
    c. both static and dynamic scoring should be replaced by a new method of scoring.
    d. the method of scoring does not matter.

APPENDIX

26. The national income and product accounts statistics are published by the
    a. Office of Management and Budget.
    b. Council of Economic Advisors.
    c. Bureau of Economic Analysis.
    d. Internal Revenue Service.

27. The income approach and the expenditures approach to GDP accounting result in
    a. two different values of GDP, called real GDP and nominal GDP.
    b. two GDP figures, called income GDP and expenditures GDP, with income GDP always greater than expenditures GDP.
    c. two kinds of GDP figures, called income GDP and expenditures GDP, with income GDP always less than expenditures GDP.
    d. a single figure for GDP regardless of approach.

28. The incomes approach to GDP includes
    a. consumption spending.
    b. gross investment.
    c. net interest.
    d. net exports.

29. The incomes approach to GDP includes a compensation of employees portion, which is based on
    a. wages and salaries.
    b. corporate profits.
    c. net interest.
    d. a statistical discrepancy.

30. Income that individuals actually have available to spend is termed
    a. net national product.
    b. net domestic product.
    c. national income.
    d. disposable personal income.

MEASURING NATIONAL OUTPUT

GRASPING THE GRAPHS
Fill in each box with a concept that applies.

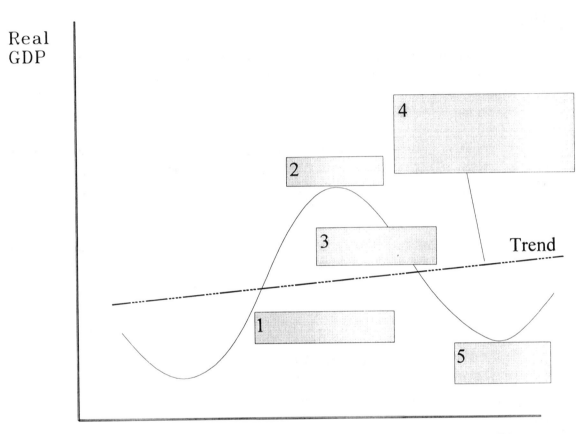

**For additional practice in grasping this chapter's graphs, visit
http://www.prenhall.com/ayers and try *Active Graph* 21.**

ANSWERS

STUDYCHECKS

1. Wages, rent, interest, and profit.

2. Leading indicators change direction before the economy changes direction. An example is the index of building permits. Coincident indicators change direction about the same time as the economy. An example is the prime interest rate. Lagging indicators change direction after the economy has already changed direction.' An example is the unemployment rate.

3. Static scoring assumes the behavior of the macroeconomy does not respond to a policy change. Dynamic scoring builds in changes in macro behavior in response to a policy change. The advantage to static scoring is that even though the estimates of the effects of a policy change will be wrong, the estimates cannot be manipulated for political purposes.

4. GNP is computed by taking GDP and then adding income received by U.S. firms and citizens outside the country, and then subtracting income received by foreign firms and workers in the United States.

FILL IN THE BLANKS

1. Economic growth, full employment, low inflation
2. growth
3. 2.5, 5
4. rule of seventy-two, 14.4
5. inflation, inflation rate
6. households, businesses, government, foreign, market
7. final, gross domestic product, intermediate
8. expenditures, income
9. consumption, investment, capital, new houses, business inventories
10. transfer payments
11. net exports, imports, exports
12. *Per capita*
13. Value added
14. gross national product, foreign-owned
15. underground, household, intangibles, welfare
16. Nominal, real
17. nominal GDP

18. business cycle, trough, expansion, recession
19. leading, lagging, coincident
20. deficit
21. Gramm-Rudman-Hollings
22. Budget Enforcement
23. static scoring, dynamic scoring,
24. Preliminary, Revised
25. expenditures, incomes
26. gross national product, net national product, national income, personal income, disposable personal income

---

TRUE/FALSE/EXPLAIN

1. False, the goal is high employment, or equivalently, low unemployment.
2. False, the rule computes doubling times.
3. False, only the value of final goods and services is counted.
4. False, consumption spending makes up about 70 percent of total spending.
5. False, spending by consumers on durable goods is included in consumption.
6. False, only the value of new houses is counted.
7. False, net investment subtracts depreciation from gross investment.
8. False, transfer payments are excluded since they are not payments for goods or services.
9. False, net exports equals the value of exports minus the value of imports.
10. True.
11. True.
12. True.
13. True.
14. True.
15. False, since the value of output in the underground economy is difficult to measure.
16. True.
17. False, the bottom turning point is called the trough.
18. False, the trend is up.
19. False, recessions occur infrequently and typically are short lived.
20. False, it is a coincident indicator.
21. True.
22. True.
23. True.
24. True.
25. False, some conservatives support static scoring and others dynamic scoring. The same is true of liberals.
26. False, revised data is adjusted for corrections.
27. False, the incomes approach adds up incomes to obtain GDP.

28. False, the difference between GDP and GNP is that GDP looks at output in the United States regardless of ownership, while GNP looks at outputs produced by U.S.-owned resources, regardless of in what country production occurs.
29. True.
30. True.

MULTIPLE CHOICE

1.	a.	9.	c.	17.	d.	25.	b.
2.	d.	10.	d.	18.	b.	26.	c.
3.	c.	11.	b.	19.	b.	27.	d.
4.	c.	12.	d.	20.	d.	28.	c.
5.	a.	13.	c.	21.	b.	29.	a.
6.	c.	14.	a.	22.	d.	30.	d.
7.	b.	15.	c.	23.	b.		
8.	b.	16.	a.	24.	c.		

GRASPING THE GRAPHS
Examples of correct answers

1. Expansion
2. Peak
3. Recession
4. Trough
5. The economy fluctuates around an upward trend.

Visit the Ayers/Collinge companion Website at http://www.prenhall.com/ayers for further activities and exercises for this chapter.

Chapter 6

UNEMPLOYMENT

CHAPTER REVIEW

6.1 Measuring Unemployment

- An economy with unemployment is wasting resources and producing at a point inside its production possibility frontier. The concept of unemployment applies to any resource that lies idle. In common usage, however, unemployment refers to idle labor rather than idle capital.

- The U.S. civilian **labor force** is composed of individuals age 16 and over, excluding those in the military, who are either employed or actively looking for work. The labor force typically expands as the population of persons age 16 and up increases because many of them look for work. The labor force also expands as job opportunities improve and some of the people not in the labor force become part of it by looking for work.

- **The labor force can be divided into two parts, consisting of the employed and the unemployed. The employed are those who work for pay, and the unemployed are those who do not work, but are seeking jobs.**

StudyCheck 1

Draw a pie chart where the pie represents the adult population. Then slice the pie into parts showing the unemployed, employed, and those not in the labor force. Each slice of the pie you draw should approximate the actual slices in the text.

- The **unemployment rate** is the fraction of the labor force who are unemployed, expressed in percentage terms:
    Unemployment rate = Number of unemployed ÷ Labor force.

- When we take the ratio of the civilian labor force to the population age 16 and over, the result is the **labor force participation rate** (or just the *participation rate*).

- Because more Americans enter the labor force each month, the economy must steadily create more jobs—enough jobs to provide each of the new entrants with a job. **If job creation lags behind the increase in the labor force, then some hopeful job seekers will be disappointed by their inability to find work and the unemployment rate will increase.**

- There are many influences on the labor force participation rate. Increased opportunities for women and minorities have led to an increase in the participation rate over time. Concurrently, opportunities for workers to take early retirement have grown. The health of workers plays a role. Various aspects of government policy have affected the size of the labor force. Individual attitudes toward labor are also important.

- As already mentioned, to be counted as unemployed a person must be at least 16 years of age and without work, but actively looking for a job. Separating the employed from the unemployed would seem easy, but there are many details to consider. For example:
    - Does an individual who works only an hour per week for pay have a job? Yes, because people are counted as employed regardless of how few hours they work, just so long as it's 1 hour a week or more for pay.
    - Can someone who works without pay be counted as employed? Again, yes, just so long as that person is working in a family business for at least 15 hours a week.
    - Does going to school count as having a job? No. For students, school may seem to be a full-time job, but it's not considered in that light by government statisticians. Neither are students counted among the unemployed, unless they are looking for jobs.

- Some workers who have part-time jobs would like to have full-time jobs. Those workers are *underemployed.* Other workers would like to have a job, but have tried unsuccessfully to find one in the past and have given up looking. Because they have stopped looking, they are not counted in the unemployment statistics. Such would-be workers are called **discouraged workers.** Government estimates put the number of discouraged workers at 317,000 in mid 2002. **The presence of discouraged workers would cause the reported unemployment rate to understate true unemployment because discouraged workers are not in the labor force.**

- Some other people who are unemployed are actually earning incomes in the underground economy. **The underground economy causes the reported unemployment rate to overstate true unemployment.**

- Unemployment rates may be different for different groups. For example, the unemployment rate among African-Americans, is consistently higher than that of whites. Historically, male unemployment rates have been close to female unemployment rates. However, when married men, with spouse present, are compared to women who maintain families, we see a dramatically higher unemployment rate among the group of women.

- The unemployment rate does not tell us the *duration of unemployment*—how long a person has been unemployed. Short spells of unemployment among workers are of less concern than long-term unemployment. The median duration of unemployment in 2001 was just under 7 weeks.

StudyCheck 2

If short-term unemployment includes unemployment of up to two months, is it more common than long-term unemployment? Why would short-term unemployment be of less concern that long-term unemployment?

- There is some tendency for unemployment rates to rise and fall together across countries. This tendency for unemployment rates to move together reflects the modern global economy that has led to the economic interrelatedness of countries. Note, however, that this tendency is not a hard and fast rule.

6.2 Identifying Types of Unemployment
- Unemployment can be divided into the following four types:
    - **Frictional**—unemployment that occurs when someone enters the labor market or switches jobs.
    - **Seasonal**—unemployment that can be predicted to recur periodically, according to the time of year.
    - **Structural**—unemployment caused by a mismatch between a person's human capital and that needed in the workplace. This mismatch can be caused by an evolving structure of the economy as some industries rise and others fall. It can also be caused by minimum wage laws or other structural *rigidities* that inhibit job creation or the movement of workers into new jobs.
    - **Cyclical**—resulting from a downturn in the business cycle and affecting workers simultaneously in many different industries.

> **StudyCheck 3**
> What is an example of each type of unemployment?
>
> Frictional: _____
>
> Seasonal: _____
>
> Structural: _____
>
> Cyclical: _____

- Structural and cyclical unemployment are usually of most concern, because they represent *involuntary unemployment*, meaning that employees have little choice in the matter. In contrast, frictional and seasonal unemployment frequently represent *voluntary unemployment*, which can be planned for and more easily overcome.

- Seasonal unemployment affects workers in agriculture, many tourism-related occupations, education, tax accounting, professional sports, and some other industries. There is usually little concern over this unemployment, because it can be planned for—it is part of the job. Workers are not even counted as unemployed if they have labor contracts that restart after the off-season, such as often occurs in teaching and professional sports.

- Frictional unemployment occurs when people are between jobs, either because they were fired and have yet to line up new jobs or have quit voluntarily, such as in preparation for moving somewhere else or trying something new. Either way, their stay on the unemployment roles is likely to be brief. Frictional unemployment also includes many young people entering the labor market for the first time and older workers reentering the workforce after an absence to rear children.

- Changing jobs does not imply frictional unemployment. Most voluntary job switching is done without it; people line up new jobs before leaving their old ones. However, involuntary job changes, such as in response to layoffs and firings, commonly do result in frictional unemployment. In the case of involuntary frictional unemployment, publicly provided unemployment compensation acts as a safety net. It allows the job seeker to hold out longer in search of the best job opportunity.

- Changes in the structure of the economy can give rise to structural unemployment, as demands for some types of goods and services give way to demands for others. This change in structure arises from such factors as technological change, international trade, and changing ways of doing business. For example, computers and telecommunications have opened doors to many types of jobs, but have cost many types of jobs, too.

- Rigidities that inhibit labor movement and the creation of new jobs can also cause structural unemployment. For example, the federal minimum wage law introduces a rigidity by making it difficult for workers with little human capital to find a job. Further rigidities arise from the regional nature of many jobs. For example, there may be pockets of unemployment in inner cities and some regions of the country, while there are plenty of job openings in suburbia or other states. If regional migration were without cost, such locational rigidities would vanish.

- Human capital is often specific to a particular firm or kind of job—**specific human capital**—and does not apply readily to other firms or in other jobs. Workers with specific human capital are most prone to structural unemployment. It is a risk that people take voluntarily, since the best-paying jobs usually involve specific human capital.

- In contrast, **general human capital** involves such skills as communication, reasoning, and math. General human capital is easily transferred from job to job. Those who possess it are less likely to be structurally unemployed. For most students, an undergraduate economics education represents general human capital.

StudyCheck 4

While an undergraduate degree in economics is most likely general human capital, explain why a doctoral degree in economics tends to be specific human capital.

- Government sometimes offers job-training programs to cushion the blows of structural unemployment.

- A troublesome form of unemployment is caused by downturns in the business cycle. The increase in U.S. unemployment in 1991 and 1992 and again in 2001 and 2002 exemplifies cyclical unemployment since those increases were associated with the mild recession that occurred at that time. Cyclical unemployment is a temporary phenomena since recessions are temporary.

160   CHAPTER 6

6.4 Unemployment Insurance and the Natural Rate of Unemployment

- Unemployed workers who qualify are able to collect government-provided *unemployment insurance* payments to help tide them over during a spell of unemployment. By making it easier for the unemployed to stay unemployed, unemployment insurance contributes to a higher unemployment rate. If there were no unemployment insurance the unemployed would be forced to take work or apply for welfare benefits as soon as their savings ran out, even if they were not happy with the jobs available to them.

- Unemployment insurance affords workers the time to find a congenial job opportunity, thus increasing the *duration of unemployment*. However, human nature being what it is, some workers may choose to stay unemployed longer than necessary, enjoying a period of idleness at taxpayer expense. Unemployment insurance programs recognize this perverse incentive and build in some provisions that are designed to discourage idleness on the part of the unemployed. These provisions include a requirement that recipients must demonstrate evidence of applying for work each week, and a limit on how long unemployment insurance can be received. Typically, unemployment insurance benefits are exhausted after one year or less.

- In countries around the globe, unemployment rates average significantly closer to zero than to 100 percent. This is no coincidence. People look for ways to work because work puts food on the table. Even in the Great Depression of the 1930s, unemployment in the United States reached as high as 25 percent of the workforce for only one year, 1930, and as high as 20 percent for only 3 years, 1930 to 1932. Given that income is critical to living, however, it does not take many percentage points of unemployment to cause severe human trauma. The Great Depression was proof of the misery that high unemployment can bring.

- Even in the long run, the unemployment rate does not tend toward zero, exactly. Rather, the long-run tendency is for unemployment to settle at a few percentage points above zero, due to the inevitable presence of seasonal, frictional, and structural unemployment. The minimum long-run sustainable level of unemployment is termed the **natural rate of unemployment,** and is thought to be in the vicinity of 4 to 5 percent of the U.S. work force today.

- The economy would tend toward a lower natural rate in the absence of social *safety net* programs, which include unemployment compensation, Medicaid, food stamps, and additional programs designed to cushion the impact of unemployment or poverty. Without the safety net, the unemployed would be subject to greater misery, and a correspondingly greater incentive to grasp at any job offer, without regard to its long-term consequences for their future prospects. From an employer's perspective, minimum wage laws, liability laws, and many other policies discourage job formation because of the cost of complying with them. Other government policies, such as employment-related tax breaks for businesses, can have the opposite effect. Thus, government policies can and do affect the level of employment. Because of government actions, it is likely that the natural rate of unemployment has risen

UNEMPLOYMENT 161

from a little over 2 percent a century ago to 4 or 5 percent today, about the same as it was in the 1960s. In the 1970s, in contrast, the natural rate had climbed to about 7 percent.

- The flip side of the natural rate of unemployment is **full employment,** which equals 100 percent minus the natural rate of unemployment. Because the natural rate of unemployment exceeds zero, **full employment occurs when the employment rate is less than 100 percent.**

StudyCheck 5

Explain why changes in the natural rate of unemployment cause the threshold value for full employment to change.

E♦A 6.4 Employing Labor—The Hidden Consequences of the Law

- Employers incur expenses associated with complying with employment laws and regulations. Hiring new employees is no longer as simple as advertising a job, interviewing the applicants, checking the references, and making the best choice.

- Firms must be careful to avoid lawsuits in this process. The lawsuits could come from the federal government, perhaps guarding against discrimination. A lawsuit could also come from someone who was not hired. Such a lawsuit might allege an unfair hiring process. While many lawsuits involve an honest difference of opinion, frivolous lawsuits designed to harass defendants have resulted in the common use of the phrase "lawsuit abuse." Many people today seem to be willing to sue another, often with only a slim justification.

- Jobs nowadays must be advertised using very careful wording. Prior to passage of the flurry of anti-discrimination laws in the mid-1960s, if a particularly appealing applicant came along, an employer could tailor the job to suit that applicant's unique abilities. Such actions today would wave the red flag of lawsuit over discriminatory treatment of those who were not hired. Hiring exactly according to a written advertisement avoids this problem, but also lowers the expected payoff to the firm from advertising a new opening. This caution increases the cost of producing the firm's output. These costs are not measured in official statistics.

- Information about prospective employees is increasingly hard to come by. The Equal Employment Opportunity Commission (EEOC) issues detailed guidelines about questions that are or are not appropriate to ask of job candidates. The same questions must be asked of each candidate. The employer cannot revise the list once interviewing has started, even if it becomes obvious that some pertinent questions have been overlooked. This very formal process makes it difficult for an employer to get a feel for whether an employee will fit into the organization.

- Letters of recommendation are often nearly devoid of meaningful information. The threat of lawsuits bears much of the blame. After all, previous employers or others who know of reasons why someone should not be hired have no incentive to reveal it. Even if their information is true, they might still be sued for slander, defamation of character, or some other charge. There could even be dangers of lawsuits from future employers if letters of recommendation are misleadingly glowing.

- Since the certain expense and uncertain outcome of a lawsuit is something few letter writers wish to face, letters of recommendation are often little more than reports on such dry, objective facts as a job applicant's previous position and duration of employment. The upshot is that, when hiring, firms face an increasingly risky process, and are less likely to find the best-qualified person for the job. This process increases per unit production costs above what would be possible had the best person for the job been hired. It also affects the marginal decision about whether to hire. The hassles of hiring can be avoided by working current employees longer hours or more efficiently. The result is fewer employees per unit of output.

- Government regulations and mandates have also increased employment costs. For example, the Americans with Disabilities Act mandates that firms accommodate a variety of employee disabilities. Thus, a firm cannot simply fire a worker for showing up to work inebriated, since that might be a symptom of alcoholism. Alcoholism is a covered disability. Health and safety regulations, anti-discrimination laws, family leave requirements, and other government actions are intended to make the workplace better. They also increase per unit real production costs.

- Such cost increases even arise from government-mandated protections for employees about to lose their jobs. For example, consider the requirement that firms notify their employees at least 60 days prior to closing a production facility and laying off employees that work there. In those 60 days, firms can expect to see both productivity and quality drop, perhaps precipitously. After all, employees are not usually motivated to do their best if they know that they will be out of work shortly. If they choose to produce at all, firms must be prepared for high absenteeism, low productivity, and even sabotage. In these ways, legislation designed to cushion the blow of unemployment has the unintended side effect of increasing firms' real production costs. Of course, if workers think they have a chance to change the company's mind, they might work harder to convince the firm to keep the plant open!

- Despite all the government presence in the employment process, life on the job isn't necessarily any easier. This is not surprising. The same incentives that reduce the number of employees firms wish to hire also motivate firms to obtain more productivity from the employees they already have. From the employees' perspective, finding new jobs is more difficult. Because all employers face similar incentives to increase productivity, employees have little recourse but to bear down and be more productive. Thus, we see the rise of workweeks that are much longer than the traditional 40 hours. Incongruously, we also see more temporary and part-time positions. The reasons for both trends are similar. Part-time and temporary workers are easier to hire and fire and require fewer federally mandated benefits. For example, firms will go to extraordinary lengths to stay below 50 full-time employees. By law, firms that exceed that threshold find themselves subject to an array of costly mandates and regulations. Part-time and temporary workers often provide the flexibility to avoid that threshold.

- Taken as a whole, then, the increasing presence of well-intentioned laws pertaining to the workplace is threatening one of the mainstays of middle-class American existence, the 40-hour workweek. Part-time and overtime work is on the rise. Whether or not these changes are for the long-term good, is it any wonder that jobs seem stressful? Employment statistics measure the quantity of employment. We have no federal measure of its quality. The increasingly common reports of violence in the workplace give reason to wonder. According to the BLS, workplace violence accounted for 16 percent of the 5915 workplace fatalities in 2000. Additionally, there were over 23,000 assaults and violent acts that did not end in fatalities.

FILL IN THE BLANKS

1. An economy with unemployment is wasting resources and producing at a point _____ its production possibility frontier.

2. The U.S. civilian _____ _____ is composed of individuals age 16 and over, excluding those in the military, who are either employed or actively looking for work.

3. The labor force can be divided into two parts, consisting of the _____ and the _____. The _____ are those who work for pay, and the _____ are those who do not work, but are seeking jobs.

4. The _____ _____ is the fraction of the labor force who are unemployed, expressed in percentage terms.

5. When we take the ratio of the civilian labor force to the population age 16 and over, the result is the labor force _____ _____. If job creation lags behind the increase in the labor force, then some hopeful job seekers will be disappointed by their inability to find work and the _____ _____ will increase.

6. People are counted as _____ regardless of how few hours they work, just so long as it's 1 hour a week or more for pay. Someone who works without pay be counted as employed so long as that person is working in a family business for at least _____ hours a week.

7. Some workers who have part-time jobs would like to have full-time jobs. Those workers are _____. Other workers would like to have a job, but have tried unsuccessfully to find one in the past and have given up looking. Because they have stopped looking, they are not counted in the unemployment statistics. Such would-be workers are called _____ workers. The presence of these workers would cause the reported unemployment rate to understate _____ true unemployment because they are not in the labor force.

8. Unemployment rates may be different for different groups. For example, the unemployment rate among African-Americans, is consistently _____ than that of whites. Historically, male unemployment rates have been _____ female unemployment rates. However, when married men, with spouse present, are compared to women who maintain families, we see a dramatically _____ unemployment rate among the group of women.

9. The unemployment rate does not tell us the _____ ____ unemployment—how long a person has been unemployed. Short spells of unemployment among workers are of less concern than long-term unemployment.

10. Unemployment can be divided into the following four types:
    _____—unemployment that occurs when someone enters the labor market or switches jobs.
    _____—unemployment that can be predicted to recur periodically, according to the time of year.
    _____—unemployment caused by a mismatch between a person's human capital and that needed in the workplace. This mismatch can be caused by an evolving structure of the economy as some industries rise and others fall. It can also be caused by minimum wage laws or other structural *rigidities* that inhibit job creation or the movement of workers into new jobs.
    _____—resulting from a downturn in the business cycle and affecting workers simultaneously in many different industries.

11. Structural and cyclical unemployment are usually of most concern, because they represent _____ unemployment, meaning that employees have little choice in the matter. In contrast, frictional and seasonal unemployment frequently represent _____ unemployment, which can be planned for and more easily overcome.

12. Human capital is often specific to a particular firm or kind of job— _____ human capital—and does not apply readily to other firms or in other jobs. In contrast, _____ human capital involves such skills as communication, reasoning, and math.

13. Unemployed workers who qualify are able to collect government-provided _____ insurance payments to help tide them over during a spell of unemployment. By making it easier for the unemployed to stay unemployed, unemployment insurance contributes to a _____ unemployment rate. If there were no unemployment insurance the unemployed would be forced to take work or apply for welfare benefits as soon as their savings ran out, even if they were not happy with the jobs available to them. Unemployment insurance affords workers the time to find a congenial job opportunity, thus increasing the _____ of unemployment.

14. The long-run tendency is for unemployment to settle at a few percentage points above zero, due to the inevitable presence of _____, _____, and _____ unemployment. The minimum long-run sustainable level of unemployment is termed the _____ _____ of unemployment, and is thought to be in the vicinity of ____ to ____ percent of the U.S. work force today.

15. The economy would tend toward a lower natural rate in the absence of social _____ programs, which include unemployment compensation, Medicaid, food stamps, and additional programs designed to cushion the impact of unemployment or poverty.

16. The flip side of the natural rate of unemployment is _____ _____, which equals 100 percent minus the natural rate of unemployment. Because the natural rate of unemployment exceeds zero, full employment occurs when the employment rate is less than 100 percent.

17. Employers incur _____ associated with complying with employment laws and regulations.

18. Firms must be careful to avoid lawsuits in this process. While many lawsuits involve an honest difference of opinion, frivolous lawsuits designed to harass defendants have resulted in the common use of the phrase "lawsuit _____." Many people today seem to be willing to sue another, often with only a slim justification.

19. Hiring exactly according to a written advertisement avoids the problem of lawsuits, but also lowers the expected payoff to the firm from advertising a new opening. This caution increases the _____ of producing the firm's output.

20. Information about prospective employees is increasingly hard to come by. The _____ _____ _____ _____ (EEOC) issues detailed guidelines about questions that are or are not appropriate to ask of job candidates. The same questions must

166 CHAPTER 6

be asked of each candidate. The employer cannot revise the list once interviewing has started, even if it becomes obvious that some pertinent questions have been overlooked.

21. Since the certain expense and uncertain outcome of a lawsuit is something few letter writers wish to face, letters of recommendation are often little more than reports on such dry, objective facts as a job applicant's previous position and duration of employment. The upshot is that, when hiring, firms face an increasingly _____ process, and are less likely to find the best-qualified person for the job. This process increases per unit production _____ above what would be possible had the best person for the job been hired. It also affects the marginal decision about whether to hire. The hassles of hiring can be avoided by working current employees longer hours or more efficiently. The result is fewer employees per unit of output.

22. Government regulations and mandates have also increased employment costs. For example, the _____ _____ _____ Act mandates that firms accommodate a variety of employee disabilities. This also _____ per unit real production costs.

23. Consider the requirement that firms notify their employees at least _____ days prior to closing a production facility and laying off employees that work there. Firms can expect to see both productivity and quality drop, perhaps precipitously. After all, employees are not usually motivated to do their best if they know that they will be out of work shortly.

24. We see the rise of workweeks that are much longer than the traditional 40 hours. Incongruously, we also see more temporary and part-time positions. The reasons for both trends are similar. Part-time and temporary workers are easier to hire and fire and require fewer federally mandated benefits. For example, firms will go to extraordinary lengths to stay below ___ full-time employees. By law, firms that exceed that threshold find themselves subject to an array of costly _____ and regulations. Part-time and temporary workers often provide the flexibility to avoid that threshold.

25. Taken as a whole, then, the increasing presence of well-intentioned laws pertaining to the workplace is threatening one of the mainstays of middle-class American existence, the 40-hour workweek. Part-time and overtime work is on the rise. Whether or not these changes are for the long-term good, is it any wonder that jobs seem stressful? According to the BLS, workplace violence accounted for _____ percent of the 5,915 workplace fatalities in 2000. Additionally, there were over 23,000 assaults and violent acts that did not end in fatalities.

TRUE/FALSE/EXPLAIN
If false, explain why in the space provided.

1. The labor force excludes persons under age 16 and over age 65.

2. The unemployed are not counted in the labor force.

3. The ratio of the labor force to the population age 16 and over equals the labor force participation rate.

4. The participation rate in the United States equals approximately 80 percent.

5. In the United States, the participation rate for men is approximately equal to the participation rate for women.

6. To be counted as employed, an individual must work at least 10 hours a week for pay.

7. People who work in a family business for 15 hours or more a week are not considered to be part of the labor force.

8. Discouraged workers are counted as in the labor force, but unemployed.

9. The existence of an underground economy causes the reported unemployment rate to be higher than if there were no underground economy.

10. The median duration of unemployment is about seven weeks.

11. Most other countries have an unemployment rate that is very close to the unemployment rate in the U.S.

12. Frictional unemployment is associated with the business cycle.

13. Structural unemployment occurs when job skills become obsolete.

14. Knowing where to find the copying machine at your current work place is an example of general human capital.

15. Unemployment caused by a recession is termed seasonal unemployment.

16. The time a person is without a job while looking for a first job is called cyclical unemployment.

17. Unemployment insurance benefits replace 100 percent of the pay that an unemployed worker previously earned.

18. Because of unemployment insurance, the unemployed stay unemployed for shorter periods of time than would be the case if there were no unemployment insurance.

19. The natural rate of unemployment is zero percent in the United States today.

20. Full employment occurs when the unemployment rate is zero percent.

E&A 21. Complying with employment laws is costly to employers.

22. According to the EEOC, it is permissible to ask job applicants any question.

23. Laws that require employers to notify employees of a plant closure have no effect on the productivity of affected workers.

24. Workers who work long hours measure about 50 percent of all workers.

25. About 40,000 people lose their lives on the job each year.

MULTIPLE CHOICE
Circle the letter preceding the one best answer.

1. Unemployment is identified with a point
   a. on a production possibilities frontier.
   b. inside a production possibilities frontier.
   c. outside a production possibilities frontier.
   d. on the horizontal axis of the production possibilities graph.

2. The labor force excludes
   a. senior citizens who work.
   b. anyone looking for a job.
   c. those between 16 and 18 years of age.
   d. people without jobs who are not looking for work.

170 CHAPTER 6

3. If we know that out of an adult population of women that numbers 100, 42 of the women hold jobs, 8 have no job but are looking for one, and the rest are in school, then
   a. women's labor force participation rate cannot be known, given the data.
   b. women's labor force participation rate equals 42 percent.
   c. women's labor force participation rate equals 50 percent.
   d. women's and men's labor force participation rates are equal.

4. The unemployment rate is computed as
   a. the number of unemployed, regardless of whether they are looking for a job or not.
   b. the number of adults over the age of 16 who do not have a job.
   c. the number of unemployed divided by the labor force.
   d. the ratio of the number of unemployed to the number of employed.

5. A graph of women's labor force participation over time would
   a. be horizontal.
   b. slope downward.
   c. slope upward.
   d. look like a graph of the business cycle.

6. A graph of men's labor force participation over time would
   a. slope mildly downward.
   b. slope steeply downward.
   c. slope upward.
   d. look like a graph of the business cycle.

7. A pie chart that shows the U.S. labor force would show that the largest slice of the pie is made up of
   a. the employed.
   b. the unemployed.
   c. teens.
   d. discouraged workers.

8. Suppose that Reba is an eighteen-year-old college student who is looking for a job, but has not yet found one. Reba would be
   a. not part of the labor force because eighteen year olds are excluded from the labor force.
   b. not part of the labor force because students are excluded from the labor force.
   c. counted among the unemployed.
   d. a discouraged worker.

9. Stoney has an advanced degree in rocket science, but drives a cab for a living. Stoney is
    a. unemployed.
    b. a discouraged worker.
    c. underemployed.
    d. overemployed.

10. Blacks and whites tend to have
    a. similar unemployment rates.
    b. dissimilar unemployment rates, with black unemployment lower than white unemployment.
    c. dissimilar unemployment rates, with black unemployment higher than white unemployment.
    d. dissimilar unemployment rates, with black unemployment sometimes higher and sometimes lower than white unemployment.

11. The duration of unemployment refers to
    a. the fraction of the labor force that is unemployed.
    b. changes in the unemployment rate.
    c. how long people are unemployed.
    d. the cost of unemployment in terms of lost earnings.

12. Granger Baldwin, the star of the soap opera *The Young and the Narcissistic,* is out of work because the network canceled his show. Assuming that Granger specializes in playing the lead in soap operas, and that the networks are canceling all soap operas in favor of game shows, we would say that Granger is _____ unemployed.
    a. frictionally
    b. structurally
    c. cyclically
    d. seasonally

13. Voluntary unemployment is exemplified by
    a. Jonathan, the unemployed typewriter repairer who lost his job when word processors replaced typewriters.
    b. Herbert, who lost his job because of the recession.
    c. Liza, the manicurist who quit her job at the beauty shop to look for a job in the medical field.
    d. La-Rain, who became unemployed when the company she worked for moved its production facilities to Mexico.

14. General human capital
    a. is impossible to transfer from one job to another.
    b. is hard, but not impossible, to transfer from one job to another.
    c. is easy to transfer from one job to another.
    d. makes a person more likely to become structurally unemployed.

15. Specific human capital
    a. involves skills like knowing how to read.
    b. is hard to transfer from one job to another.
    c. is associated with graduation from college with an undergraduate degree.
    d. is exemplified by the specific computer a worker has sitting on his or her desk at work.

16. Unemployment insurance is paid for by
    a. workers, who generally insure themselves with the same company that insures their house or car.
    b. workers, who are taxed by government to pay for unemployment insurance.
    c. employers, who are taxed by government to pay for unemployment insurance.
    d. the federal government, which taxes state and local governments to pay for the insurance.

17. Unemployment insurance benefits typically last
    a. one month.
    b. six months.
    c. one year.
    d. for an unlimited amount of time.

18. During the Great Depression, the highest level reached by the unemployment rate was
    a. 90 percent.
    b. 50 percent.
    c. 25 percent.
    d. 14 percent.

19. The minimum long-run sustainable unemployment rate is called the
    a. cyclical rate of unemployment.
    b. structural rate of unemployment.
    c. seasonal rate of unemployment.
    d. natural rate of unemployment.

20. The number that comes closest to the best estimate of the natural rate of unemployment today is
    a. 2 percent.
    b. 5 percent.
    c. 9 percent.
    d. 12 percent.

E&A 21. In advertising a job, an employer must word advertisements carefully and hire according to the wording, which
    a. has no effect on the cost of production.
    b. decreases the cost of production.
    c. increases the cost of production.
    d. affects the cost of production in unpredictable ways.

22. Today, letters of recommendation
    a. are very useful to employers in evaluating job candidates.
    b. are usually the basis upon which an applicant is selected to fill a job.
    c. are regulated by the government to ensure truthful content.
    d. might lead to lawsuits, so are nearly devoid of meaningful information.

23. The Americans with Disabilities Act mandates that firms
    a. notify charities that work with the disabled 60 days in advance of any new job openings to give the disabled the first chance to land a job.
    b. hire the disabled even when they are unable to perform a job.
    c. accommodate employee disabilities.
    d. pay the medical expenses of their disabled employees.

24. If Superior Fishing Lures plans to close the plant where its Type 101 lures have been made for the last 90 years,
    a. the firm has no obligation to gives its workers advance notice.
    b. the firm must give its workers 60 days notice.
    c. the firm must give it workers one-year's notice.
    d. government must approve the plant closing, and find jobs for the workers before the plant will be allowed to close.

25. The career that shows the highest percentage of workers who put in long hours on the job is
    a. firefighter.
    b. minister.
    c. police officer.
    d. physician.

174 CHAPTER 6

ANSWERS

STUDYCHECKS

1. The slice for the unemployed should be 6.7 million people, the slice for the employed 141.8 million people, and the slice for those not in the labor force 63.4 million people.

2. If short-term unemployment duration includes up to two months of unemployment, then most of the unemployed in 2001 would fall into this category. They are less of a concern than the long-term unemployed because they are able to re-establish their own incomes. The long-term unemployed are more likely to need assistance.

3. An example of frictional unemployment is anyone who is unemployed while looking for a first job and anyone who is unemployed while looking for a job after being out of the labor force for a while.

4. An undergraduate degree in economics qualifies a graduate for a career in a variety of fields including many business occupations, including finance, management and marketing positions. In that sense, it is general human capital. A doctoral degree qualifies a graduate who holds that degree for a career in college teaching, research, and in business economics. In order words, a doctoral degree prepares the graduate for a career in economics.

5. Since full employment is defined as 100 percent minus the natural rate of unemployment, any change in the natural rate will change what is considered as full employment. For example, a natural rate of 7 percent implies full employment at 93 percent of the labor force. However, 96 percent of the labor force represents full employment when the natural rate changes to 4 percent.

FILL IN THE BLANKS

1. inside
2. labor force
3. employed, unemployed, employed, unemployed
4. unemployment rate
5. participation rate, unemployment rate
6. employed, 15
7. underemployed, discouraged
8. higher, close to, higher
9. duration of
10. Frictional, Seasonal, Structural, Cyclical

11. involuntary, voluntary
12. specific, general
13. unemployment, higher, duration
14. seasonal, frictional, structural, natural rate, 4, 5
15. safety net
16. full employment
17. expenses
18. abuse
19. cost
20. Equal Employment Opportunity Commission
21. risky, costs
22. Americans with Disabilities, increases
23. 60
24. 50, mandates
25. 16

TRUE/FALSE/EXPLAIN

1. False, only those under age 16 are excluded.
2. False, the unemployed who are looking for a job are counted in the labor force.
3. True.
4. False, the participation rate equals about 67 percent.
5. False, the participation rate for women is lower than that for men.
6. False, to be employed a person must work one hour a week for pay.
7. False, these people are considered to be employed, and thus part of the labor force.
8. False, discouraged workers are not part of the labor force because they are not employed and not looking for work.
9. True.
10. True.
11. False, unemployment rates vary significantly from country to country.
12. False, cyclical unemployment is associated with the business cycle.
13. True.
14. False, the location of a copying machine is specific human capital.
15. False, cyclical unemployment is created by recessions.
16. False, unemployment while looking for a first job is frictional.
17. False, unemployment benefits replace only a fraction of previous pay.
18. False, unemployment insurance allows people to stay unemployed longer.
19. False, the natural rate of unemployment is around 4 to 5 percent.
20. False, full employment is achieved when the actual unemployment rate equals the natural rate of unemployment.
21. True.

22. False, selected topics cannot be asked about in a job interview.
23. False, the negative effect on morale can lead to lower productivity.
24. False, the percentage of workers who work long hours is about 10 percent for men and 3 percent for women.
25. False, the number killed on the job equals about 5900 people each year.

MULTIPLE CHOICE

1.	b.	8.	c.	15.	b.	22.	d.
2.	d.	9.	c.	16.	c.	23.	c.
3.	c.	10.	c.	17.	c.	24.	b.
4.	d.	11.	c.	18.	c.	25.	d.
5.	c.	12.	b.	19.	d.		
6.	a.	13.	c.	20.	b.		
7.	b.	14.	c.	21.	c.		

Visit the Ayers/Collinge companion Website at http://www.prenhall.com/ayers for further activities and exercises for this chapter.

Chapter 7

INFLATION

CHAPTER REVIEW

7.1 The Goal of Low Inflation

- There are three fundamental goals for our economy: economic growth, high employment, and low inflation.

- The *price level* refers to the prices of goods and services, when considered in the aggregate. Most of the time the price level increases from one year to the next so that it moves progressively higher over time.

- **Inflation** is a persistent increase in the price level. Thus, inflation is not the same as a one-time increase in the prices of a few products. Rather, inflation is a chronic ailment that bedevils the economy. It involves widespread price increases, affecting the prices of many goods and services. Inflation can be mild, meaning that price increases are typically small for most goods, or severe, in which case price increases tend to be large. Any amount of inflation robs people of their purchasing power, *ceteris paribus*.

- The **inflation rate** is the annual percentage increase in the price level. We can compare the inflation rate in one year to the inflation rate in other years. In the U.S. so long as the inflation rate stays at approximately 3 percent or less, most Americans are satisfied that the goal of low inflation has been accomplished. Once the inflation rate gets much over 3 percent, people become more worried about inflation.

- As the inflation rate rises beyond the 3 percent threshold, people expect the federal government to "fight" inflation. In the U.S., the last bout of relatively high inflation occurred in the 1970s. The inflation rate can rise significantly from one year to the next.

- Inflation is not confined just to the U.S. The Central Intelligence Agency (CIA) estimates that the average inflation rate in the world in 2000 was 25 percent. Throughout recent history, inflation has been much more severe in many other countries than in America. These countries have tended to be developing nations, with a variety of economic and social problems. The CIA estimates that developing countries had inflation rates between 5 percent and 60 percent in 2000, which is markedly higher than the typical 1 percent to 3 percent inflation rate in developed countries. To a large extent the high inflation rates in developing countries reflect policies that inadvertently promote inflation.

- Seeking a solution to its high inflation, Ecuador adopted a policy of *dollarization* in 2001. Dollarization replaces a country's currency with the U.S. dollar. By dollarizing its economy Ecuador expects to be better off because its inflation rate should mirror the relatively low U.S. inflation rate. Dollarization should also provide for a more stable economy and government. Following dollarization the inflation rate in Ecuador fell sharply from the value in the table.

- When the inflation rate is negative, *deflation* is said to occur. That would happen if the price level declined from one year to the next. Severe, persistent deflation has yet to occur in modern U.S. history, although the inflation rate showed slight deflation in 1949 and 1955. More recently, prices of raw materials and some other goods, such as personal computers, fell significantly in the late 1990s, but not enough that we could say there was deflation.

- In spite of the good news for consumers when we see persistently falling prices, deflation is not a macroeconomic goal. Why not? You might reason that if inflation hurts some people by reducing their purchasing power, then deflation would benefit people by increasing their purchasing power. For example, if deflation caused prices to drop by 10 percent then everyone's income would buy 10 percent more. Surely, people would be better off if the economy were characterized by deflation. The catch is that everyone's income would have to stay the same for deflation to be beneficial to consumers. In fact, deflation is associated with economies in trouble.

- Disinflation differs from either inflation or deflation. *Disinflation* means that the rate of inflation declines. Disinflation is sometimes confused with deflation, but they are not the same.

StudyCheck 1

Suppose that annual inflation rates in the country of Stabilia are: Year 1: 5%; Year 2: 4%; Year 3: -1%; Year 4: 0%; Year 5: 2%. In which years, if any, did Stabilia experience either deflation or disinflation?

INFLATION 179

7.2 The Harm from Inflation

- In spite of relatively little inflation in the U.S. in recent years, the fear of higher inflation persists. This fear causes people to pay attention to inflation data. Toward the middle of each month, the government makes public the inflation rate for the previous month—a news release that is reported by all media.

- Energy and food prices are subject to wide fluctuations caused by temporary shifts in their supplies. Excluding food and energy prices from the computation of the inflation rate reveals what is termed *core inflation*. The core rate of inflation is of special interest when food and energy inflation rates differ significantly from the overall inflation rate. Otherwise, core inflation and the overall inflation rate will not differ much.

StudyCheck 2

Suppose that in a particular year, food and energy prices each increased by 6 percent, and in that same year the overall inflation rate was 4 percent. Was the core inflation rate in that year higher or lower than the overall inflation rate?

- Even with relatively low inflation, as in recent years, Inflation can hurt select groups of people. There will be some people whose incomes do not keep up with inflation and other people whose incomes keep up with or exceed inflation. The first group will be hurt. The latter group probably will not be.

- Most workers expect and receive an annual raise in pay. To them a good pay raise is one that provides them with an increase in their purchasing power—one that exceeds the inflation rate. In contrast, people who live on a fixed income see no increase in their income. Thus, inflation eats away at their purchasing power. Over time, through no fault of their own their standard of living declines. **Inflation hurts those on fixed incomes.**

- One group that can benefit from inflation is borrowers. Because inflation erodes the purchasing power of money, borrowers repay their debts with dollars that are worth less and less. Of course, on the other side are the lenders who receive those devalued dollars as the debts of the borrowers are paid off. Thus, when lenders and borrowers are compared, it is the lenders that are hurt by inflation.

180   CHAPTER 7

- **Perhaps the greatest harm from inflation is the opportunity cost of the time and other resources spent trying to avoid some of the harm inflicted by inflation.** One obvious response by consumers to inflation is to seek out substitute goods whose prices have not risen as much as the prices of similar goods. Shoppers must spend time, energy, gasoline, and other resources trying the dodge the inflation bullet.

- By making the distinction between anticipated inflation and unanticipated inflation, we can more easily discuss the gains and losses produced by inflation. *Anticipated inflation* is expected by the public. *Unanticipated inflation* is inflation that catches the public by surprise.

- People can take anticipated inflation into account in wage negotiations, mortgage loans, the tax system, and a variety of other contractual agreements. In theory at least, everyone is thus able to defend against losses imposed by anticipated inflation. For example, if workers anticipate the inflation rate will be 3 percent next year, they can try to negotiate 3 percent wage increases to offset that inflation.

- When inflation is unanticipated, the story changes. An increase in inflation that causes the inflation rate to be higher than expected provides borrowers with a windfall. Because borrowers win, lenders lose. To see this possibility, suppose I borrowed $1,000 from you to be repaid in 1 year. We both anticipate an inflation rate of 2 percent over the year, and agree that an additional 3 percent interest to compensate you for the use of your money is fair. Thus, we strike a deal that I will repay you $1,050, the original sum I borrowed, plus $20 (2 percent of $1,000) to make you whole for the loss of purchasing power you suffer because of inflation, plus another $30 (3 percent of $1,000) for giving up the use of your money for the year.

StudyCheck 3

Suppose that a borrower and a lender both expect an inflation rate of 0 percent over the next year, and that both parties agree that a 3 percent interest payment is fair compensation for the use of borrowed money. Explain why the borrower will repay $30 of interest for each $1,000 borrowed. Would this $30 remain the same if both parties revise their expectations to expect an inflation rate of 1 percent?

- Now suppose inflation proves greater than we anticipated. For example, suppose inflation rises to 5 percent. The $1,050 I repay you provides you with no reward for giving up the use of your money. You lose. I win, because I was able to use your money without having to pay you for its use. In other words, I used your purchasing power, and later returned the same purchasing power to you. If inflation had risen to a rate greater than 5 percent, I would have returned less purchasing power to you than you had before. You would be an even bigger loser, and I would be a bigger winner.

- A solution to the winners and losers problem created by unanticipated inflation is called **indexing**—automatically adjusting the terms of an agreement to account for inflation. If we indexed our loan agreement, we would agree to adjust the amount I repaid you according to the behavior of the inflation rate. If the inflation rate were to be 5 percent over the year of our loan agreement, I would be required to repay you $1,080, equal to the $1,000 I borrowed, plus the additional 3 percent interest you wanted, or $30, plus the 5 percent, or $50, to make up for the reduction in purchasing power caused by inflation. In other words, an interest rate that is indexed to inflation rises when inflation rises and falls when inflation falls.

- A number of high-inflation countries have resorted to indexation to deal with inflation. In the U. S., variable-rate home mortgages are a form of indexing. When market interest rates rise because of inflation, home buyers find their monthly payments also rising because the interest rate built into their mortgage agreement rises accordingly. Traditional fixed-rate home mortgages are not indexed. Lenders who make fixed-rate loans take the risk of inflation-induced losses in exchange for a higher interest rate than is initially attached to a variable-rate mortgage that is otherwise similar.

- Indexing can benefit savers. Millions of Americans have loaned money to the federal government by buying U.S. Savings Bonds, receiving fixed interest payments in return. The fixed interest payments mean that these bonds are not indexed for inflation. Inflation thus reduces the purchasing power of the interest payments as the years go by. Because of people's fears of inflation, the U. S Treasury began to offer in 1997 indexed bonds called *Treasury Inflation-Protected Securities (TIPS)*. Savers who buy TIPS bonds will find their interest earnings rise as inflation rises and fall as inflation falls. This feature of these bonds makes them attractive to savers who worry about unanticipated inflation. Meanwhile, the old-fashioned savings bond is still available for other less worried savers.

- In the 1970s *cost of living adjustment (COLA)* clauses in labor agreements were a popular form of wage indexing. COLAs call for periodic upward adjustments in the wages of workers to match increases in inflation. With labor unions losing power and inflation losing steam during the 1980s, COLAs lost popularity. Social Security payments, however, still feature a COLA. People who receive monthly Social Security checks find those checks get larger each year because of the built-in COLA.

7.3 Measuring Inflation

- A *price index* measures the average level of prices in the economy. There are several price indexes, each created for a specific purpose, with a different set of prices measured.

- The **Consumer Price Index (CPI),** the best known price index among the public, measures prices of typical purchases made by consumers living in urban areas. It is computed by the federal government's Bureau of Labor Statistics (BLS).

- The **Producer Price Index (PPI)** measures wholesale prices, which are prices paid by firms. It, too, is computed by the BLS.

- The **GDP chain-type price index** and the **GDP deflator** are the most broadly based price indexes because they include prices across the spectrum of GDP. They are computed by the Department of Commerce.

- To understand the CPI, let's start with the concept of the base period. **The *base period* is an arbitrarily selected initial time period against which other time periods are compared.** The CPI is assigned a value of 100 during the base period. For instance, the base period for the CPI is presently 1982 to 1984, and the CPI has been assigned an average value of 100 over that period of time.

- We can use the CPI data to compute the inflation rate. The inflation rate is calculated by taking the percentage change in the CPI as follows:
    Inflation rate = [change in price index ÷ initial price index] × 100

- The calculation of the CPI is based upon the prices of selected goods and services that consumers typically purchase. **The collection of goods and services used in the calculation of the CPI is called the *market basket.*** The market basket represents a sampling of the items that consumers buy that make up a significant part of their budgets.

- The market basket is based on extensive surveys of consumer purchases. There are around 200 specific categories of goods and services in the market basket, ranging from apples to women's dresses. Each item in the market basket is assigned a *weight* that reflects its importance in consumers' budgets. For example, personal care items such as shampoo have a smaller weight than gasoline. The BLS computes the CPI for the market basket every month. This effort requires BLS employees in 87 urban areas to collect a total of 80,000 different prices.

- The 200 or so specific categories of goods in the CPI market basket are divided into eight broad expenditure categories. All goods and services in the market basket belong to one of these categories. The weight on each category, which reflects the relative importance of the categories to consumers, is also shown in the table. The relative importance is stated as a percentage of total spending by the average consumer. For example, housing expenditures are the largest component of the expenditure categories, amounting to 40.9 percent of expenditures by average consumers. The weights are so important in contributing to the accuracy of the CPI that they are now updated every two years, rather than every 10 years, as in the past. Current weights help to ensure that the CPI reflects how people are spending their money.

- Weights can be used to identify the sources of inflation. For example, suppose that there is a price increase of 10 percent in housing, with no price changes for the other expenditure categories. The inflation rate as measured by the CPI would equal 4.09 percent, computed as 10 percent multiplied by 0.409 (the weight on housing, after it is converted from a percent to decimal form). The knowledge that the increase in the CPI is concentrated in the price of housing can be used to design policies that target inflation from that source.

- Let's see how to compute a price index based on a market basket of items. The simplified formula for the Consumer Price Index is:

    $$\frac{\text{Cost of market basket at current prices}}{\text{Cost of market basket at base period prices}} \times 100$$

- **The Consumer Price Index measures the increase in the price of the market basket between the current year and the base period.** It uses base period quantities throughout. A simplified example in which this price index is calculated for a market basket of three goods can help clarify the procedure. Suppose we wish to calculate the price index for a market basket of apples, oranges, and bananas. In the base period 5 apples, 4 oranges, and 2 bananas are purchased. The prices in the base period were 30 cents each for apples, 20 cents each for oranges, and 10 cents each for bananas. Currently, apples are still 30 cents each, but oranges have also risen to 30 cents each, while bananas have risen to 20 cents each. These prices and quantities are presented in Table 7-4.

Table 7-4 Computing a Simplified Price Index

Base Period Quantities	Base Period Prices	Current Prices
Apples: 5 Oranges: 4 Bananas: 2	Apples: 30 cents each Oranges: 20 cents each Bananas: 10 cents each	Apples: 30 cents each Oranges: 30 cents each Bananas: 20 cents each

- Convert the prices to decimal form and then perform the calculation as follows:

    $$\frac{(.30 \times 5) + (.30 \times 4) + (.20 \times 2)}{(.30 \times 5) + (.20 \times 4) + (.10 \times 2)} = \frac{3.10}{2.50} = 1.24 \times 100 = 124$$

In the base year the market basket cost $2.50. Now that same market basket costs $3.10. The index number of 124 indicates that the market basket costs 24 percent more than in the base year. The computation of this simplified price index gives you an idea of how the CPI is computed. The actual CPI calculation follows this procedure, but is more complicated because of some problems with price indexes that we discuss a little later in the chapter.

184   CHAPTER 7

StudyCheck 4

Suppose that base period quantities are as follows: apples: 5; oranges: 4; bananas: 2. Suppose base period prices for these items are 15 cents each, 10 cents each, and 5 cents each, respectively, and that current period prices are 30 cents each, 30 cents each, and 20 cents each, respectively. What is the value of the price index?

- Increases in economic variables may occur as a consequence of inflation, which "pumps up" the value of macro variables. For example, an increase in GDP due solely to price increases does not increase economic welfare, just as an increase in wages that is completely offset by higher prices leaves workers no better off. We can use a price index to adjust economic measures for the effects of inflation.

- The **nominal value** of a variable is expressed in current dollar terms. Nominal values may be considered as "what you see is what you get," because nominal values are not adjusted for inflation. The **real value** of a variable adjusts for inflation. The real value is expressed in terms of the value of the dollar during a selected base period. The time period chosen as the base period is not very important. What is important is that each year's measuring units be the same—dollars with the same purchasing power.

- The distinction between real and nominal values is important not only to the study of macroeconomics, but also to individuals. Consider a worker whose weekly pay increases from $100 to $110. That worker has experienced a 10 percent increase in nominal income. If the price level remained constant, the worker's real income is also 10 percent greater. However, if the price level increased by 10 percent, the $110 of current income will purchase only as much as $100 purchased in the past. That means that the real income has not changed.

- The following formula shows how to use a price index to compute a real value:
Real value = [nominal value/price index] × 100

- For example, suppose Jack earned nominal incomes of $39,000 a year in the base period and $40,500 in the current year, a 3.8 percent increase over the base period. Is Jack better off in the current year than in the base period? If the price index in the current year equals 105, then:
Jack's real income = ($40,500/105) × 100 = $38,571.43

- Jack's real income, which measures his purchasing power, has fallen since the base year. In terms of his real income he is not better off. Although Jack's earnings indicate he is paid more than the federal minimum wage, millions of workers toil at that wage. Figure 7-4 shows the nominal and real values of the minimum wage since its enactment in 1938. As the figure shows, the purchasing power of the minimum wage has been in a long-term decline, with periodic slight upticks when the minimum is increased by Congress.

- The distinction between a nominal and a real value is important in other instances. A *nominal interest rate* is the payment from a borrower to a lender, expressed in percentage terms. A *real interest rate* measures the percentage payment in terms of its purchasing power. To compute a real interest rate it is not necessary to know the value of a price index. Instead, all that is needed is knowledge of the inflation rate and the nominal interest rate:
Real interest rate = nominal interest rate − inflation rate.

- Recall our earlier example in this chapter where I borrow $1,000 from you to be repaid in one year. We agree that I am to repay you $1,050. The $50 more than I borrow that I repay you is the interest. The nominal interest rate is 5 percent (the interest payment divided by the amount borrowed). Recall, though, that the inflation rate is 2 percent, meaning that the purchasing power of money is declining by 2 percent a year. When we subtract the inflation rate from the nominal interest rate on the loan, we are left with 3 percent. As you can tell by the formula, this 3 percent is the value of the real interest rate. You, the lender in this example, will increase your purchasing power by 3 percent when the loan is repaid. The real interest rate in the U.S. is contrasted to the nominal interest rate in Figure 7-5. The real interest rate and the nominal rate typically move in the same direction, but the nominal rate is higher than the real rate.

- Let's consider the three other price indexes mentioned earlier: the Producer Price Index, the GDP chain-type price index, and the GDP deflator. The Producer Price Index (PPI) focuses on the prices received by U.S. producers, as measured by the revenue they receive. The prices are those of the outputs sold by producers to other producers as intermediate goods, and sold directly to consumers. The PPI often foretells increases in the CPI because price increases at the producer level will usually be passed on later to consumer prices. Thus, the PPI is watched for hints about the future course of consumer prices.

- The GDP chain-type price index and the GDP deflator, as you would guess from their names, are for gross domestic product. Both indexes, published by the Department of Commerce, use 1996 as the base period, meaning that the values of the indexes are equal to 100 in that year.
  Let's look at the GDP deflator first. It is computed as:
  $$\text{GDP deflator} = \text{Nominal GDP} \div \text{Real GDP}$$

- Let's apply the formula. In 2001 nominal GDP equaled $10,218 billion and real GDP equaled $9,333.8 billion. Substituting in the formula, we have:
  $$\text{2001 GDP deflator} = 10{,}208.1 \div 9{,}333.8 = 109.37$$

- This value of the GDP deflator says that the price level has risen over 9 percent since the 1996 base year, since the 2001 GDP deflator differs by 9.37 points from the value of 100 in the base year. The GDP deflator is broad-based because it reflects price changes in the entire spectrum of good and services that go into GDP. For contrast, consider what the CPI reveals about price changes between 1996 and 2001. From Table 7-3, the CPI stood at 156.9 in 1996 and 177.1 in 2001. Using the formula for the inflation rate, we have:
  $$\text{Inflation Rate}_{\text{CPI 1996 - 2001}} = [\text{change in price index/initial value of price index}] \times 100$$
  $$= [(177.1 - 156.9)/156.9] \times 100 = 12.8 \text{ percent}$$

- The CPI computes the price level as having risen over 12 percent during the 1996 to 2001 time period. It is normal for the four price indexes, which measure different prices and are computed differently, to give results that are not identical.

- At first glance, the GDP chain-type price index is computed in a similar manner to the GDP deflator:
  $$\text{GDP chain-type price index} = \text{Nominal GDP} \div \text{Real chained GDP}$$

  There is a difference, however in that real chained GDP is used in the computation. The chained price index uses chained weights in the computation of real GDP, which is termed real chained GDP. A chain index offers advantages over other types of indexes, as discussed in the next section.

- The term *chain weight* comes about because the GDP chain-type price index links quantities (weights) in two successive years, then moves forward a year and does that link again, and so forth. This continuous linking, two years at a time, forms a chain, and hence the name. For example, the calculation of 2002 GDP involves prices and quantities for 2001 and 2002. Similarly, the calculation of 2003 GDP involves prices and quantities for 2002 and 2003.

- Prior to 1999 the CPI was calculated using *fixed weights* throughout the market basket. Fixed weight price indexes provide consistently incorrect results because they assume that people do not change their consumption when prices rise. In fact, as prices change, people

INFLATION 187

typically substitute relatively cheaper goods for goods that have become relatively more expensive. The inaccuracy introduced into the CPI by this behavior is termed the *substitution bias*. **The substitution bias causes inflation to be overstated**. This bias is inherent in a fixed weight price index like the old CPI. Other biases creep into price indexes because it is difficult to account for quality changes that improve products. Similarly, unless a price index immediately takes account of the introduction of new products, it will be biased.

- It was long recognized that the substitution bias caused the CPI to overstate inflation, and a solution to the problem was sought. Through the years since its inception in 1913 the method of computing the CPI has been improved repeatedly. In January 1999 the CPI was improved again to provide a partial solution to the substitution bias. That change better measures the cost of living when people respond to inflation by cutting their consumption of goods whose prices have risen the most, and increasing their consumption of items whose prices have not. The new method of computing the CPI uses geometric means, but does not go all the way toward a chained CPI. The use of geometric means does not perfectly correct for substitution bias. The effect has been, however, to lower the computed inflation rate slightly, providing a more accurate, if not perfect, assessment of the cost of living.

- In an effort to provide even more accurate inflation data, the BLS introduced another CPI in August, 2002. This CPI is called the C-CPI, with the first C standing for Chained. A chained price index uses updated expenditure weights. As discussed in relation to Figure 7-3, the CPI updates its weights every two years. The new C-CPI will be chained monthly. In effect, the weights for the C-CPI will be updated continuously.

- The C-CPI supplements, but does not replace the older CPI. Both price indexes are useful, but the method of computation is different. The current CPI assumes that the share of the consumer's budget spent on an item stays fixed for the two years between updates in the weights. Thus, it retains some of the disadvantage of a fixed weight index. The C-CPI makes no such assumption, and instead assumes that consumers substitute freely among items as prices change. Thus, the C-CPI may be viewed as an effort to overcome fully the problem of substitution bias.

7.4 Living With Inflation

- The Consumer Price Index (CPI) is used in three ways:
  - As an economic indicator. The CPI is the most popular indicator of inflation. As such, it is used by government and the public to determine whether the nation is meeting its goal of low inflation.
  - To convert nominal economic values into real values. The average real income of the American worker is a superior measure of economic progress than is nominal income. The CPI is the most popular price index used to compute real incomes.
  - To adjust selected monetary payments upward as prices increase. The annual cost-of-living adjustment in Social Security payments is an example.

- *Hyperinflation* is inflation out of control, with prices rising quickly. The most widely documented hyperinflation occurred in post-World War I Germany in the years 1922-1923.

- Imagine a hyper-inflated world. It would be difficult to carry enough cash to make a simple purchase since a simple purchase might cost you millions of dollars. You might want your wages paid daily, or even more often. That's because a dollar received now would have more purchasing power than a dollar received later—even a few hours later. You would also want to budget enough time to spend your money. You might take time off from work during the day to go spend your wages as soon as you receive them. Hyperinflation turns money into a hot potato. Get rid of it quickly before it loses more value.

- With prices changing quickly, everyone tries to adjust. One type of adjustment is the behavioral changes that individuals make in order to try to cope with inflation. Individual adjustments can be as simple as searching out cheaper places to shop, and substituting chicken for steak. Some people barter—they enter into direct exchanges of goods and services with other people, with no need for money to change hands. Other people exchange their country's currency for foreign currencies that are stable in value, as Mexicans and Russians have done with the dollar during recent inflations in their countries. These adjustments can be stressful and costly in terms of a person's time.

- Another type of adjustment revolves around the changes in business practices that increase the cost of doing business. For example, businesses must devote resources to constantly keep track of prices, making changes as often as necessary. Other businesses may be forced into costly redesigns of their products in response to higher labor and materials prices. These costs are likely to be passed on in the form of higher consumer prices. Higher prices followed by higher costs followed by even higher prices can result in an *inflationary spiral*, with inflation feeding on itself.

- With all these examples of individual and business behavioral changes, you can see that hyperinflation would be a giant headache. The time needed to cope with it decreases individual productivity, which reduces the production of goods and services, in turn reducing the standard of living. Some of the adjustments that people make in response to hyperinflation may be made in response to even ordinary levels of inflation, but on a smaller scale.

- The changes in behavior we've discussed make it more difficult to measure the inflation rate accurately. Since the CPI is widely used, it should reflect price changes as precisely as possible. Changes in product design present a particular challenge to the accurate measurement of inflation. To understand this point, recall the example in the chapter in which the prices of apples, bananas, and oranges were used to illustrate the computation of the CPI. Those computations implicitly assumed that the three products remained unchanged. Suppose, however, that improved varieties of all three goods have been introduced in the marketplace since the base period. The improvements offer consumers greater satisfaction,

INFLATION 189

which they are willing to pay for. In this context, the value of the CPI does not accurately reflect inflation, but a willingness to pay for improvements in product quality. Thus, unless a price index adjusts for product quality improvements, the price index will overstate the inflation rate.

- The CPI adjusts price changes for product improvements. The method is called an *hedonic model*. Although hedonic models use statistical methods and are complicated in practice, in concept they are quite simple. In an hedonic model each product is viewed as a bundle of characteristics and the model is used to estimate the value of each characteristic. Although hedonic models help improve the accuracy of the CPI they are not perfect.

- Even if the CPI were perfectly accurate, your personal inflation experience would probably be different. The CPI measures changes in average prices. You may live in an area of the country that is experiencing price increases that outstrip the average. For a variety of reasons your purchasing may not mirror that of the average consumer. If you are chronically ill, you may spend a larger than average fraction of your income on medicines. If you are in college, increases in tuition will hit you harder than the average citizen. If you have a long commute between home and work, it is increases in the price of gasoline that make your personal inflation experience different from the CPI.

- Even relatively low inflation can add up over time. The rule of seventy-two allows an estimate of how many years it would take prices to double for any inflation rate. The calculation involved in the rule of seventy-two is simple: Take an inflation rate and divide it into 72. The result is the time it takes prices to double. Figure 7-6 shows doubling times for selected annual inflation rates between 1 percent and 16 percent.

- Figure 7-6 shows that an increase in the inflation rate can have dramatic long-term effects. For instance, a sustained 2 percent inflation rate would mean that it would take almost half of the average person's lifetime for prices to double. At a 4 percent inflation rate, not much higher than in recent U.S. experience, prices would double about four times over a lifetime. At a 10 percent inflation rate, prices would double a total of ten times for someone living into his or her seventies. No matter the inflation rate, living with inflation is what people must do.

StudyCheck 5
Compute the approximate number of years it would take for the price level to double if the inflation rate were 11 percent annually.

FILL IN THE BLANKS

1. The _____ _____ refers to the prices of goods and services, when considered in the aggregate. _____ is a persistent increase in the price level. Any amount of inflation robs people of their purchasing power, *ceteris paribus*.

2. The _____ _____ is the annual percentage increase in the price level.

3. Inflation is not confined just to the U.S. The Central Intelligence Agency (CIA) estimates that the average inflation rate in the world in 2000 was ____ percent. The CIA estimates that developing countries had inflation rates between 5 percent and 60 percent in 2000, which is markedly higher than the typical ____ percent to ____ percent inflation rate in developed countries. Seeking a solution to its high inflation, Ecuador adopted a policy of _____ in 2001, which replaces a country's currency with the U.S. dollar.

4. When the inflation rate is negative, _____ is said to occur. That would happen if the price level declined from one year to the next. _____ means that the rate of inflation declines. Energy and food prices are subject to wide fluctuations caused by temporary shifts in their supplies. Excluding food and energy prices from the computation of the inflation rate reveals what is termed _____ _____.

5. Inflation hurts those on _____ incomes. One group that can benefit from inflation is _____. Perhaps the greatest harm from inflation is the opportunity cost of the time and other resources spent trying to avoid some of the harm inflicted by inflation. One obvious response by consumers to inflation is to seek out _____ goods whose prices have not risen as much as the prices of similar goods.

6. _____ inflation is expected by the public. _____ inflation is inflation that catches the public by surprise. People can take _____ inflation into account in wage negotiations, mortgage loans, the tax system, and a variety of other contractual agreements. In theory at least, everyone is thus able to defend against losses imposed by anticipated inflation. When inflation is _____, borrowers receive a windfall. A solution to the winners and losers problem created by unanticipated inflation is called _____—automatically adjusting the terms of an agreement to account for inflation.

7. In the 1970s _____ ____ _____ _____ *(COLA)* clauses in labor agreements were a popular form of wage indexing. COLAs call for periodic upward adjustments in the wages of workers to match increases in inflation. With labor unions losing power and inflation losing steam during the 1980s, COLAs lost popularity. Social Security payments, however,

still feature a COLA. People who receive monthly Social Security checks find those checks get larger each year because of the built-in COLA.

8. A _____ _____ measures the average level of prices in the economy. The **Consumer Price Index (CPI),** the best known price index among the public, measures prices of typical purchases made by consumers living in urban areas. It is computed by the federal government's Bureau of Labor Statistics (BLS). The **Producer Price Index (PPI)** measures wholesale prices, which are prices paid by firms. It, too, is computed by the BLS. The **GDP chain-type price index** and the **GDP deflator** are the most broadly based price indexes because they include prices across the spectrum of GDP. They are computed by the Department of Commerce.

9. The _____ _____ is an arbitrarily selected initial time period against which other time periods are compared. The CPI is assigned a value of _____ during the base period.

10. We can use the CPI data to compute the inflation rate. The inflation rate is calculated by taking the percentage change in the CPI as follows:
    Inflation rate = [_____ __ _____ _____ ÷ _____ _____ _____] × 100

11. The collection of goods and services used in the calculation of the CPI is called the _____ _____, representing a sampling of the items that consumers buy that make up a significant part of their budgets. Each item in the sample is assigned a -_____ that reflects its importance in consumers' budgets.

12. The formula for the Consumer Price Index is: Cost of market basket at _____ prices/Cost of market basket at base period prices × 100.

13. The _____ of a variable is expressed in current dollar terms. Nominal values may be considered as "what you see is what you get," because nominal values are not adjusted for inflation. The _____ _____ of a variable adjusts for inflation. The real value is expressed in terms of the value of the dollar during a selected base period.

14. The following formula shows how to use a price index to compute a real value:
    Real value = [nominal value/_____ _____] × 100

15. The distinction between a nominal and a real value is important in other instances. A _____ interest rate is the payment from a borrower to a lender, expressed in percentage terms. A _____ interest rate measures the percentage payment in terms of its purchasing power.

16. To compute a real interest rate it is not necessary to know the value of a price index. Instead, all that is needed is knowledge of the inflation rate and the nominal interest rate:
    Real interest rate = _____ interest rate − _____ rate.

192   CHAPTER 7

17. The _____ _____ _____ (PPI) focuses on the prices received by U.S. producers, as measured by the revenue they receive.

18. The GDP chain-type price index and the GDP deflator, as you would guess from their names, are for _____ _____ _____. The GDP deflator is computed as:
GDP deflator = _____ GDP ÷ _____ GDP

19. The GDP chain-type price index is computed as:
GDP chain-type price index = _____ GDP ÷ chained _____ GDP

20. The term *chain weight* comes about because the GDP chain-type price index links quantities (weights) in two successive years, then moves forward a year and does that link again, and so forth. This continuous linking, two years at a time, forms a chain, and hence the name. For example, the calculation of 2002 GDP involves prices and quantities for _____ and _____. Similarly, the calculation of 2003 GDP involves prices and quantities for _____ and _____. Prior to 1999 the CPI was calculated using _____ weights throughout the market basket, which provides consistently incorrect results because they assume that people do not change their consumption when prices rise. The inaccuracy introduced into the CPI by this behavior is termed the _____ bias, which causes inflation to be _____.

21. In an effort to provide even more accurate inflation data, the BLS introduced another CPI in August, 2002. This CPI is called the C-CPI, with the first C standing for _____. A chained price index uses updated expenditure weights. In effect, the weights for the C-CPI will be updated continuously. The C-CPI supplements, but does not replace the older CPI. The C-CPI may be viewed as an effort to overcome fully the problem of substitution bias.

E&A 22. _____ is inflation out of control, with prices rising quickly. The most widely documented case occurred in post-World War I Germany _____ in the years 1922-1923.

23. _____ turns money into a hot potato. Get rid of it quickly before it loses more value. With prices changing quickly, everyone tries to adjust. Individual adjustments can be as simple as searching out cheaper places to shop, and substituting chicken for steak. Some people _____—they enter into direct exchanges of goods and services with other people, with no need for money to change hands. Another type of adjustment revolves around the changes in business practices that _____ the cost of doing business. Higher prices followed by higher costs followed by even higher prices can result in an _____ _____, with inflation feeding on itself.

24. The CPI adjusts price changes for product improvements. The method is called an, _____ _____ which uses statistical methods. Each product is viewed as a bundle of characteristics and the model is used to estimate the value of each characteristic.

25. Even relatively low inflation can add up over time. The _____ __ _____-____ allows an estimate of how many years it would take prices to double for any inflation rate.

TRUE/FALSE/EXPLAIN
If false, explain why in the space provided.

1. The price level refers to prices in the aggregate.

2. Inflation involves a persistent increase in the price level.

3. The inflation rate is the annual percentage increase in the price level.

4. According to CIA estimates, recently the world inflation rate have been about 5 percent.

5. Dollarization involves a country other than the U.S. adopting the U.S. dollar as its currency.

6. Disinflation is another word for deflation.

7. Deflation is clearly preferred by the public and economists to inflation.

8. The core rate of inflation can be higher or lower than the overall inflation rate.

9. The core rate of inflation excludes food and energy prices in the computation of the inflation rate.

10. Anticipated inflation is ignored by workers since it is expected.

11. Indexing is a response to anticipated inflation.

12. Social Security payments feature an annual cost of living adjustment.

13. The GDP deflator and the GDP chained price index are two price indexes that measure prices in the market basket.

14. The Consumer Price Index is computed by the White House.

15. The CPI is computed and made available to the public every six months.

16. The CPI is able to measure inflation, but cannot measure deflation.

17. The CPI market basket has not been changed since 1965.

18. To a worker living during a period of significant inflation, the nominal value of the worker's salary is more important than the real value.

INFLATION 195

19. The substitution bias in the CPI refers to the tendency of the CPI to understate the true rate of inflation.

20. The chained version of the CPI replaces the old version of the CPI.

21. The CPI cannot be used to compute a real value from a nominal value.

22. In a period of hyperinflation, one response is to exchange the currency that is losing purchasing power for a more stable foreign currency.

23. There is no method available to adjust the CPI for changes in product quality.

24. Each person's personal inflation rate is accurately reflected by the CPI.

25. The rule of seventy two is used to compute a real value from a nominal value.

MULTIPLE CHOICE
Circle the letter preceding the one best answer.

1. The price level refers to
   a. the price of a single good.
   b. the price of a small group of similar goods.
   c. prices in the aggregate.
   d. prices that remain level, and thus do not change.

2. Inflation _____ purchasing power.
   a. increases
   b. decreases
   c. has no effect on
   d. has unpredictable effects on

3. Regarding inflation, the 1990s are best characterized by
   a. high and rising inflation.
   b. extremely variable inflation rates.
   c. zero inflation in many years.
   d. low inflation.

4. Because Ecuador's inflation rate was _____, the country adopted a policy of _____.
   a. low; revising the method of computing its price index
   b. low, changing its market basket
   c. high, using a chained price index
   d. high, dollarization

5. The difference between deflation and disinflation
   a. is nil since they measure the same thing.
   b. is that deflation measures price increases and disinflation measures price decreases.
   c. occurs because deflation refers to the price level, but disinflation refers to specific prices.
   d. is that deflation occurs when the price level drops, but disinflation occurs when the inflation rate drops.

6. The core rate of inflation will be _____ the overall inflation rate when food and energy prices are rising more rapidly than other prices.
   a. the same as
   b. lower than
   c. higher than
   d. of no value compared to

7. Regarding the harm from inflation, which statement is the most accurate?
   a. Inflation harms no one.
   b. Inflation harms everyone to an equal degree.
   c. Inflation harms borrowers.
   d. Inflation harms those on fixed incomes.

8. If the public believes that the inflation rate is about to rise, then this type of inflation is best characterized as
   a. anticipated.
   b. unanticipated.
   c. hyperinflation.
   d. disinflation.

9. Suppose you negotiate a deal to borrow money from a lender today. A year from now when you repay the loan, the amount repaid plus interest has less purchasing power than the original amount borrowed. Based on these facts, the best conclusion is that
   a. inflation was perfectly anticipated.
   b. there was some unanticipated inflation.
   c. all inflation is unanticipated.
   d. no inflation is anticipated.

10. The purpose of indexing is to
    a. cut the inflation rate to zero.
    b. increase inflation to stimulate the economy.
    c. create winners and losers in the event of unanticipated inflation.
    d. adjust contracts according to the actual amount of inflation that occurs.

11. The base period for a price index refers to
    a. a time when the inflation rate was zero.
    b. before the price index was computed.
    c. a time period to which other time periods are compared.
    d. the year 2000.

12. An inflation rate is computed by the formula
    a. change in the price index
    b. change in price index divided by the initial price index, and then multiplied by 100.
    c. change in price index multiplied by the initial price index, and then divided by 100.
    d. square root of the change in the price index.

13. The CPI market basket refers to
    a. all goods and services that consumers buy.
    b. goods that are necessities, but not goods that are luxuries.
    c. goods that go up in price the fastest.
    d. 200 categories of goods and services typically bought by consumers.

14. The CPI is computed using the formula
   a. cost of market basket at base period prices divided by cost of market basket at current period prices, and then multiplied by 100.
   b. cost of market basket at base period prices multiplied by cost of market basket at current period prices, and then divided by 100.
   c. cost of market basket at current period prices divided by cost of market basket at base period prices, and then multiplied by 100.
   d. cost of all goods and services today divided by cost of all goods and services last year.

15. A real value is computed by
   a. multiplying a nominal value by a price index
   b. dividing a nominal value by a price index, and then multiplying by 100.
   c. dividing a real value by a nominal value, and then multiplying by 100.
   d. dividing the current value of a price index by a past value of the same index, and then multiplying by 100.

16. A real interest rate
   a. is always identical to a nominal interest rate.
   b. is computed using a price index.
   c. exists in theory but is impossible to compute.
   d. is the difference between a nominal interest rate and the inflation rate

17. Regarding the real value of the minimum wage,
   a. it is higher today than at any time in history.
   b. it is lower today than at any time in history
   c. it is kept the same every year when the government adjusts it each January for inflation.
   d. it is lower today than in the 1960s.

18. The GDP implicit price deflator is computed
   a. in the same way as the CPI.
   b. as nominal GDP divided by real GDP, and then multiplied by 100.
   c. as real GDP divided by nominal GDP, and then multiplied by 100.
   d. as real GDP minus nominal GDP.

19. To obtain real GDP
   a. a price index is not required.
   b. the consumer price index is used.
   c. the producer price index is used.
   d. the GDP chained price index is used.

20. Substitution bias refers to
    a. the effect on the CPI when people replace goods whose prices are increasing most rapidly with goods that cost less.
    b. the tendency of people to buy higher quality goods when their incomes increase.
    c. the loss of purchasing power resulting from inflation.
    d. the idea that people like a substitute less than they like an item that they usually buy.

21. With hyperinflation
    a. prices rise slowly.
    b. prices rise rapidly.
    c. prices do not rise.
    d. people become hyper over higher prices.

22. In 1922-1923 hyperinflation was experienced by
    a. the U.S.
    b. England.
    c. France.
    d. Germany.

23. Which of the following would NOT be a possible adjustment to inflation?
    a. Barter
    b. Redesigned products.
    c. Substituting chicken for steak.
    d. An increase in saving.

24. Changes in product quality
    a. are ignored in computing the CPI.
    b. have no effect on the price of a product.
    c. have an insignificant effect on the price of a product.
    d. may have a significant effect on the price of a product, and are adjusted for when the CPI is computed.

25. The rule of seventy-two is used to
    a. compute the amount of inflation since 1972.
    b. estimate how many more years of life a 72-year-old man can expect.
    c. estimate how much inflation will occur over a newborn baby's lifetime.
    d. compute doubling times.

200 CHAPTER 7

ANSWERS

STUDYCHECKS

1. In years 2 and 3 Stabilia experienced a lower inflation rate than the previous years. Thus, those years could be characterized as showing disinflation. However, in year 3 the inflation rate was negative, so in year 3 Stabilia also experienced deflation.
2. Since food and energy price inflation exceeded overall inflation, by excluding food and energy prices, the core inflation rate will be less than 4 percent.
3. The $30 of interest for each $1,000 borrowed represents a 3 percent interest rate on the loan. With 0 percent inflation expected, there is no reason for this 3 percent to be adjusted upward. However, when inflation expectations are revised to 1 percent, an additional 1 percent interest must be tacked on to the interest payment. Thus, the borrower will pay $40 in interest for each $1,000 borrowed when inflation is expected to be 1 percent.
4. The value of the price index is 248. The cost of the market basket at base period prices is $1.25, while it is $3.10 at current prices. The computation of the price index is as follows: $(3.10/1.25) = 2.48 \times 100 = 248$.
5. Dividing 72 by 11, we have 6.55. Thus, the price level would double in 6.55 years at an inflation rate of 11 percent annually.

FILL IN THE BLANKS

1. price level, inflation
2. inflation rate
3. 25, 1 to 3 percent, dollarization
4. deflation, Disinflation, core inflation
5. fixed, substitute
6. Anticipated, Unanticipated, anticipated, unanticipated, indexing
7. cost of living adjustment
8. price index, 100
9. base period
10. change in price index, initial price index
11. market basket
12. current
13. nominal value, real value
14. price index
15. nominal, real
16. nominal, inflation
17. producer price index
18. gross domestic product, nominal, real

19. nominal, real
20. 2001, 2002, 2002, 2003, fixed, substitution, overstated
21. chained
22. Hyperinflation, Germany
23. Hyperinflation, barter, increase, inflationary spiral
24. hedonic model
25. rule of seventy-two

TRUE/FALSE/EXPLAIN

1. True.
2. True.
3. True.
4. False, 25 percent.
5. True.
6. False, disinflation is a decrease in the inflation rate, while deflation is a negative inflation rate.
7. False, since there is fear that deflation involves recession.
8. True.
9. True.
10. False, although anticipated inflation is expected, that expectation results in changes in worker behavior, such as a desire for increased wages to offset the amount of inflation that is anticipated.
11. False, indexing is a method to deal with unanticipated inflation.
12. True.
13. False, the CPI measures prices of items in the market basket, while the GDP price indexes are broad based.
14. False, the CPI is computed by the Bureau of Labor Statistics.
15. False, the CPI is computed monthly.
16. False, the CPI can measure both price increases and price decreases, and so can measure both inflation and deflation.
17. False, the market basket was updated in 1999.
18. False, the real value of wages is more important to a worker than the nominal value.
19. False, the substitution bias causes inflation to be overstated.
20. False, the chained version of the CPI supplements, but does not replace, the older CPI.
21. False, the CPI can be used to compute real values of income from nominal values.
22. True.
23. False, hedonic methods are used to adjust for product quality.
24. False, personal inflation rates can differ from the CPI.
25. False, the rule of seventy-two is used to compute the time it takes for a value to double.

MULTIPLE CHOICE

1	c	8.	a	15.	b	22.	d
2.	b	9.	b	16.	d	23.	d
3.	d	10.	d	17.	d	24.	d
4.	d	11.	c	18.	b	25.	d
5.	d	12.	b	19.	d		
6.	b	13.	d	20.	a		
7.	d	14.	c	21.	b		

Visit the Ayers/Collinge companion Website at http://www.prenhall.com/ayers for further activities and exercises for this chapter.

Part 3

AGGREGATE SUPPLY AND AGGREGATE DEMAND

Chapter 8

A FRAMEWORK FOR MACROECONOMIC ANALYSIS

CHAPTER REVIEW

8.1 Keynesian Short-Run and Classical Long-Run Perspectives

- The **long run** involves underlying economic forces that make themselves felt over time. For example, economic growth is a long-run consideration.

- In contrast, the **short run** represents more immediate and transitory economic developments, such as the increased unemployment in the months following the September 11 attacks. Much of the difference of opinion within the economics profession concerns how much weight to attach to short-run versus long-run outcomes. The issues are especially contentious when the policies that are best for long-run economic health come at the price of short-run problems.

- In 1936, John Maynard Keynes authored *The General Theory of Employment, Interest, and Money*. Instead of accepting that government should sit back and wait for the economy to pull itself out of recession, he proposed ways in which government could actively manage the economy toward prosperity.

- Keynesian theory came to define the field of macroeconomics for nearly half a century. Before it, the field and term *macroeconomics* did not even exist.

- After World War II, it appeared that government had a duty to shepherd the economy through times of economic distress. When the problem was too little spending and too few people employed, government could go far toward solving the problem through spending more itself and giving its citizens incentives to do likewise. At the time, there seemed to be no macroeconomic tradeoffs in this course of action.

- As time progressed, however, efforts by government to keep unemployment low started to cause the unwanted side effect of inflation. The emphasis in economics shifted away from short-run cures toward looking for policies that would facilitate smooth long-run economic growth without significant inflation. From this perspective, government should not adjust its policies in order to promote spending when unemployment rises, but should rather provide the stability that allows the economy to adjust on its own.

- Macroeconomic theory can be placed within either of two broad categories, depending on whether the emphasis is on short-run or long-run processes. These schools of thought are:
  - **Keynesian**, which suggests that government action is an appropriate response to short-run macroeconomic problems;
  - **Classical**, which suggests that a steady policy aimed at the long run best allows the economy to take care of itself.
- Keynes was emphatic about the difference between these perspectives. He vigorously argued that the short run should be our focus because, as he put it, "In the long run we are all dead." Economists today commonly tap into both schools of thought, with their emphasis depending on the degree of short-run problems encountered.

StudyCheck 1

Describe the classical school of macroeconomic thought, distinguishing it from the Keynesian perspective.

- Aggregate supply and aggregate demand analysis was motivated by the Phillips curve, named after British economist A.W. Phillips who first identified it. The **Phillips curve** is a graphical representation of data that, from the 1960s in the United States, depicted a distinct curvilinear tradeoff between low unemployment and low inflation. The evidence seemed so convincing that many economists at the time hailed the Philips curve as a newly revealed fundamental truth.

- Data past the decade of the 1960s showed no systematic relationship between unemployment and inflation. The Phillips curve is now viewed as a short-run phenomenon that did not hold up in the long run. The reason is thought to revolve around how people form their expectations.

- Whether we are particularly conscious of it or not, we each have **inflationary expectations**, meaning expectations about how much higher or lower prices will be in the future.

- There are two ways for people to form their inflationary expectations. One way is to have **adaptive expectations**, where we form our expectations as to future prices according to what our experiences have been in the past. If something disruptive happens in the macro economy that requires prices to rise or fall in a manner inconsistent with the past, adaptive expectations could lead to our being fooled and slow to adjust our wage demands.

- By the 1970s, people and businesses had learned to factor the effects of inflation into their personal and business plans. Government could no longer inflate its way to lower unemployment. This limitation on government's ability to manage the economy was shown by the combination of inflation and unemployment—**stagflation**—experienced in that decade. People had learned to predict more accurately the impacts of public policy.

- These days, public policy is unlikely to succeed if it depends on assuming that government knows more than participants in the marketplace. With the instant communications of the modern world, people are more likely to have **rational expectations** in which they correctly predict the implications of government policy action and thus cannot be systematically tricked. With rational expectations, we keep up with the news analyses and base our expectations on the best information available to us.

- Rational expectations explains the demise of the Phillips Curve relationship of the 1950s and 60s. In those years, government actions that caused inflation also caused people to work more because they didn't recognize that inflation. People at the time were tricked by higher wages into working more. They later came to understand that the higher wages were only in nominal terms, not in real terms, because prices were rising to match. From then on, it became standard practice for workers to compare wage increases to their expected cost-of-living increases. The more experience they had with being surprised, the more attention they paid to inflation predictions in the media and the better those predictions became.

- If people have rational expectations, government policy that is intended to stimulate the economy will have no predictable effect. In other words, the best guess is that policy actions will not change the economy much in either direction. The idea of rational expectations provides support to the classical argument that government should step back and let the macro economy take care of itself.

8.2 Modeling the Long Run with Aggregate Supply and Aggregate Demand

- A fundamental macroeconomic goal is for the economy to obtain **full-employment output**, also termed **full-employment GDP**, which is the real GDP the economy produces when it fully employs its resources. At any given point in time, actual output can be either above or below the amount associated with full-employment amount.

- The economy can temporarily exceed full-employment output if workers accept overtime, work more than one job, or find new jobs exceptionally quickly. Whether actual GDP is above or below full-employment GDP, **the existence of a natural rate of unemployment implies that the long-run tendency is toward full-employment GDP.**

- For most of its history, the U.S. economy has been successful at living up to its potential. In other words, actual GDP has been in the vicinity of *potential GDP*, which is the amount that we can expect the economy to achieve at full employment.

- Periods of unemployment in which actual GDP falls short of full-employment GDP represent transition times in a market economy—the time markets take to adjust to their market-clearing equilibriums. During these times, there is a surplus of workers in the labor market. As they compete for jobs, workers drive down wages until the labor surplus is absorbed. In response to lower labor costs, competition forces output prices to fall, too. These wage and price adjustments reflect supply and demand in action in the many markets that make up the economy as a whole. These adjustments can take time, however, the significance of which forms the crux of the debate between classical and Keynesian economists.

- The economy supplies full-employment output in the long run, no matter the price level, as shown by the **long-run aggregate supply**. Because the price level is irrelevant to the potential for full-employment output, **long-run aggregate supply is always vertical.** The logic is the same as the logic behind the natural rate of unemployment. Specifically, **in the long run, the desire of people to receive income pushes unemployment down toward its natural rate and leads to full-employment output.**

- The vertical long-run aggregate supply curve means that the same quantity of real GDP will be produced whether the price level is low, high, or in-between. In other words, the price level does not make a difference in determining the full-employment level of GDP.

- Over time, long-run aggregate supply shifts in response to changes in the amount of resources available to the economy and in the technology available to use these resources.

- Economic growth increases full-employment output and thus shifts long-run aggregate supply to the right.

- **Aggregate demand** tells us how much real GDP consumers, businesses, and government will purchase at each price level. In the overall economy, an increase in the price level will also cut back the aggregate quantities that consumers purchase. Likewise, a decrease in the price level will increase aggregate purchases.

- At a lower price level, money buys more goods and services. In other words, even if all of us continue to spend the same amount of money, a lower price level causes the real GDP we purchase to be greater. Second, a lower price level increases the inflation-adjusted value of money that has been saved. When people think that they have more wealth, they spend more of their current income.

- The two effects of a price level change are summed up as follows:
    - **purchasing power effect:** A lower price level allows consumers to receive more goods and services for any given number of dollars they spend. A higher price level means consumers receive fewer goods and services for any given number of dollars they spend;
    - **wealth effect:** A lower price level causes consumers to spend more money out of their current incomes because the lower price level increases the value of the money they have saved. Conversely, a higher price level would reduce the real value of savings and lead consumers to spend less out of current income.

- Both the purchasing power effect and the wealth effect cause there to be an inverse relationship between the price level and the quantity of GDP demanded. Thus, **aggregate demand slopes down.**

- The intersection of aggregate demand and aggregate supply represents a long-run macroeconomic equilibrium, termed the **full-employment equilibrium** because it occurs at the full-employment output. The figure labels both the full-employment equilibrium and the price level that supports it.

- At any price level above the full-employment price level, aggregate spending will be insufficient to support full-employment output. Unemployed workers will compete for jobs, which will drive down wages. Competition in the output market will force firms to lower prices in response to these lower wages. The lower price level that results means that spending will buy more output and thus lead to greater employment. The process continues until the economy reaches full employment and the corresponding full-employment GDP.

- If the actual price level were below the equilibrium, the economy would "overheat," with aggregate purchasing power exceeding the economy's ability to produce. Firms would compete for workers, thus driving their wages up. Competitive firms would pass on these higher wages to consumers by raising their prices. The resulting increase in the price level would soak up the excess purchasing power, thus leading the economy back to its long-run equilibrium.

> **StudyCheck 2**
> Using the model of aggregate supply and aggregate demand, explain how a natural disaster could influence GDP and the price level.

8.3 Root Causes of Inflation

- Aggregate demand tends to increase—shift to the right—over time. This shift occurs in response to general growth in purchasing power as consumer spending increases, government spending increases, or, most generally, as more money circulates throughout the economy. *Ceteris paribus*, in the long run, the effect is to keep output the same and increase the price level. This effect is known as **demand-side inflation**.

- Alternatively, if aggregate demand were to shift to the left, the effect would be **demand-side deflation.** Many economists point to the difficulties of adjusting to a lower price level as being a root cause of the 1930s' Great Depression.

- Changes on the supply side of the economy can also cause either inflation or deflation. If long-run aggregate supply were to shift to the left, we would see **supply-side inflation** in which the same amount of spending is able to buy fewer goods at higher prices. Note that full-employment GDP decreases as long-run aggregate supply shifts to the left.

A Framework for Macroeconomic Analysis 211

StudyCheck 3
Using two graphs, show demand-side inflation and demand-side deflation.

- One possible source of supply-side inflation is a **supply shock**, which is an unexpected event that is major enough to affect the overall economy. Supply shocks, such as caused by wars or natural disasters, cause real changes in productive capacity. Supply shocks are behind what is called the **real business cycle,** in which GDP rises or falls in response to major events that cannot be foreseen.

- Aggregate supply might alternatively shift to the left in response to a change in the laws governing business practices within a country. Recent years have witnessed a number of laws and lawsuits that have changed the way firms can operate. Most notably, firms have seen their production costs increase in response to higher indirect employee costs, higher costs of complying with government regulations, and higher legal costs.

- Technological change or an increase in the economy's resources increases the output associated with full employment. The result is a rightward shift in long-run aggregate supply. As aggregate supply shifts to the right, the economy moves down the aggregate demand curve to a lower equilibrium price level. This process is called **supply-side deflation**. It is associated with an increase in full-employment GDP, as shown in Figure 8-7(b).

212   CHAPTER 8

StudyCheck 4

Using two graphs, show supply-side inflation and supply-side deflation.

8.4 Classical versus Keynesian—The Great Debate

- As President Richard Nixon phrased it in 1972, "We are all Keynesians, now." However, just as Nixon was proclaiming that Keynes had won, the economics profession was focusing in a more classical direction. It began to emphasize its microeconomic foundations, such as incentives facing individuals and firms that can influence the performance of the overall economy.

- Economic analysis influences people's politics and vice versa. For example, political liberals often adopt Keynesian policy prescriptions. A similar analysis applies to political conservatives, who tend to adhere to a classical perspective on the role of government. Classical analysis suggests that much government action does more harm than good to the macro economy, which is in keeping with the conservative perspective.

- While some controversy in macroeconomics is positive, concerning factual issues of cause and effect, most disagreement among macro economists is normative. For example, modern Keynesian models incorporate classical analysis of the long run. What makes these economists and their models Keynesian is that they discount the significance of the long run, preferring instead to emphasize practical issues in the workplace that inhibit adjustments to full employment. Thus, the disagreement between modern Keynesians and classical economists

A FRAMEWORK FOR MACROECONOMIC ANALYSIS 213

often boils down to the degrees to which they are willing to trade off short- and long-run objectives.

8.5 Fighting Terrorism—What Price Does the Economy Pay?

- The added costs for security services causes an increase in the real cost of producing the final goods and services recorded in GDP.

- The economy's limited resources are thus not capable of producing as much final output, meaning that full-employment output falls. Note that full employment itself remains the same, but the output associated with it is less. The result is a shift to the left in the long-run aggregate supply curve which leads to a new full-employment equilibrium at a higher price level and a lower level of output.

- This shift can be moderated or even completely offset by advances in technology, which increases productivity. For example, advances in monitoring and scanning cameras can reduce the need for security personnel, freeing them up to be productive in other ways. More generally, technology is applied to the workplace in order to increase productivity. To the extent it does so, the effect is to increase full-employment output and shift aggregate demand to the right.

- Other influences might also shift aggregate supply to the right. Looking back to World War II, we find that patriotism led to far more hours of work from the general population than was the norm either before or after the war. In effect, wartime full employment was higher than peacetime full employment. Taken by itself, the result is an increase in long-run aggregate supply, with consequences opposite to those shown in Figure 8-8.

- Figure 8-8 shows aggregate demand as constant, with only aggregate supply shifting to the left. Under those assumptions, the economy would experience supply-side inflation as shown in that figure. However, the economy is rarely so simple.

- The 2001 terrorist attacks had a significant effect on the demand side of the economy. The shock and uncertainty caused businesses to postpone new investment and consumers to postpone new purchases. The result was a leftward shift in aggregate demand. In other words, for any given price level, less output was demanded.

- Taken by itself, this leftward shift in aggregate demand would have the effect of pushing prices lower, as shown. Before the price level would have a chance to adjust downward, output would fall and unemployment rise. Were aggregate demand and aggregate supply both shifting left simultaneously, however, their influences would tend to offset each other in regard to price—only output would fall.

- There was considerable question following the September 2001 attacks as to how long it would take for consumers to resume their former patterns of spending. The answer was significant in terms of what government should do. In particular, the government was not only spending additional money to combat the terrorists, but was also taking actions to lower borrowing costs and increase the amount of money circulating in the economy. The idea was to offset any drop in aggregate demand.

- While intended to merely offset a drop in aggregate demand, such government actions ran the risk of going too far and actually increasing aggregate demand above what it had been before, particularly once the initial fears subsided and people returned to more normal spending patterns. If aggregate demand were to increase, demand-side inflation would be the result as shown on the left side of Figure 8-10. The right side of Figure 8-10 shows how the situation could easily get out of hand, with demand-side inflation adding to the supply-side inflation shown in Figure 8-8. This situation is stagflation, in which output falls even as prices rise.

- In application to the war against terrorism, there are also important macroeconomic consequences that lie hidden beneath the surface of the aggregate-demand/aggregate-supply model. For example, for the purposes of this model, it does not matter whether GDP is composed of military spending that we wish was unnecessary or spending on consumer goods and services that would be the alternative in peacetime. It matters to our standard of living, but we do not see these things in the aggregate economic analysis.

StudyCheck 5

Using a graph of aggregate supply and aggregate demand, explain the macroeconomic consequences of the war on terrorism's requirement that security be improved throughout the economy.

FILL IN THE BLANKS

1. The _____ involves underlying economic forces that make themselves felt over time. The _____ represents more immediate and transitory economic developments.

2. 1936, John Maynard _____ authored *The General Theory of Employment, Interest, and Money*. Instead of accepting that government should sit back and wait for the economy to pull itself out of recession, he proposed ways in which government could actively _____ the economy toward prosperity.

3. Efforts by government to keep unemployment low may cause the unwanted side effect of _____.

4. Macroeconomic theory can be placed within either of two broad categories, depending on whether the emphasis is on short-run or long-run processes. These schools of thought are: _____, which suggests that government action is an appropriate response to short-run macroeconomic problems; _____, which suggests that a steady policy aimed at the long run best allows the economy to take care of itself.

5. Keynes was emphatic about the difference between these perspectives. He vigorously argued that the _____ should be our focus.

6. Aggregate supply and aggregate demand analysis was motivated by the _____ curve, a graphical representation of data that, from the 1960s in the United States, depicted a distinct curvilinear tradeoff between low unemployment and low inflation. Data past the decade of the 1960s showed no systematic relationship between unemployment and inflation.

7. Whether we are particularly conscious of it or not, we each have inflationary _____, meaning beliefs about how much higher or lower prices will be in the future. One way to form these beliefs is to have _____, where we form our views as to future prices according to what our experiences have been in the past.

8. These days, public policy is unlikely to succeed if it depends on assuming that government knows more than participants in the marketplace. With the instant communications of the modern world, people are more likely to have _____ in which they correctly predict the implications of government policy action and thus cannot be systematically tricked. This idea provides support to the classical argument that government should step back and let the macro economy take care of itself.

216 CHAPTER 8

9. A fundamental macroeconomic goal is for the economy to obtain full-employment output, also termed full-employment _____. At any given point in time, actual output can be either above or below the amount associated with full-employment amount.

10. Whether actual GDP is above or below full-employment GDP, the existence of a _____ _____ ____ _____ implies that the long-run tendency is toward full-employment GDP.

11. For most of its history, the U.S. actual GDP has been in the vicinity of _____ _____, which is the amount of output that we can expect the economy to achieve at full employment. The economy supplies full-employment output in the long run, no matter the price level, as shown by the _____-_____ _____ _____.

12. Because the price level is irrelevant to the potential for full-employment output, long-run aggregate supply is always_____.

13. The vertical long-run aggregate supply curve means that the same quantity of real GDP will be produced whether the_____ _____ is low, high, or in-between.

14. Over time, long-run aggregate supply _____ in response to changes in the amount of resources available to the economy and in the technology available to use these resources. Economic growth increases full-employment output and thus shifts long-run aggregate supply to the_____.

15. _____ _____ tells us how much real GDP consumers, businesses, and government will purchase at each price level. In the overall economy, an increase in the price level will also cut back the aggregate quantities that consumers purchase. Likewise, a decrease in the price level will increase aggregate purchases.

16. The two effects of a price level change on aggregate demand are: _____ _____effect: A lower price level allows consumers to receive more goods and services for any given number of dollars they spend. A higher price level means consumers receive fewer goods and services for any given number of dollars they spend; _____ effect: A lower price level causes consumers to spend more money out of their current incomes because the lower price level increases the value of the money they have saved. Conversely, a higher price level would reduce the real value of savings and lead consumers to spend less out of current income.

17. Both the purchasing power effect and the wealth effect cause there to be an inverse relationship between the price level and the quantity of GDP demanded. Thus, aggregate demand slopes _____.

18. The intersection of aggregate demand and aggregate supply represents a long-run macroeconomic _____. Aggregate demand tends to increase—_____ __ ___ _____—over time. This shift occurs in response to general growth in purchasing power as consumer spending increases, government spending increases, or, most generally, as more money circulates throughout the economy. *Ceteris paribus*, in the long run, the effect is to keep output the same and increase the _____ _____. This effect is known as demand-side inflation. If aggregate demand were to shift to the left, the effect would be demand-side_____.

19. Changes on the supply side of the economy can also cause either inflation or deflation. If long-run aggregate supply were to shift to the left, we would see supply-side _____ in which the same amount of spending is able to buy fewer goods at higher prices. Note that full-employment GDP decreases as long-run aggregate supply shifts to the left.

20. One possible source of supply-side inflation is a_____ _____, which is an unexpected event that is major enough to affect the overall economy. Such events are behind what is called the _____ _____ _____, in which GDP rises or falls in response to major events that cannot be foreseen.

21. Aggregate supply might shift to the_____ in response to higher indirect employee costs, higher costs of complying with government regulations, and higher legal costs. Technological change or an increase in the economy's resources_____ the output associated with full employment. The result is a rightward shift in long-run aggregate supply. As aggregate supply shifts to the right, the economy moves down the aggregate demand curve to a lower equilibrium price level. This process is called supply-side_,_____.

22. Economic analysis influences people's politics and vice versa. For example, political liberals often adopt_____ policy prescriptions. A similar analysis applies to political conservatives, who tend to adhere to a_____ perspective on the role of government.

23. The added costs for security services causes an _____ in the real cost of producing the final goods and services recorded in GDP. The economy's limited resources are thus not capable of producing as much final output, meaning that full-employment output_____. The result is a shift to the_____ in the long-run aggregate supply curve which leads to a new full-employment equilibrium at a higher price level and a lower level of output. This shift can be moderated or even completely offset by advances in_____, which increases productivity. To the extent it does so, the effect is to_____ full-employment output and shift aggregate demand to the _____.

24. The 2001 terrorist attacks had a significant effect on the demand side of the economy. The shock and uncertainty caused businesses to postpone new investment and consumers to postpone new purchases. The result was a _____ shift in aggregate demand. In other words, for any given price level, less output was demanded. Were aggregate demand and

aggregate supply both shifting left simultaneously, however, their influences would tend to offset each other in regard to _____—only output would fall.

25. With demand-side inflation adding to the supply-side inflation, the situation is _____, in which output falls even as prices rise.

TRUE/FALSE/EXPLAIN
If false, explain why in the space provided.

1. U.S. unemployment after World War II was more than 10 percent lower than unemployment before the war.

2. The economic aftershocks from the terrorist attacks of September 11th 2002 increased public interest in how the economy works and what could be done to help it.

3. Much of the difference of opinion within the economics profession concerns how much weight to attach to short-run versus long-run outcomes.

4. *The General Theory of Employment, Interest, and Money* was written by Adam Smith, and published during the Great Depression.

5. Macroeconomic theory can be placed within either of two broad categories, depending on whether the emphasis is on short-run or long-run processes.

6. Keynesian economists emphasize the government should keep its hands out of the economy as much as possible.

7. Classical economists argue that the desire of people to work will eventually lead to full employment, even if the unemployment rate is temporarily quite high.

8. Economists today commonly tap into both Keynesian and classical schools thought, with their emphasis depending on the severity of short-run problems encountered.

9. The Phillips curve refers to the trade-off between the short run and the long run.

10. The U.S. economy in the 1960s was characterized by rational expectations.

11. Rational expectations refers to the idea that we use our past experiences to predict the future.

12. The price level is irrelevant to the potential for full-employment output.

13. The position of the long-run aggregate supply curve can change only in response to changes in the natural rate of unemployment.

14. As economies gain resources and improved technology over time, they see economic growth that shifts long-run aggregate supply to the right.

15. The downward slope of aggregate demand is explained by both the purchasing power affect and the wealth effect.

16. The idea that a lower price level causes consumers to spend more of their current incomes because the lower price level increases the value of savings is referred to as the purchasing power affect.

17. Aggregate demand slopes downward because of the law of demand, which states that price and quantity must vary inversely.

18. Demand-side inflation involves a movement up the long-run aggregate supply curve.

19. The supply shock is a transitory event that arousals public concern but causes no real changes in production capacity.

20. Technological change tends to push the economy toward supply-side deflation.

E&A 21. The war on terrorism causes the output associated with full employment to decrease.

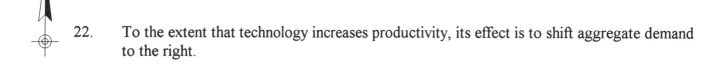

22. To the extent that technology increases productivity, its effect is to shift aggregate demand to the right.

23. If patriotism causes people to increase the number of hours that they are willing to work, long-run aggregate supply would shift to the right.

24. Following the September 11 terrorist attacks, there were significant concerns that aggregate demand was too high.

25. If the economy experiences stagflation, output falls even as prices rise.

MULTIPLE CHOICE
Circle the letter preceding the one best answer.

1. The Keynesian school of thought suggests that
    a. a steady policy aimed at the long run best allows the economy to take care of itself.
    b. the best cure for unemployment is inflation.
    c. the best cure for inflation is unemployment.
    d. government action is an appropriate response to short-run macroeconomic problems.

2. According to classical economic theory,
    a. government should seek to move the economy to full-employment output.
    b. consumers should spend more and save less if the economy suffers from unemployment.
    c. sticky wages prevent the economy from reaching full employment.
    d. government action is unnecessary for the economy to achieve full-employment output.

3. The Phillips curve represents a trade-off between
    a. employment and output.
    b. unemployment and output.
    c. employment and inflation.
    d. unemployment and inflation.

4. The Phillips curve fit reality best in the
    a. 1920s.
    b. 1940s.
    c. 1960s.
    d. 1980s.

5. If people rely primarily upon their past experiences to predict future inflation, they are said to have
    a. adaptive expectations.
    b. rational expectations.
    c. precautionary expectations.
    d. exuberant expectations.

6. Long-run aggregate supply is shifted outward by
    a. an improvement in technology.
    b. an expansion of the labor force.
    c. a reduction in social safety net programs, such as elimination of the minimum-wage law.
    d. all of the above.

7. Aggregate demand slopes downward because,
   a. as prices rise, people substitute less expensive goods and services.
   b. as the price level rises, people begin to expect inflation.
   c. as the price level rises, people are fooled because they did not expect it.
   d. an increase in the price level reduces the real value of intended spending, which causes the expenditure equilibrium to occur at a lower real GDP.

8. In the long-run, supply-side inflation is shown by
   a. a movement up the long-run aggregate supply curve in response to a shift in aggregate demand.
   b. a movement down the aggregate demand curve in response to a rightward shift in long-run aggregate supply.
   c. a movement up aggregate demand in response to a leftward shift in long-run aggregate supply.
   d. a movement down the long-run aggregate supply in response to a shift in aggregate demand.

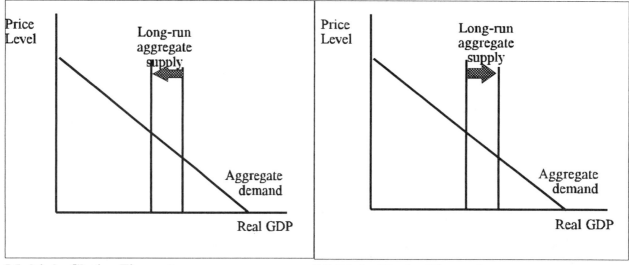

Multiple Choice Figure 1 **Multiple Choice Figure 2**

9. Multiple Choice Figure 1 shows a situation that will result in
   a. supply-side inflation.
   b. supply-side deflation.
   c. demand-side inflation.
   d. demand-side deflation.

10. Multiple Choice Figure 2 shows a situation that will result in
    a. supply-side inflation.
    b. supply-side deflation.
    c. demand-side inflation.
    d. demand-side deflation.

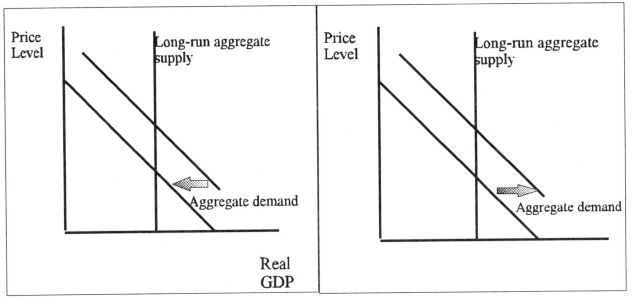

Multiple Choice Figure 3   **Multiple Choice Figure 4**

11. Multiple Choice Figure 3 shows a situation that will result in
    a. supply-side inflation.
    b. supply-side deflation.
    c. demand-side inflation.
    d. demand-side deflation.

12. Multiple Choice Figure 4 shows a situation that will result in
    a. supply-side inflation.
    b. supply-side deflation.
    c. demand-side inflation.
    d. demand-side deflation.

13. In the long run, demand-side inflation causes
    a. an increase in output.
    b. a decrease in output.
    c. no change in output.
    d. unpredictable effects on output.

14. In the long run, supply-side inflation causes
    a. an increase in output.
    b. a decrease in output.
    c. no change in output.
    d. unpredictable effects on output.

15. In the long run, demand-side deflation causes
    a. an increase in output.
    b. a decrease in output.
    c. no change in output.
    d. unpredictable effects on output.

16. In the long run, supply-side deflation causes
    a. an increase in output.
    b. a decrease in output.
    c. no change in output.
    d. unpredictable effects on output.

17. An unexpected event that is major enough to affect the overall economy is termed
    a. a Keynesian crisis.
    b. a classical crisis.
    c. the real business cycle.
    d. a supply shock.

18. The real business cycle is caused by
    a. demand shocks.
    b. demand-side inflation.
    c. supply shocks.
    d. supply-side inflation.

19. Classical economic analysis is most frequently embraced by
    a. conservatives.
    b. communists.
    c. Keynesians.
    d. liberals.

20. Keynesian economic analysis is most frequently embraced by
    a. conservatives.
    b. communists.
    c. libertarians.
    d. liberals.

The following five questions refer to Multiple Choice Figure 5.

21. Supply-side inflation is represented by arrow
    a. B.
    b. D.
    c. G.
    d. H.

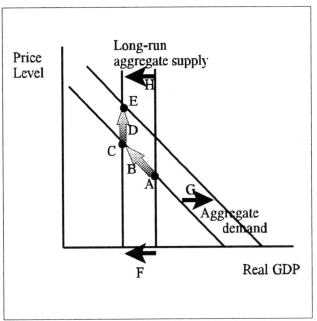

Multiple Choice Figure 5

22. The movement associated with arrow H is most likely caused by
    a. destruction of resources in warfare or from terrorist attacks.
    b. the increased willingness of a country citizens to work during times of warfare.
    c. a loss of confidence on the part of consumers, which reduces their willingness to spend.
    d. and increasing consumer willingness to spend, perhaps motivated by a desire to help the economy.

23. Arrow F represents a decrease in
    a. actual employment.
    b. full employment.
    c. the output associated with full employment.
    d. the price level.

24. The total effect of changes shown in the figure is that the macroeconomic equilibrium changes from
    a. point A to point C.
    b. point A to point E.
    c. point C to point E.
    d. arrow G to arrow H.

25. The combination of all of the changes shown in Multiple Choice Figure 5 would cause the economy to experience
    a. both a boom and a bust.
    b. deflation.
    c. economic growth.
    d. both supply-side inflation and demand-side inflation.

GRASPING THE GRAPHS
Fill in each box with a concept that applies.

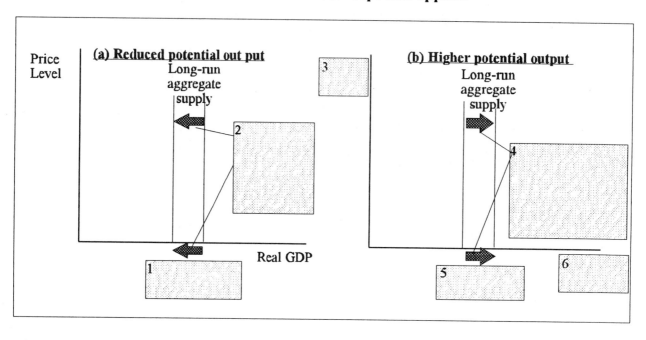

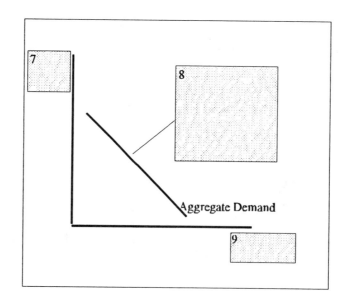

A FRAMEWORK FOR MACROECONOMIC ANALYSIS 227

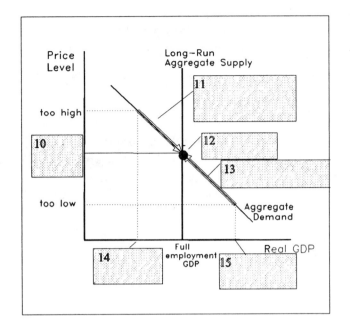

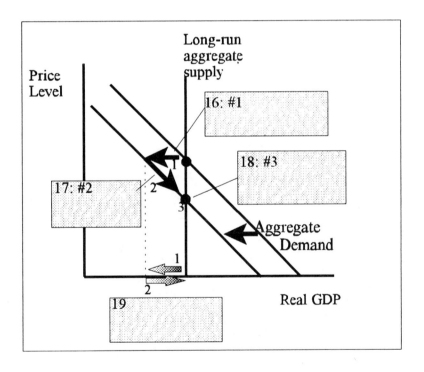

**For additional practice in grasping this chapter's graphs, visit
http://www.prenhall.com/ayers and try *Smart Graph*s 10 and 11,
along with *Active Graphs* 22, and 23.**

228 CHAPTER 8

ANSWERS

STUDYCHECKS

1. Classical economists rely upon the adjustment of market wages and prices to bring the economy to a full-employment equilibrium. A full-employment equilibrium is defined as the amount of real GDP produced by a fully employed workforce. Full employment occurs at the natural rate of unemployment. Unlike the short-run focus of Keynesians, classical economists focus on the long run and downplay the possibilities for government action to help the economy.
2. A natural disaster is an economic shock that policy makers cannot foresee and can do nothing about. It can cause long-run cost-push inflation, in which the long-run aggregate supply curve shifts to the left. Along with inflation comes a lower GDP.
3. See StudyCheck 3 Figure.

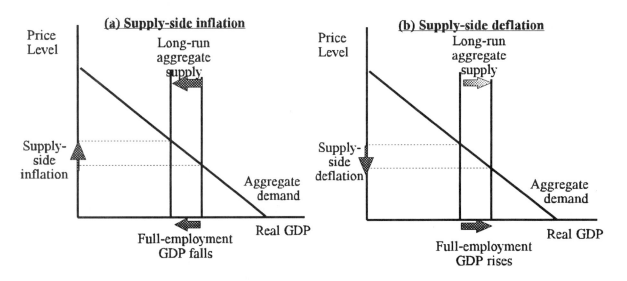

StudyCheck 4 Figure

4. See StudyCheck 4 Figure.

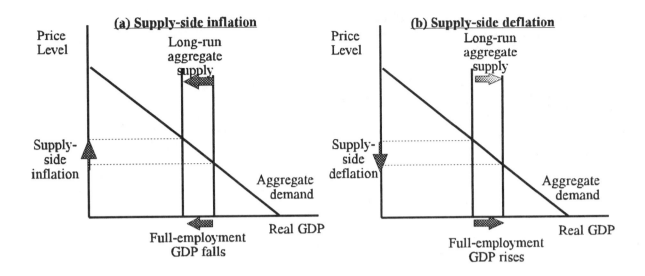

StudyCheck 4 Figure

5. The war on terrorism causes firms to spend more on security, which takes resources that could otherwise produce final goods and services. For this reason, the output associated with full employment decreases and shifts long-run aggregate supply to the left, as shown in StudyCheck 3 Figure. The macro equilibrium adjusts from *A* to *B*, reflecting a higher price level and less output. The adoption of improved technologies holds the potential to offset these effects.

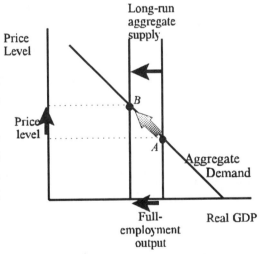

StudyCheck 5 Figure

FILL IN THE BLANKS

1. long run, short run
2. Keynes, manage
3. inflation
4. Keynesian, Classical
5. short run

6. Phillips
7. expectations, adaptive expectations
8. rational expectations
9. GDP
10. natural rate of unemployment
11. potential GDP, long-run aggregate supply
12. vertical
13. price level
14. shifts, right
15. Aggregate demand
16. purchasing power, wealth
17. down
18. equilibrium, shift to the right, price level, deflation
19. inflation
20. supply shock, real business cycle
21. left, increases, deflation
22. Keynesian, classical
23. increase, falls, left, technology, increase
24. leftward, price,
25. stagflation

TRUE/FALSE/EXPLAIN

1. True.
2. True.
3. True.
4. False, while the book was written during the great Depression, the author was John Maynard Keynes, not Adam Smith.
5. True.
6. False, Keynesian economists emphasize the government should take action when there are problems of unemployment in the short run.
7. True.
8. True.
9. False, the Phillips curve refers to the trade-off between unemployment and inflation.
10. False, it was characterized by adaptive expectations.
11. False, rational expectations refers to the idea that we use the best information available to us in order to predict the future.
12. True.
13. False, that is only one possible shift factor.
14. True.
15. True.
16. False, that is the wealth effect.

A FRAMEWORK FOR MACROECONOMIC ANALYSIS   231

17. False, aggregate demand slopes down for different reasons than the demand for individual goods or services.
18. True.
19. False, a supply shock changes the economy's productive capacity.
20. True.
21. True.
22. False, the effect is to shift aggregate supply to the right.
23. True.
24. False, the concerns were that aggregate demand might be too low.
25. True.

MULTIPLE CHOICE

1.	d	8.	c	15.	c	22.	a
2.	d	9.	a	16.	a	23.	c
3.	d	10.	b	17.	d	24.	b
4.	c	11.	d	18.	c	25.	d
5.	a	12.	c	19.	a		
6.	d	13.	c	20.	d		
7.	d	14.	b	21.	a		

GRASPING THE GRAPHS
Examples of correct answers

1. Full-unemployment output
2. Caused by fewer resources
3. Price level
4. From more resources or better technology
5. Full-employment output
6. Real GDP
7. Price level
8. Slopes down due to the wealth effect and the purchasing power effect
9. Real GDP
10. Equilibrium price level
11. Unemployment causes wages and prices to fall.
12. Long-run equilibrium
13. Overheating causes wages and prices to rise.
14. GDP with unemployment

15. GDP with overheating
16. Reduced demand hits output and employment.
17. The price level is pressured down.
18. The long-run equilibrium ends up lower.
19. Output falls only temporarily.

Visit the Ayers/Collinge companion Website at <http://www.prenhall.com/ayers> for further activities and exercises for this chapter.

Chapter 9

SHORT-RUN INSTABILITY

CHAPTER REVIEW

9.1 Short-Run Stickiness along Aggregate Demand

- The debate over macro policy often comes down to the question of nothing more than whether to wait for a movement along aggregate demand or to take action to *manage aggregate demand*, meaning to shift the aggregate demand curve itself.

- If a market is not at equilibrium, forces of supply and demand will cause price to change until the equilibrium comes about. That is the classical analysis: wage and price adjustments will lead to a long-run macro equilibrium that is characterized by both full employment and its associated full-employment output. Keynesians agree, but dismiss this analysis as irrelevant in the short run, which is the time period that they consider to be the most significant. Their rationale is the existence of downwardly **sticky wages** and **sticky prices**, where downwardly sticky refers to an inflexibility that makes it difficult for wages and prices to fall. If wages are sticky, the downward movement in wages required to reach a long-run equilibrium could take too long to wait for.

StudyCheck 1
Explain why Keynesians are anxious for government to take action when times are tough, rather than just wait for the economy to make its own adjustments.

- One reason for wage and price stickiness is that some markets might not move to equilibrium easily. Changes in demand for outputs make it appropriate for some wages and prices to rise or fall relative to other wages and prices. However, there is resistance to change—*rigidities*—within both labor and output markets. Stores have leases and contracts that are not easily adjusted. In some cases, the contracts are with unions that refuse to negotiate wage cuts.

- In principle, wage and price stickiness might occur in either direction—whether for price increases or for price decreases. In practice, wage and price stickiness is most pronounced in a downward direction, meaning that the market pressure is toward lower wages and prices. For example, it is natural for workers to resent a wage cut, no matter what the macroeconomic circumstances might be.

- By preventing movement down the aggregate demand curve to a full-employment equilibrium, wage and price stickiness can mean a prolonged period in which both output and employment are below the economy's potential.

9.2 Fiscal Policy To Stabilize The Business Cycle

- Suppose the economy starts at an **unemployment equilibrium,** characterized by a price level that is too high to achieve full employment GDP, but that refuses to fall because of sticky prices. If the price level cannot fall to correct the unemployment equilibrium, the only solution is to shift aggregate demand rightward by increasing spending power. The shift can be accomplished by **fiscal policy,** which is government policy toward taxation and spending. It can also be accomplished through *monetary policy*, which has to do with varying the quantity of money that is available to spend.

StudyCheck 2

Discuss how the model of aggregate demand and aggregate supply can be used as the context to discuss the Keynesian perspective relative to that of the classical economists.

- When the economy finds itself stuck at an unemployment equilibrium, Keynesians advocate using **expansionary fiscal policy**, also called a **fiscal stimulus**, which is increased government spending or reduced taxation to *stimulate* aggregate demand and return the economy to full-employment. The Works Progress Administration and other New Deal public works programs of President Franklin Roosevelt are examples of stimulative fiscal policies. Indeed, World War II seemed to prove the validity of Keynesian economics, since the massive amount of government spending it involved paved the way from the Depression of the 1930s to the prosperity of the 1950s.

StudyCheck 3
Using a graph of aggregate demand, show the effect of an expansionary fiscal policy.

- Alternatively, when the economy *overheats*—growing so fast that inflation threatens—government can use **contractionary fiscal policy**, also called a **fiscal drag**, to slow it down. Contractionary fiscal policy can shift aggregate demand to the left and avoid overheating.

- Both expansionary and contractionary fiscal policy are examples of **discretionary policy**—public policy adjusted at the discretion of lawmakers. Unfortunately, even the best intentioned discretionary public policy is unlikely to follow the Keynesian policy prescription. The reason has to do with the three *fiscal policy lags*:
    - The **recognition lag**—It takes time to know that the economy is in a recession. For example, it usually takes approximately three consecutive quarters of declining GDP

before the authoritative National Bureau of Economic Research (NBER) declares a recession. In late November of 2001, the NBER declared that the economy was in a recession that started in March of that year.
- The **action lag**—Tax and spending bills are not passed overnight. The fiscal stimulus aimed at the 2001 recession was not passed until 2002.
- The **implementation lag**—It's great to build a highway, but most people expect to have it planned out before crews are sent to lay asphalt! Planning government spending takes time. It also takes time before tax changes can take effect.

- Because of fiscal policy lags, the business cycle may have turned by the time the money starts flowing. The spending may be more likely to cause inflation than to reduce unemployment. Policy lags make it very difficult, if not impossible, to *fine tune* the economy to even out the ups and downs of the business cycle. Fine tuning would require that contractionary fiscal policy start when the economy pushes above full-employment GDP. Likewise, when the economy sinks to less than full-employment GDP, then finely tuned fiscal policy should be expansionary.

- Instead of discretionary policy, lawmakers can rely on **automatic stabilizers.** Automatic stabilizers are components of existing fiscal policies that stimulate the economy when it is sluggish and act as a drag when it overheats. The U.S. economy has automatic stabilizers embedded within its system of taxation and spending.

- Consider automatic stabilizers on the tax side. As personal and corporate incomes fall during recession, so too does the amount collected by the U.S. personal and corporate income taxes. The reduced tax burden on individuals and companies helps reduce the severity of that recession. Alternatively, if the economy is booming, income taxes collect more revenue, which is contractionary because it removes some of the excess purchasing power. No policy action is necessary.

- On the spending side, payments for welfare, unemployment compensation, and other social programs rise as the economy slows and more people seek these safety-net services. Conversely, this spending falls when the economy heats up, just as Keynesian policy prescribes. Again, the action to stabilize the economy is automatic; no policy adjustments are needed.

- Taken as a whole, the automatic stabilizers are intended to be expansionary if the economy is below full employment and contractionary when the economy is overheating. If the economy is at full employment, fiscal policy should be neutral, since there is no need to either stimulate or slow down economic activity. If the economy is at full employment, the neutral fiscal policy could generate a **balanced budget**, meaning that tax revenue inflows just equal government expenditure outflows—government spending and revenues being recorded in the *federal budget*.

- Economists often suggest that, whether fiscal policy is by automatic stabilizers or discretionary, it should be set so that the budget roughly balances over the course of the business cycle. The idea is that, when the economy is overheated and contractionary policy is in order, the government would run a **budget surplus** in which tax revenue exceeds government spending. When economic health is poor and expansionary policy is needed, the government would then choose a **budget deficit** in which government spending exceeds tax revenue. The surpluses could help pay for the deficits.

- In practice, however, there is a significant tilt toward the expansionary side, even when the economy is doing well. To assess this tilt, we can look at the **full-employment budget,** which is an estimate of what government revenue and spending would be were there to be full employment. The full employment budget has usually been in deficit in recent years.

9.3 The Short-Run Adjustment Process

- In principle, expansionary fiscal policy can shift aggregate demand rightward until it achieves full-employment output at the current price level. In practice, however, the economy does not behave quite this simply. The most notable complexity is a tendency toward inflation when policymakers try to stimulate aggregate demand. In order to understand this response, we will distinguish between aggregate supply in the short run and aggregate supply in the long run.

- Recall that aggregate supply tells how much output the economy has to offer at each possible price level, based on the potential productivity of its resources. In the long run, the price level does not matter to this potential. In the long run, higher wages that are merely the result of inflation will have no influence on behavior as workers recognize that the higher wages are merely necessary to pay for higher costs of living. So, in the long run, aggregate supply is unaffected by the price level, causing it to be vertical. However, **short-run aggregate supply**—the amount of output the economy has to offer in the short run—will slope upwards.

- Two reasons for the upward slope of aggregate supply are as follows:
  - **Structural rigidities**—as new spending power is added to the economy, it tends to raise wages and prices where it first hits, before eventually diffusing throughout the economy. Wages and prices in the sectors of the economy most directly affected by the spending will rise before the extra spending can circulate more generally throughout the economy. The result is a higher output in those sectors, but also a higher overall price level.
  - **The production effect**—when the price level rises and labor supply curves remain unchanged, firms can profit by increasing output and employment. If the economy is already at full employment, firms will employ workers overtime, thus allowing the economy to exceed full-employment output temporarily. The production effect relies upon workers being fooled by inflation or deflation.

- In the event of inflation, individual wage requirements should rise, thus shifting each worker's labor supply curve upward. However, while it is easy for workers to know past rates of inflation, it is much more difficult to recognize contemporaneous price-level changes. People seeing wages going up are likely to respond by offering to work more first and then adjusting their inflationary expectations later. Since an increased price level is associated with higher wages, a higher price level brings forth more work effort as workers are fooled by inflation, but only in the short run. For the economy to be in long-run equilibrium, workers must have accurate wage and price expectations. For this reason, **short-run aggregate supply always intersects long-run aggregate supply at the expected price level.**

- The intersection of aggregate demand and short-run aggregate supply constitutes a **short-run macroeconomic equilibrium**. In this case, the macro equilibrium is also an unemployment equilibrium, because it occurs at less than full-employment GDP. The short-run macro equilibrium consists of an equilibrium price level and an equilibrium GDP. These are labeled in the figure as actual price level and actual GDP, since the short run is where the economy actually is at any given point in time. As before, short-run aggregate supply intersects long-run aggregate supply at the expected price level. The long-run aggregate supply is a reference toward which the economy tends over time. So, whereas the long-run equilibrium occurs where aggregate demand intersects long-run aggregate supply, the short-run equilibrium is where aggregate demand intersects short-run aggregate supply.

StudyCheck 4

Graph a long-run aggregate supply curve (LRAS) and a short-run aggregate supply curve (SRAS), where the expected price level is 100. Label the axes, "100," LRAS, and SRAS. On the same graph, add an aggregate demand (AD) curve such that the actual price level is 125. Label AD and "125." Show the short-run equilibrium output, GDP*.

SHORT-RUN INSTABILITY 239

StudyCheck 5

On an Aggregate Supply - Aggregate Demand graph, show a situation in which the expected price level exceeds the actual price level. Label: 1) EP as the expected price level; 2) AP as the actual price level; 3) GDPFE as the full-employment GDP; 4) GDPA as the actual GDP; 5) LRAS as long-run aggregate supply; 6) SRAS as short run aggregate supply; 7) AD as aggregate demand; 8) the axes.

- Chapter 8 discussed demand-side and supply-side inflation in the context of changes in either aggregate demand or long-run aggregate supply. Changes in aggregate demand or in short-run aggregate supply can also have inflationary effects, those being in the short run. Consider first **demand-pull inflation**, which is caused by an increase in aggregate demand that pulls the economy up short-run aggregate supply. **Demand-pull inflation occurs when a rightward shift in aggregate demand moves the economy to both a higher output and a higher price level.** Demand-pull inflation might be caused by expansionary fiscal policy that is meant to move the economy toward full employment.

- Inflation could also arise from an upward shift in the short-run aggregate supply curve. Because the short-run aggregate supply curve intersects long-run aggregate supply at the expected price level, a change in the expected price level will shift short-run aggregate supply vertically. For example, if the expected price level increases, short-run aggregate supply shifts vertically upward until its intersection with long-run aggregate supply occurs at the new expected price level. Likewise, if the expected price level decreases, short-run aggregate supply shifts downward, intersecting long-run aggregate supply at the new expected price level. Such shifts are likely because workers revise their expectations over time.

240 CHAPTER 9

StudyCheck 6

Using a graph, show the effect in the short run of an increase in inflationary expectations.

- When aggregate supply shifts up, the economy moves up the aggregate demand curve to a point of higher prices and lower output, as shown in Figure 9-11. Inflation that is caused in this way is called **cost-push inflation. Cost push inflation reduces output and increases the price level.** Recall from chapter 8, this combination is known as *stagflation*—the simultaneous occurrence of inflation and economic stagnation.

9.4 Short-Run Paths to Long-Run Stability

- The shifting short-run aggregate supply becomes a moving target for government policymakers. If government chases an upwardly shifting aggregate supply with ever more stimulative policies that shift out aggregate demand, the result would be the reinforcement of inflationary expectations. As inflationary expectations rise, short-run aggregate supply shifts up and output falls, which prompts more fiscal stimuli in an ever-repeating cycle. The result is an ongoing **inflationary spiral** of rising and falling output along with continually accelerating inflation, as shown in Figure 9-12.

- In the inflationary spiral, demand-pull and cost-push inflation feed upon each other. Cost-push inflation is caused by past experiences with inflation, which was most likely caused by policies that had allowed aggregate demand to increase. To counter cost-push inflation and keep the economy near full employment, policymakers might choose to expand aggregate demand again. That would reinforce inflationary expectations in future periods, causing another round of cost-push inflation. Thus, if government responds to cost-push inflation by stimulating aggregate demand, the result is likely to be an inflationary spiral of demand-pull inflation followed by more cost-push inflation, continuing in a cycle that goes on and on.

StudyCheck 7

Describe the process of an inflationary spiral.

- A sustainable long-run macro equilibrium occurs when the expected and actual price levels are equal. The expected price level is given by the intersection of short- and long-run aggregate supply. The actual price level is given by the intersection of short-run aggregate supply and aggregate demand. Because these intersections both occur at the same point, a point on long-run aggregate supply, the economy is at full employment. Whether achieved through government policy intended to manage aggregate demand, or through a hands-off policy of giving short-run aggregate supply time to adjust on its own, this long-run macro equilibrium is usually considered to be the ideal outcome of macro policy.

- **To achieve long-run stability and avoid the inflationary spiral, classical economists advocate a hands-off policy to let inflationary expectations subside.** The U.S. followed that policy in the early 1980s, after a decade when inflation had risen to the double-digit range. The result was a short-lived recession during which people adjusted their inflationary expectations downward. Afterward, the economy returned to full employment, but at a much lower rate of inflation.

- Table 9-1 summarizes the differences between the classical and Keynesian approaches. Bear in mind that both schools of thought have the same goal for the economy, which is to reach full employment output without inflation. The essential difference is that the Keynesians will set aside long-run goals to combat the short-run suffering of the unemployed, while classical economists "keep their eyes on the horizon" to obtain a sustainable long-run equilibrium of stable prices and full employment.

Table 9-1 Summary of Classical and Keynesian Views

	Classical	**Keynesian**
Focus:	long-run issues, especially economic growth	short-run issues, especially unemployment
Prices and Wages:	Prices and wages will adjust upward or downward as needed to reach a full-employment equilibrium.	Prices and wages adjust upward without difficulty, but are downwardly sticky and thus unable to lead the economy from an unemployment equilibrium to full employment.
Government Role:	Government should not attempt to manage aggregate demand.	Government should actively adjust taxes and spending in order to manage aggregate demand.
Shortcoming:	Remedying unemployment requires patience.	Remedying unemployment can lead to demand-pull inflation and possibly an inflationary spiral.

9.5 Deficits and Debt—Do We Spend Too Much?

- On average, $21,000 is how much debt Uncle Sam has already rung up for each U.S. citizen. The federal Government continues to add to that national debt each year in which it runs a budget deficit. In 2002, the budget deficit was $106.2 billion, and the gross national debt stood at $6.14 trillion.

- The national debt can be thought of as the *stock* or inventory of accumulated past budgetary imbalances, and the deficit as a *flow* that adds to that debt. That debt represents almost 60 percent of the $10.4 trillion value of U.S. GDP. Interest payments alone account for about 14 percent of total federal government spending.

- When the government measures how much Americans save, it subtracts from that savings figure the amount that is owed on mortgages. The value of the homes is left out because it is difficult to measure. Since there are so many homeowners with mortgages in the U.S., America's savings rate then appears artificially low when compared with that of other countries.

- Likewise, when the government reports its own debt, it does not offset this debt with the value of the assets it owns. After all, how do you value assets of the government? Those assets include such things as parks, highways, military bases, military equipment, a judicial system, and much more. Taken as a whole, we know the value is quite high. We also know that new babies born as U.S. citizens will obtain benefits from these assets for years to come. From this perspective, expecting future citizens to bear some of the costs does not seem so bad.

- Would the next generation accept this deal, to be born with both the privileges and obligations of being a U.S. citizen? While we cannot ask them, we can observe their parents answering that question with their actions. It would be most unusual to find an expectant mother seeking to leave the U.S. so that her baby would be born elsewhere. In contrast, immigrant couples frequently seek entry into the U.S. so their babies can be born as U.S. citizens.

- Just because most people believe that, on balance, there is a positive value to living in the U.S. does not tell us that the U.S. has the right amount of debt. If the accumulation of debt exceeds the accumulation of assets, the value of our country diminishes over time. Conversely, if the U.S. holds down debt by cutting back on public investments, the country runs the risk of missing out on investment opportunities that would look good in hindsight. U.S. opportunities for economic growth would diminish, meaning that long-run aggregate supply would not shift rightward as rapidly as it could.

StudyCheck 8

Is a national debt justified? Explain.

- As a country, we often accuse ourselves of being on a spending binge, one we will have to pay for later. As evidence, we point to both the federal budget deficit and the U.S. *trade deficit*. The trade deficit is the amount by which the value of goods we import exceeds the value of goods we export. Because we spend more of our dollars on foreign goods than foreigners return in exchange for American goods, foreigners have extra dollars left over to invest in the U.S. Those investments represent future obligations of this country to other countries. Yet, while it is the collection of our individual actions that leads us to a trade deficit, we don't usually consider ourselves to engage personally in irresponsible spending.

- The $106 billion budget deficit differs from the amount of the trade deficit, which has been running well over $400 billion in recent years. Still, the two are related, so much so that they have been dubbed the *twin deficits*. By running a budget deficit, the U.S. government leaves more money in the pockets of consumers, some of which they spend on imports. Those U.S. dollars that consumers spend on imports come back to the U.S., such as when foreigners buy U.S. exports or invest in the U.S.

- When the government borrows money to finance the budget deficit, that borrowing tends to draw more investment dollars into the U.S. in response to the expanded investment opportunities. To obtain dollars to invest in the U.S., foreign investors must bid them away from other uses, such as foreign purchases of U.S. products. For this reason, holding all else constant, the higher is the federal budget deficit, the higher is the trade deficit.

- The existence of the twin deficits runs counter to the idea that government fiscal policy can spend the economy out of an unemployment equilibrium. The problem is illustrated in Figure 9-13. If the government attempts to shift aggregate demand to the right through deficit spending, it generates offsetting effects that shift aggregate demand back to the left. Specifically, the higher U.S. trade deficit reflects a reduction in spending on U.S. goods as foreigners substitute purchases of U.S. debt for purchases of U.S. products.

- By the same token, the same higher interest rates that caused foreigners to invest in the U.S. rather than buy U.S. goods will likewise prompt U.S. citizens to save more and spend less. Higher interest rates also *crowd out* private sector investment, because the more that investors put their money into secure government debt, the less is left over for private-sector investments. Together, these effects might offset government's expansionary fiscal policy and leave the economy back where it started, as seen in Figure 9-13.

> **StudyCheck 9**
> Explain the relationship between the national debt and the trade deficit.

- Over 80 percent of government debt is owed to U.S. citizens. Nevertheless, as the federal government adds to its debt, so too do U.S. citizens. Attracting additional foreign investment accumulates obligations to repay that debt in the future, even if the debt is in the form of foreign ownership of land, buildings, and factories. After all, it becomes their assets that we hold in this country. Is that dangerous? The problems Argentina and many other impoverished countries had in repaying their debts are legendary. But when it comes to the U.S., the dangers of foreign debt are overstated.

- Some people worry over a sudden exodus of foreign investment, possibly as a means to exert political pressure. Such worries are unfounded. If foreigners for some reason wish to stampede out of the U.S., they would have to leave behind all but a small fraction of their assets. By investing in the U.S., foreigners allow us political and economic control over things of great value to them. In that way, foreigners acquire a strong interest in having our economy perform well and in maintaining good political relations.

- We have seen that a budget deficit and consequent increase in the federal debt can be justifiable. We have also seen that this expansionary fiscal policy tends to increase the trade deficit and international debt, but that the consequences of those increases are not as worrisome as many people think. Just how much debt is the right amount, however, remains an open question.

246 CHAPTER 9

StudyCheck 10

Why is it difficult to control the federal budget deficit and national debt? Would a balanced budget amendment to the U.S. constitution resolve this problem?

FILL IN THE BLANKS

1. The debate over macro policy often comes down to the question of nothing more than whether to wait for a movement along aggregate demand or to take action to *manage aggregate demand*, meaning to _____ the aggregate demand curve.

2. If a market is not at equilibrium, the forces of supply and demand will cause price to change until the equilibrium comes about. That is the classical analysis: _____ and _____ adjustments will lead to a long-run macro equilibrium that is characterized by both full employment and its associated full-employment output. Keynesians agree, but dismiss this analysis as irrelevant in the _____ _____, which is the time period that they consider to be the most significant. Their rationale is the existence of downwardly _____ _____ and sticky prices, where downwardly sticky refers to an inflexibility that makes it difficult for wages and prices to fall. If wages are sticky, the downward movement in wages required to reach a long-run equilibrium could take too long to wait for.

3. One reason for wage and price stickiness is that some markets might not move to equilibrium easily. Changes in demand for outputs make it appropriate for some wages and prices to rise or fall relative to other wages and prices. However, there is resistance to change—_____—within both labor and output markets.

4. By preventing movement down the aggregate demand curve to a full-employment equilibrium, wage and price stickiness can mean a prolonged period in which both _____ and _____ are below the economy's potential.

5. Suppose the economy starts at an unemployment equilibrium, characterized by a price level that is too high to achieve full employment GDP, but that refuses to fall because of sticky prices. If the price level cannot _____ to correct the unemployment equilibrium, the only solution is to shift aggregate demand rightward by increasing spending power. The shift can be accomplished by _____ policy, which is government policy toward taxation and spending. It can also be accomplished through *monetary policy*, which has to do with varying the quantity of money that is available to spend.

6. When the economy finds itself stuck at an unemployment equilibrium, Keynesians advocate using _____ fiscal policy, also called a fiscal stimulus, which is increased government spending or reduced taxation to *stimulate* aggregate demand and return the economy to full-employment. With more government spending, aggregate demand shifts to the _____. The Keynesian idea is to shift it just enough to reach full-employment output, thus solving unemployment problems without causing _____.

7. Alternatively, when the economy _____—growing so fast that inflation threatens—government can use _____ fiscal policy, also called a fiscal drag, to slow it down, by shifting aggregate demand to the left.

8. Both expansionary and contractionary fiscal policy are examples of _____ policy—public policy adjusted at the discretion of lawmakers. Unfortunately, even the best intentioned discretionary public policy is unlikely to follow the Keynesian policy prescription. The reason has to do with the three *fiscal policy lags*:
   a. The _____ lag—It takes time to know that the economy is in a recession.
   b. The _____ lag—Tax and spending bills are not passed overnight.
   c. The _____ lag. Planning government spending takes time. It also takes time before tax changes can take effect.

9. Because of fiscal policy lags, the business cycle may have turned by the time the money starts flowing. The spending may be more likely to cause inflation than to reduce unemployment. Policy lags make it very difficult, if not impossible, to *fine tune* the economy to even out the ups and downs of the business cycle. Fine tuning would require that _____ fiscal policy start when the economy pushes above full-employment GDP. Likewise, when the economy sinks to less than full-employment GDP, then finely tuned fiscal policy should be _____. Instead of discretionary policy, lawmakers can rely on _____ _____, components of existing fiscal policies that stimulate the economy when it is sluggish and act as a drag when it overheats.

248   CHAPTER 9

10. Taken as a whole, the automatic stabilizers are intended to be _____ if the economy is below full employment and _____ when the economy is overheating. If the economy is at full employment, fiscal policy should be neutral_____, since there is no need to either stimulate or slow down economic activity. If the economy is at full employment, the neutral fiscal policy could generate a balanced _____ budget, meaning that tax revenue inflows just equal government expenditure outflows—government spending and revenues being recorded in the *federal budget*.

11. Economists often suggest that, whether fiscal policy is by automatic stabilizers or discretionary, it should be set so that the budget roughly balances over the course of the business cycle. The idea is that, when the economy is overheated and contractionary policy is in order, the government would run a budget surplus in which tax revenue exceeds government _____. When economic health is poor and expansionary policy is needed, the government would then choose a budget deficit in which government spending exceeds tax revenue. The surpluses could help pay for the deficits.

12. There is a significant tilt toward the expansionary side, even when the economy is doing well. To assess this tilt, we can look at the full-employment budget, which is an estimate of what government revenue and spending would be were there to be full employment. The full employment budget has usually been in _____ in recent years.

13. Despite being in the vicinity of full employment for much of the past two decades, the U.S. government has run substantial budget deficits in the large majority of those years. The result of the accumulation of past budget deficits and surpluses is, on balance, a U.S. _____ _____ of $6.14 trillion. This is money owed by the U.S. Government, mostly to American citizens. In principle, expansionary fiscal policy can shift aggregate demand _____ until it achieves full-employment output at the current price level. In practice, however, the economy does not behave quite this simply. The most notable complexity is a tendency toward inflation when policymakers try to stimulate aggregate demand.

14. The short-run aggregate supply is _____ sloping, while the long-run aggregate supply is always vertical_____ at full employment GDP. In the short run, the amount of output offered can even exceed full employment GDP, as workers offer to work overtime or seek out extra jobs. Conversely, if workers expect more inflation than actually occurs, the output they would offer at the actual price level would be less than full employment GDP.

15. Two reasons for the upward slope of aggregate supply are as follows:
    a. _____ _____—as new spending power is added to the economy, it tends to raise wages and prices where it first hits, before eventually diffusing throughout the economy. Wages and prices in the sectors of the economy most directly affect by the spending will rise before the extra spending can circulate more

generally throughout the economy. The result is a higher output in those sectors, but also a higher overall price level.

b. The _____ _____—when the price level rises and labor supply curves remain unchanged, firms can profit by increasing output and employment. If the economy is already at full employment, firms will employ workers overtime, thus allowing the economy to exceed full-employment output temporarily.

16. The production effect relies upon workers being fooled by inflation or deflation. For the economy to be in long-run equilibrium, workers must have accurate wage and price expectations. For this reason, short-run aggregate supply always intersects long-run aggregate supply at the _____ price level.

17. _____-_____ inflation is caused by an increase in aggregate demand that pulls the economy up short-run aggregate supply.

18. Demand-pull inflation occurs when a rightward shift in aggregate demand moves the economy to both a higher output and a higher price level. Demand-pull inflation might be caused by _____ fiscal policy that is meant to move the economy toward full employment. The result is shown as a movement up the short-run aggregate supply curve in the general direction of full-employment output, but also in the direction of a higher price level.

19. When aggregate supply shifts up, the economy moves up the aggregate demand curve to a point of higher prices and lower output. Inflation that is caused in this way is called _____-_____ inflation.

20. Cost push inflation reduces output and increases the price level. Recall from chapter 8, this combination is known as _____—the simultaneous occurrence of inflation and economic stagnation.

21. The shifting short-run aggregate supply becomes a moving target for government policymakers. If government chases an upwardly shifting aggregate supply with ever more stimulative policies that shift out aggregate demand, the result would be the reinforcement of inflationary expectations. As inflationary expectations rise, short-run aggregate supply shifts up and output falls, which prompts more fiscal stimuli in an ever-repeating cycle. The result is an ongoing _____ _____ of rising and falling output along with a continuing rise in the price level.

22. A sustainable long-run macro equilibrium is one in which the expected and actual price levels are _____. The expected price level is given by the _____ of short- and long-run aggregate supply. The actual price level is given by the _____ of short-run aggregate supply and aggregate demand. Because these intersections both occur at the same point, a point on long-run aggregate supply, the economy is at _____ _____.
Whether achieved through government policy intended to manage aggregate demand, or

through a hands-off policy of giving short-run aggregate supply time to adjust on its own, this long-run macro equilibrium is usually considered to be the ideal outcome of macro policy.

23. To achieve long-run stability and avoid the inflationary spiral, _____ economists advocate a hands-off policy to let inflationary expectations subside.

E&A 24. The national debt can be thought of as the _____ or inventory of accumulated past budgetary imbalances, and the deficit as a _____ that adds to that debt. As a country, we often accuse ourselves of being on a spending binge, one we will have to pay for later. As evidence, we point to both the federal budget deficit and the U.S. *trade deficit*. The trade deficit is the amount by which the value of goods we _____ exceeds the value of goods we _____. Because we spend more of our dollars on foreign goods than foreigners return in exchange for American goods, foreigners have extra dollars left over to invest in the U.S. Those investments represent future obligations of this country to other countries. Yet, while it is the collection of our individual actions that leads us to a trade deficit, we don't usually consider ourselves to engage personally in irresponsible spending.

25. The $106 billion budget deficit differs from the amount of the trade deficit, which has been running well over $400 billion in recent years. Still, the two are related, so much so that they have been dubbed the _____ _____ . By running a budget deficit, the U.S. government leaves more money in the pockets of consumers, some of which they spend on imports. Those U.S. dollars that consumers spend on imports come back to the U.S., such as when foreigners buy U.S. _____ or _____ invest in the U.S.

TRUE/FALSE/EXPLAIN
If false, explain why in the space provided.

1. According to Keynesians, downward movement of the price level happens relatively quickly, but only if that movement is along the aggregate demand curve.

2. Keynesians argue that sticky wages will prevent the economy from reaching full employment in the long run.

3. Keynesian analysis focuses primarily on the supply side of the economy.

4. Classical analysis suggests that much government action does more harm than good.

5. A fiscal drag is the opposite of a fiscal stimulus.

6. When the economy overheats, government can use a contractionary fiscal policy to slow it down.

7. The three policy lags are termed the recognition lag, action lag, and implementation lag.

8. Automatic stabilizers avoid the problems of policy lags associated with discretionary fiscal policy.

9. Automatic stabilizers are contractionary when the economy is at less that a full employment equilibrium.

10. A budget deficit is the same thing as the national debt.

11. If the government balances its budget over the course of business cycle, that would involve surpluses in some years paying for deficits in others.

12. The full-employment budget is, by definition, neither in surplus nor deficit.

13. Aggregate demand slopes downward because of structural rigidities and the production effect.

CHAPTER 9

14. The short-run macroeconomic equilibrium occurs at the intersection of short-run aggregate supply and long-run aggregate supply.

15. Short-run aggregate supply intersects long-run aggregate supply at the expected price level.

16. Demand-pull inflation is associated with an increase in unemployment.

17. Inflation is likely to reduce the effectiveness of expansionary fiscal policy.

18. Demand-pull inflation is associated with a higher GDP in the short run.

19. Short-run aggregate supply will shift upward if people have inflationary expectations.

20. Keynesian analysis is usually adopted by political conservatives.

21. The national debt can be thought of as a stock of accumulated past budgetary imbalances.

22. It is very difficult to *force* Congress to balance the budget, because Congress has the power to hide taxes, such as by issuing unfunded mandates.

23. The value of a country's capital can be used to justify a national debt.

24. The budget deficit and the national debt are termed the "twin deficits."

25. Unless the U.S. trade deficit declines, there is a real danger that the U.S. government will be forced to default on its debt.

MULTIPLE CHOICE
Circle the letter preceding the one best answer.

1. And unemployment equilibrium is characterized by
   a. unionization.
   b. budget deficits.
   c. budget surpluses.
   d. sticky prices.

2. According to Keynesian economic theory,
   a. there is no such thing as full-employment output.
   b. consumers should spend less and save more if the economy suffers from unemployment.
   c. sticky wages prevent the economy from reaching full employment.
   d. government action is unnecessary for the economy to achieve full-employment output.

3. Keynesians argue that
   a. the government's power to spend and tax should be used to promote full employment.
   b. the capitalist system has an automatic mechanism that generates a high level of employment quickly and dependably.
   c. the means of production should be allocated in accord with a central plan.
   d. there should be no private property.

4. The primary focus of Keynesian economics is on
   a. inflation.
   b. economic growth.
   c. aggregate demand.
   d. aggregate supply.

254 CHAPTER 9

5. If the economy starts at the point indicated in Multiple Choice Figure 1 and government takes no action, the economy is likely to move in the direction given by the arrow labeled
   a. A.
   b. B.
   c. C.
   d. D.

6. If the economy starts at the point indicated in Multiple Choice Figure 1 and government pursues a contractionary fiscal policy, the economy is likely to move in the direction given by the arrow labeled
   a. A.
   b. B.
   c. C.
   d. D.

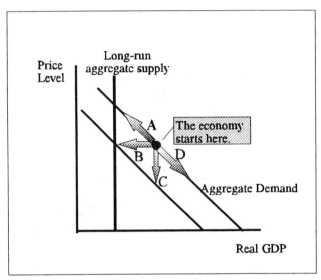

Multiple Choice Figure 1

7. Keynesian analysis emphasizes that
   a. government can best achieve its objectives of high employment and low inflation by staying out of the marketplace, and by keeping its budget balanced.
   b. equilibrium in the economy can occur at less than full employment.
   c. it is better for government to cut taxes than to increase spending.
   d. the government should always balance its budget.

8. In Multiple Choice Figure 2, the best time to implement a contractionary fiscal policy would be at the point labeled
   a. A.
   b. B.
   c. C.
   d. D.

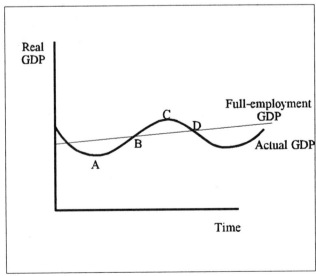

Multiple Choice Figure 2

9. In Multiple Choice Figure 2, the best time to implement an expansionary fiscal policy would be at the point labeled
   a. A.
   b. B.
   c. C.
   d. D.

10. Which of the following is the best example of an automatic stabilizer?
    a. The U.S. income tax system as a whole.
    b. Foreign aid.
    c. Passing legislation during recessions to cut tax rates.
    d. Passing legislation during recessions to cut government spending.

11. Automatic stabilizers have an advantage over discretionary fiscal policies in that they largely avoid the problem of
    a. inflation.
    b. government interference in the private marketplace.
    c. multiplier effects.
    d. policy lags.

12. Short-run aggregate supply holds _____ constant.
    a. expected inflation
    b. actual inflation
    c. unemployment
    d. taxes and government spending

13. Starting at a long-run equilibrium, a shift in aggregate demand will cause a movement to a new long-run equilibrium by eventually causing a shift in
    a. the short-run aggregate supply curve, but not the long-run aggregate supply curve.
    b. the long-run aggregate supply curve, but not the short-run aggregate supply curve.
    c. both the long-run and short-run aggregate supply curves.
    d. neither the long-run nor short-run aggregate supply curves.

14. A revision upward in the expected rate of inflation would will cause the actual rate of inflation to _____ and the unemployment rate to _____.
    a. rise; fall
    b. fall; rise
    c. rise; rise
    d. fall; fall

15. If the price level rises and output stays constant in the long run, this is most likely caused by
    a. demand-pull inflation when the economy is at full employment.
    b. demand-pull inflation when there is unemployment.
    c. cost-push inflation when the economy is at full employment.
    d. cost-push inflation when there is unemployment.

16. Cost-push inflation is associated with
    a. lower real GDP.
    b. lower prices.
    c. tax cuts.
    d. automatic stabilizers.

17. In Multiple Choice Figure 3, the arrow labeled A is most likely to be the
    a. actual effect of expansionary fiscal policy.
    b. intended effect of expansionary fiscal policy.
    c. actual effect of contractionary fiscal policy.
    d. intended effect of contractionary fiscal policy.

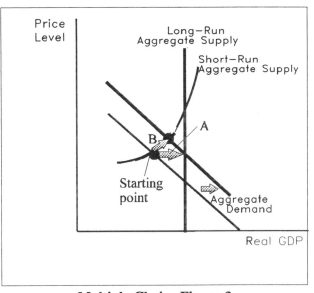

Multiple Choice Figure 3

18. In Multiple Choice Figure 3, the arrow labeled B is most likely to be the
    a. actual effect of expansionary fiscal policy.
    b. intended effect of expansionary fiscal policy.
    c. actual effect of contractionary fiscal policy.
    d. intended effect of contractionary fiscal policy.

19. In Multiple Choice Figure 3, the arrow labeled B is associated with
    a. a long-run macroeconomic equilibrium.
    b. demand-pull inflation.
    c. cost-push inflation.
    d. an automatic stabilizer.

20. Demand-pull inflation can lead to cost-push inflation as
    a. the shift in aggregate demand becomes difficult to slow down.
    b. firms increase output to meet increased demand.
    c. firms raise prices in response to increased demand.
    d. firms and workers revise upwards their expectations of the price level.

E&A 21. The national debt most convincingly can be justified by pointing to
   a. the equity of redistributing income.
   b. the value of owing other countries money so as to keep the peace.
   c. the many valuable assets that the debt has helped pay for.
   d. The national debt cannot be justified by any reasonable analysis.

22. About _____ percentage of the U.S. national debt is owed to U.S. citizens.
   a. 20
   b. 40
   c. 60
   d. 80

23. The presence of foreign-owned assets on U.S. soil
   a. increases the risk that foreign countries will wage war against the United States.
   b. decreases the risk that foreign countries will wage war against the United States.
   c. increases the risk that foreign countries will wage war against each other.
   d. has no bearing on the risk of warfare.

24. Multiple Choice Figure 4 is most likely to show the
   a. actual effect of expansionary fiscal policy.
   b. intended effect of expansionary fiscal policy.
   c. actual effect of contractionary fiscal policy.
   d. intended effect of contractionary fiscal policy.

25. In Multiple Choice Figure 4, the most likely reason for the shift back to the left in aggregate demand is
   a. inflation.
   b. exceeding full-employment output.
   c. the effect of government borrowing.
   d. cost-push inflation.

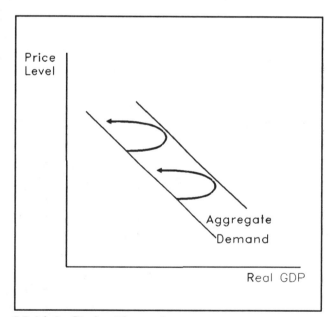

Multiple Choice Figure 4

GRASPING THE GRAPHS
Fill in each box with a concept that applies.

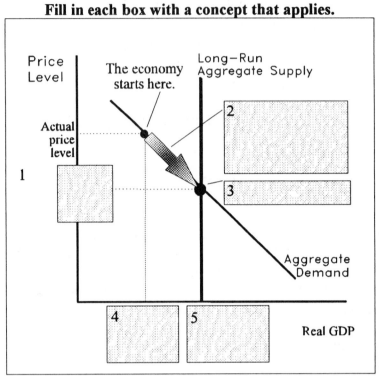

Fill in the boxes in this graph to show how fiscal policy is meant to cure an unemployment equilibrium.

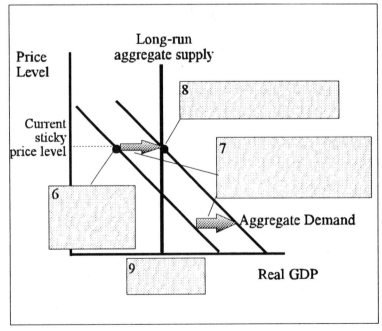

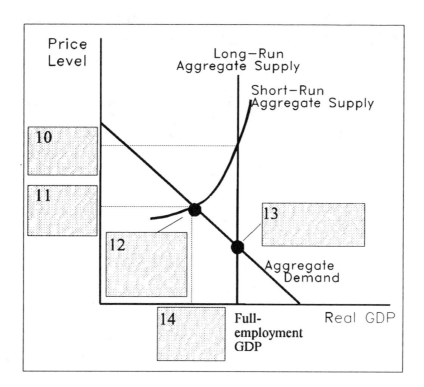

Fill in the boxes in this graph to show an inflationary spiral.

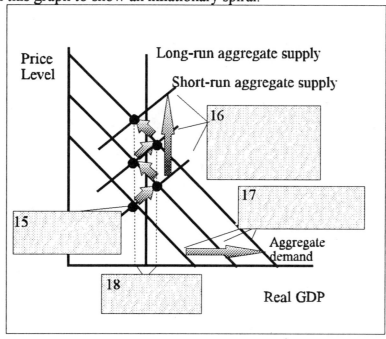

For additional practice in grasping this chapter's graphs, visit
http://www.prenhall.com/ayers and try *Smart Graph* 1,
along with *Active Graphs* 1, 2, 3, 4, and 5.

ANSWERS

STUDYCHECKS

1. Keynesian economists believe that sticky wages and prices prevent the economy from moving out of recession to a lower price level and full-employment equilibrium in the short run. Since there is urgency to unemployment needs, Keynesians argue for government action.

2. The model of aggregate demand and aggregate supply can be used as the context to discuss the Keynesian perspective relative to that of the classical economists. For example, the model reveals how an increase in aggregate demand will bring inflation. While the evidence suggests that this inflation is likely in practice following fiscal policies to stimulate the economy, Keynes himself did not envision prices rising until the economy had actually reached full employment.

3. See StudyCheck 3 Figure.

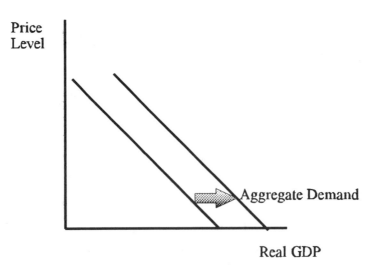

StudyCheck 3 Figure

4. See StudyCheck 4 Figure.

5. See StudyCheck 5 Figure.

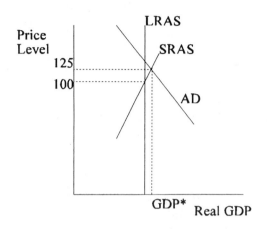

StudyCheck 4 Figure

StudyCheck 5 Figure

6. See StudyCheck 6 Figure.

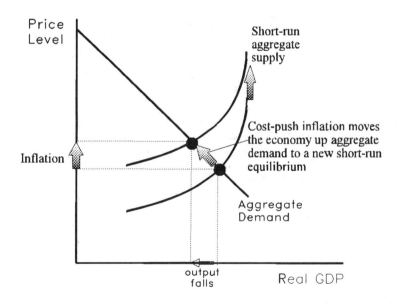

StudyCheck 6 Figure

262 CHAPTER 9

7. The inflationary spiral is that demand-pull inflation, such as caused by fiscal stimulus, can lead to a higher GDP in the short run, but not in the long run. Long-run cost-push inflation, in which the long-run aggregate supply curve shifts to the left, leads to lower GDP. An inflationary spiral can occur in which fiscal stimulus causes demand-pull inflation, that in turn counters the initial effect of the stimulus, possibly leading to a continuously repeating cycle.

8. Some national debt is justified on the basis of valuable assets that accompany it. However, there is no consensus on how much is the right amount.

9. As the federal debt rises, it draws in capital from both domestic and foreign sources. Foreign investment money could otherwise have gone to buy U.S. exports and is thus associated with an increase in the trade deficit.

10. Politicians are under pressure to spend, since the benefits are clear while the costs are somewhat hidden. Constituencies fight for specific components of spending. The desire to control it is more abstract and carries less weight in the political process. It is difficult to control this spending because it can be hidden by Congress, either through its internal accounting or through substituting unfunded mandates for direct government expenditures. A balanced-budget amendment to the U.S. constitution would thus be unlikely to eliminate the problem.

FILL IN THE BLANKS

1. shift
2. wage, price, short run, sticky wages
3. rigidities
4. output, employment
5. fall, fiscal
6. expansionary, right, inflation
7. overheats, contractionary
8. discretionary, recognition, action, implementation
9. contractionary, expansionary, automatic stabilizers
10. expansionary, contractionary, neutral
11. spending
12. deficit
13. national debt, rightward
14. upward, vertical
15. Structural rigidities, production effect
16. expected
17. Demand-pull
18. expansionary
19. cost-push

20. stagflation
21. inflationary spiral
22. equal, intersection, intersection, full employment
23. classical
24. stock, flow, import, export
25. twin deficits, exports, invest

TRUE/FALSE/EXPLAIN

1. False, Keynesians emphasize that prices are likely to be downwardly sticky as they try to adjust along aggregate demand.
2. False, Keynesians argued that sticky wages will prevent the economy from reaching full employment in the short run.
3. False, Keynesian analysis focuses on the demand side of the economy.
4. True.
5. True.
6. True.
7. True.
8. True.
9. False, automatic stabilizers are expansionary if the economy is not full employment.
10. False, a budget deficit represents additions to the national debt.
11. True.
12. False, the full-employment budget has been in deficit in recent years, which suggests that fiscal policy is expansionary.
13. False, it is short-run aggregate supply that slopes upward because of these effects.
14. False, the short-run macroeconomic equilibrium occurs at the intersection of aggregate demand and long-run aggregate supply.
15. True.
16. False, demand-pull inflation is associated with a decrease in the unemployment.
17. True.
18. True.
19. True.
20. False, classical analysis is usually adopted by conservatives and Keynesian analysis by liberals.
21. True.
22. True.
23. True.
24. False, it is the budget deficit and trade deficit that are termed the twin deficits.
25. False, the U.S. government's debt is in dollars, which it has no need to acquire through exports.

MULTIPLE CHOICE

1.	d	8.	b	15.	a	22.	d
2.	c	9.	d	16.	a	23.	a
3.	a	10.	a	17.	b	24.	a
4.	c	11.	d	18.	a	25.	c
5.	a	12.	a	19.	b		
6.	b	13.	a	20.	d		
7.	b	14.	c	21.	c		

GRASPING THE GRAPHS
Examples of correct answers

1. equilibrium price level
2. Sticky wages and prices prevent movement to equilibrium.
3. Long-run equilibrium, or full-employment equilibrium
4. Unemployment equilibrium
5. Full-employment GDP
6. Unemployment equilibrium
7. Effect of a fiscal stimulus
8. Full-employment equilibrium
9. Full-employment GDP
10. Expected price level
11. Actual price level
12. Unemployment equilibrium
13. Full-employment equilibrium
14. Actual GDP
15. Start of the inflationary spiral
16. Upward shifts caused by inflationary expectations
17. Effect of expansionary fiscal policy
18. Fluctuations in output

Visit the Ayers/Collinge companion Website at http://www.prenhall.com/ayers for further activities and exercises for this chapter.

Chapter 10

AGGREGATE EXPENDITURES

CHAPTER REVIEW

10.1 "In the Long Run, We are All Dead"
- With the famous line above, John Maynard Keynes (1883-1946) spotlighted the need to address immediate problems facing the unemployed. In response to the pressing problems of the Great Depression, Keynes offered a new, short-run perspective that came to be called *Keynesian economics*. Prior to that time, economists emphasized long-run economic tendencies, viewing short-run fluctuations around the long-run trends as transitory problems that would correct themselves. That long-run way of looking at the macro economy became known as *classical economics*. Both classical and Keynesian perspectives are used today.

- The Keynesian model is based around understanding how much spending is likely to occur at different levels of GDP and how government can influence that spending to make sure that the economy lands at full employment.

- The Great Depression was a long time ago, beginning in 1929 and ending with the U.S. entry into World War II in 1942. Since Keynesian analysis seemed to explain how the economy went from depression to prosperity in that period, it should come as no surprise that the Keynesian model was popular in the 1950s and 1960s. But the model did not seem to apply in the 1970s, during which time the U.S. economy faced serious problems of both inflation and unemployment.

- The 2001 recession and the eagerness of politicians to embrace Keynesian remedies in the months that followed propelled the Keynesian model into the spotlight once more. George W. Bush implemented a Keynesian style policy of tax rebate checks mailed out in the summer of 2001. Then, following the terrorist attacks of September 11th, both the president and Congress were eager to spend, with the justification that extra spending was needed to spur the economy.

10.2 The Income-Expenditure Model
- **One person's spending is another person's income**—the two go hand in hand. Likewise, the circular flow model from chapter 2 tells us that aggregate income and output must be equal.

    Aggregate national income = aggregate national output

266 CHAPTER 10

- The **aggregate expenditure function** tells what the economy's planned spending will be at each level of real GDP. There will be only one GDP that does match up planned spending and actual spending. That GDP occurs at the **expenditure equilibrium,** which is given by the intersection of the aggregate expenditure function and the 45-degree line in the income-expenditure model.

StudyCheck 1

Graph an aggregate expenditure (AE) function, where autonomous spending is $1 and the marginal propensity to consume is 4/5. Label: 1) the axes of the graph; 2) AE; 3) autonomous spending ($1); 4) the number equaling equilibrium national income.

- The aggregate expenditure function shows that the economy's planned spending depends upon its income, the latter measured by actual GDP. Aggregate expenditures can be divided into the following two types:
    - **Autonomous spending** would occur even if people had no incomes;
    - **Induced spending** depends upon income.

- Autonomous spending includes both investments and goods and services that will be purchased no matter what national income might be. For example, if it became necessary, people would draw upon their accumulated wealth to buy such necessities of life as food and shelter.

- Aggregate expenditures equal the sum of autonomous and induced spending. Autonomous spending by itself shows up graphically as a horizontal line, since it does not vary with income. In contrast, induced spending is entirely dependent upon income. So the line showing induced spending starts at zero GDP and rises from there. When autonomous spending and induced spending are added together, the result is in aggregate expenditure function that has both a positive vertical intercept and a positive slope.

> **StudyCheck 2**
> Using a graph, show the components of the aggregate expenditure function.

- The components of aggregate expenditures are merely the components of GDP, which are:
    GDP = consumption + investment + government purchases + (exports − imports)
  or, for short,
    GDP = C + I + G + (X - M)
  Exports minus imports is alternatively termed *net exports*.

- Far and away the largest component of GDP is consumption. Plotting consumption spending against GDP gives the **consumption function**. Because of autonomous spending, the consumption function has a positive vertical intercept. From there, it slopes upward because of the **marginal propensity to consume (mpc)**, which is the fraction of incremental income that people spend. It is computed as the slope of the consumption function.

- The fraction of additional income that people save is termed the **marginal propensity to save** (mps). Adding together the marginal propensity to save and the marginal propensity to consume must yield of total of one, since there is nowhere else for income to go:

  mpc + mps = 1

- Investment and government purchases are of roughly comparable size. For simplicity planned government purchases and planned investment spending are assumed to be completely autonomous and thus to be constant as GDP changes. For this reason, the slope of the aggregate expenditure function and consumption function are the same, both equaling the marginal propensity to consume.

- Recall that the expenditure equilibrium occurs where the aggregate expenditure function intersects the 45-degree line. At the expenditure equilibrium, the economy's actual GDP equals its planned spending. **When the economy is not at equilibrium, actual GDP and planned spending differ. The difference shows up in business inventories.** In particular, businesses plan to maintain some amount of inventories, but cannot predict exactly how much of their products consumers will buy. Unintended inventory changes show up as the difference between planned and actual investment, as follows:

  Expenditure equilibrium: aggregate expenditures = actual GDP,

  where

  Aggregate expenditures = consumption + planned investment + government + net exports

  and

  GDP = consumption + actual investment + government + net exports

  which implies

  Expenditure equilibrium: planned investment = actual investment.

- Another way to understand the expenditure equilibrium is to consider what would happen if real GDP were either above or below it. If the economy produced less than the equilibrium, planned spending would exceed output. With buyers clamoring for more than the economy in fact produces, businesses would see their inventories decline. The next step after a decline in inventories is a surge in orders to suppliers. Businesses would want to replace those inventories. In response, manufacturers and other suppliers would increase output. The result is not only an increase in GDP produced. The process does not stop there. The workers in the factories would take home more pay. They would spend some of that pay. That extra spending is induced consumption, induced by the extra income. So inventories are drawn down again, which means that firms will again increase output. This process continues, but not forever. At each round, the output increases and income increases get smaller until, eventually, an equilibrium is reached.

- Conversely, if production were to exceed the equilibrium, planned spending would not keep pace with production and inventories would build up. In response to the buildup in

AGGREGATE EXPENDITURES 269

inventories, firms would cut back output and jobs. The output cuts cause income to drop. In turn, induced spending falls and inventory levels would continue to be high. Firms would continue to postpone ordering and GDP would continue to fall until an expenditure equilibrium is reached. At the expenditure equilibrium, there are no further unplanned changes in inventories.

10.3 Changing the Expenditure Equilibrium

- An expenditure equilibrium implies that there are no unplanned inventory buildups or drawdowns that would prompt a change in business plans. To achieve this result, all businesses would need to correctly forecast the demands for their products. The world is not that precise. Because there will always be some forecasting errors, the economy can achieve an equilibrium only approximately. In addition, that equilibrium will change when the aggregate expenditure function changes, such as in response to people changing their consumption preferences or businesses changing their investment preferences. The reasons could be as simple as attitudes toward world events, with planned expenditures increasing when we are optimistic and decreasing when we are pessimistic. Then there is government, which can change the aggregate expenditure function directly by altering its spending policies, or change it indirectly by altering tax policies that affect consumer spending or business investment.

- When there are changes in autonomous spending, the changes are magnified by the **multiplier effect**, which is a sequence of cause and effect, much like the ones shown in Figure 10-5. However, instead of taking us from a disequilibrium to an equilibrium as in that figure, the multiplier effect takes the economy from one equilibrium to another.

- The multiplier effect works as follows: Adding autonomous spending causes a higher GDP, which causes more induced spending. That's because money that one person spends autonomously adds to the income of others, which in turn induces them to buy more output. This process generates an ongoing cycle of greater income and greater output. At each stage in this cycle, however, some income is likely to be saved, thus eventually bringing the cycle to a halt.

- The strength of the multiplier effect depends upon the proportion of income that is devoted to consumption. To the extent that people save their incomes, for example, those savings represent a *leakage* out of the multiplier process. Table 14-2 illustrates how the value of the marginal propensity to consume determines the increase in spending as income rises from zero to $5,000. The table assumes that autonomous spending is $1,000. Although actual values of mpc and mps depend upon consumer confidence, the table will for simplicity assume that the mpc is a constant 0.6, meaning people spend 60 cents out of each additional dollar of income. Savings are also shown in the table, because income not spent is saved. Thus, the mpc of 0.6 implies an mps of 0.4. A negative value for savings, which occurs at lower income values in the table, means that there is *dissaving*—spending out of existing saving.

Table 10-1 Spending Depends Upon the Marginal Propensity to Consume (mpc)
(Assume autonomous spending = $1,000, mpc = 0.6, mps = 0.4)

Income	Spending	Savings
$0	$1,000	-$1,000
$1,000	$1,600	-$600
$2,000	$2,200	-$200
$3,000	$2,800	$200
$4,000	$3,400	$600
$5,000	$4,000	$1,000

- The multiplier effect works through the following formula: Change in autonomous spending × expenditure multiplier = change in equilibrium GDP, where the **expenditure multiplier** is the multiple by which equilibrium real GDP grows as a result of an increase—an *injection*—of new autonomous spending. The expenditure multiplier is sometimes called the *autonomous expenditure multiplier* for clarity or merely just the *multiplier* for short. If autonomous spending rises, **the expenditure equilibrium will rise by the increase in autonomous spending multiplied by the expenditure multiplier.** The price level is assumed to remain unchanged. For example, if investors gain confidence in the economy and so increase their autonomous investment spending, equilibrium GDP would rise by more than that amount. Specifically, the equilibrium GDP would equal the increase in autonomous investment multiplied by the multiplier. Conversely, if autonomous spending were to decrease, the expenditure multiplier would reveal how much real GDP would fall.

- If people always spend every penny of income they receive, the expenditure multiplier would be infinite and the multiplier formula would lead to an infinite GDP. For example, if Ann were to receive $1,000 in income, she would spend $1,000. That would provide others with $1,000 in income, which they would spend, thus providing others with $1,000 in income, and so forth. In practice, however, leakages and possible price increases eventually bring the multiplier process to a halt. For example, if the mps were to equal 0.2, Ann would only spend $800, and 20 percent of that $800 would be saved by those receiving it, so that the next round of spending would amount to only $640.

- The multiplier is computed as the reciprocal of the percentage of new income that isn't spent on consumption. If the only options for using additional income are to spend it or save it, the multiplier formula becomes the reciprocal of the marginal propensity to save:
$$\text{expenditure multiplier} = 1/(1 - \text{mpc})$$
or, equivalently,
$$\text{expenditure multiplier} = 1/\text{mps}.$$

- Again, **the multiplier is multiplied by a change in autonomous spending to reveal the change in equilibrium GDP.** The change in autonomous spending could be undertaken by government, businesses, or consumers. For example, if government spending rises by $10 billion, and the marginal propensity to save is 0.2, the expenditure equilibrium will rise by (1/0.2) multiplied by $10 billion, which equals 5 multiplied by $10 billion, or $50 billion.

StudyCheck 3

Suppose that the marginal propensity to save is 0.2. Using the expenditure multiplier and assuming that GDP is $100 billion less than full-employment GDP, how much extra government spending would be required to bring the economy to full employment?

- Note that nothing in the foregoing analysis indicates whether the expenditure equilibrium occurs at full employment. However, **there must be some idle resources for the multiplier effect to occur.** If an injection of new spending occurs when the economy is already at full employment, consumers and others bid up prices by seeking to buy more output than the economy is capable of sustaining. The result is inflation, implying a rising price level that offsets the multiplier effect by making money not go as far in real terms. Thus, rising prices thwart the multiplier effect, even to the extent that extra spending might cause no increase at all in real GDP.

- If the expenditure equilibrium occurs below full-employment GDP, there will be unemployment, and thus downward pressure on prices until full-employment GDP is achieved. However, this point is where Keynes draws the line from his classical predecessors. Regarding the expenditure equilibrium, Keynes wrote, "There is no reason for expecting it to be *equal* to full employment." Keynes went so far as to dismiss any possibility for prices to fall, because that process would only occur in the long run. Remember, "In the long run, we are all dead." Accordingly, **Keynesian multiplier analysis assumes a constant price level.**

- If the expenditure equilibrium lies below full-employment GDP, it is called an **unemployment equilibrium.** Along with the unemployment equilibrium comes an **output gap**, in which actual GDP falls below full-employment GDP, as shown in Figure 10-7. At an unemployment equilibrium, there is too little planned spending for the economy to achieve full employment GDP. The shortfall in spending is called a **recessionary gap**, which is a shortfall in the aggregate expenditure function below that necessary to achieve a full-employment equilibrium.

- Keynes suggested that government could increase spending by just this amount and the multiplier effect would do the rest. More generally, an increase in autonomous spending in an amount equal to the recessionary gap would shift up the aggregate expenditure function by just enough to lead to a full-employment equilibrium. This result assumes a constant price level. As we saw in chapter 9, expansionary fiscal policy might raise the price level and have a diminished effect on output, particularly as the economy approaches full-employment GDP.

- If the expenditure equilibrium occurs past full-employment GDP, multiplier analysis does not apply because inflation will not allow it to stay there. This possibility is referred to as an **inflationary gap**, which is the excess of the aggregate expenditure function above that consistent with a full-employment equilibrium. The inflationary gap is shown in Figure 10-8. Because the productive capacity of the economy could not keep up with the economy's appetite to buy, the result would be inflation. Inflation would continue until it eroded the real value of planned aggregate expenditures and shifted the aggregate expenditure function down to intersect the 45-degree line at a full-employment equilibrium.

- To prevent an unemployment equilibrium, in which the economy is stuck in recession, Keynesians argue that either autonomous spending or the multiplier itself must be increased. The multiplier will increase to the extent that people decrease their marginal propensity to save. Because savings represent a leakage out of the multiplier process, Keynesians emphasize the value of consumption. If people consume a greater fraction of their income, the multiplier increases and equilibrium occurs at a higher GDP.

- For example, if the marginal propensity to save were to equal 1, that would mean that people save every dollar they receive. In that case, the expenditure multiplier would equal $1/1 = 1$, meaning that the effect of an extra dollar of spending is that dollar and no more. If the mps equals 0.2, in contrast, people save only twenty cents per dollar of additional income. In that case, an extra dollar of spending would generate $1 multiplied by (1/0.2), giving a result of $1 multiplied by 5, which equals a $5 increase in equilibrium spending and output. Thus, a decrease in the marginal propensity to save means that equilibrium income will be a greater multiple of autonomous spending.

- How can the multiplier be increased or autonomous spending be stimulated? According to Keynes, when business conditions are bad, the private sector is unlikely to make it better! Because he doubted increases in private-sector spending, Keynes was a strong advocate of increasing government spending during recessions.

- Keynesian analysis also suggests that government can use tax cuts to stimulate the economy. However, Keynesians note that people might save some of their higher after-tax income rather than spend it all. In other words, the **tax multiplier**—the expansionary effect of a tax cut or contractionary effect of a tax increase—would be less than the expenditure multiplier by the amount of the initial round of spending.

- For example, if government spends a dollar, taxpayers with an mpc of 70 cents will get that dollar and proceed to spend 70 cents. If government merely cuts taxes by a dollar, the first effect to be felt on the economy is that taxpayers will spend their mpc of, in this case, 70 cents. So the tax multiplier starts at the marginal propensity to consume and proceeds from there. The result is that, instead of a multiplier of $1/(1-mpc)$, the tax multiplier formula is:

    Tax multiplier = $-mpc/(1-mpc)$

    and

    Change in taxes owed to government × tax multiplier = change in equilibrium GDP.

- The tax multiplier is preceded with a negative sign because an increase in taxation reduces after-tax income and thus reduces aggregate expenditures. Because the tax multiplier is smaller than the expenditure multiplier, **Keynesians view extra government spending as the most effective policy to cure a recession.**

- In this model, financing extra government spending with an identical increase in taxation would have an expansionary effect because the expenditure multiplier exceeds the tax multiplier. The **balanced-budget multiplier** combines the expenditure multiplier for an increase in government spending and the tax multiplier because taxes would increase to finance that spending. Adding these multipliers together gives a balanced budget multiplier of 1, as follows:

    Balanced budget multiplier = $1/(1-mpc) - mpc/(1-mpc) = (1-mpc)/(1-mpc) = 1$

    and

    Change in balanced-budget government spending × 1 = change in equilibrium GDP.

    In other words, when financed by a tax increase, an increase in government spending increases equilibrium GDP by exactly the amount of that extra spending, without further multiplier effect.

- **Critics of Keynesian analysis contend that Keynesian multiplier analysis is flawed because it ignores the impact of how government spending is financed.** Specifically, the tax multiplier and balanced-budget multiplier analysis assumes that tax rates have no effect on incentives to work or invest. For example, to the extent that higher taxes reduce expected after-tax returns on investments, tax increases might be expected to reduce investment. Alternatively, if government spending is financed by borrowing, the borrowing is likely to drive up interest rates and cause a *crowding out effect*, which means that less money will go to private-sector investments because it is going to finance government instead. Such reductions in investment spending are not included in the Keynesian multipliers, but will be considered in chapter 12.

274 CHAPTER 10

> **StudyCheck 4**
> Using the concepts in this chapter, summarize Keynesian fiscal policy.

10.4 Aggregate Demand—An Expenditure Equilibrium for Each Price Level

- When the price level changes, the aggregate expenditure function shifts and generates a different expenditure equilibrium. The reason is that a change in the price level changes the real value of consumer wealth. For example, a higher price level represents inflation that erodes wealth and purchasing power. In response, there is less planned spending at each level of GDP, meaning that the aggregate expenditure function shifts down. Autonomous and induced spending are both less, because inflation has diminished the real value of savings. The expenditure equilibrium drops to a lower GDP.

- If we were to plot the expenditure equilibrium for each price level, the result would be the aggregate demand curve that we've used in the previous two chapters. A higher price level is associated with the lower expenditure equilibrium, the same information as above but now plotted explicitly. This relationship between the price level and the expenditure equilibrium is nothing more nor less than aggregate demand.

- If the price level remains constant and the aggregate expenditure function shifts for any other reason, aggregate demand shifts as well. The reason is that the price level, while not itself changed, would now be associated with a different expenditure equilibrium.

- Holding the price level unchanged, suppose the aggregate expenditure function shifts down in response to a decrease in autonomous spending. Perhaps the decrease is the result of lower government spending or higher taxation. The decrease in the autonomous expenditure function causes the expenditure equilibrium to occur at a lower real GDP. Since the price level has not changed, the result is that aggregate demand shifts to the left. There is now a lower expenditure-equilibrium GDP at the current price level. The equilibrium GDP would be lower at any other price level, as well.

StudyCheck 5

Using two possible price levels, derive the aggregate demand curve from the income/expenditure diagram. This will require two graphs. Proceed as follows:

a. On an income/expenditure diagram, graph an aggregate expenditure function. Label this AE1. Denote the equilibrium GDP by GDP1. Be sure to label the axes of the graph.

b. Suppose the price level rises from P1 to P2. On the same graph as above, graph a second AE function reflecting this change. Label this AE2. Denote equilibrium GDP by GDP2.

c. On a separate graph, draw an aggregate demand curve which is consistent with the information in parts a and b. Label this AD. Label two points on AD to show its consistency with the information above. Again, label the axes.

E&A 10.5 The Great Depression—At the Time and with the Benefit of Time

- In August of 1929 the U.S. economic expansion reached its peak. Just another bump on the road to permanent prosperity? Most people, if they even noticed the economic downturn at all, thought so. Then came October 23, "Black Thursday." The stock market crashed and did not soon recover.

- The "Roaring 20s" witnessed unprecedented prosperity as the average American family seized the opportunity to buy its first automobile, a radio that would tune in the soap operas, dramas, and comedies offered by the expanding web of network-affiliated stations. Many also dabbled in stocks, shares of ownership in the booming businesses around them. It was a new age of permanent prosperity in which the consumer and investor both shared in the wealth.

- A couple of brief, mild economic downturns did occur along with a more severe recession at the beginning of the decade of the 20s. Farmers in particular did not share in the general prosperity. But the wealthy made out quite well. The Revenue Act of 1926 legislated huge tax cuts, fueling the demand for stocks issued by companies like General Motors (GM), General Electric (GE), and the Radio Corporation of America (RCA).

- The crash of the stock market in 1929 was followed by deepening economic troubles. Most people blamed the market crash for those troubles. The economy did not begin to recover until 1933. The recovery, never strong enough to convince the country that its troubles were behind it, was interrupted by a second severe downturn in 1937.

- The tools of Keynesian economic analysis can help us understand the problems of recession and its meaner relative, depression. Suppose GDP starts far short of that needed for full employment. In order for the economy to produce full-employment GDP, the aggregate expenditure function must be shifted upward to intersect the 45-degree line at the higher level of GDP. Keynes called for government to make this shift happen by filling the recessionary gap with extra autonomous spending. If the government would just spend this extra amount, the multiplier effect would take over and bring the economy to full employment.

- Unfortunately, this analysis does not answer several important questions. If we grant that the crash of the stock market destroyed enough wealth to push the aggregate expenditure function down from the full employment level, why did the aggregate expenditure function continue to shift downward until 1933? Once the economy did begin to recover in 1933 why was the recovery so weak? What could have been done to strengthen the recovery? The Keynesian analysis neither tells us why the depression occurred, nor why the economy remained trapped so long.

- Even today, economists differ over the cause or causes of the Great Depression. The simplest explanation is that the stock market crash caused the aggregate expenditure function to shift downward as described above. However, economists are well aware of the dangers of the *fallacy of causation* in which an event is attributed to another event that preceded it. Just because one event occurs before a second one does not mean that the first event caused the second one. Many economists would label the stock market explanation as an example of the fallacy of causation. After all, the economic downturn began in August of 1929, while the market did not crash until October.

- What else could have caused the depression? In the 1992 presidential debate that CNN broadcast on *Larry King Live*, candidate Al Gore presented candidate Ross Perot with a framed picture of Senators Smoot and Hawley, authors of the Smoot-Hawley Tariff Act, passed in 1930. Gore criticized Perot for favoring raising tariffs on imports into the U.S. Many analysts believe that the Smoot-Hawley tariffs turned what might have been an ordinary recession into an economic disaster. By smothering international trade with high tariffs and precipitating retaliation by other countries, the Smoot-Hawley Act disrupted commerce. Soon the depression had spread to become a world wide phenomenon.

- We know that other suspects lurk in the pages of history. Economist Milton Friedman points his finger at the Federal Reserve, America's central bank. The Federal Reserve failed to rescue the banking system and allowed bank failures to multiply. By the time President Roosevelt declared a so-called bank holiday on his Inauguration Day, March 4, 1933, about a third of the country's money had been swallowed by bank failures. As one survivor of the era, Vince Olsen, put it, "A nickel would go a long way in those days. The problem was that nobody had a nickel." If the Fed had acted decisively to save the nation's banks and its money supply the depression would not have occurred.

- Others point to the nation's unequal distribution of wealth as the culprit, decrying such actions as The Revenue Act of 1926 that cut the federal income tax on a million dollar income from $600,000 to $200,000. As the rich took a larger fraction of national income and wealth, some argue that the nation began to save too much, resulting in too little aggregate demand. In addition to advocating government spending, for example, Keynes also urged consumers to increase the marginal propensity to consume and in that way get more money circulating in the economy.

- There was a widespread belief early on that a balanced federal budget would be the soundest fiscal policy. Thus, the Revenue Act of 1932 raised tax rates from a 25 percent maximum rate to 63 percent. Keynes abhorred that policy.

- With the passing of the Hoover presidency into history on March 4, 1933 President Franklin D. Roosevelt took the oath of office while promising the American people a New Deal. The nation witnessed an energetic, if not always successful effort, to banish the depression through legislation. The first theme of action was to reform the nation's financial and banking system to make banks stronger and safer. However, government did not repay the money lost when banks failed. A program of deposit insurance was not enacted until June of 1933, and that program was not retroactive.

- A second theme of the New Deal, the one for which it is most widely known, is embodied in various pieces of legislation to provide "relief" in the form of money and services for those in distress. Government attempted to set up a social safety net so that business downturns would no longer bring such personal devastation.

- A third theme is government influence over market prices. Prime examples are minimum wage laws and agricultural price floors. The purpose of these actions was to put purchasing power into the hands of workers and farmers, a very large group in those days. Support for workers was also embodied in legislation that supported the efforts of labor unions to organize workers.

- Even years prior to its publication date in 1936, drafts of Keynes' *General Theory of Employment, Interest, and Money* were the talk of the town in Washington. The ideas of this already well-known English economist offered the best hope that the country could find a way out of the depression. Keynes suggested that an economy ought to use government deficit spending to stimulate the economy and close any recessionary gap. A tax cut might achieve the same result, but with less certainty because taxpayers might save the money received from a tax cut rather than spend it. Thus, the Keynesian remedies for unemployment can be summarized as "spend, spend, spend." Only government has deep enough pockets for that.

- Keynes recommended that the deficit spending that governments use to fight off recessions should be balanced by a budget surplus during good economic times. The problem is that the Keynesian medicine of deficit spending has proved to be an addictive drug for governments around the world. Severe, protracted unemployment such as in the Great Depression has not been seen since.

- Economists today are indebted to Keynes for his powerful logic and insights into the role of aggregate demand in the macro economy. But economists also recognize the importance of money, taxes, aggregate supply, property rights, international trade, and other factors in promoting a healthy economy.

AGGREGATE EXPENDITURES 279

StudyCheck 6
Critique the idea that the stock market crash was the cause of the Great Depression. Be sure to mention the fallacy of causation and other possible causes of the recession in your answer.

FILL IN THE BLANKS

1. In response to the pressing problems of the Great Depression, Keynes offered a new, short-run perspective that came to be called _____ _____. Prior to that time, economists emphasized long-run economic tendencies, viewing short-run fluctuations around the long-run trends as transitory problems that would correct themselves. That long-run way of looking at the macro economy became known as _____ _____. Both perspectives are used today.

2. In keeping with a short-run perspective, Keynes chose to ignore long-run tendencies toward _____ _____. The Keynesian model is based around understanding how much _____ is likely to occur at different levels of GDP and how government can influence that spending to make sure that the economy lands at full employment.

3. One person's spending is another person's income—the two go hand in hand. Likewise, the circular flow model from chapter 2 tells us that: Aggregate national income = _____ _____ _____. The 45-degree line in the income expenditure graph maps _____ _____ _____ from the horizontal axis to the vertical axis.

280   CHAPTER 10

4. The _____ _____ function tells what the economy's planned spending will be at each level of real GDP. There will be only one GDP that does match up planned spending and actual spending. That GDP occurs at the expenditure equilibrium, which is given by the intersection of the aggregate expenditure function and the 45-degree line in the income-expenditure model.

5. The aggregate expenditure function shows that the economy's planned spending depends upon its income, the latter measured by actual GDP. Aggregate expenditures can be divided into the following two types:
   _____ spending would occur even if people had no incomes;
   _____ spending depends upon income.

6. _____ _____ equal the sum of autonomous and induced spending. Autonomous spending by itself shows up as a horizontal line, since it does not vary with income. In contrast, induced spending is entirely dependent upon income. So the line showing induced spending starts at zero GDP and rises from there. When autonomous spending and induced spending are added together, the result is in aggregate expenditure function that has both a positive vertical intercept and a positive slope. The components of aggregate expenditures are merely the components of GDP, which are: GDP = consumption + investment + government purchases + (exports − imports) or, for short, GDP = C + I + G + (X - M) Exports minus imports is alternatively termed *net exports*. Far and away the largest component of GDP is _____.

7. Plotting consumption spending against GDP gives the consumption function. Because of _____ _____, the consumption function has a positive vertical intercept. From there, it slopes upward because of the _____ _____ __ _____, which is the fraction of incremental income that people spend. It is computed as the slope of the consumption function.

8. The fraction of additional income that people save is termed the _____ _____ __ _____. Adding together the marginal propensity to save and the marginal propensity to consume must yield of total of _____, since there is nowhere else for income to go.

9. The slope of the aggregate expenditure function and consumption function are the same, both equaling the _____ _____ __ _____.

10. Recall that the expenditure equilibrium occurs where the aggregate expenditure function intersects the _____-_____ _____. At the expenditure equilibrium, the economy's actual GDP equals its planned spending. When the economy is not at equilibrium, actual GDP and planned spending differ. The difference shows up in business inventories.

AGGREGATE EXPENDITURES 281

Unintended inventory changes show up as the difference between planned and actual investment, as follows:

Expenditure equilibrium: aggregate expenditures = actual GDP,
  where
Aggregate expenditures = consumption + planned investment + government + net exports
  and
GDP = consumption + actual investment + government + net exports
  which implies
Expenditure equilibrium: _____ investment = _____ investment.

11. An expenditure equilibrium implies that there are no _____ inventory buildups or drawdowns that would prompt a change in business plans. Thus, all businesses must correctly forecast demands for their products. The world is not that precise. Because there will always be some forecasting errors, the economy can achieve an equilibrium only approximately.

12. When there are changes in autonomous spending, the changes are magnified by the _____ effect, which is a sequence of cause and effect taking us from a disequilibrium to an equilibrium. The strength of the multiplier effect depends upon the proportion of income that is devoted to consumption. To the extent that people save their incomes, for example, those savings represent a _____ out of the multiplier process. The multiplier effect works through the following formula: Change in _____ _____ × expenditure multiplier = change in equilibrium GDP.

13. In the short run, equilibrium GDP can grow as a result of an increase—an _____—of new autonomous spending. The expenditure multiplier is sometimes called the autonomous expenditure multiplier for clarity or merely just the multiplier for short. If autonomous spending rises, the expenditure equilibrium will rise by the increase in autonomous spending multiplied by the expenditure multiplier. The price level is assumed to remain _____.

14. The multiplier is computed as the reciprocal of the percentage of new income that isn't spent on consumption. If the only options for using additional income are to spend it or save it, the multiplier formula becomes the reciprocal of the marginal propensity to save:
  expenditure multiplier = 1/(1 − mpc)
or, equivalently,
  expenditure multiplier = 1/_____.
Keynesian multiplier analysis assumes a _____ price level.

15. If the expenditure equilibrium lies below full-employment GDP, it is called an _____ equilibrium. Along with the unemployment equilibrium comes an _____ gap, in which actual GDP falls below full-employment GDP. At an unemployment equilibrium, there is too little spending for the economy to achieve full employment GDP. The shortfall in spending is called a _____ gap, which is a

282 CHAPTER 10

shortfall in the aggregate expenditure function below that necessary to achieve a full-employment equilibrium. An increase in autonomous spending in an amount equal to the recessionary gap would shift up the _____ _____ function by just enough to lead to a full-employment equilibrium.

16. If the expenditure equilibrium occurs past full-employment GDP, multiplier analysis does not apply because inflation will not allow it to stay there. This possibility is referred to as an _____ gap, which is the excess of the aggregate expenditure function above that consistent with a full-employment equilibrium.

17. To prevent an unemployment equilibrium, in which the economy is stuck in recession, Keynesians argue that _____ _____ or the _____ must be increased. The multiplier will increase to the extent that people decrease their marginal propensity to save. Because savings represent a leakage out of the multiplier process, Keynesians emphasize the value of consumption. If people consume a greater fraction of their income, the multiplier increases and equilibrium occurs at a higher GDP.

18. How can the multiplier be increased or autonomous spending be stimulated? According to Keynes, when business conditions are bad, the private sector is unlikely to make it better! Because he doubted increases in private-sector spending, Keynes was a strong advocate of increasing government spending during _____.

19. Keynesian analysis also suggests that government can use tax cuts to stimulate the economy. However, Keynesians note that people might save some of their higher after-tax income rather than spend it all. In other words, the _____ multiplier—the expansionary effect of a tax cut or contractionary effect of a tax increase—would be less than the expenditure multiplier by the amount of the initial round of spending.
The tax multiplier formula is:
    Tax multiplier = − _____/(1−mpc)
and
    Change in taxes owed to government × tax multiplier = change in equilibrium GDP.

20. In this model, financing extra government spending with an identical increase in taxation would have an expansionary effect because the expenditure multiplier exceeds the tax multiplier. The **balanced-budget multiplier** combines the expenditure multiplier for an increase in government spending and the tax multiplier because taxes would increase to finance that spending. Adding these multipliers together gives a balanced budget multiplier, as follows:
Balanced budget multiplier = 1/(1−mpc) − mpc/(1−mpc) = (1−mpc)/(1−mpc) = ____
    and
Change in balanced-budget government spending × 1 = change in equilibrium GDP.

AGGREGATE EXPENDITURES 283

21. If government spending is financed by borrowing, the borrowing is likely to drive up interest rates and cause a _____ _____ effect, which means that less money will go to private-sector investments because it is going to finance government instead.

22. If we were to plot the expenditure equilibrium for each price level, the result would be the _____ _____ curve.

23. The tools of Keynesian economic analysis can help us understand the problems of recession and its meaner relative, depression. Consider a situation in which GDP starts far short of that needed for full employment. In order for the economy to produce full-employment GDP, the aggregate expenditure function must be shifted upward to intersect the 45-degree line at the higher level of GDP. Keynes called for government to make this shift happen by filling the _____ gap with extra _____ spending by government.

24. Even today, economists differ over the cause or causes of the Great Depression. The simplest explanation is that the stock market crash caused the aggregate expenditure function to shift downward as described above. However, economists are well aware of the dangers of the _____ ____ _____ in which an event is attributed to another event that preceded it. Just because one event occurs before a second one does not mean that the first event caused the second one.

25. Even years prior to its publication date in 1936, drafts of Keynes' *General Theory of Employment, Interest, and Money* circulated among policymakers. Keynes suggested that an economy ought to use government _____ spending to stimulate the economy and close any recessionary gap. A tax cut might achieve the same result, but with less certainty because taxpayers might save the money received from a tax cut rather than _____ it. Thus, the Keynesian remedies for unemployment can be summarized as "spend, spend, spend." Only government has deep enough pockets for that. Keynes recommended that the spending that governments use to fight off recessions should be balanced by a budget _____ during good economic times.

TRUE/FALSE/EXPLAIN
If false, explain why in the space provided.

1. Keynes chose to ignore long-run tendencies toward full employment.

2. The axes of the income-expenditure model show GDP and the price level.

3. The expenditure equilibrium occurs when total spending equals total consumption.

4. An expenditure equilibrium occurs at the intersection of the aggregate expenditure function and the 45-degree line.

5. Induced spending depends upon income.

6. When the economy is not at equilibrium, the difference between actual GDP and planned spending shows up in business inventories.

7. If production were to exceed the equilibrium GDP, inventories would be drawn down.

8. If the marginal propensity to save is 0.25, and government adds $1 million to autonomous spending, the expenditure equilibrium will rise by $0.75 million.

9. If the expenditure multiplier is 5, a $1,000 increase in autonomous spending will increase the expenditure equilibrium by $5,000.

10. If the marginal propensity to consume is 0.8 and government increases spending by $100 million, then the expenditure multiplier formula suggests that equilibrium GDP will increase by $500 million.

11. If the marginal propensity to consume is 0.8 and government increases taxes by $100 million, then the expenditure multiplier formula suggests that equilibrium GDP will increase by $400 million.

12. The formula for the expenditure multiplier assumes that the price level is constant.

13. Keynesian multiplier analysis assumes that higher tax rates reduce incentives to work or invest.

14. Keynes viewed extra government spending as more effective than tax cuts as a means to cure a recession.

15. In Keynesian analysis, the balanced budget multiplier equals zero.

16. According to the balanced budget multiplier, an increase in government spending of $100 million along with an increase in taxation of $100 million will increase GDP by $100 million.

17. Keynesian analysis encourages less saving and more consumption if the economy is at an unemployment equilibrium.

18. A higher price level shifts the aggregate expenditure function down and causes a movement up the aggregate demand curve.

19. If the aggregate expenditure function shifts in response to a change in something other than the price level, the aggregate demand curve will also shift.

20. The income-expenditure model underlies the idea that aggregate supply slopes upward in the short run.

286   CHAPTER 10

E&A 21.   Tax cuts in the 1920s fueled the demand for stocks, such as those of General Motors and General Electric.

22.   Within five years of the stock market crash on October 29, 1929, the economy had fully recovered.

23.   John Maynard Keynes called for government to increase autonomous spending so as to fill the recessionary gap in the 1930s.

24.   Keynes was pessimistic about the ability of government to help the economy through extra spending, because he thought that the multiplier effect would offset most of the good done by government spending.

25.   The Smoot-Hawley Tariff Act was instrumental in bringing the economy out of the Great Depression.

MULTIPLE CHOICE
Circle the letter preceding the one best answer.

1. Autonomous investment
   a. depends upon the amount of GDP.
   b. depends upon the amount of current sales.
   c. is independent of GDP.
   d. is another name for government investment.

2. In Multiple Choice Figure 1, autonomous spending is shown by arrow
   a. A.
   b. B.
   c. C.
   d. D.

3. In Multiple Choice Figure 1, induced spending is shown by arrow
   a. A.
   b. B.
   c. C.
   d. D.

4. In the income-expenditure graph, the 45-degree line represents
   a. intended spending.
   b. possible points of equilibrium.
   c. induced consumption.
   d. intended investment.

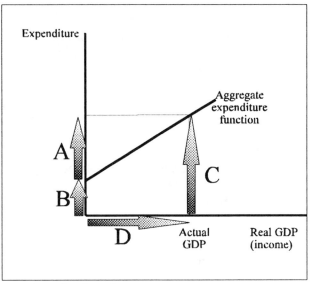

Multiple Choice Figure 1

5. Unintended depletion of inventories
   a. indicates that real output is likely to fall, as price increases drive away consumers.
   b. indicates that real output is likely to increase as firms seek to replenish those inventories.
   c. is unrelated to output, as inventories are preexisting, and thus not a part of current or future production.
   d. would be impossible in the Keynesian model, as intended and actual investment must always be equal.

6. In Multiple Choice Figure 2, the marginal propensity to consume is
   a. 1/4.
   b. 1/3.
   c. 1/2
   d. 2.

7. The sum of the marginal propensity to consume and the marginal propensity to save equals
   a. 0.
   b. 1.
   c. equilibrium GDP.
   d. no single specific number every time.

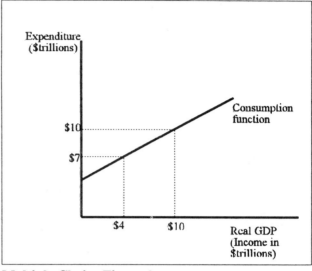
Multiple Choice Figure 2

8. The sequence of events shown in Multiple Choice Figure 3 represents
   a. closing a recessionary gap.
   b. closing an inflationary gap.
   c. achieving full-employment output.
   d. moving to an expenditure equilibrium.

9. Suppose the marginal propensity to consume is .75 and that the economy has unemployed resources. According to Keynesian multiplier analysis, an increase in autonomous spending of $1 billion would cause equilibrium GDP to rise by
   a. nothing at all.
   b. $1 billion.
   c. $1.333 billion.
   d. $4 billion.

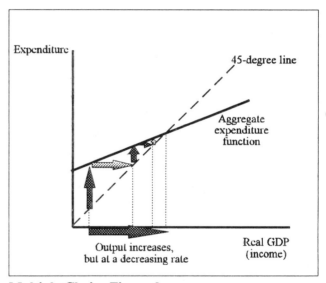
Multiple Choice Figure 3

10. Suppose that equilibrium national income is $1 million below full-employment national income. Suppose the marginal propensity to consume is 0.8. To achieve an equilibrium at full employment, autonomous expenditures would need to increase by a minimum of
   a. $5 million.
   b. $1 million.
   c. $800,000.
   d. $200,000.

11. The formula for the expenditure multiplier
   a. applies only when there are some idle, unemployed resources and the price level remains constant.
   b. implies that the price level rises as spending rises.
   c. indicates that the multiplier will be 5 if the marginal propensity to consume is 1/5.
   d. assumes full employment.

12. A balanced-budget multiplier equal to one implies that
   a. increasing both taxation and government spending by the same amount will have no effect upon the economy.
   b. increasing both taxation and government spending by the same amount will stimulate the economy by the amount of the spending increase, but no more.
   c. balancing the federal budget has no effect upon economic activity.
   d. balancing the federal budget will stimulate economic activity.

13. In Multiple Choice Figure 4, arrow A represents an increase in
   a. autonomous spending.
   b. induced spending.
   c. equilibrium GDP.
   d. full-employment GDP.

14. In Multiple Choice Figure 4, the multiplier effect of spending is best described by
   a. arrow A.
   b. point B.
   c. point C.
   d. arrow D.

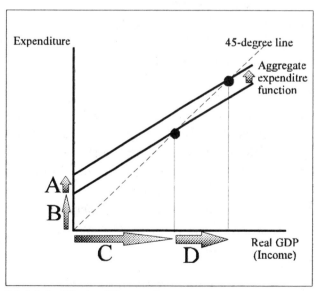

Multiple Choice Figure 4

15. In Multiple Choice Figure 5, arrow A represents the
    a. inflationary gap.
    b. recessionary gap.
    c. output gap.
    d. multiplier effect.

16. In Multiple Choice Figure 5, arrow B represents the
    a. inflationary gap.
    b. recessionary gap.
    c. output gap.
    d. multiplier effect.

17. If the economy is in the situation shown in Multiple Choice Figure 5, which of the following would be most likely to achieve a full-employment equilibrium?
    a. A tax increase.
    b. More government spending.
    c. Less government spending.
    d. Inflation.

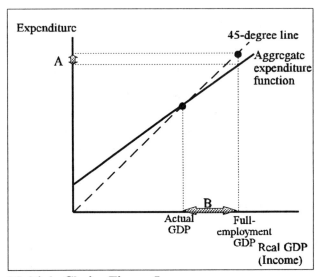
Multiple Choice Figure 5

18. The arrow shown in Multiple Choice Figure 6 is called the
    a. inflationary gap.
    b. recessionary gap.
    c. output gap.
    d. multiplier effect.

19. If the economy is in the situation shown in Multiple Choice Figure 6, which of the following would be most likely to achieve a full-employment equilibrium?
    a. A tax increase.
    b. More government spending.
    c. Less government spending.
    d. Inflation.

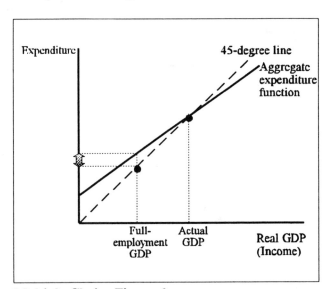
Multiple Choice Figure 6

20. In the income-expenditure graph, an increase in the price level will tend to
    a. increase aggregate expenditures.
    b. reduce aggregate expenditures.
    c. not change aggregate expenditures.
    d. have an unpredictable effect on aggregate expenditures.

E&A 21. The Revenue Act of 1926 legislated
a. tax increases.
b. tax cuts.
c. unemployment insurance.
d. Keynesian monetary policies.

22. A Keynesian remedy for the Great Depression was
a. tax cuts.
b. tax increases.
c. a balanced budget
d. extra autonomous spending by government.

23. The U.S. President who proposed a "New Deal" for the American people was
a. Abraham Lincoln.
b. Herbert Hoover.
c. Franklin D. Roosevelt.
d. Richard M. Nixon.

24. The Smoot-Hawley Act
a. aimed to increase stock prices.
b. made the federal government responsible for bad bank loans.
c. decreased trade between the U.S. and other countries.
d. provided soup kitchens for the poor.

25. Keynes view on deficit spending is that the government
a. should not fall into the trap of deficit spending.
b. should always run a budget deficit, no matter how well the economy performs.
c. should practice deficit spending during recessions.
d. the effects of deficit spending are too difficult to predict, leaving Keynes confused about his views on deficit spending.

GRASPING THE GRAPHS
Fill in each box with a concept that applies.

292 CHAPTER 10

Fill in the boxes to describe the income-expenditure model..

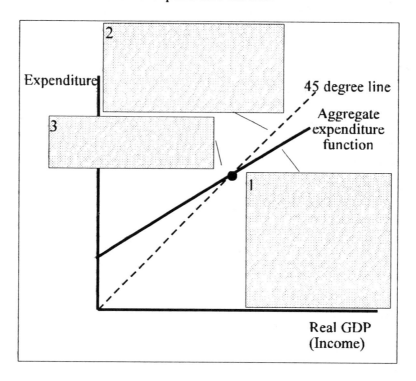

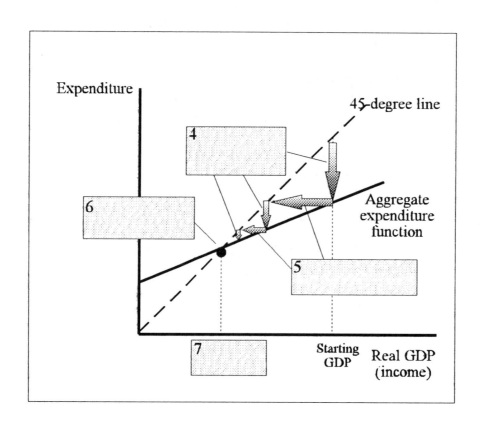

Aggregate Expenditures 293

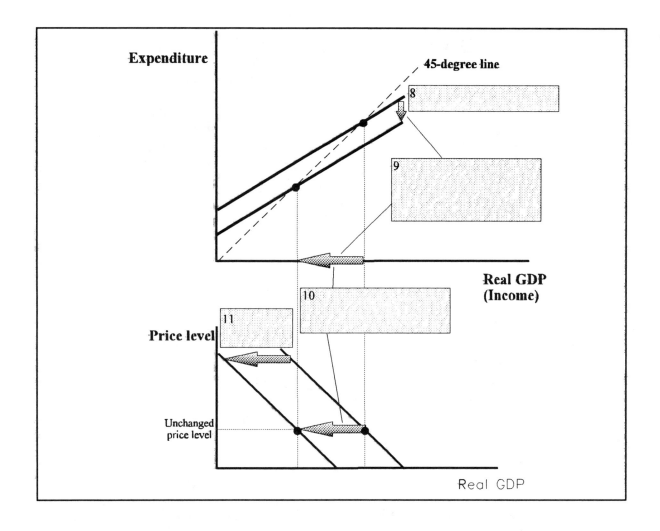

294 CHAPTER 10

E&A Fill in the boxes to describe Keynes' idea of how to end the Great Depression.

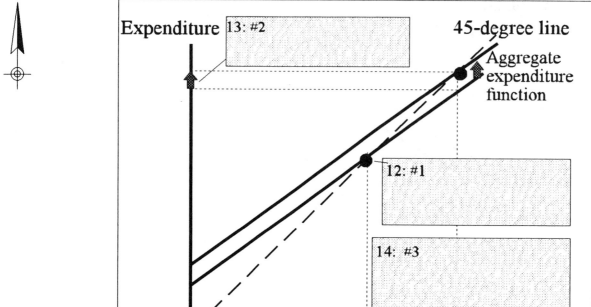

For additional practice in grasping this chapter's graphs, visit
http://www.prenhall.com/ayers and try *Smart Graph* 14,
along with *Active Graphs* 26, 27, an 28.

ANSWERS

STUDYCHECKS

1. See StudyCheck 1 Figure.

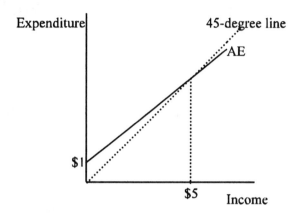

StudyCheck 1 Figure

2. See StudyCheck 2 Figure.

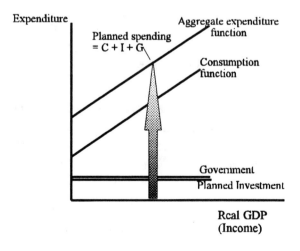

StudyCheck 2 Figure

3. The multiplier is 1/0.2, which equals 5. The question then becomes: What number, when multiplied by 5, gives a product of $100 billion? The answer is $100 billion divided by 5, which equals $20 billion.

4. Keynesian analysis focuses on the demand side of the economy. Keynesians suggest that the most effective policy to increase aggregate demand is to increase autonomous spending. An increase in autonomous spending, such as an increase in government spending, causes a multiplier effect as it leads to subsequent rounds of increased induced spending. Tax cuts also increase aggregate demand, although the multiplier effect is less.

5. See StudyCheck 5 Figure.

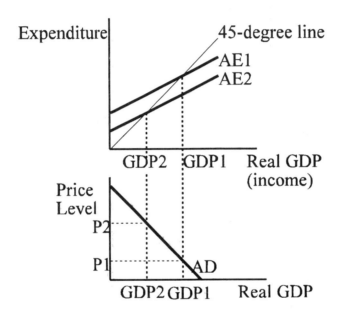

StudyCheck 5 Figure

6. The fallacy of causation is attributing causality to an event that precedes another event. Since the stock market crash occurred at the early in the recession that began in 1929, the market crash has been named as a cause of the depression. However, the Smoot-Hawley Act, the Revenue Act of 1926, and the Federal Reserve have also been cited as causes of the depression.

FILL IN THE BLANKS

1. Keynesian economics, classical economics
2. full employment, spending

3. aggregate national output, gross domestic product
4. aggregate expenditure
5. autonomous, induced
6. Aggregate expenditures, consumption
7. autonomous spending, marginal propensity to consume
8. marginal propensity to save, one
9. marginal propensity to consume
10. 45-degree line, planned, actual
11. unplanned
12. multiplier, leakage, autonomous spending
13. injection, unchanged
14. mps, constant
15. unemployment, output, recessionary, aggregate expenditure,
16. inflationary
17. autonomous spending, multiplier
18. recessions
19. tax, mpc
20. 1
21. crowding out
22. aggregate demand
23. recessionary, autonomous
24. fallacy of causation
25. deficit, spend, surplus

TRUE/FALSE/EXPLAIN

1. True.
2. False, the axes show real GDP (income) and expenditure.
3. False, the expenditure equilibrium occurs when planned expenditures equal actual GDP.
4. True.
5. True.
6. True.
7. False, inventories would build up.
8. False, the expenditure equilibrium would rise by $4 million.
9. True.
10. True.
11. False, equilibrium GDP would decrease by $400 million.
12. True.
13. False, Keynesian analysis ignores incentive effects.
14. True.
15. False, the balanced budget multiplier equals 1.

16. True.
17. True.
18. True.
19. True.
20. False, in contrast to the upward slope of the short-run aggregate supply curve, the income-expenditure model assumes that the price level will not change unless the economy exceeds full-employment GDP.
21. True.
22. False, the U.S. economy remain mired in the Great Depression throughout the 1930s.
23. True.
24. False, Keynes pointed to the multiplier effect as a way that the impact of government spending would be much larger than the spending itself.
25. False, the protectionist Smoot-Hawley tariff act probably made matters worse.

MULTIPLE CHOICE

1.	c	8.	d	15.	b	22.	d
2.	b	9.	d	16.	c	23.	c
3.	a	10.	d	17.	b	24.	c
4.	b	11.	a	18.	a	25.	c
5.	b	12.	b	19.	d		
6.	c	13.	a	20.	b		
7.	b	14.	d	21.	b		

GRASPING THE GRAPHS
Examples of correct answers

1. Shows how much the economy plans to spend that each possible GDP
2. Shows actual GDP
3. Expenditure equilibrium were planned GDP = actual GDP
4. Excess inventories
5. Output reductions
6. Expenditure equilibrium
7. Ending GDP
8. Aggregate expenditure function
9. A lower aggregate expenditure function reduces equilibrium GDP.
10. If the price level is constant, the result is a leftward shift in aggregate demand.
11. Aggregate demand
12. #1 The economy starts at an unemployment equilibrium.

13.   #2 Government increases spending to close the recessionary gap.
14.   #3 The multiplier effect leads to full-employment GDP.

**Visit the Ayers/Collinge companion Website at http://www.prenhall.com/ayers
for further activities and exercises for this chapter.**

Part 4

INCENTIVES FOR PRODUCTIVITY

Chapter 11

FISCAL POLICY IN ACTION

CHAPTER REVIEW

11.1 Policy in Practice

- Government spending in the U.S. encompasses a vast array of programs. Some of these programs go towards the purchase of goods and services, such as highways or national defense. Others are regulatory programs, such as conducted by the Occupational Safety and Health Administration or the Environmental Protection Agency. In addition, a large fraction of government spending goes towards **transfer payments** that redistribute income. Transfer payments include unemployment compensation, welfare, and other *safety-net programs* that provide economic security. Transfer payments account for approximately 44 percent of total federal spending.

- Because taxes take roughly 30 percent of gross domestic product (GDP), taxpayers are acutely concerned that they not be taken advantage of—that all pay their fair share. This is the goal of equity. Because taxes can discourage work effort and investment, a second goal in taxation is efficiency. To achieve efficiency, taxes which are intended to raise revenues should do so in a manner that affects our behavior the least. Efficiency in taxation gives citizens the greatest possible incentive to be productive.

- The personal income tax is the single largest revenue source for the U.S. federal government, providing 50 percent of all revenues. As U.S. citizens accumulate income over the course of the year, the federal personal income tax claims those earnings at incremental rates that increase from 10 percent to 15 percent, to 27 percent, to 30 percent, to 35 percent, and to 38.6. This incremental tax rate on incremental income is known as the **marginal tax rate**:
    Marginal tax rate = additional taxes owed as a percentage of additional income

- Note that the marginal tax rate differs from the *average tax rate*, which equals a person's total tax liability divided by total income at the end of the year. The amount of income withheld from your paycheck is based on your projected average tax liability.
    Average tax rate = total taxes owed as a percentage of total income

- Social Security taxes, inclusive of the hospitalization portion of *Medicare*—health insurance for the elderly—account for 35 percent of federal revenues, second only to the share of the personal income tax.

- The Social Security tax is a *payroll tax,* in which the government deducts a flat 7.65 percent from the amount of money the employer pays, plus another 7.65 percent from the amount of money the employee receives. Taken together, the Social Security tax collects 15.3 percent of a worker's payroll income, up to a maximum individual income of $84,900 in 2002, after which only the 2.9 percent Medicare hospitalization tax continues to be collected.

- The largest category of federal spending is on transfer payments. Other federal spending goes to purchase goods and services, pay the interest on the national debt, provide grant monies to state and local governments, and a variety of other government subsidy programs.

- The corporation income tax takes approximately 30 percent of corporate profits, and brought in revenues of $151.1 billion in 2001, equaling about 7.5 percent of total federal revenues. The corporation income tax has proven to be quite controversial over time because, while it may seem fair to tax corporations as though they are people, the **tax incidence** of the corporation income tax—meaning who ultimately winds up paying the tax—is on real people who directly or indirectly own the corporations.

- Most states rely heavily on a combination of individual income taxes, sales taxes, revenue from the federal government, and other charges. Major sources of revenue at the local level include property taxes and sales taxes. The Other category is very large because it includes many types of expenditures. Examples include libraries, hospitals, police protection, fire protection, and much more. States have to be careful not to tax any one source of revenue much more heavily than do other states, or that revenue source will migrate to the less-taxing state.

- When all the revenues received by all units of government are added together, the result is that government revenues in the USA are over 30 percent of the value of production. Another way of looking at this is that the average American must work until "Tax Freedom Day" each year—declared by the Tax Foundation to be April 27 as of 2002—in order to have enough money to pay the government.

- Taxes are used to redistribute income from the haves to the have-nots, and in the process remedy some of the inequities that arise in a free market economy. People's views on equity vary widely, however, which means that issues of equity in taxation—*tax equity*—become a matter of hot debate. Some basic principles can help frame this debate.

- The two most fundamental principles of tax equity are as follows:
    - The **benefit principle** states that a fair tax is one that taxes people in proportion to the benefits they receive when government spends the tax revenues.
    - The **ability-to-pay principle** states that those who can afford to pay more taxes than others should be required to do so.

- The gasoline tax would appear to satisfy the benefit principle of tax equity, because gasoline tax revenues are *earmarked* for—restricted to—highway construction and repair. In general, *user fees* are designed to meet the benefit principle of tax equity. The benefit principle cannot be applied to programs whose purpose is to redistribute income.

- To justify redistributional programs, a different principle of tax equity is invoked—the ability-to-pay principle. The idea of the ability-to-pay principle is that the more a person is able to pay, the more that person should pay.

- Many people interpret the ability-to-pay principle to mean that taxes designed for redistributing income should be progressive. A **progressive tax** collects a higher percentage of high incomes than of low incomes. In contrast, a **regressive tax** collects a higher percentage of low incomes than of high incomes. A **proportional tax** collects the same percentage of income, no matter what the income is. A *flat tax* that taxes all income at the same tax rate would be proportional. In practice, proposals for a so-called flat tax almost always provide for some exemptions that make the tax progressive overall.

StudyCheck 1
List two advantages and two disadvantages of replacing the U.S. personal income tax code with a flat tax.

- Economic efficiency involves getting the most valuable output from the inputs available. It bakes the biggest economic pie that is possible, given the economy's scarce resources. In general, taxes are efficient to the extent that they do not change our behavior, with the most efficient tax being the one we cannot influence or escape.

- To see how taxes cause inefficiency, consider an increase in the income tax. Some workers, especially those who are not heads of households, would cut back their work efforts. Even those who do not cut back would find that getting ahead in the workplace would bring less reward. For this reason, people are less likely to invest their time and money to acquire more human capital. Corporate income taxes mean that businesses also don't invest as much, either, because the corporation income tax cuts down on the return to that investment. For an efficient tax, we can turn to the *head tax*. In short, if you have a head, you pay the tax!

- Not only are tax laws written with an eye toward equity, but government spending is often meant to promote equity directly through provision of a social safety net. This safety net targets the needy with both cash transfers and **in-kind benefits**, which are any benefits other than money. Social Security is far and away the largest cash transfer program, redirecting a significant amount of current earnings to current retirees. The largest in-kind program is Medicaid, which provides health insurance for the impoverished.

- **A trade-off between efficiency and equity pervades our system of tax and spending programs.** Ideally, to provide a broad and generous safety net, government might guarantee good housing, good food, and good health insurance for everyone. The better the guarantees, however, the more the programs will cost and the less will be the incentives to work and invest.

- There are three reasons for this inefficient reduction in work incentives, as follows:
  - There is less need to better yourself to the extent that government guarantees you a comfortable lifestyle.
  - If you choose to forge ahead anyway, your greater ability to take care of yourself causes you to lose eligibility for many welfare-type programs.
  - Obtaining the money for safety net programs requires the government to either tax or borrow, which would need to be repaid with from future tax revenue. With taxes comes less incentive to work and invest.

- There is no ready answer to the dilemma of choosing between a generous safety net and incentives for economic productivity. This is an area of seemingly endless political debate and compromise. We don't want the income tax burden to be so high that our economy stagnates because we have little to gain personally by being productive. On the other hand, our economy can afford to provide some degree of economic security for those in need. Choices of this sort are why policymakers face what has been called *the big tradeoff* between efficiency and equity in the design of government tax and spending programs.

> **StudyCheck 2**
> Why is there a tradeoff between efficiency and equity in the design of tax policies and associated income redistribution?

11.2 Social Security

- Social Security collects taxes on all payroll income, and allots the proceeds for *OASDI* and *HI*, which stands for old age, survivors, and disability insurance, and hospitalization insurance, respectively. The hospitalization portion is more commonly known as Medicare. The combined employer and employee Social Security tax rate is 15.3 percent of the first $84,900 of that income in 2002, where the threshold has been adjusted upward over time in response to wage inflation. For income over that threshold, the Social Security tax is eliminated except for the 2.9 percent Medicare component. The rates have risen over time, as shown in Figure 11-4.

- Requiring the firm to pay Social Security taxes causes the equilibrium wage to be lower by exactly the amount of the tax. In effect, the tax burden has been *shifted* from employers to employees. The result is that workers effectively pay the full 15.3 percent Social Security tax. Many employees are unaware of the true magnitude of the Social Security tax, because only half of the combined 15.3 percent rate appears on their pay stubs.

StudyCheck 3
Explain why Social Security taxes are higher than most workers realize.

- Social Security is primarily **pay-as-you-go**, meaning that current workers pay for people who are currently retired. In this way, **Social Security redistributes income from one generation to another.**

- **Social Security also redistributes income within generations.** The ratio of payments to retirees relative to the amount they contributed in their working years is much higher for the low income than for the high income.

- On an after-tax basis, Social Security may even pay the retired low-income worker more than he or she earned when working. A worker at the maximum income subject to Social Security tax, in contrast, is likely to receive only about 30 percent as much as when employed. The upshot is that, when Social Security taxes and payments are combined, the Social Security system is highly progressive. Low-income workers have money redistributed their way from the tax dollars paid by higher-income workers. The redistribution from higher-income workers to lower-income workers is one reason participation in Social Security is required by law. If it were optional, workers with above-average incomes would quit, leaving no money to redistribute.

- There is a **Social Security trust fund,** which is the depository for Social Security tax revenues. The Trust Fund is currently building up because tax revenues exceed Social Security payouts. However, the size of that trust fund pales in comparison to the expected future demands against it. Moreover, all savings held in the Social Security trust fund take the form of special government bonds. Since a bond is merely a promise to pay in the future, savings within the Social Security trust fund are nothing more than government IOUs. To pay those IOUs, government must either create extra money or collect extra tax dollars in the future.

- Social Security also reduces private savings to the extent that people expect to receive Social Security checks in the future. Workers substitute government's promises for their own savings. Moreover, because the Social Security tax reduces take-home pay, current workers have less money that could be saved. The reduction in the national saving rate because of Social Security means there is less money for investment, and thus less economic growth.

- For the Social Security trust fund to represent real savings, it must generate real capital that will increase the country's production possibilities in years to come. This could come about either directly through investment in capital or indirectly through a paydown in other government debt.
- Rather than use the trust fund to pay down other government debt, the federal government might directly invest the Social Security trust fund in the production of real capital. It could take one of two routes:
    - **Government could produce the necessary capital itself.** Government production may be justified to the extent that the needed investment applies to the provision of public goods, such as highway infrastructure needed for smoothly flowing traffic. Beyond this, however, direct government investment would lead the economy in the direction of command and control.
    - **Government could invest the money in the marketplace, perhaps establishing or designating mutual funds to buy stock in private companies.**

  In either case, the danger is that the investments would move the economy toward inefficient central planning and be allocated to firms based on politics rather than economic merit.

- For the Social Security trust fund to be **fully funded**—able to pay off all its future obligations without recourse to future taxation—it would need to own well over a year's worth of GDP. In other words, the buildup of savings in the Social Security trust fund would need to greatly expand the country's current productive capacity for that savings to be real in a macroeconomic sense.

- Individuals do save for their own retirement. **Individual retirement accounts (IRAs)** promote that saving by allowing a limited amount of tax-free or tax-prepaid (for *Roth IRAs*) contributions. The limit in 2002 is $3,000, scheduled to rise to $4,000 in 2005. If government wants to promote private saving, its options include:
    - increasing or eliminating the contribution cap on IRAs.
    - eliminating the taxation of income that is saved.
    - requiring that individuals save some fraction of their earnings for their own retirement.

- The third option has led to proposals for **Personal Security Accounts**, which would be financed by a payroll tax but be under the individual's own control and ownership. **Personal Security Accounts could only supplement, not replace, Social Security as it now stands**, for three reasons:

- **Social Security depends on current workers to support current retirees.** With Personal Security Accounts, workers are saving to support themselves.
- **Social Security redistributes income from wealthier workers to poorer ones.** With Personal Security Accounts, workers keep their own savings.
- **Personal Security Accounts are riskier**, with workers making their own investment choices. They would still need a Social Security fallback in case their personal investment choices lose their value.

StudyCheck 4

Describe the notion of mandatory personal security accounts as a supplement to Social Security, differentiating it from the more general Social Security tax. List two advantages and one disadvantage to this approach.

11.3 Tax Reform

- A tax is efficient only if it does not *distort* relative prices within the economy, since price signals are what allocate resources to their highest-valued uses. By taxing all income equally, distortions are minimized. Efficiency thus calls for a *broadly based tax,* meaning one that it is difficult to escape, where the **tax base** refers to that which is taxed.

- **It is less disruptive to the workings of the economy to tax as wide a spectrum of income or consumption as possible at a low rate, rather than single out a few things for especially high rates of taxation.** By spreading taxes broadly, people have few ways to escape them and not as much incentive to try; inefficient changes in behavior are kept to a minimum. Much of the complexity of the current income tax code stems from innumerable provisions that remove income from taxation, thus narrowing the tax base.

- The ability-to-pay principle of equity suggests that some income should be taxed more than other income, depending on how needy the person is. Exempting low incomes concentrates the tax base and leads to inefficiencies. Thus, the personal income tax is a compromise between efficiency and equity. Unfortunately, the compromise accomplishes neither goal fully and is also complicated.

- **A comprehensive measure of income** would subtract a person's wealth at the beginning of the year from wealth at the end of the year, and then add back in the person's consumption during the course of that year. Consumption is added because it represents income that is spent. Government does not use this comprehensive measure of income in computing the amount of personal income taxes to collect. It would be too complicated and intrusive for government to attempt assessing how valuable each person's assets are at the end of each year.

- The result is that the tax code looks at only a subset of comprehensive income, that which is liquid. If people sell their illiquid assets, they obtain liquidity and are subject to taxation on their *realized capital gains*, the increase in the value of assets between when they were bought and when they were sold. Even here, however, there are exceptions.

- So-called *loopholes* include the various exemptions, deductions, exclusions, and credits that complicate the tax code. Despite their notoriety, there are often economic principles behind these **tax expenditures**, so termed because they sacrifice tax dollars. The basis of tax expenditures frequently revolves around equity. For example, the concepts of vertical equity and horizontal equity are two ways to judge whether a tax meets the ability-to-pay principle.

- **Vertical equity** concerns the proper tax burden for people of differing abilities to pay. It involves determining how *much* more someone with more ability to pay should in fact pay. That determination is not easy. For example, it seems vertically equitable for the top 10 percent of taxpayers ranked by income to pay more in federal taxes than any other percentile. However, is it vertically equitable to ask them to pay approximately twice as much as all other percentiles combined? That is in fact the situation in the U.S. when it comes to federal taxes. While the richest 10 percent might think it an undue burden for them to finance two-thirds of federal spending, the majority of voters do not appear to mind.

- **Horizontal equity**, which suggests that people with equal means should pay equal taxes, is more straightforward. Yet, even ignoring differences in wealth, equal monetary incomes do not imply an equal ability to pay. Differences in the abilities to pay of households with identical incomes explain why there are tax exemptions for children, deductions for major medical expenses, and other features of the tax code that attempt to compensate for facets of life that hit some people harder than others.

- There are many alternatives to the particular set of taxes chosen in the United States. For example, some have suggested that the United States should adjust its income tax to become a **consumed-income tax**, in which dollars that are saved would not be counted as income when the tax is applied. The consumed-income tax would remove the bias against saving that is present in a more general income tax, which taxes money when it is earned and also taxes interest on that money when it is saved. The flip side is that, although a consumed-income tax would promote saving, some people view it as a tax deduction for the rich and not for the poor, because the ability to save rises sharply with income.

- Most of us are familiar with state or local *sales taxes* that collect a percentage of the value of the sale for government. Sales taxes are one form of **consumption tax,** which takes money as you spend it rather than as you earn it. This tax gives people a greater incentive to save, and may be partly responsible for the higher saving rates in other countries relative to the United States. Most countries of the world, including Canada and countries of Europe and the Far East, rely much more heavily on consumption taxes as a source of public revenues than does the United States.

- The most common form of consumption tax in other countries is the **value-added tax (VAT).** A VAT collects the difference between what companies earn in revenues and what they pay out in previously taxed costs, which would mostly be the cost of material inputs. For example, the wheat farmer would pay a tax on the difference between revenues from the sale of the crop and the costs of fertilizer and other materials used to grow it. Taxing value-added yields the same tax revenues as a retail sales tax set at the same rate, since the price of a final product is nothing more than the sum of the values added.

11.4 Paying for Homeland Security

- Who is to pay for security measures? One possibility is to use general tax revenues, such as the $28 billion of financing budgeted in 2002 for the Office for Homeland Security. Another possibility is to levy taxes on specific industries for which the federal government provides security. For example, air travelers are assessed a surcharge to help defray the expenses of federally provided airport security. That approach is in keeping with the benefit principle of taxation, in which the beneficiaries of government spending are the ones who pay the taxes. A third possibility is that industries facing terrorist threats are themselves held responsible for security, with any costs merely absorbed by the companies or passed along to their customers.

- To the extent that heightened concerns over security cause companies to increase spending on security, supply shifts to the left and the quantity of air travel increases. Alternatively, the federal government could give airlines *subsidies,* in which government picks up some of the cost of providing security.

- Comparing the alternative approaches requires us to specify our goals. The two most fundamental goals in economics are efficiency and equity, both of which might come into play in considering the best policy. Meeting the goal of the efficiency requires that each good be produced only up to the point for which its marginal benefit equals its marginal cost. As discussed in chapter 4, the market accomplishes this mission to the extent that the intersection of demand and supply is also the intersection of marginal benefit and marginal cost. However, if the costs of necessary security measures are paid for by government subsidies, the market supply will no longer represent the complete marginal cost. Instead, the output will be greater than the efficient quantity and the price will be lower than the price that achieves efficiency.

- When government gets directly involved in providing security, such as with screening mail for anthrax or checking airline passengers for weapons, the same principles of market pricing apply here as well. With the mail, screening costs are reflected in the postage we pay. With airline security, there is a user charge of $2.50 added to each passenger's ticket. Both of these practices are consistent with market efficiency.

- Government action and taxation cannot replace the marketplace in one element of efficiency, however. In particular, the government lacks competition to insure that its actions are technologically efficient. Possible inefficiencies represent a cost of government actions, not a definitive reason against taking those actions.

- The upshot of this discussion is that when government does take action, efficiency suggests that it should tailor its practices as closely as possible to those of the marketplace. Rather than just using general tax revenues to provide government services, the implementation of user fees tailors price adjustments from industry to industry to match the costs of increased security in the various industries.

- Politics does not always ensure that user charges are assessed in the right amount or even assessed at all. In that case, distortions can occur in the pattern of economic activity away from what is efficient. In particular, if the costs to government of providing security are not reimbursed by user fees, the result is a subsidy to the industries government is protecting. This subsidy comes from general tax revenue, which reduces the amount of income that customers, who are also taxpayers, have to spend throughout the rest of the economy. When incomes are reduced by the taxes that pay for security, the demand for many goods and services will decrease, such as shown in Figure 11-9. For those industries, output is reduced.

312   CHAPTER 11

- The myriad of new security measures to safeguard against terrorism have costs that cannot be avoided. Whether it be taxpayers or customers, someone will pay. Economic analysis can provide guidance to policymakers on how to design taxes in an efficient manner. Whether policymakers follow this advice is of course up to them.

StudyCheck 5
Which approach to paying for homeland security embodies the benefits approach to taxation. Explain.

FILL IN THE BLANKS

1. A large fraction of government spending goes towards _____ _____ that redistribute income to the needy. These include unemployment compensation, welfare, and other *safety-net programs* that provide economic security, and account for approximately 44 percent of total federal spending.

2. Because taxes take roughly 30 percent of gross domestic product (GDP), taxpayers are acutely concerned that they not be taken advantage of—that all pay their fair share. This is the goal of _____. Because taxes can discourage work effort and investment, a second goal in taxation is _____.

3. The _____ _____ tax is the single largest revenue source for the U.S. federal government, providing 50 percent of all revenues. As U.S. citizens accumulate income over the course of the year, the federal personal income tax claims those earnings at incremental rates that increase from 10 percent to 15 percent, to 27 percent, to 30 percent, to 35 percent, and to 38.6. This incremental tax rate on incremental income is known as the _____ _____ _____, which equals 27 percent for most American taxpayers.

FISCAL POLICY IN ACTION   313

4. Note that the marginal tax rate differs from the _____ _____ _____ , which equals a person's total tax liability divided by total income at the end of the year. The amount of income withheld from your paycheck is based on your projected average tax liability.

5. _____ _____ taxes, inclusive of the hospitalization portion of Medicare—health insurance for the elderly—account for 35 percent of federal revenues, second only to the share of the personal income tax. The Social Security tax is a _____ _____ , in which the government deducts a flat 7.65 percent from the amount of money the employer pays, plus another 7.65 percent from the amount of money the employee receives. Taken together, the Social Security tax collects 15.3 percent of a worker's payroll income, up to a maximum individual income of $84,900 in 2002, after which only the 2.9 percent Medicare hospitalization tax continues to be collected.

6. The corporation income tax takes approximately 30 percent of corporate profits, and brought in revenues of $151.1 billion in 2001, equaling about 7.5 percent of total federal revenues. The corporation income tax has proven to be quite controversial over time because, while it may seem fair to tax corporations as though they are people, the _____ _____ of the corporation income tax—meaning who ultimately winds up paying the tax—is on real people who directly or indirectly own the corporations.

7. When all the revenues received by all units of government are added together, the result is that government revenues in the USA are over _____ percent of the value of production. Another way of looking at this is that the average American must work until "Tax Freedom Day" each year—declared by the Tax Foundation to be April 27 as of 2002—in order to have enough money to pay the government.

8. The two most fundamental principles of tax equity are as follows:
   - The _____ _____ states that a fair tax is one that taxes people in proportion to the benefits they receive when government spends the tax revenues.
   - The _____-___-_____ _____ states that those who can afford to pay more taxes than others should be required to do so.

9. The gasoline tax would appear to satisfy the benefit principle of tax equity, because gasoline tax revenues are _____ for—restricted to—highway construction and repair. In general, _____ fees are designed to meet the benefit principle of tax equity. The benefit principle cannot be applied to programs whose purpose is to redistribute income. To justify redistributional programs, a different principle of tax equity is invoked—the ability-to-pay principle.

10. Many people interpret the ability-to-pay principle to mean that taxes designed for redistributing income should be progressive. A _____ tax collects a higher percentage of high incomes than of low incomes. In contrast, a _____ tax collects

a higher percentage of low incomes than of high incomes. A _____ tax collects the same percentage of income, no matter what the income is. A flat tax that taxes all income at the same tax rate would be proportional.

11. Economic _____ involves getting the most valuable output from the inputs available. It bakes the biggest economic pie. In general, taxes are efficient to the extent that they do not change our behavior, with the most efficient tax being the one we cannot influence or escape. For an efficient tax, we can turn to the _____ tax. In short, if you have a head, you pay the tax! While efficient, the head tax satisfies neither the benefit principle nor the ability-to-pay principle of equity.

12. Not only are tax laws written with an eye toward equity, but government spending is often meant to promote equity directly through provision of a social safety net. This safety net targets the needy with both cash transfers and ____-_____ benefits, which are any benefits other than money.

13. A trade-off between _____ and _____ pervades our system of tax and spending programs.

14. Requiring the firm to pay Social Security taxes causes the equilibrium wage to be lower by exactly the amount of the tax. In effect, the tax burden has been _____ from employers to employees. The result is that workers effectively pay the full 15.3 percent Social Security tax. Many employees are unaware of the true magnitude of the Social Security tax, because only half of the combined 15.3 percent rate appears on their pay stubs.

15. Social Security is primarily _____-____-_____-____, meaning that current workers pay for people who are currently retired. In this way, Social Security redistributes income from one generation to another. Social Security also redistributes income within generations. The ratio of payments to retirees relative to the amount they contributed in their working years is much higher for the low income than for the high income.

16. There is a Social Security _____ _____, which is the depository for Social Security tax revenues. Currently, tax revenues exceed Social Security payouts. However, the size of that trust fund pales in comparison to the expected future demands against it. Moreover, all savings held in the Social Security trust fund take the form of special government bonds. Since a bond is merely a promise to pay in the future, savings within the Social Security trust fund are nothing more than government IOUs. To pay those IOUs, government must either create extra money or collect extra tax dollars in the future. Either way, future taxpayers pay. For the Social Security trust fund to be fully funded—able to pay off all its future obligations without recourse to future taxation—it would need to own well over a year's worth of GDP. In other words, the buildup of savings in the Social Security trust fund would need to greatly expand the country's current productive capacity for that savings to be _____ in a macroeconomic sense.

17. Individuals do save for their own retirement. _____ _____ _____ (IRAs) promote that saving by allowing a limited amount of tax-free or tax-prepaid contributions. The third option has led to proposals for _____ _____ _____, which would be financed by a payroll tax but be under the individual's own control and ownership.

18. A tax is _____ only if it does not *distort* relative prices within the economy, since price signals are what allocate resources to their highest-valued uses. By taxing all income equally, distortions are minimized. Efficiency thus calls for a _____ _____ tax, meaning one that it is difficult to escape. The _____ _____ refers to that which is taxed.

19. Even the concept of income is not altogether easy to pin down, since income is more than money. For example, if you drill a water well in your backyard and inadvertently strike oil, your wealth spikes upward. That change in wealth is income, even if you do not sell any of that newly discovered oil until next year or beyond. A _____ _____ of income would subtract a person's wealth at the beginning of the year from wealth at the end of the year, and then add back in the person's consumption during the course of that year.

20. So-called loopholes include the various exemptions, deductions, exclusions, and credits that complicate the tax code. Despite their notoriety, there are often economic principles behind these _____ _____, so termed because they sacrifice tax dollars. The basis of tax expenditures frequently revolves around equity. For example, the concepts of vertical equity and horizontal equity are two ways to judge whether a tax meets the ability-to-pay principle.

21. _____ equity concerns the proper tax burden for people of differing abilities to pay. It involves determining how much more someone with more ability to pay should in fact pay. _____ equity suggests that people with equal means should pay equal taxes.

22. There are many alternatives to the particular set of taxes chosen in the United States. For example, some have suggested that the United States should adjust its income tax to become a _____ _____ tax, in which dollars that are saved would not be counted as income when the tax is applied.

23. Most of us are familiar with state or local *sales taxes* that collect a percentage of the value of the sale for government. Sales taxes are one form of _____ tax, which takes money as you spend it rather than as you earn it. This tax gives people a greater incentive to save, and may be partly responsible for the higher saving rates in other countries relative to the United States. The most common form of consumption tax in other countries is the _____ _____ tax (VAT). A VAT collects the difference between what

companies earn in revenues and what they pay out in previously taxed costs, which would mostly be the cost of material inputs.

24. Air travelers are assessed a surcharge to help defray the expenses of federally provided airport security. That approach is in keeping with the _____ principle of taxation. Alternatively, the federal government could give airlines _____, in which government picks up some of the cost of providing security.

25. Comparing the alternative approaches requires us to specify our goals. The two most fundamental goals in economics are _____ and _____, both of which might come into play in considering the best policy. Government action and taxation cannot replace the marketplace in one element of efficiency, however. In particular, the government lacks _____ to insure that its actions are technologically efficient.

TRUE/FALSE/EXPLAIN
If false, explain why in the space provided.

1. The Social Security tax accounts for a little over one third of federal tax revenue and the personal income tax accounts for most of the rest.

2. Corporation income taxes account for about one-fourth of the revenues collected by the federal government.

3. Tax exporting is more commonly known as foreign aid.

4. Efficiency requires that companies be taxed at the same rate as individuals.

5. Government programs that are designed to redistribute income from the rich to the poor are usually justified on the basis of the ability-to-pay principle of taxation.

6. The U.S. personal income tax is equitable according to the benefit principle of taxation.

7. The personal income tax in the United States is progressive.

8. If your income increases from $10,000 to $30,000, and your tax payments increase from $2,000 to $4000, the tax is regressive.

9. If a rich person pays more taxes than a poor person, the tax system must be progressive.

10. Workers in effect pay the employer portion of the Social Security tax, and often do not know it.

11. When taxes paid by the employer and employee are combined, the Social Security tax collects about 5 percent of payroll income, up to a maximum income of about $100,000.

12. The Social Security Trust Fund has enough savings built up to last for approximately fifteen years.

13. Social Security redistributes income both within and between generations.

14. The idea of personal security accounts is to require workers to save for their own retirement, but leave control of those savings in the workers own hands rather than in the hands of the Social Security administration.

15. When Social Security taxes and payments are combined, the Social Security system is highly progressive.

16. One reason for the appeal of the flat tax is that it is transparent.

17. A flat tax would be regressive.

18. A comprehensive measure of income would add the value of a person's consumption to the change in that person's net worth.

19. Value added taxes and sales taxes are both consumption taxes.

20. Narrowing the tax base increases the efficiency of taxation.

E&A 21. Assessing air travelers a surcharge to help pay for the expenses of federally provided airport security is in keeping with the benefit principle of taxation.

22. To the extent that heightened concerns over security cause companies to increase spending on security, demand in the affected industry shifts to the left.

23. Meeting the goal of equity requires that each good be produced only up to the point for which its marginal benefit equals its marginal cost.

24. If the costs of necessary security measures are paid for by government subsidies, the market supply will not represent the complete marginal cost.

25. Government subsidies to particular industries can be expected to increase the amount of income taxpayers have available to spend throughout the rest of the economy.

MULTIPLE CHOICE
Circle the letter that corresponds to the one best answer.

1. Taxes take roughly _____ percent of GDP in the United States.
   a. 10
   b. 30
   c. 50
   d. 75

2. The two largest revenue sources for the federal government are the personal income tax and
   a. the corporate income tax.
   b. the Social Security tax.
   c. sales taxes.
   d. tariffs.

3. The marginal income tax rate for most Americans is about
   a. 15 percent.
   b. 27 percent.
   c. 40 percent.
   d. 52 percent.

4. From an economic standpoint, the Social Security payroll tax rate is
   a. 10 percent, after all exemptions, exclusions, and deductions are accounted for.
   b. 7.65 percent.
   c. 15.3 percent, of which only half appears on the worker's pay stub.
   d. zero percent, because workers get it all back.

5. The goal of tax equity is to see that
   a. everyone pays a fair share of taxes.
   b. taxes do not harm the incentive to produce.
   c. taxes are collected efficiently.
   d. government benefits are distributed efficiently.

6. Of the following, the most efficient tax would be the
   a. corporate income tax.
   b. personal income tax.
   c. sales tax.
   d. head tax.

7. In general, _____ suggests that taxes should be designed to raise revenues in ways that have the fewest effects on people's behavior.
   a. static scoring
   b. equity
   c. efficiency
   d. dynamic scoring

8. The benefit principle of taxation is most likely to justify the
   a. personal income tax.
   b. corporate income tax.
   c. tax on cigarettes.
   d. tax on gasoline.

9. If income increases from $10,000 to $20,000, and tax on that income increases from $5,000 to $7,000, the tax system would be termed
   a. progressive.
   b. proportional.
   c. regressive.
   d. flat.

10. If a person's income rises and the tax system is regressive, the amount of money a person pays in taxes
    a. will rise.
    b. will fall.
    c. will stay the same.
    d. may rise, fall, or stay the same, but will definitely fall as a percentage of income.

11. Which of the following is NOT a reason that income redistribution reduces the incentive to work and invest?
    a. Taxes decrease a person's return (payoff) from work and investment.
    b. Eligibility for Medicaid or other redistributional programs is available only to the poor.
    c. The social "safety net" makes it easier to live without working or investing.
    d. People work and invest in order to feel good about themselves.

12. Which of the following does NOT explain why participation in the Social Security System is mandated by law?
    a. Social Security redistributes income from wealthier taxpayers to poorer taxpayers.
    b. Social Security relies primarily on a pay-as-you-go method of financing.
    c. Most current workers could expect a better return on their Social Security contributions if they invested their money themselves.
    d. The Social Security Administration has been plagued by scandal and corruption.

13. The pay-as-you-go nature of Social Security _____ national savings.
    a. increases
    b. decreases
    c. does not affect
    d. eliminates the need for

14. Which of the following is NOT a problem in converting Social Security financing from pay-as-you-go to fully funded?
    a. Current workers would face double taxation.
    b. There would be less ability to redistribute income within a generation.
    c. Social Security investments are in government bonds.
    d. Future taxpayers would be forced to pay higher payroll taxes.

15. A comprehensive measure of income is
    a. the same as the "adjusted gross income" line reported by all taxpayers to the Internal Revenue Service.
    b. the increase in the value of assets between when they were bought and when they were sold.
    c. what the government would use to calculate deductions and exemptions under a flat tax.
    d. the change in a person's wealth from the beginning of the year to the end of the year, plus consumption spending during that year.

16. Which of the following is the best example of a tax expenditure?
    a. Building a new interstate highway.
    b. Deducting charitable contributions from income before taxes are assessed.
    c. The Medicaid program, in which medical services are offered only to the poor.
    d. Social Security payments to the elderly.

17. A totally flat tax would
    a. apply the same tax rate to all income, without exception.
    b. bring in the exact same amount of revenue from each taxpayer.
    c. be equivalent to a poll tax.
    d. provide people with no incentive to work or invest.

18. Which of the following is a form of consumption tax?
    a. Sales tax.
    b. Income tax.
    c. Property tax.
    d. Social Security tax.

19. So-called loopholes represent
    a. tax expenditures.
    b. consumed income.
    c. had taxes.
    d. a comprehensive measure of income.

20. To achieve the efficiency, value added taxes and sales taxes should be
    a. horizontally equitable.
    b. vertically equitable.
    c. progressive.
    d. broadly based.

21. If a federal government gives airlines subsidies in order to increase security, that means that the government
    a. holds airlines financially responsible for passengers' security.
    b. picks up some of the cost of providing security.
    c. places a tax on airplane tickets.
    d. restrict competition from foreign airlines.

22. If the costs of necessary security measures in an industry are paid for by government subsidies, then the market supply curve in that industry will no longer represent the complete
    a. marginal cost.
    b. marginal benefit.
    c. total cost.
    d. total benefit.

23. Inefficiencies can arise when the government takes direct responsibility for security services, because the government
    a. is too big.
    b. does not pay enough.
    c. lacks competition.
    d. does not have enough money.

24. The hidden cost of government subsidies to selected industries is
    a. that those subsidies never appear in the government budget.
    b. the decrease in after-tax consumer income available to be spent on other industries' products.
    c. the higher wages that are likely to result in those industries.
    d. the inequities that inevitably accompany taxation.

25. Rather than using general tax revenues to finance security measures, it is likely to be more efficient for government to use
   a. the Armed Forces.
   b. the power of persuasion.
   c. user fees that vary from industry to industry.
   d. money from the Social Security trust fund.

GRASPING THE GRAPHS
Fill in each box with a concept that applies.

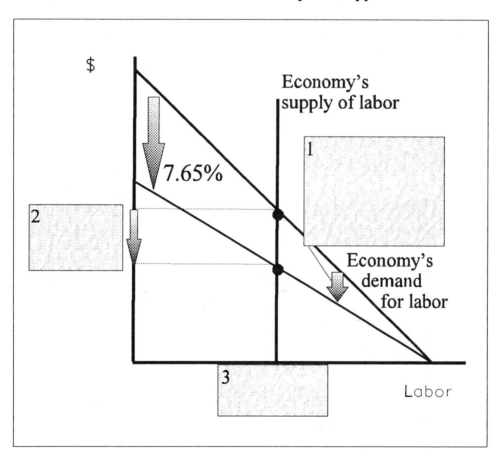

324 CHAPTER 11

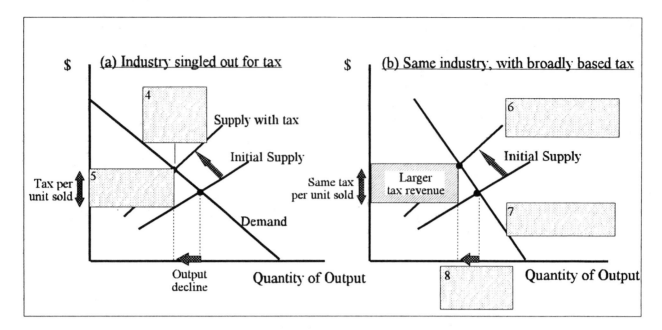

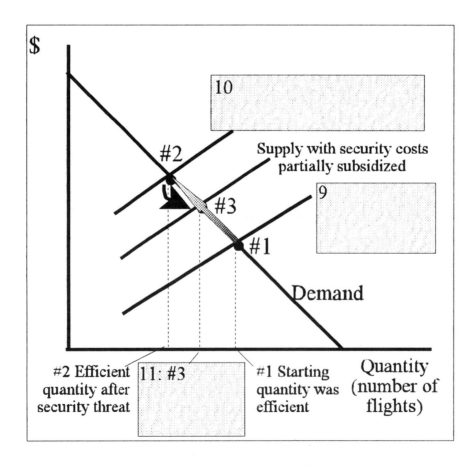

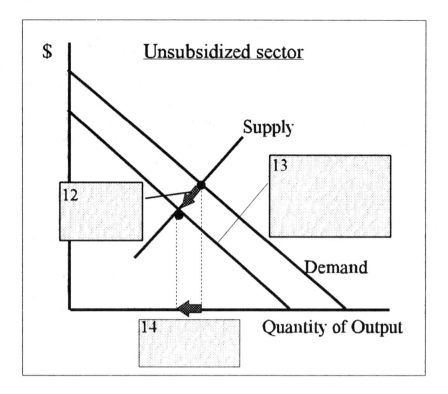

ANSWERS

STUDYCHECKS

1. One advantage is lower transaction costs. Another is that the marginal tax rate would be lower, which would promote investment and growth. One disadvantage is that ignoring differences in personal situations in the use of income could violate the principle of horizontal equity. Another is that the government would have less ability to promote its social and economic agenda through the tax system.

2. The answer revolves around incentives. The combination of taxation and income redistribution illustrates that there is usually a tradeoff between efficiency and equity. The more generous is income redistribution, the more fair it may seem to the recipients, but the more taxes are required to pay for it. Both the safety net that supports those who do not work and the taxes upon those who do work serve to reduce the incentives for citizens to acquire human capital and to be productive workers.

3. Social Security taxes are higher than most people recognize, because they are split evenly between the employer and employee, with only the latter half appearing on pay stubs.

326 CHAPTER 11

However, from an economic standpoint, the employer and employee portions should be added together, yielding a combined rate of 15.3 percent.

4. Personal security accounts would be financed by a mandatory tax similar to the Social Security tax. The difference is that, whereas a worker's Social Security tax payment goes to fund current retirees, the payments into a personal security account would be kept under the control of the worker and would go to finance that worker's own retirement. One advantage would be less need to modify Social Security later to prevent its insolvency. Another advantage is that it would increase real economic saving and investment. A disadvantage is that the worker would be paying twice, once to finance his or her own retirement and once to finance current retirees.

5. When airline travelers are charged for security measures, such as with a ticket surcharge, the benefit principle of taxation is satisfied. Passenger ticket surcharges are an example of the benefit principle because the people who receive the benefits are paying for them, rather than spreading the costs to others.

FILL IN THE BLANKS

1. transfer payments
2. equity
3. personal income, marginal tax rate
4. average tax rate
5. Social Security, payroll tax
6. tax incidence
7. 30
8. benefit principle, ability-to-pay principle
9. earmarked, user
10. progressive, regressive, proportional
11. efficiency, head
12. in-kind
13. efficiency, equity
14. shifted
15. pay-as-you-go
16. trust fund, real
17. Individual retirement accounts, personal security accounts
18. efficient, broadly based, tax base
19. comprehensive measure
20. tax expenditures
21. Vertical, Horizontal
22. consumed-income

23. consumption value-added
24. benefit, subsidies
25. equity, efficiency, competition

TRUE/FALSE/EXPLAIN

1. True.
2. False, the Corporation income tax accounts for less than 10 percent of federal revenue.
3. False, tax exporting it is when tax revenues are collected from nonresidents, such as from visitors paying taxes on their motel rooms.
4. False, taxing companies at the same rate as individuals would be double taxing the individuals who own the companies.
5. True.
6. False, the benefit principle would not allow for income redistribution.
7. True.
8. True.
9. False, the tax system is progressive only if the percentage taken from the rich person is greater than a percentage taken from the poor person.
10. True.
11. False, the combined tax rate is 15.3 percent, and the maximum is somewhat over $80,000.
12. False, the Social Security trust fund has enough savings to last only a couple of years.
13. True.
14. True.
15. True.
16. True.
17. False, a truly flat tax that did not exempt any income would be proportional.
18. True.
19. True.
20. False, broadening the tax base increases the efficiency of taxation.
21. True.
22. False, supply would shift to the left.
23. True.
24. True.
25. False, consumers would have less income remaining after taxes, which would decrease their purchases in other sectors of the economy.

MULTIPLE CHOICE

1.	b	8.	d	15.	d	22.	a
2.	b	9.	c	16.	b	23.	c
3.	b	10.	d	17.	a	24.	b
4.	c	11.	d	18.	a	25.	c
5.	a	12.	d	19.	a		
6.	d	13.	b	20.	d		
7.	c	14.	d	21.	b		

GRASPING THE GRAPHS
Examples of correct answers

1. Because they must pay taxes, firms are less willing to pay wages.
2. Lower wage rate
3. Full employment
4. Equilibrium with tax
5. Tax revenue
6. Supply with tax
7. Steeper demand
8. Smaller output decline
9. Supply without security costs or with full subsidy
10. Supply with security costs and without subsidies
11. Actual quantity with security costs partly subsidized
12. Change in market equilibrium
13. Reduced demand resulting from reduced after-tax incomes
14. Reduced output in unsubsidized industry

**Visit the Ayers/Collinge companion Website at http://www.prenhall.com/ayers
for further activities and exercises for this chapter.**

Chapter 12

ECONOMIC GROWTH

CHAPTER REVIEW

- Government tax and spending policies could change incentives, such as incentives to work, to save, and to acquire physical capital and human capital. In turn, these changes affect **economic growth**, which is usually measured by the change in GDP over time. (Sometimes a GNP measure is used, instead.) If the growth is in per-capita GDP, a country can look forward to a better standard of living for its people.

12.1 The Seeds of Growth

- Countries around the world exhibit significant differences in their standards of living and growth rates.

- Looking at high-growth countries shows a common factor that accounts for their rapid growth—a significant role for the marketplace. However, even countries that assign markets a significant role have variations in their growth rates and variations in the specific ways in which government influences their economies. Digging deeper into the data can reveal both the features of the economy that are important to growth and how government policies can influence the incentives for the development of those features.

- From 1947 to 1973, the average GDP growth rate averaged around 4 percent. GDP growth diminished in the 1970's to under 3 percent by the time of the Carter administration. GDP growth picked up steam a couple years into the Reagan administration, resulting in an annual growth rate average for Reagan's eight years of 3.5 percent. It then stumbled again to less than two percent in the following four years under George Bush. Growth was picking up in the final months of the first Bush administration to average a bit under four percent in the eight years of the Clinton administration. Shortly before Clinton left office and growth slowed, falling into negative territory in the recession that took hold in President George W. Bush's first year in office.

- While growth is stated above in terms of presidential administrations, growth is not directed from top down. It is also sometimes hard to know what the economy's growth rate is at any given point in time, because it takes time to compile the data used to report GDP. This lag can have political repercussions. For example, following the election of President Bill Clinton in 1992, it was widely speculated that President Bush would have instead been re-elected if only voters had recognized the then-occurring economic recovery just a little sooner.

- Most U.S. economic growth is attributable to increases in labor and capital, and to technological change. Both technological change and additional capital increase **labor productivity**, output per hour worked. Although there is still some question as to why U.S. economic growth began turning upward in the mid-1990s, many analysts believe that technological change, embodied in the personal computer and the Internet, played a significant role. In turn, technological change increased labor productivity.

- Labor productivity does not necessarily increase each year. Why does the growth rate in productivity decrease in some years, and even fall in others? One important factor is economic slowdowns. When the economy slows down, or enters a recession, labor productivity tends to fall at first. That is because businesses decrease the production of goods and services in response to reduced aggregate demand, but try to retain their workers in order to avoid the costs of recruiting and training new workers when aggregate demand picks back up. Thus, less production combined with the same amount of labor must decrease labor productivity. Later, when a recession nears its end, production is at first increased without a corresponding increase in labor employed. Thus, labor productivity rises at that point in the business cycle.

- Labor productivity is associated with how much capital—both physical capital and human capital—labor has at its disposal. The labor productivity statistics suggest correctly that the United States has been quite successful at accumulating capital. The creation of new capital is termed **capital formation.** Capital formation requires initiative, since to produce capital requires that people identify what additional outputs need to be produced or technologies employed. In market economies, entrepreneurs make these choices based on their best judgements of what is most profitable, meaning of most value to both consumers and producers. The struggle for profit weeds out entrepreneurs who do not make these choices well. Thus, one of the keys to capital formation is to allow this competitive search for profit. Where central planning is practiced, that key is lost. Thus, in Cuba, North Korea, and other economies in which government exercises too heavy a hand, the quantity and quality of capital formation is impaired.

- Capital formation requires investment. Investment can be coordinated centrally, through government. For example, government ordinarily finances the construction of highways, because it would be very difficult for private investors to acquire rights of way or to charge for highway usage. Indeed, rebuilding highways, especially bridges on the U.S. interstate highway system, is thought to be one of the major investment needs in the United States today.

- More typically, investment is a decentralized process that responds to supply and demand in the marketplace. Investors finance the capital formation that is necessary to take advantage of market opportunities. For example, investors who expect to profit from the sale of gum balls, livestock feeders, big-screen televisions, or any other product must first finance the capital necessary to produce that product. Firms invest when they wish to do any of the following:
    - expand their scale of operations;
    - implement better production techniques;
    - produce new goods that their old factories are ill-suited to manufacture.

- **To acquire human capital, individuals invest in themselves.** This investment includes the time and money it takes to attend college or otherwise acquire new skills.

- Private investors have a strong personal incentive to invest wisely. Because their own resources are on the line, private investors can be relied on to investigate closely which products are likely to succeed and which are not. While no one can foresee the future with certainty, investors who judge the best are rewarded in the marketplace with additional funds for further investment.

- Central to understanding the process of capital formation is the observation that **saving provides the funding for investment.** In general, the more saving, the more investment. Sometimes people invest their savings themselves, such as when they buy houses or stocks. Other times, savers deposit their money into financial intermediaries, such as banks and mutual funds, which are then responsible for investing that money.

- Savers look to invest for good returns without excessive risk. Without aiming to do so, **government reduces private saving and investment.** This reduction happens in two ways. First, **government taxes away income that might be saved.** Second, **government taxes the returns on investments**, thus making them less attractive. In contrast, **government also adds to investment** to the extent that it directly invests the tax revenues it receives. The government investment in highways is an example. So, too, are government investments in schools, the criminal justice system, and elsewhere in the economy. In turn, these investments are used in the private sector.

- Without government, aggregate saving and investment would be equal. This equality would be true because money saved would either be directly invested or would find its way into investment through banks and other financial institutions. With government, the situation is more complicated because tax dollars can be directed toward government investment or government consumption. Thus, the total amount saved plus the total amount taken in taxes must equal the sum of private investment, government investment, and government spending on consumption items. Lumping together private and government investment, and simply calling the sum investment, we have the following equality: Investment + government consumption = saving + taxation or, equivalently, Investment = saving + taxation −

- government consumption. Some investment funds also come from abroad and, likewise, some saving becomes investment in other countries.

- Investment is a current expense that is made in the expectation of receiving income in the future. When firms borrow to finance new investment, the expected future income must be sufficient to pay off the amount borrowed, plus interest. How much interest depends upon the interest rate. **Higher real interest rates raise the cost of investing.** Some investments that would be undertaken at low real interest rates will not be undertaken when those rates are high. This result causes the investment demand curve to slope downward.

- The money for investment comes from saving. While people will save some money no matter if they are paid interest or not, the higher the interest rate, the greater will be the quantity supplied of saving. For this reason, the supply of saving curve is shown as upwardly sloping. There is only one point of equilibrium, which determines the actual interest rate. The market equilibrium equates the quantity of saving supplied to the quantity of investment demanded.

- In addition to being affected by the interest rate, investment is also affected by such other factors as business confidence, which encompasses expectations about the future, current economic growth, and opportunities presented by technological change. Increases in any of these variables would shift the investment demand curve to the right. Decreases would shift it to the left.

- Government fiscal policy—changes in taxes or government spending—can also shift investment demand. An expansionary fiscal policy can stymie the capital formation needed for economic growth. Specifically, when government increases spending or cuts taxes in order to stimulate the economy, it often finances the difference with borrowing. It borrows by selling government bonds to investors.

- **Government borrowing is in competition with private-sector borrowing, and thus can cause higher interest rates.** The resulting reduction in private investment spending is called the **crowding-out effect** of expansionary fiscal policy. In other words, the crowding-out effect represents money that would have gone to private-sector investment, but instead goes to finance government borrowing. However, because so much goes on at once in the macro economy, it is difficult to interpret from investment data whether and to what extent the crowding-out effect actually occurs.

> **StudyCheck 1**
> List three government actions that reduce the incentive to save, and explain in each case why this is so.

12.2 Influencing Growth through Public Policy

- The world's economies represent a mix of markets and government, with government actions holding the potential to either help or hinder economic growth. To understand the likely effects of public policy requires, first, an understanding of the incentives facing prospective investors. The key elements are risk and return.

- Private investors do not know with certainty which products will sell and which will not. They accept some risk of failure, in the hopes of getting a return that compensates for that risk. There is always risk ex ante, meaning before the outcome is known. Investors assess the **expected return**—the value of the investment if successful, multiplied by the probability of success. The **actual return** can be viewed ex post, meaning after the fact. Ex post, an investment might have turned out fabulously, or it might have failed miserably.

- In addition to regulation, taxes also can affect growth. The U. S. federal government relies on the personal income tax for the bulk of its revenues. This tax takes a fraction of an individual's income. If the taxpayer uses the remaining income to buy goods and services, no additional income tax is collected from that person. However, if the taxpayer saves some of the remaining income, the government comes back to tax the interest or other return on that saving. The result is that the personal income tax discourages saving by taxing saved income twice—one when it is earned and again when it is put aside for saving instead of used for current consumption. This tax has the effect of discouraging investment by increasing the market interest rate.

- A tax on saving increases the market interest rate and discourages investment. Savers face a lower return because of the tax, which causes them to be willing to save less at each real interest rate. For this reason, taxing the return to saving shifts the supply of saving curve to the left, resulting in a higher equilibrium interest rate and less saving and investment. In this way, taxation of the return on saving discourages both saving and investment.

- Because saving is so important to economic growth, there is concern over the low *personal saving rate* in the U.S. in recent years. In 2000 and 2001 the personal saving rate plunged to lows not seen since the Great Depression. The low personal saving rate provided one of the arguments for cutting income taxes in 2001.

- Investment is also discouraged by other taxes, such as the tax on capital gains. **Capital gains** represent the difference between the current market value of an investment and its purchase price. The **capital gains tax** takes a percentage of this difference when the investment is sold. Because investors know about the capital gains tax when making investment decisions, it too diminishes capital formation. The reduction in investment demand means that banks pay lower interest rates on savings. Likewise, individuals who invest directly in stocks or anything else subject to capital gains taxation also see their expected returns reduced. The upshot is that the capital gains tax leads to less saving and investment.

- Even without the inhibiting effects of taxes and regulations, the private sector may not devote an efficient amount of financial capital toward increasing future productivity. This shortfall occurs when there are external benefits from investment in research and development). An **external benefit** occurs when some benefits are received by third parties who are not directly involved in the decision to research or invest. In effect, these third parties siphon off benefits that would otherwise have gone to the firms undertaking the R&D. This reduces the expected benefit to investors, and is thus likely to reduce the amount of resources they devote to R&D.

- While often lumped together, there is a significant distinction between research and development. **Research** is aimed at creating new products or otherwise expanding the frontiers of knowledge and technology. **Development** occurs when that technology is embodied into capital or output. For example, research may be aimed at uncovering a superconducting material that allows electricity to flow unimpeded at ordinary temperatures. If the research is successful, many companies could then incorporate the advance in knowledge to design their own products, such as transmission lines, electromagnets, or computers.

- External benefits are most prominent at the research stage, especially when the research involves creation of knowledge that can be applied to the production of many different products, as in the example just given. It is difficult for any one investor or group of investors to assert ownership—**property rights**—over the range of applications from basic advances in knowledge. For this reason, given that the odds of achieving a significant knowledge breakthrough are quite small, private investors usually avoid investments in basic research.

- To correct this market failure, and perhaps as a counterweight to the general distortion against investment in the federal taxes, government subsidizes research. Sometimes government funds research directly, such as cancer research at the National Institutes of Health. Sometimes subsidies are indirect, such as public support of universities that require faculty to conduct research along with their teaching. There is controversy over how generous these subsidies should be, however, since the diffusion of knowledge throughout the economy makes measuring the value of basic research practically impossible.

- Much more controversy exists when government subsidizes development. For example, the U.S. Department of Energy funded a variety of alternative energy demonstration projects after the dramatic rise in world oil prices in 1973. However, most of the investments in windmills, solar energy, shale oil, and other forms of alternative energy were never commercially viable. Even gasoline blended with ethanol (alcohol made from corn) survives in the marketplace only because of ongoing government subsidies.

- Such investments are development rather than basic research. Development by one firm does give other firms ideas about what will be successful and what will not, and thus involves external benefits. However, this situation holds true for airline services, fast-food locations, new toys, and a host of other goods and services offered in the marketplace—competitors learn from each others' successes and mistakes. Such minor external benefits pervade any market economy. It would be inefficient to single out some and not others.

StudyCheck 2

Explain how government promotes research and development, and why it is more likely to subsidize research than development.

12.3 Property Rights and the New Growth Theory

- The prospect for business profits in the future can lead to research and development in the present. While not new in itself, that idea is a cornerstone of what is called **new growth theory**. New growth theory stresses the association between productivity growth over time and technological advances that are embodied in new capital.

- According to new growth theory, the ideas behind new technologies are promoted most effectively by allowing individuals to claim property rights, and the associated monopoly power, over ideas they have. The excess profit associated with monopoly power provides the incentive to create ever better ways of doing things. The idea that private property is the key to growth, however, is far from new.

- New growth theory contrasts with mainstream prescriptions for growth in the decades following the Great Depression of the 1930s and World War II. The viewpoint at that time was that government is the centerpiece of economic development. This view of growth was consistent with the high degree of confidence in government that characterized that period in history. For example, the American public works projects and World War II itself were seen as instrumental to moving the economy from the ravages of depression to decades of peace and prosperity. Aid to Europe under the Marshall plan was also credited with getting that continent back on its feet.

- Confidence in the ability of government to direct the economy along a pathway of growth rose in the 1930s with the New Deal, and peaked during the period from the 1950s through the early 1970s. Although new in contrast to the prevailing economic wisdom of that period, new growth theory actually taps into themes that have been central to economic analysis for centuries. For example, private property is central to Adam Smith's idea of the invisible hand of the marketplace, discussed in chapter 1, which gives entrepreneurs an incentive to invest and grow the economy in their search for profit. Likewise, private property and the unfettered freedom to use it form a central theme of the *Austrian school* of economic thought, which got its start with the writings of Ludwig von Mises in the early twentieth century. Von Mises emphasized that government rules and regulations that restrict the use of private property impede progress, which "is precisely that which the rules and regulations did not foresee."

12.4 Supply-Side Policy

- Economists are generally well aware of the importance of growth. Those economists who particularly emphasize policies aimed at growth are called **supply-side economists**, or **supply siders** for short. Supply siders focus on increasing the value of what the economy can produce in the long run (the supply side), rather than on any desire to change consumers' spending behavior (the demand side). Supply-siders figure that the short-run business cycle will sort itself out over time, and will lead to a larger economic pie in the long run if government does not intrude. This long-run, free-market orientation places supply siders squarely within the classical school of economic thought.

- **The objective of supply-side policy is to ensure that the output associated with full employment is as high as possible.** Supply-side policies are designed to increase productivity, such as through increasing capital formation. The intended effect of such policies is to shift long-run aggregate supply to the right.

- **Full-employment output will change in response to changes in *structural features of the economy*, including resources and technology. Structural features also include government policies that change how workers and firms behave.** Examples include unemployment compensation, minimum-wage laws, and other public policies that affect the natural rate of unemployment.

- **Supply siders are concerned with any government policies that might cut productivity** or lead to structural unemployment. They look with suspicion at the work disincentives embedded in many safety-net programs, and at regulations that make it more costly for firms to hire and fire employees. They emphasize that regulations should be designed with an eye toward minimizing their impact on productivity. However, supply siders are most known for their focus on tax policies.

- Supply siders recommend keeping marginal tax rates low in order to leave a higher fraction of incremental earnings in the hands of individuals and investors. In this way, there is more incentive to invest and be productive. The result is a higher full-employment output. The reason is partly that there will be more work effort provided at the full-employment equilibrium in response to greater marginal rewards for that effort. Mostly, however, output will be greater because investors will have greater incentives to build up the economy's stock of physical and human capital, and thereby increase the productivity of its labor.

- Because the concern of the supply siders is with the long run, they have little use for activist fiscal policies designed for short-run goals. Supply siders often see an expansionary fiscal policy as an excuse for a greater government presence in the economy, and worry about the increased regulatory and tax burdens that presence may bring.

- Following the election of President Ronald Reagan, the U.S. Congress passed sweeping changes in the tax code. The 1982 tax changes adopted the supply-side agenda of cutting marginal tax rates in order to promote growth. Such growth was intended to provide greater prosperity in the future, as well as a greater tax base over time. Beginning in 1983, after the tax cuts took effect, and lasting through the end of that decade, the economy witnessed real economic growth every year along with an inflation rate that was much lower than in the preceding decade.

- Because Congress did not curtail spending in line with its tax cuts, the federal government ran a large budget deficit in the 1980s. The budget deficit exceeded 6 percent of GDP in 1983, although it fell to just under 3 percent by 1989. The Reagan-era budget deficits look like fiscal policy run amok, with the fiscal stimulus of a tax cut applied to marginal tax rates at the high end of the income spectrum, rather than to rates paid by those struggling to make a good life for themselves. **Critics thus refer to supply-side policies as *trickle-down economics.*** The term seems to suggest that the policies were intended to make the rich richer, so that they might spend a bit more and help the rest of us. In fact, that was not the process that the supply siders had in mind. Supply siders aim at productivity, not spending.

- The U.S. economy grew in the 1980s after the tax cuts. The rich did indeed get disproportionately richer, at least in terms of the income they reported to the IRS. They also became more productive and paid more taxes. While the tax cuts of the 1980s reduced real federal tax revenues from most groups in the economy, the tax cuts greatly increased tax revenues from the highest income groups. The top 5 percent of income earners increased their share of total income tax payments from 36 percent in 1980 to 43 percent in 1990. Upward mobility also became more commonplace as a result of the lower tax rates. Looking at the lowest fifth of the income distribution in 1980, for example, 86 percent had advanced beyond that by 1988, with 16 percent even making it all the way to the top fifth of the income distribution.

StudyCheck 3
Describe the goals of supply-side economics and the policy means to accomplish these goals. Why do some people criticize supply-side economics as sacrificing equity for the sake of growth?

E&A 12.5 The New Economy—Is it Real?

- American prosperity seemed strong and enduring in the 1990s. The vitality of the economic boom indicated that the economy had changed in some fundamental way. The media needed a catch phrase that would describe what was happening and help define the decade for posterity. In this way, America's economy became the "new economy." Today, the question is whether the new economy is still alive, or ever was.

- The new economy is about high tech and its promise to revolutionize everyday life. How much about the new economy is ballyhoo? Consider that new economy centerpiece, the Internet. Over half of U.S. households are connected, and their number is growing fast. The Internet provides access to information and entertainment, and allows people to communicate instantly with each other. For buyers and sellers the Internet provides opportunities to meet in cyberspace to transact business, which can reduce transaction costs and make the economy more efficient. The problems and failures associated with the Internet are often glossed over, however, when these benefits are raised in conversation.

- The Internet bubble, exemplified by a host of other failed online firms, began to deflate near the end of the longest economic expansion in U.S. history. The upswing in the economy began in the early 1990s and ended with the recession that started in March 2001. Some economists began to question whether the new economy was dead, or even whether it ever existed at all. Let's try to answer their questions, using the framework of macroeconomics.

- The three macro goals of high growth, high employment, and low inflation all fell into place for the U.S. during the Presidency of William Jefferson Clinton (1993-2001). Economists will study this era for years to come, seeking to establish with certainty all the factors that accounted for the nation's superior economic performance. Economist Alan Greenspan, Chairman of the Federal Reserve at the time, commented that the economy has been revitalized by fundamental changes in the 1990s. Behold technology.

- The new economy is characterized by the application of technology to increase business productivity. The growth of computers in the workplace increases the productivity of labor. More productive labor means incomes rise in the long run. Furthermore, increased productivity is the closest thing to a "magic bullet" for the economy. Increased productivity can translate into meeting the three macro goals. Strong productivity growth can keep the economy growing, keep workers employed, and act as a brake on inflation.

- Before we discuss how productivity growth can strengthen the economy, let's examine U.S. productivity. Cheaper and easier to use technology was provided to workers throughout the economy in the 1990s, allowing workers to become more efficient. Output per worker increased and the *per-unit cost* of production dropped. Businesses increased production in response.

- The table below tracks economic performance for three separate time periods: 1979 to 1990, 1990 to 1995, and 1995 to 2000. Row (1) shows the acceleration in the growth rate of labor productivity between 1995 and 2000 relative to the earlier years in the table. In the 1995 to 2000 time period, each year American workers produced 2.7 percent more output per hour worked than in the previous year. Compared to the earlier periods, labor productivity roared ahead in the mid-to-late 1990s.

Sources of Changes in United States Labor Productivity, 1979-2000

Item	1979 to 1990	1990 to 1995	1995 to 2000
(1) Output per hour (labor productivity)	1.6	1.5	2.7
(2) Contribution of capital	0.8	0.5	1.1
(2a) Contribution of information technology capital	0.5	0.4	0.9
(2b) Contribution of other capital	0.3	0.1	0.2
(3) Contribution of labor	.03	0.4	0.3
(4) Contribution of technological change and other factors	0.5	0.6	1.4

- Rows (2) through (4) in the preceding table explain the sources of growth in labor productivity: increases in capital, labor, and technological change. Row (2a) shows that additions to information technology capital, computers, fax machines, and so forth, contributed significantly to soaring labor productivity in the 1995 to 2000 period. The same is true of technological change, as shown in row (4). The data in this table allow us to separate the hoopla about the new economy from the substance. What we see is that something fundamental did indeed change in the mid 1990s. Technological change, especially as it related to increases in information technology capital such as computers, contributed mightily to the burst in labor productivity, which in turn contributed mightily to the nation's increased prosperity.

ECONOMIC GROWTH   341

StudyCheck 4
Describe what happened to labor productivity between 1995 and 2000, and why.

FILL IN THE BLANKS

1. Government tax and spending policies could change incentives, such as incentives to work, to save, and to acquire human capital. In turn, these changes affect economic growth, which is usually measured by the change in _____ _____ _____ over time.

2. The U.S. economy has probably been studied more extensively than that of any other country. Evidence from the United States reveals quite a bit about what factors are important to growth. The United States has a history of _____ real GDP.

3. Most U.S. economic growth is attributable to increases in labor and capital, and to technological change. Both technological change and additional capital increase _____ _____, output per hour worked. Although there is still some question as to why U.S. economic growth began turning upward in the mid-1990s, many analysts believe that technological change, embodied in the personal computer and the Internet, played a significant role. In turn, technological change increased labor productivity.

4. The table makes clear that labor productivity does not necessarily increase each year. Why does the growth rate in productivity decrease in some years, and even fall in others? One

important factor is economic slowdowns. Labor productivity is associated with how much _____ labor has at its disposal.

5. The labor productivity statistics suggest correctly that the United States has been quite successful at accumulating capital. The creation of new capital is termed capital _____.

6. Capital formation requires _____. To acquire _____ capital, individuals invest in themselves. This investment includes the time and money it takes to attend college or otherwise acquire new skills. Central to understanding the process of capital formation is the observation that _____ provide the funding for investment.

7. Without aiming to do so, government reduces private saving and investment. This reduction happens in two ways. First, government _____ away income that might be saved. Second, government _____ the returns on investments, thus making them less attractive. In contrast, government also adds to investment to the extent that it directly invests the tax revenues it receives.

8. Without government, aggregate _____ and _____ would be equal. This equality would be true because money saved would either be directly invested or would find its way into investment through banks and other financial institutions.

9. With government, the situation is more complicated because tax dollars can be directed toward government investment or government consumption. Thus, the total amount saved plus the total amount taken in taxes must equal the sum of private investment, government investment, and government spending on consumption items. Lumping together private and government investment, and simply calling the sum investment, we have the following equality: Investment + government consumption = saving + taxation or, equivalently, _____ = saving + taxation − government consumption.

10. Higher real interest rates raise the cost of investing. Some investments that would be undertaken at low real interest rates will not be undertaken when those rates are high. This result causes the investment demand curve to slope _____.

11. The money for investment comes from saving. While people will save some money no matter if they are paid interest or not, the higher is the interest rate, the greater will be the quantity of saving supplied. For this reason, the supply of saving curve is shown as _____ sloping. There is only one point of equilibrium, which determines the actual interest rate. The market equilibrium _____ the quantity of saving supplied to the quantity of investment demanded.

12. Government borrowing is in competition with private-sector borrowing, and thus can cause higher interest rates. The resulting reduction in private investment spending is called the _____-_____ effect of expansionary fiscal policy.

13. The tax on saving increases the market interest rate and discourages investment. Savers face a lower return because of the tax, which causes them to be willing to save less at each real interest rate. For this reason, taxing the return to saving shifts the supply of saving curve to the _____, resulting in a _____ equilibrium interest rate and less saving and investment. In this way, taxation of the return on saving discourages both saving and investment.

14. Investment is also discouraged by other taxes, such as the tax on capital gains. Capital gains represent the difference between the current market value of an investment and its _____ _____. The capital gains tax takes a percentage of this difference when the investment is sold. Because investors know about the capital gains tax when making investment decisions, it too diminishes capital formation.

15. An _____ _____ occurs when some benefits are received by third parties who are not directly involved in the decision to research or invest. In effect, these third parties siphon off benefits that would otherwise have gone to the firms undertaking the R&D. This reduces the expected benefit to investors, and is thus likely to reduce the amount of resources they devote to R&D. While often lumped together, there is a significant distinction between research and development. _____ is aimed at creating new products or otherwise expanding the frontiers of knowledge and technology. _____ occurs when that technology is embodied into capital or output. External benefits are most prominent at the _____ stage. It is difficult for any one investor or group of investors to assert ownership—_____ _____—over the range of applications from basic advances in knowledge. To correct this market failure, and perhaps as a counterweight to the general distortion against investment in the federal taxes, government _____ research.

16. The prospect for business profits in the future can lead to research and development in the present. While not new in itself, that idea is a cornerstone of what is called _____ _____, which stresses the association between productivity growth over time and technological advances that are embodied in new capital.

17. Economists are generally well aware of the importance of growth. Those economists who particularly emphasize policies aimed at growth are called supply-side economists, or supply siders for short. The objective of supply-side policy is to ensure that the output associated with full employment is as high as possible. Supply-side policies are designed to increase productivity, such as through increasing capital formation. The intended effect of such policies is to shift long-run aggregate supply to the _____.

18. Supply siders recommend keeping marginal tax rates _____ in order to leave a higher fraction of incremental earnings in the hands of individuals and investors. In this way, there is more incentive to invest and be productive. The result is a higher full-employment output.

The reason is partly that there will be more work effort provided at the full-employment equilibrium in response to greater marginal rewards for that effort. Mostly, however, output will be greater because investors will have greater incentives to build up the economy's stock of physical and human capital, and thereby increase the productivity of its labor.

19. Because the concern of the supply siders is with the long run, they have little use for activist fiscal policies designed for short-run goals. Supply siders often see an expansionary fiscal policy as an excuse for a greater government presence in the economy, and worry about the increased regulatory and tax burdens that presence may bring. Following the election of President Ronald Reagan, the U.S. Congress passed sweeping changes in the tax code. The 1982 tax changes adopted the supply-side agenda of cutting marginal tax rates in order to promote growth. Because Congress did not curtail spending in line with its tax cuts, the federal government ran a large budget _____ in the 1980s.

20. Critics refer to supply-side policies as _____-_____ economics. The term seems to suggest that the policies were intended to make the rich richer, so that they might spend a bit more and help the rest of us. In fact, that was not the process that the supply siders had in mind. Supply siders aim at productivity, not spending.

21. While the tax cuts of the 1980s reduced real federal tax revenues from most groups in the economy, the tax cuts greatly _____ tax revenues from the highest income groups.

E&A 22. The three macro goals of high_____, high_____, and low_____ all fell into place for the U.S. during the Presidency of William Jefferson Clinton (1993-2001). Economists will study this era for years to come, seeking to establish with certainty all the factors that accounted for the nation's superior economic performance. Economist Alan Greenspan, Chairman of the Federal Reserve at the time, has commented that the economy has been revitalized by fundamental changes in the 1990s. Behold technology.

23. The new economy is characterized by the application of _____ to increase business productivity.

24. In the 1995 to 2000 time period, each year American workers produced _____ percent more output per hour worked than in the previous year. Compared to earlier periods examined, labor productivity _____ in the mid-to-late 1990s.

25. The sources of growth in labor productivity are: increases in _____, _____, and _____ _____.

TRUE/FALSE/EXPLAIN
If false, explain why in the space provided.

1. Economic growth is usually measured as a change in real GDP over time.

2. An increase in capital increases labor productivity.

3. A country's labor productivity is primarily related to its culture.

4. To acquire human capital, individuals invest in themselves.

5. Higher real interest rates lower the cost of investing.

6. When the real interest rates drop, firms invest more and consumer save less.

7. Without government, the amount saved and the amount invested would be equal.

8. Saving plus investment equals taxation plus government spending.

9. Actual investment equals the replacement of depreciated capital, plus capital formation, plus inventory changes.

10. Most investment comes from government.

11. The crowding-out effect represents money that would have gone to private-sector investment, but instead goes to finance government borrowing.

12. If prices on pharmaceutical drugs are controlled to allow the producer to cover manufacturing expenses plus a slight profit, the marketplace will ensure an efficient amount of investment into new products.

13. Government taxes the return on saving in order to bring in extra revenue.

14. A tax on interest income lowers the amounts of both saving and investment.

15. The capital gains tax discourages investment because it takes away some of the expected return on that investment.

16. It is usually more efficient for government to subsidize development rather than subsidize basic research.

17. New growth theorists emphasize the importance of lower tax rates so that full-employment output will increase over time.

18. The objective of supply-side policy is to ensure that full employment is associated with the greatest possible amount of output.

19. Supply-side economists favor increasing government spending in order to generate more profits for business and thus help the economy grow.

ECONOMIC GROWTH 347

20. The term "trickle-down economics" accurately captures the essence of supply-side tax policies, which is that lowering the tax rate on the rich will cause them to spend more and thus help the economy as their spending trickles down to workers.

E&A 21. The so-called new economy refers to the renewed tendency for people around the world to cut back on their consumption in favor of saving for retirement.

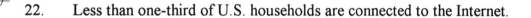

22. Less than one-third of U.S. households are connected to the Internet.

23. The three macro goals of high growth, high employment, and low inflation all fell into place for the United States during the presidency of Bill Clinton.

24. When cheaper and easier-to-use technology was provided to workers in the 1990s, the evidence shows that the workers became less productive.

25. In the late 1990s, the new economy was filled with hype, speculation, and excess.

MULTIPLE CHOICE
Circle the letter preceding the one best answer.

1. The labor productivity growth rate in the United States has
   a. been positive, but dropping off in recent years.
   b. increased dramatically in recent years.
   c. not changed in the last two centuries, with the exception of minor cyclical variations.
   d. been steadily negative since the industrial revolution.

2. Most economic growth can be accounted for by
   a. technological change and increases in labor and capital.
   b. expansionary fiscal policy.
   c. increases in the money supply.
   d. contractionary fiscal policy.

3. Creation of new capital is termed
   a. a capital construct.
   b. a capital idea.
   c. capital formation.
   d. capitalizing.

4. Typically, funds for investment come from
   a. government.
   b. the trade deficit.
   c. saving.
   d. corporate profits.

5. Aggregate investment equals
   a. saving + all government spending.
   b. taxation + all government spending.
   c. saving + taxation − government consumption.
   d. saving − taxation + government spending for investment.

6. Without government or foreign commerce, the amount saved is about the same as the amount
   a. invested.
   b. consumed.
   c. taxed.
   d. earned.

7. The investment demand curve illustrates how the amount of investment depends on the
   a. price of capital, such as plants and equipment.
   b. nominal interest rate.
   c. real interest rate.
   d. inflation rate.

8. The investment demand curve would shift in response to each of the following, EXCEPT
   a. business confidence.
   b. a change in the interest rate.
   c. current economic growth.
   d. opportunities presented by technological change.

9. When the crowding-out effect occurs,

a. foreign investors replace domestic investors in the market for borrowed funds.
b. younger workers replace older workers who are "crowded out" of the job market.
c. firms choose to raise money in the bond market instead of the stock market.
d. less saving is channeled into investment, and more is channeled into government.

10. The interest rate equilibrium occurs at the intersection of
    a. investment demand and saving demand.
    b. investment supply and saving supply.
    c. investment supply and saving demand.
    d. investment demand and saving supply.

11. The tax on interest income and capital gains has the effect of _____ interest rates and _____ investment.
    a. increasing; increasing
    b. increasing; decreasing
    c. decreasing; increasing
    d. decreasing; decreasing

12. The difference between the revenue received when an investment is sold and its purchase price is called
    a. value added.
    b. a realized capital gain.
    c. marginal revenue.
    d. the crowding-out effect.

13. The capital gains tax is likely to
    a. increase investment, because the tax revenues are earmarked for research subsidies.
    b. decrease investment, because the tax reduces the expected return on that investment.
    c. increase saving, because more saving is needed in order to pay the tax.
    d. increase saving, because investment alternatives are less attractive.

14. Government subsidies for basic research can be economically justified on the grounds that basic research
    a. redistributes income to the poor.
    b. provides external benefits, but less than would development.
    c. provides external benefits, more than would development.
    d. would otherwise be monopolized by the private sector.

15. New growth theory highlights the association between

350 CHAPTER 12

    a. labor and income.
    b. labor and leisure.
    c. productivity growth and technological advance.
    d. privatization and economic growth.

16. Technological advance would shift the economy's
    a. long-run aggregate supply curve to the left.
    b. long-run aggregate supply curve to the right.
    c. aggregate demand curve to the left.
    d. aggregate demand curve to the right.

17. Supply-side economics focuses upon
    a. providing incentives for economic growth (baking a bigger economic pie).
    b. increasing opportunities for minorities.
    c. redistributing income from the haves to the have-nots (slicing the economic pie more equally).
    d. increasing the number of exemptions, deductions, and other "loopholes" in the federal tax code.

18. Supply-side economists are LEAST likely to favor
    a. broadening the tax base so that marginal tax rates can be reduced.
    b. eliminating taxes on saving so as to spur investment and growth.
    c. eliminating the corporate income tax, so that the return on investment is higher.
    d. the use of government mandates to force businesses to spend their own money to accomplish social objectives.

19. In Multiple Choice Figure 12-1, the goal of supply side economics is best characterized by the arrow labeled
    a. A.
    b. B.
    c. C.
    d. D.

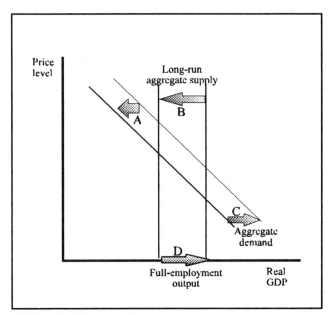

Multiple Choice Figure 12-1

20. If the tax rate is increased incrementally from 0 percent to 100 percent, tax revenues will rise from 0 to a maximum, and then drop back to zero. This relationship is known as
    a. new growth theory.
    b. the capital gains tax.
    c. the Laffer curve.
    d. the trade-off between the risk and return.

E&A 21. The new economy emphasizes
    a. the application of technology to increase productivity and raise living standards.
    b. higher unemployment, because there are more ways of working.
    c. the same things that have been emphasized by the old economy.
    d. personal accountability and integrity.

22. The decade most associated with the emergence of the new economy is the
    a. 1920s.
    b. 1930s.
    c. 1960s.
    d. 1990s.

23. Relative to earlier periods, labor productivity in the mid-to-late 1990s
    a. was very strong.
    b. was very weak.
    c. was about the same.
    d. could not being measured because the benchmarks had all changed.

24. In the late 1990s, information technology capital is likely to have contributed and extra ____ percent to the U.S. economic growth rate.
    a. 0.9
    b. 19
    c. 59
    d. 99

25. Most fundamentally, the new economy is a building block for
    a. permanently higher employment.
    b. permanently lower inflation.
    c. permanently higher taxes.
    d. economic growth.

GRASPING THE GRAPHS
Fill in each box with a concept that applies.

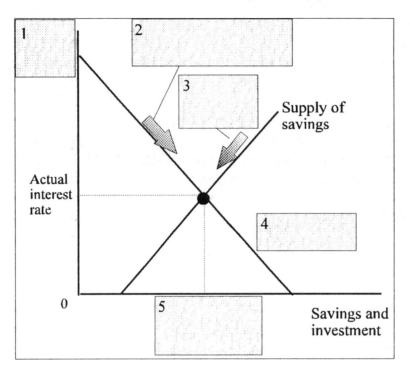

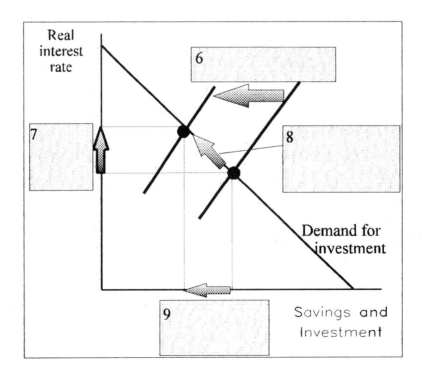

ECONOMIC GROWTH 353

Fill in the boxes to show the effect of a tax on interest income.

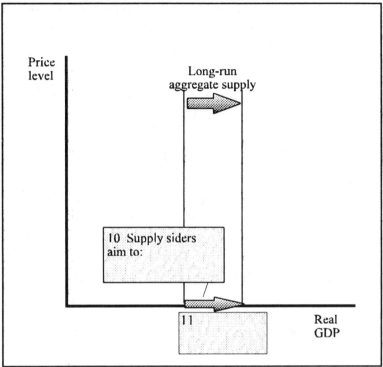

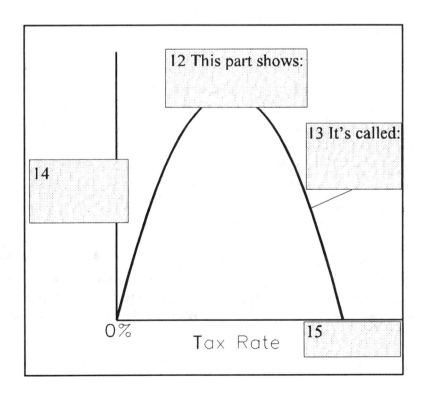

For additional practice in grasping this chapter's graphs, visit
http://www.prenhall.com/ayers and try *Smart Graph* 15,
along with *Active Graphs* 29 and 30.

ANSWERS

STUDYCHECKS

1. Taxation of capital gains reduces the return on successful investments and thus reduces the incentive to save. Similarly, taxation of interest and dividend payments as personal income also reduces the after-tax returns to saving and investing, and thereby reduces the incentive to save. Thirdly, actions that lower business profits reduce the demand for investment and the return to saving. Such actions include the corporate income tax and many costly regulations.

2. New capital often embodies new technology, which allows resources to be used more productively. To the extent that basic research is a public good, the market produces less than an efficient amount of new technology. To partially remedy this inefficiency, government offers subsidies, such as subsidies to higher education. Government also sometimes subsidizes development. However, the marketplace is more efficient when it comes to development because returns on development can often be captured by firms or individuals. This protection is achieved by establishing property rights to the development, such as with patents.

3. Supply-side economists emphasize ways in which government policies could be changed to increase the incentives for capital formation and other forms of productivity improvement. Accomplishing these goals would shift aggregate supply outward over time, and thus lead to more output to divide. However, the policies that increase the size of the economic pie often slice that pie in very unequal pieces, an outcome that is commonly viewed as inequitable. For example, reducing the marginal tax rate encourages capital formation but also rewards the wealthy who can afford to invest. Thus, supply-side policies are sometimes seen as sacrificing short-run equity for long-run growth.

4. As cheaper and easier to use technology was provided to workers throughout the economy in the 1990s, workers became more efficient. Output per worker increased and the *per-unit cost* of production dropped. Additions to information technology capital, such as computers and fax machines, contributed significantly to soaring labor productivity in the 1995 to 2000 period. The same is true of technological change

ECONOMIC GROWTH 355

FILL IN THE BLANKS

1. gross domestic product
2. increasing
3. labor productivity
4. capital
5. formation
6. investment, human, saving
7. taxes, taxes
8. saving, investment
9. Investment
10. downward
11. upward, equates
12. crowding-out
13. left, higher
14. purchase price
15. external benefit, Research, Development, research, property rights, subsidies
16. new growth theory
17. right
18. low
19. deficit
20. trickle-down
21. increased
22. growth, employment, inflation
23. technology
24. 2.7, increased
25. capital, labor, technological change

TRUE/FALSE/EXPLAIN

1. True.
2. True.
3. False, labor productivity is primarily related to the amount of capital and technology the labor has to work with.
4. True.
5. False, higher real interest rates mean higher borrowing costs for investors.
6. True.
7. True.
8. False, saving plus taxation equals investment plus government spending.
9. True.

10. False, most investment comes from the private sector.
11. True.
12. False, unless the perspective profits are substantial, there would be little investment in new drugs that might or might not be effective and approved for sale.
13. True.
14. True.
15. True.
16. False, it is more efficient for government to subsidize basic research because there are more externalities associated with basic research than with development.
17. False, it is supply-siders who emphasize lower tax rates as a means to increase full-employment output over time.
18. True.
19. False, that position is more closely associated with new growth theory.
20. False, that would be a Keynesian interpretation of how tax cuts would affect the economy. Supply siders emphasize that tax cuts encourage additional work effort and investment, including investment in human capital that would make workers more productive and cause output to grow.
21. False, the so-called new economy emphasizes the application of technology to raise living standards.
22. False, more than half of U.S. households are connected to the Internet.
23. True.
24. False, workers became more productive.
25. True.

MULTIPLE CHOICE

1.	a	8.	b	15.	c	22.	d
2.	a	9.	d	16.	b	23.	a
3.	c	10.	d	17.	a	24.	a
4.	c	11.	b	18.	d	25.	d
5.	c	12.	b	19.	d		
6.	a	13.	b	20.	c		
7.	c	14.	c	21.	a		

GRASPING THE GRAPHS
Examples of correct answers

1. Real interest rate
2. More investment at lower interest rate

3. Less saving at lower interest rate
4. Investment demand
5. Actual saving and investment
6. Shift in the supply of saving
7. Change in market equilibrium
8. Higher real interest rate
9. Less saved and invested
10. Increase full-employment output
11. Full-employment output
12. Maximum tax revenue
13. The Laffer Curve
14. Tax revenue
15. 100 percent

Visit the Ayers/Collinge companion Website at http://www.prenhall.com/ayers for further activities and exercises for this chapter.

Part 5

MONEY IN THE MACROECONOMY

Chapter 13

MONEY, BANKING, AND THE FEDERAL RESERVE

CHAPTER REVIEW

- Commercial banks are the banks we find on Main Street. The Federal Reserve (the Fed) is the U.S. *central bank*, a special kind of bank charged with regulating money and commercial banks. Together, the commercial banks and the Federal Reserve make up the U.S. banking system. Meeting the macro goals of high employment, low inflation, and economic growth is made easier by the existence of money and banks, including a central bank.

13.1 Money

- **Money** is whatever is commonly used in an economy to buy and sell things. To put money into perspective, imagine a world in which it did not exist. To fulfill our wants, we would have to either swap one good for another—**barter**—or produce on our own all the goods and services we consume. Both alternatives are inefficient.

- Among the important qualities of money are *portability* and *divisibility*. Money should be easy to carry around, and divisible to make it convenient to spend and receive change.

- Money performs the following functions:
  - *Medium of exchange.* Money is used to make purchases. Money must be acceptable to sellers, who will find it so only if they believe that others will too.
  - *Store of value.* Money is a means of holding wealth, but by no means the only one.
  - *Unit of account.* The market values of goods and services are expressed as prices, which are stated in terms of money.

- **Fiat money** is money because the law says it is. Paper currency and current U.S. coins are examples. Because the government accepts fiat money, individuals and businesses do too.

- Gold and silver coins, once a commonplace form of money in the U.S., are examples of *commodity money*. Commodity money is made from precious metals. Coins today are made from cheaper metals.

- Unfortunately, commodity money is subject to **Gresham's law**—bad money drives out good. In other words, people have the incentive to nick, shave, or otherwise reduce the metallic content of coins.

- The governments of virtually all nations today hold a monopoly on the production of fiat money. The profit from the difference between the value of money and the cost of producing it is called *seigniorage*.

StudyCheck1
What distinguishes fiat money from commodity money?

- When paper money and coins are deposited in banks, money changes form. Deposits into checking accounts create **demand deposits,** also termed *checkable deposits*. More money is held in the form of checkable deposits than in any other form. These deposits are money because checks—orders to a bank to make payment—are generally accepted by sellers. Traveler's checks are also generally accepted by sellers of goods and services.

- **Liquidity** refers to how easily and quickly something of value can be converted into spendable form. An item is highly liquid if it is spendable without delay. Money is highly liquid.

- Three definitions of money, termed the *monetary aggregates,* categorize various types of money according to how liquid they are. The monetary aggregates include M1, M2, and M3. The specific components of each category are as follows:
    - **M1:** The sum of currency and coin in the hands of the public, demand deposits, other checkable deposits, and traveler's checks. These forms of money are the most easily and immediately spendable. **Currency stored in bank vaults is not counted in the money supply because it is not available to make purchases.**
    - **M2:** M1 plus the balances in savings deposits, "small" time deposits and balances in money market mutual funds. *Time deposits* are certificates of deposit (CDs), which can be withdrawn without penalty only after some period of time, such as one or five years. The Fed considers CDs small if they are less than $100,000!

- **M3:** M2 plus large time deposits (at least $100,000), and several other near monies. These additional components of M3 are even less likely to be spent than the items in M2.

StudyCheck 2
List the items that make up the M1 money supply. Which item is the largest?

13.2 Money and Banking in the United States

- Since the mid-1980s the number of banks in the U.S. has plummeted because of bank failures and bank mergers. More specifically, the number of banks fell an astonishing 41 percent between 1986 and 2000. During this period the U.S. has seen the rise of megabanks—large banks that do business in many locations. Megabanks thrive in today's climate of *interstate banking* as legal barriers against branching across state lines have fallen.

- Banks are regulated by both state and federal governments. Bank regulation is designed to protect against unsound banking practices that could bankrupt both depositors and government insurance funds.

- Bank regulation is controversial. Since regulations inhibit banks from responding to the demands of their customers, regulations can lead to inefficiencies in the financial system. For example, under the Glass-Steagall Act of 1933, banks were barred from offering insurance and brokerage services. The act was intended to keep banks away from risky investment activities that could endanger the banking system. Over time, the inefficiencies created by Glass-Steagall were recognized and a number of its provisions were relaxed because of changes in the law, regulatory interpretations, and court decisions. Congress finally killed off the Glass-Steagall Act in 1999 after 12 attempts to do so in the prior 25 years.

- To understand how our banking system operates, it is useful to consider a simplified *balance sheet* showing the assets and liabilities of a bank, as seen in the following table. The assets are things that a bank owns and show how banks use funds. In a balance sheet, assets are always listed on the left side. The liabilities show how a bank raises funds, and are listed on the right side. The value of the sum of the assets must by definition equal the value of the sum of the liabilities plus net worth for any balance sheet.

A Balance Sheet—Major Assets and Liabilities of Banks

Assets	Liabilities
Vault cash (part 1 of bank reserves)	Customer Deposits
Deposits held by the Federal Reserve (part 2 of bank reserves)	Federal funds
Loans	Discount loans
Securities	Net worth
Other	

- The two most liquid assets, vault cash and deposits held by the Federal Reserve, are normally lumped together to form what are called cash assets. The sum of vault cash plus deposits with the Fed is called **bank reserves**. Bank reserves are highly liquid and so are available immediately to meet depositor withdrawals.

- Banks hold some fraction of their deposits on reserve to meet the cash needs of their customers. Individual banks are also required by law to meet the *reserve requirements* imposed by the Fed. The current reserve requirement of approximately 10 percent for demand deposits means that banks must hold at least $10 in reserves for every $100 of customer deposits. Reserves in excess of **required reserves** are called **excess reserves.** Hence, total reserves equal required reserves plus excess reserves.

> **StudyCheck 3**
>
> What two items make up bank reserves? Why are bank reserves important to bankers?

- The next asset in the table is loans, which represent promises by borrowers to repay borrowed funds. Bank loans go to both the household and business sectors. Banks lend to borrowers in order to earn income in the form of interest. The interest rate on bank loans that is widely known to the public is the *bank prime lending rate*. This interest rate applies to short-term business loans to the banks' most valued customers.

- *Securities*, in the form of **bonds**, are interest-paying investments. The government issues bonds when it borrows money from investors in order to pay the expenses of government that are not covered by tax collections. Banks mostly purchase federally issued short-term bonds called *T-bills*, which is short for *Treasury bills*.

- The *Federal Deposit Insurance Corporation (FDIC)* insures deposit accounts up to $100,000. This insurance reduces the likelihood of bank runs, in which numerous depositors simultaneously seek to withdraw funds because of fears about the financial soundness of a bank. The tradeoff is that FDIC insurance allows banks to make riskier loans without scaring away their depositors.

- Banks also own other assets, such as their buildings, equipment, and fixtures. These assets are needed in order to do business with the public.

- Bank deposits are liabilities because they are funds owed to depositors. Banks also raise funds by borrowing, both from each other and from the Federal Reserve.

- Funds borrowed from other banks are called *federal funds*. The interest rate that banks charge on loans to other banks is called the **federal funds rate.** The federal funds rate is determined by the supply and demand in the marketplace for federal funds.

- Borrowings by banks from the Federal Reserve are called *discount loans* because the Federal Reserve is said to "discount" its loans. To discount a loan means that banks are required to pay the interest on loans from the Fed when they are made rather than as they are repaid. The rate of interest charged is termed the **discount rate.** The discount rate is set by the Fed.

StudyCheck 4
How are bank reserves acquired in the federal funds market different from bank reserves acquired through discount loans?

- The final liability on the balance sheet in the table is *net worth*. This entry represents the funds invested in a bank by its owners, the stockholders. In order to start a bank, investors in the bank must put up capital in the amount set by regulation. This amount of money varies by the type of bank and its location.

- In addition to banks, there are other *financial intermediaries,* bank-like institutions that accept funds from savers in order to make loans or investments. Insurance companies, mutual funds, pension funds, and finance companies are examples of nonbank financial intermediaries, because, although they are not banks, they invest the funds they raise.

- **When a bank makes a loan, the quantity of money in the economy increases.** To see how, suppose you borrow the cost of a new PT Cruiser, $18,000, from your bank, Homestate University National Bank. We can illustrate the effect of a loan on a bank's balance sheet by referring to the changes in Homestate University National Bank's balance sheet, seen below. The bank acquires an asset, your IOU promising to repay the loan. Customer deposits increase on the other side of the balance sheet because the bank increases your account by $18,000 when the loan is made.

Homestate University National Bank: Balance Sheet Changes When a Loan is Made

Assets	Liabilities
Loans + $18,000	Customer deposits + $18,000

MONEY, BANKING, AND THE FEDERAL RESERVE 365

StudyCheck 5
When a bank makes a loan what two items on its balance sheet change, and by how much?

- When you pay for your new car, the bank's balance sheet will change again. Customer deposits decrease by $18,000 since you no longer have that money in your account. Bank reserves will also fall by $18,000 since the bank will either lose $18,000 in vault cash, or see its deposits at the Fed reduced by that amount. The balance sheet effects are shown below.

Homestate University National Bank: Balance Sheet Changes When a Loan is Spent

Assets	Liabilities
Reserves −$18,000	Customer deposits −$18,000

- When borrowers repay bank loans, the quantity of money falls. If a loan is repaid with currency, the money supply decreases because there is less currency in the hands of the public. If a loan is repaid by writing a check, the money supply falls due to fewer demand deposits. Say that you repay your $18,000 loan all at once. That wipes out your IOU and increases the bank's reserves, as shown.

Homestate University National Bank: Balance Sheet Changes When a Loan is Repaid

Assets	Liabilities
Reserves + $10,000 Loans − $10,000	

13.3 Meet the Fed

- In the U.S., it is the Federal Reserve that performs the central banking functions at the heart of the monetary system. The Fed is known to the public for engineering changes in short-term interest rates. However, the Fed does much more.

- A central bank is a bank that is an arm of the government charged with seeing to it that the monetary system functions efficiently. The U.S. central bank is called the Fed, short for **Federal Reserve System**. It was created by the *Federal Reserve Act of 1913* in response to recurring problems of bank failure and the belief that a central bank could contribute to U.S. economic stability.

- The Fed does the following:
  - **Functions as a banker's bank.** The Fed holds reserves for commercial banks.
  - **Functions as a lender of last resort.** The Fed lends reserves to sound banks that are temporarily short of reserves.
  - **Supervises banks.** Banks are held accountable for complying with the federal laws and regulations that apply to banks.
  - **Conducts monetary policy.** Monetary policy involves the Fed in changing short-term interest rates and the quantity of money.
  - **Issues currency.** Currency is printed by the U.S. Treasury, but put into circulation by the Fed.
  - **Clears checks.** When you write a check, the check must clear, meaning that your bank must reduce your account by the amount of the check. The Fed operates facilities that process and transport checks to the banks upon which they are written.

- Congress sought to keep the Fed *independent,* meaning free from political pressures that might lead it to take actions that would harm the economy in the long run. Because the Fed does not depend upon Congress for its income, but instead earns income from its investments and from providing banking services, the Fed is one of the more independent central banks around the world.

StudyCheck 6
Why was the Federal Reserve created to be independent?

- To further insulate the Fed from the political process, the Fed is divided into three components:
  - **The *Board of Governors***, which is responsible for the overall direction of the Federal Reserve and its policies.
  - **The *Federal Open Market Committee (FOMC)***, which conducts monetary policy.
  - **The *Federal Reserve Banks***, which regulate and provide a variety of services for banks.

- There are seven members of the Board of Governors. They are appointed to 14-year nonrenewable terms by the president, with the advice and consent of the Senate. The chairperson serves a 4-year renewable term. The chairperson is the most powerful individual in the Fed and among the most powerful people in the world because of the Fed's influence over the most widely used currency in the world.

- The FOMC consists of twelve members, the seven members of the Board plus four rotating district bank presidents, and the president of the New York District Bank. The president of the New York Fed is always a member of the Committee because New York City is the hub of the Nation's financial markets. The FOMC usually meets at intervals of approximately four to six weeks, making adjustments in the conduct of monetary policy in accordance with its assessment of economic conditions.

StudyCheck 7
Which branch of the Federal Reserve conducts monetary policy? Describe it.

- There are twelve regional Federal Reserve Banks. Together with their branches, these Banks perform the routine functions of the Fed.

- National banks—those chartered by the federal government—are automatically members of the Federal Reserve. Banks with state charters may join at their option.

- The principle method the Fed uses to influence the money supply is called open market operations. **Open market operations** occur when the Fed enters the financial marketplace to buy or sell government securities, such as Treasury bonds. The Fed does not itself issue government securities; the U.S. Department of the Treasury issues Treasury bonds, for example. The Fed can only obtain them in the open market, hence the name. Open market operations allow currency, in the form of Federal Reserve Notes, to make its way into circulation.

- When an individual buys a bond sold by the Fed, the money supply decreases. Suppose the buyer pays for the bond by writing a check. When the buyer's bank pays the Fed, the buyer's checking account is reduced by the amount of the check. Thus, demand deposits decrease, as does the money supply.

- The bulk of the Fed's open market operations involve banks directly. An open market sale to a bank by the Fed decreases bank reserves. Fewer reserves mean that the bank is able to do less lending. Thus, open market sales tend to reduce the money supply. A greater volume of open market sales is consistent with a tighter policy.

- An open market purchase by the Fed from a bank increases bank reserves, which in turn tends to increase the money supply because banks have more money to loan. However, whether loans are actually made and the money supply actually increased depends on the willingness of banks to make loans and on the desire of the public to borrow. **Thus, the Fed influences but does not control the money supply.**

- However, by conducting open market operations, **the Fed controls the monetary base.** The **monetary base** is the sum of currency held by the public plus bank reserves. **An open market purchase by the Fed always increases the monetary base by the amount of the purchase; an open market sale always decreases the monetary base by the amount of the sale.**

- Case 1: Suppose the Fed buys a $10,000 bond from a member of the public, and the seller deposits the funds received in a commercial bank.

Bank Balance Sheet Changes: Public sells bond

Assets		Liabilities
Reserves	+ $10,000	Customer deposits + $10,000

- Case 2: Suppose the Fed buys a $10,000 bond from a commercial bank.

Bank Balance Sheet Changes: Bank sells bond

Assets		Liabilities
Bonds	− $10,000	
Reserves	+ $10,000	

- Case 3: Suppose the Fed sells a $10,000 bond to a member of the public. The buyer writes a check to pay for the bond.

Bank Balance Sheet Changes: Public purchases bond

Assets		Liabilities	
Reserves	− $10,000	Customer deposits	− $10,000

- Case 4: Suppose the Fed sells a $10,000 bond to a commercial bank. The bank pays for the bond by having its account at the Fed reduced by $10,000.

Bank Balance Sheet Changes: Bank purchases bond

Assets		Liabilities
Reserves	− $10,000	
Bonds	+ $10,000	

- When the Fed buys or sells a bond to the public, the money supply changes immediately. When the transaction involved a bank, there was no immediate change in the money supply. However, when bank reserves increase, banks are able to make more loans. When bank reserves decrease, the opposite is true. This means that any open market operation has the potential to change the money supply, if not now, then later.

- In which cases did the monetary base increase? Since all four cases saw a change in bank reserves, the monetary base changed in all cases. As stated above, any open market operation changes the monetary base immediately.

StudyCheck 8
What is the effect of an open market sale of a bond by the Fed to a bank on the money supply and the monetary base?

- The effects of open market operations do not stop with the initial purchase or sale. Secondary effects magnify changes in the money supply or monetary base. **The money multiplier shows the total effect on the money supply of each dollar of open market operations.**

- What is the total of new money created when the expansion of the money supply is complete? The answer depends on the money multiplier.
  $$\text{Money supply} = \text{money multiplier} \times \text{monetary base}$$

- The money multiplier can vary according to loan prospects and people's behavior, and is thus hard to calculate with precision. However, an upper bound can be found by calculating the **deposit multiplier—the maximum possible value of the money multiplier.**

- The deposit multiplier is calculated by assuming that all money is held as demand deposits and that banks do not hold excess reserves. In practice, the true value of the money multiplier will be less than the deposit multiplier. The deposit multiplier is the reciprocal of the percentage reserve requirement, meaning
  $$1/\text{percentage reserve requirement}$$

MONEY, BANKING, AND THE FEDERAL RESERVE 371

> **StudyCheck 9**
> Suppose the reserve requirement is 20 percent. What is the size of the deposit multiplier?

- The following three factors affect the money multiplier, and thus the actual expansion of the money supply:
    - **The reserve requirement:** Changes in the reserve requirement would change the deposit multiplier, and thus the maximum value of the money multiplier. A lower reserve requirement means that banks are able to lend a greater fraction of deposits; a higher reserve requirement has the opposite effect.
    - **The public's desire to hold currency instead of deposits:** If people hold more of their money as currency and less as deposits, banks will have fewer dollars to lend. We say that a *currency drain* has occurred. **Currency drains reduce the multiplier effect.**
    - **The bank's desire to hold excess reserves:** Excess reserves may be held in order to meet unexpected depositor withdrawals, or because lending opportunities seem poor. Reserves that are not loaned out do not add to the money supply. **Excess reserves reduce the multiplier effect.**

- In response to unexpected customer withdrawals, banks may wish to borrow from the Fed in order to maintain their required reserves. Recall that loans from the Fed to banks are called discount loans, and the rate of interest charged is called the discount rate. An increase in the discount rate makes it more costly for banks to borrow; a decrease makes it less costly.

- Increases in the discount rate tend to decrease the quantity of money by prompting banks to borrow less from the Fed. Conversely, a decrease in the discount rate leads banks to borrow more from the Fed, which tends to increase the amount of money in circulation. Thus, **a change in the discount rate tends to cause the money supply to change in the opposite direction.**

- **The Fed could change the money supply dramatically by altering the reserve requirement.** A decrease in required reserves would increase the money multiplier and spur monetary growth. An increase in the reserve requirement would reduce the money multiplier and thus decrease the money supply. The Fed is reluctant to increase reserve requirements because banks without sufficient excess reserves would be forced to sell securities or call in loans—actions that could prove disruptive to the bank and its customers.

- A *tight monetary policy* is intended to slow the economy down in order to keep inflation in check. A *loose monetary policy* is intended to have an expansionary effect on the economy. Monetary policy is discussed in detail in the next chapter.

The Fed's Monetary Policy Options

Tighter Monetary Policy	Looser Monetary Policy
Open market sale of securities	Open market purchase of securities
Increase in discount rate	Decrease in discount rate
Increase in reserve requirement	Decrease in reserve requirement

13.4 The Banking Crisis of the 1980s—Could It Happen Again?

- Two rounds of legislation, 50 years apart, set the stage for the banking crisis of the 1980s. New Deal legislation created the Federal Deposit Insurance Corporation (FDIC) to insure funds deposited in banks, and the Glass-Steagall law to restrict the investment-related activities of banks. The purpose of the FDIC insurance was to restore public confidence in the banking system; the purpose of Glass-Steagall was to prevent bank failures by keeping banks away from risky investments. For many years afterward, bank failures were rare.

- Round two of the legislation that shaped today's banking system occurred with the passage of the *Depository Institutions Deregulation and Monetary Control Act of 1980 (DIDMCA)*. This legislation loosened the regulatory knot that was holding back the banks. Regulation Q, which limited the interest rates banks could pay on deposits, was also rolled back. Now banks were freer to compete for depositors' money.

- In the competition for deposits that came to characterize the latter 1970s and the 1980s, banks had to take on a large volume of what proved to be high-risk loans and investments. The alternative was to keep their rates on deposits low and see depositors flee to other banks, savings and loans, money market mutual funds, or even the bond market, all of which offered higher returns. After all, with the FDIC insurance, the only thing depositors cared about was high interest rates. If it hadn't been for the FDIC insurance, depositors would likely have shopped for banks that invested wisely.

- The problem of *moral hazard* occurs when people change their behavior because of insurance. When the price of risk goes down, people will do riskier things. It is clear that the moral hazard problem led both depositors and bankers to take on more risk than they otherwise would have accepted. For the bankers' part, they could seek out lending opportunities with higher returns but greater risk without experiencing howls of protest from depositors worried about the safety of their deposits. Depositors could sleep soundly as long as their deposits did not exceed the $100,000 FDIC limit.

- In practice if not in law, the government even guaranteed deposits above the $100,000 level by adopting a policy of "too big to fail," and by encouraging the merger of insolvent banks—those whose asset values fell below the value of their liabilities—with sound banks. Both of these government policies were equivalent to insurance.

- The market also found a way to extend deposit insurance to those with deposits of more than $100,000. The business of deposit brokering was invented. Deposit brokers could guarantee that any amount of deposits was insured by breaking up large deposits into blocks of amounts less than $100,000 and then placing these blocks with different banks. For example, a $1,000,000 deposit could be placed into ten different banks in $100,000 blocks. With this innovation, the FDIC limits became meaningless.

- Could another massive wave of bank failures occur? To the extent that bank loans are for the most part sound, banks will be able to survive an up tick in the number of loans that are not repaid. Thus, the answer to the question is equivalent to asking how sound are bank loans. So long as deposit insurance creates moral hazard issues, that answer will remain unclear.

StudyCheck 10
How could the presence of federal deposit insurance help explain the bank failures of the late 1980s?

FILL IN THE BLANKS

1. _____ banks are the banks we find on Main Street. The Federal Reserve (the Fed) is the U.S. _____ bank, a special kind of bank charged with regulating money and commercial banks.

2. Money is whatever is commonly used in an economy to buy and sell things. To put money into perspective, imagine a world in which it did not exist. To fulfill our wants, we would have to either swap one good for another—_____—or produce on our own all the goods and services we consume.

3. Money performs the following functions: (a) _____, which means that money is used to make purchases. (b) _____ __ _____, which means that money is a means of holding wealth. (c) _____ __ _____, which relates to the fact that the market values of goods and services are expressed as prices, which are stated in terms of money.

4. _____ money is money because the law says it is. Paper currency and current U.S. coins are examples. Gold and silver coins, once a commonplace form of money in the U.S., are examples of _____ money.

5. Gresham's law states that _____ money drives out _____. In other words, people have the incentive to nick, shave, or otherwise reduce the metallic content of coins. The profit from the difference between the value of money and the cost of producing it is called _____.

6. When paper money and coins are deposited in banks, money changes form. Deposits into checking accounts create _____ _____, also termed *checkable deposits*.

7. _____ refers to how easily and quickly something of value can be converted into spendable form. An item is highly liquid if it is spendable without delay.

8. Three definitions of money, termed the _____ _____, categorize various types of money according to how liquid they are. The sum of currency and coin in the hands of the public, demand deposits, other checkable deposits, and traveler's checks is called _____. When the balances in savings deposits, "small" time deposits and balances in money market mutual funds are added to the preceding items we have _____.

9. The sum of vault cash plus deposits with the Fed is called _____ _____. Banks hold some fraction of their deposits on reserve to meet the cash needs of their

customers. Individual banks are also required by law to meet the reserve requirements imposed by the Fed. The current reserve requirement is approximately _____ percent for demand deposits. Reserves in excess of required reserves are called _____ reserves.

10. Securities, in the form of bonds, are interest-paying investments owned by banks and other investors. Banks mostly purchase federally issued short-term bonds called _____-_____, which is short for Treasury bills.

11. Funds borrowed from other banks are called _____ _____. Borrowings by banks from the Federal Reserve are called _____ _____.

12. When a bank makes a loan, the quantity of money in the economy _____. When borrowers repay bank loans, the quantity of money _____.

13. A central bank is a bank that is an arm of the government charged with seeing to it that the monetary system functions efficiently. The U.S. central bank is called the Fed, short for Federal Reserve System. Among its duties, the Fed: (a) Functions as a _____ bank. The Fed holds reserves for commercial banks. (b) Functions as a lender of _____ _____. The Fed lends reserves to sound banks that are temporarily short of reserves.

14. The Fed is divided into three components: The _____ _____ _____, which is responsible for the overall direction of the Federal Reserve and its policies. The _____ _____ _____ _____ (FOMC), which conducts of monetary policy. The regional _____ _____ _____, which regulate and provide a variety of services for commercial banks in their districts.

15. There are _____ members of the Board of Governors. They are appointed to _____-year nonrenewable terms by the president, with the advice and consent of the Senate. The FOMC consists of _____ members. There are _____ regional Federal Reserve Banks.

16. The principle method the Fed uses to influence the money supply is called _____ _____ _____, which occur when the Fed enters the financial marketplace to buy or sell government securities, such as Treasury bonds. When an individual buys a bond sold by the Fed, the money supply _____. A sale of bonds to banks by the Fed tends to _____ the money supply.

17. By conducting open market operations, the Fed controls the monetary _____, the sum of currency held by the public plus bank reserves.

18. The total of new money created when the expansion of the money supply is complete is computed by:
    Money supply = _____ _____ × _____ _____

19. The deposit multiplier is
    1/_____ _____ _____

20. Currency drains _____ the multiplier effect. Excess reserves _____ the multiplier effect.

21. Increases in the discount rate tend to decrease the quantity of money by prompting banks to borrow _____ from the Fed. More generally, a change in the discount rate tends to cause the money supply to change in the _____ direction.

22. A _____ monetary policy is intended to slow the economy down in order to keep inflation in check. A _____ monetary policy is intended to have an expansionary effect on the economy.

23. New Deal legislation created the _____ _____ _____ _____ (FDIC) to insure funds deposited in banks, and also the passage of the _____ _____ law to restrict the investment-related activities of banks.

24. Legislation that helped shape today's banking system occurred with the passage of the _____ _____ _____ _____ _____ _____ Act of 1980 (DIDMCA). This legislation loosened the regulatory knot that was holding back the banks. Regulation ___, which limited the interest rates banks could pay on deposits, was also rolled back.

25. The problem of _____ _____ occurs when people change their behavior because of insurance. When the price of risk goes down, people will do riskier things.

TRUE/FALSE/EXPLAIN
If false, explain why in the space provided.

1. Fish could not serve as money.

2. Government earns a "profit" from seigniorage.

3. Gresham's Law states that good money drives bad money out of circulation.

4. Currency in bank vaults is included as part of the M1 money supply.

5. M1 is the least liquid definition of money.

6. It is legal for banks to create money.

7. If you find a $10 bill in a landfill, the money supply immediately increases by $10.

8. If you accidentally destroy a $10 bill in the laundry, the money supply immediately decreases by $10.

9. When a bank makes a loan, the money supply will not increase if the loan proceeds are taken in the form of a check.

10. When banks borrow from other banks, the borrowings are called federal funds.

11. The Federal Open Market Committee includes all members of the Federal Reserve Board.

12. Part of the Fed's job is to provide services to banks.

378 CHAPTER 13

13. Currency plus bank reserves equals the monetary base.

14. Increasing the discount rate will probably decrease the money supply.

15. The primary tool of monetary policy is open market operations.

16. If the reserve requirement equals 20 percent, the deposit multiplier equals 20.

17. The Federal Reserve Board includes all members of the Federal Open Market Committee.

18. The Federal Reserve system consists of three branches, which are the executive branch, the legislative branch, and the judicial branch.

19. If the Fed seeks to expand the money supply through open-market operations, it would buy U.S. government securities in the open market.

20. The Fed would usually like to buy more government securities than it is able to afford.

21. Federal deposit insurance is used as a rationale for federal restrictions on bank behavior.

22. In the mid 1980s, competition for deposits into federally insured bank accounts raised interest rates, and thus caused banks to take on riskier investments.

23. In the absence of careful oversight, the provision of deposit insurance by government can lead to excessively risky investing by banks.

24. According to the analysis in the text, the bank failures of the late 1980s and early 1990s were primarily the result of fraudulent activities by bankers.

25. By the late 1990s, the number of bank failures was near to the all-time high it reached in the 1980s.

MULTIPLE CHOICE
Circle the letter preceding the one best answer.

1. Which is NOT a function of money?
   a. Unit of account.
   b. Store of value.
   c. Store of account.
   d. Medium of exchange.

2. The money supply is the sum of
   a. all money incomes.
   b. the cash in banks plus the value of checks written.
   c. the currency and deposits held by the nonbanking public.
   d. the currency held by banks and the public, plus the assets of the Fed.

3. Which of the following is included in the M2 money supply?
   a. U.S. savings bonds.
   b. Currency held in bank vaults.
   c. Savings accounts.
   d. U.S. Treasury bonds.

4. Initially, the conversion of currency to demand deposits that occurs when people deposit cash into their checking accounts
   a. decreases the money supply.
   b. has no effect upon the money supply.
   c. increases the money supply.
   d. is a misdemeanor, although it becomes a felony for future convictions.

5. T-bills are
   a. short-term bonds issued by the Treasury Department.
   b. long-term bonds issued by banks.
   c. $10 bills that are issued by the Federal Reserve.
   d. long-term bonds issued by the Federal Reserve.

6. The federal funds rate is the rate of interest that
   a. the federal government pays on T-bills.
   b. the Federal Reserve charges on discount loans.
   c. banks pay on long-term bonds.
   d. banks charge on loans to other banks.

7. Suppose a bank that is currently meeting the reserve requirement and holds no excess reserves receives a deposit of $10,000. If the reserve requirement is 10 percent, how much is the bank allowed to loan out?
   a. $100,000.
   b. $9,000.
   c. $1,000.
   d. $0.00.

8. The Fed's Board of the Governors consists of
   a. the governors of all 50 states.
   b. the governor of New York and six other states.
   c. the governor of Texas and six other states.
   d. seven members who are appointed by the president, subject to Senate approval.

9. The Governors of the Federal Reserve System
   a. serve at the pleasure of the president.
   b. serve at the pleasure of Congress.
   c. are elected every three years by bankers from the Federal Reserve banks.
   d. each serve 14-year terms, staggered so that one ends every two years.

10. The regional Federal Reserve Banks do **not**
    a. set monetary policy.
    b. clear checks.
    c. supervise banks.
    d. replace worn-out currency.

11. Which is the most important tool of monetary policy?
    a. Changes in the discount rate.
    b. Changes in the federal funds rate.
    c. Changes in reserve requirements.
    d. Open market operations.

12. Which of the following is most likely to reduce the money supply?
    a. The Fed sells Treasury bills.
    b. The Fed lowers the discount rate.
    c. The Fed reduces reserve requirements.
    d. Consumers deposit cash into their checking accounts.

13. The Fed buys Treasury bills in order to
    a. raise money for government.
    b. reduce government debt.
    c. increase the money supply.
    d. decrease the money supply.

14. When the Fed buys treasury bills, one side effect is that
    a. government debt is reduced.
    b. government debt is increased.
    c. the discount rate is reduced.
    d. the discount rate is increased.

15. The Fed has the most control over
    a. M1.
    b. M2.
    c. M3.
    d. the monetary base.

16. Which of the following would increase the deposit multiplier?
    a. Banks decide to hold onto their excess reserves rather than lend them out.
    b. The Fed lowers the reserve requirement.
    c. Consumers decide to hold more cash.
    d. The Fed buys a Treasury bill.

17. Suppose the reserve requirement is 10 percent. If you unexpectedly find a $100 bill and deposit the money in the bank, the money supply could potentially increase by as much as
    a. $1000.
    b. $110.
    c. $100.
    d. $10.

18. The relationship between the deposit multiplier and the money multiplier is that
    a. the money multiplier equals the reciprocal of the deposit multiplier.
    b. the deposit multiplier equals the reciprocal of the money multiplier.
    c. the money multiplier is the maximum value of the deposit multiplier.
    d. the deposit multiplier is the maximum value of the money multiplier.

19. An increase in the discount rate would represent a
    a. tighter monetary policy.
    b. looser monetary policy.
    c. tighter fiscal policy.
    d. looser fiscal policy.

20. The reserve requirement is typically not used as a tool of monetary policy because
    a. it would be illegal to do so.
    b. changing its value would have little impact on money supply.
    c. changing its value would be too disruptive to banks and their customers.
    d. changing the reserve requirement would represent fiscal policy, not monetary policy.

E&A 21. In order to ensure depositors' money in the aftermath of the bank failures in the 1930s, the federal government created
    a. the Federal Reserve System.
    b. the Federal Deposit Insurance Corporation.
    c. the Depository Institutions Deregulation and Monetary Control Act.
    d. *Consumer Reports* magazine.

22. "When the price (of taking risks) goes down, people take more risks." This statement illustrates the problem of _____ _____ faced by the insurance industry.
    a. adverse selection
    b. universal coverage
    c. moral hazard
    d. risk transfer

23. The existence of federal deposit insurance _____ risky activity on the part of banks and _____ the cost to the federal treasury.
    a. reduces; increases
    b. reduces; reduces
    c. increases; reduces
    d. increases; increases

24. Which of the following was a factor in the bank failures in the 1980s?
    a. A hands-off attitude of federal bank regulators.
    b. Deposit insurance.
    c. Consumers acting in their own personal best interests.
    d. Competition for bank deposits.
    e. All of the above factors contributed to the bank failures.

MONEY, BANKING, AND THE FEDERAL RESERVE 383

25. From the mid-1990s into the early 2000s, the number of bank failures
   a. remained steady at about half of the number which had occurred in late 1980s.
   b. returned to numbers in line with those of the 1950s, 1960s, and 1970s.
   c. increased dramatically to near early reach the peak numbers of bank failures seen in the late 1980s.
   d. increased dramatically to reach a new, all-time high.

For practice in grasping this chapter's graphs, visit http://www.prenhall.com/ayers and try *Active Graphs* **31.**

ANSWERS

STUDYCHECKS

1. Fiat money has little intrinsic value. Commodity money, such as gold or silver coins, has intrinsic value.

2. Currency (and coin), demand deposits and other checkable deposits, and traveler's checks make up M1. Demand deposits (including other checkable deposits) are the largest part of M1.

3. Vault cash and bank deposits at the Fed are the two items that make up bank reserves. These items are highly liquid, and hence can be used to meet depositor withdrawals. Banks are required to meet the legal reserve requirement, but may keep excess reserves if they wish.

4. Reserves can be borrowed from other banks in the federal funds market. Reserves can also be borrowed from the Fed as discount loans. Thus, the source of the borrowed reserves is different in each case. However, the bank that borrows reserves must pay interest for their use. The price of federal funds is the federal funds rate, while the price of discount loans is the discount rate.

5. On the assets side of the balance sheet, loans increase. On the liabilities side, customer deposits increase. The change in both of these items equals the amount of the loan.

6. The independence of the Fed relates to the desire to see it remain above short-run political considerations. Fed independence contributes to the ability of the Fed to make decisions without taking into account politics.

7. The Federal Open Market Committee (FOMC) conducts monetary policy. It consists of 12 members. Five of these are the members of the Board of Governors. The other seven are

384 CHAPTER 13

presidents of Federal Reserve district banks. The president of the New York Fed is always a member.

8. When a bank purchases a bond from the Fed, it pays for that bond by reducing its reserves by the amount of the purchase. There is no immediate effect on the money supply because only bank reserves are affected, not M1, M2, or M3. However, the reduction in reserves reduces the ability of the bank to make loans, which tends to dampen the expansion of the money supply. Since bank reserves fall with the purchase, the monetary base is decreased by the amount of the purchase.

9. The formula for the deposit multiplier is 1 divided by the percentage reserve requirement (expressed as a decimal). Thus, a 20 percent reserve requirement results in a deposit multiplier of 5, computed as 1/.2.

10. Bank customers with FDIC-insured deposits are insulated from the risk associated with loans. These customers seek out the highest rates. When the economy is doing well, banks with high-risk loans can offer the highest rates. Competition for customers weeds out banks that do not follow these risky lending practices. However, when there is a downturn in the real estate market or other economic downturn, banks with a portfolio of risky loans are prone to failure. Such was the case in the late 1980s.

FILL IN THE BLANKS

1. Commercial, central
2. barter
3. medium of exchange, store of value, unit of account
4. fiat, commodity
5. bad, good, seigniorage
6. demand deposits
7. liquidity
8. monetary aggregates, M1, M2
9. bank reserves, 10, excess
10. T-bills
11. federal funds, discount loans
12. increases, decreases
13. banker's, last resort
14. Board of Governors, Federal Open Market Committee, Federal Reserve Banks
15. seven, 14, 12, 12
16. open market operations, decreases, reduce (decrease)
17. base,
18. money multiplier, monetary base

19. percentage reserve requirement
20. reduce, reduce
21. less, opposite
22. tight, loose
23. Federal Deposit Insurance Corporation, Glass-Steagall
24. Depository Institutions Deregulation and Monetary Control, Q
25. moral hazard

TRUE/FALSE/EXPLAIN

1. True.
2. True.
3. False, it states that bad money drives out good money.
4. False, currency is only included if it is in the hands of the public.
5. False, it is the most liquid definition of money.
6. True.
7. True.
8. True.
9. False, checking account balances are included in the money supply.
10. True.
11. True.
12. True.
13. True.
14. True.
15. True.
16. False, the deposit multiplier is the reciprocal of the reserve requirement, and so would equal 5.
17. False, it is the Federal Open Market Committee that includes all members of the Federal Reserve Board, as well as some of the district bank presidents.
18. False, the three branches are the Federal Reserve Board, the Federal Open Market Committee, and the Federal Reserve Banks.
19. True.
20. False, since the Fed in effect is able to print its own money, it can afford to buy as many government securities as it wants.
21. True.
22. True.
23. True.
24. False, they resulted from high-risk investments undertaken to pay the high interest rates that were needed to attract the FDIC-insured customers.
25. False, by the late 1990s the number bank failures was in the vicinity of historical lows.

MULTIPLE CHOICE

1.	c	8.	d	15.	d	22.	c
2.	c	9.	d	16.	b	23.	d
3.	c	10.	a	17.	a	24.	e
4.	b	11.	d	18.	d	25.	b
5.	a	12.	a	19.	a		
6.	d	13.	c	20.	c		
7.	b	14.	a	21.	b		

Visit the Ayers/Collinge companion Website at <u>http://www.prenhall.com/ayers</u> for further activities and exercises for this chapter.

Chapter 14

MONETARY POLICY AND PRICE STABILITY

CHAPTER REVIEW

14.1 The Aims of Monetary Policy

- *Low inflation*, referred to as *price stability*, is a goal of monetary policy. In its efforts to keep employment high the Fed must take care not to set off higher inflation. **Many economists argue that price stability should be the Fed's primary goal.**

- Two realities of monetary policy are: **1) There are sometimes conflicts and/or tradeoffs involved in pursing a particular monetary policy. 2) The Fed develops monetary policy surrounded by a whirl of political considerations.**

- Cyclical unemployment stems from spending that is insufficient to purchase the full-employment level of output at current prices. Thus, to cure a recession, either prices must fall or the quantity of money available to be spent must rise. In general, to maintain full employment, the quantity of money must rise to keep pace with the economy's productive potential.

- The Fed strongly influences the money supply by conducting open market operations, changing the discount rate, and changing the reserve requirement, as discussed in the previous chapter. The Fed is thus able to utilize these tools of monetary policy to achieve the goals of monetary policy.

- If the quantity of money rises too much, the problem is that too much money will be chasing the goods and services that the economy is capable of producing, thus driving up their prices and causing a general inflation. **An overwhelming amount of evidence shows excessive growth in money to be the root cause of inflation.**

- The quantity of money affects aggregate demand. An increase in the money supply is associated with an **expansionary monetary policy**, also called a *looser monetary policy* because the Fed is in effect loosening the purse strings to stimulate the economy with more money. **An increase in the money supply shifts aggregate demand to the right, and thus allows more aggregate output to be purchased at each possible price level.** However, to the extent that the increased money supply causes the price level to rise, its effect in terms of increasing real GDP will be reduced or eliminated.

- Conversely, a **contractionary monetary policy** would have the effect of drying up liquidity and tightening the economy's purse strings, and is thus alternatively called a *tighter monetary policy*.

- There are two **monetary policy targets** that the Fed can influence as part of monetary policy:
  - *The money supply.* By increasing or decreasing the growth rate of the money supply the Fed can attempt to stimulate or slow down the economy. Prior to July 2000 the Fed set target ranges for the growth of the M2 money supply. M2 targets are no longer set because the relationship between the size of the M2 money supply and economic performance is not as clear as it was in prior years.
  - **Short-term interest rates.** The Fed can also manipulate short-term interest rates up or down, such as the interest rate on short-term government securities. Lower short-term interest rates stimulate the economy, while higher rates are aimed at slowing it down.

- The Fed selects a monetary policy target based on whether adjustments in the money supply or manipulation of interest rates will be more effective in achieving the aims of monetary policy.

StudyCheck1
If the problem were inflation, which kind of monetary policy would be called for? Which monetary policy target would the Fed select?

14.2 The Money Market

- The **demand for money** is the quantities of money that people would prefer to hold at various nominal interest rates, *ceteris paribus*. Money demand slopes downward because people will hold less money when the market interest rate, the price of money, is high. Likewise, people will hold more money when the market interest rate is low.

StudyCheck2

Draw a money demand curve. Be sure to label both axes. What would cause people to decrease the quantity demanded of money?

- Three motives make people willing to pay the price of holding money:
    - **Transactions motive**: money is held because of the everyday need to buy goods and services.

- **Precautionary motive**: unforeseen circumstances motivate people to hold more money than called for by their transactions demands.
- **Speculative motive**: people may speculate with some of their money in the sense that they prefer to hold money rather than invest it when stocks, bonds, and other financial investments appear unattractive at their current returns. The *speculative demand for money* increases when people believe that future returns on investments will rise.

StudyCheck3

Using the three motives for holding money, provide three reasons why someone might hold more money.

- The **money market** is characterized by demand and supply. The money supply curve is drawn as a vertical line. A vertical money supply curve implies that the money supply is independent of the interest rate. In other words, any interest rate is consistent with the quantity of money shown.

- The intersection of demand and supply establishes the money market *equilibrium*. The equilibrium interest rate equates the quantity of money demanded to the money supply.

- The market interest rate will adjust to the equilibrium interest rate. A market interest rate that is above the equilibrium interest rate will fall until the equilibrium interest rate is reached. Similarly, a market interest rate that is below the equilibrium interest rate will rise.

- **The key to understanding interest rate changes is to realize that money, bonds, and other investments are substitutes for each other.** When people see relatively high market interest rates they will economize on their cash holdings in order to own bonds and other assets that pay those high interest rates. On the other hand, when interest rates are relatively low the opportunity cost of holding cash is low and so people will hold more cash and fewer bonds.

MONETARY POLICY AND PRICE STABILITY   391

- The quantity of money demanded is less than the quantity of money supplied when the market interest rate is above its equilibrium value, called an *excess supply of money*. People will react to an excess supply of money by purchasing bonds. In this way people rid themselves of their excess money holdings. The interest rate decreases because it does not need to be so high to attract buyers to bonds. The decrease in the interest rate will continue until it equals the equilibrium level.

- When the quantity of money demanded is greater than the money supply, the situation is called an *excess demand for money*. In their efforts to increase their holdings of money, people will sell their bonds. This increase in the supply of bonds must increase the interest rate on bonds because a higher interest rate is needed to make the additional bonds being sold attractive to investors in bonds. The market interest rate will increase until it equals the equilibrium interest rate.

StudyCheck4
Describe how an interest rate that is less than the equilibrium rate motivates people to try to increase their holdings of money.

14.3 Guiding Monetary Policy

- In recent years, observers speculate that the Fed has usually followed a **price rule,** by which it conducts monetary policy with the aim of keeping price increases among certain basic commodities, perhaps including gold, within a low target range.

- The **equation of exchange** was originally proposed in the nineteenth century as a means of explaining the link between money, prices, and output. The equation of exchange reveals that the amount of money people spend must equal the market value of what they purchase, as follows:

$$M \times V = P \times Q$$

- The equation of exchange applies to the aggregate economy. The quantity of money is indicated by M in the equation. The average number of times money changes hands in a year is called the **velocity of money** (V). Total spending is calculated by multiplying the money supply by velocity, as shown above in the left side of the equation of exchange. P is a price index, such as the GDP chained price index that shows the level of prices in the economy. The aggregate output of goods and services (real GDP) is represented by Q. When P and Q are multiplied, the result is the dollar value of aggregate purchases (nominal GDP).

- The total amount of purchasing in an economy is equivalent to the economy's nominal GDP. Thus, **the equation of exchange says that aggregate spending, the left side of the equation, equals nominal GDP, the right side. Because the value of what is bought must equal the value of what is sold, the equation of exchange is always true.** Thus, we may expand the equation of exchange to include the interpretation of each side:

    $M \times V$ [total spending] = $P \times Q$ [nominal GDP]

- The equation of exchange forms the basis for the **quantity theory of money.** The quantity theory assumes:
    - The velocity of money, V in the equation of exchange, is independent of the quantity of money in the long run. In other words, V is assumed not to change when the money supply changes, so that we can treat V as a constant value
    - Aggregate output, Q, is also independent of the quantity of money in the long run. Aggregate output depends upon the productive capacity of the economy and is assumed to be at its maximum level. This means that Q can also be treated as a constant.

- These two assumptions leave only M and P, money and the price level to vary. Thus, the effect of a change in the quantity of money must be a proportional change in the price level.

StudyCheck5
Using some numbers, show how the equation of exchange predicts a change in the quantity of money leads to a proportional change in the price level, according to the quantity theory.

- The quantity theory can be illustrated with the model of aggregate supply and aggregate demand. An increase in the money supply shifts aggregate demand to the right, because additional money provides greater purchasing power at any given price level. The long run effect is to move the economy to a new equilibrium at a higher price level. Output remains the same at its full-employment level.

- **Monetarism** is a school of economic thought, associated with Nobel-winning economist Milton Friedman (1912–), that offers a modern version of the quantity theory. Monetarists readily agree with one contention of the original quantity theory: Velocity and aggregate output are independent of the quantity of money in the long run. However, unlike the quantity theory, monetarism acknowledges the existence of a short run.

- According to the monetarist view, the quantity of money may indeed affect velocity and aggregate output in the short run. Thus, neither V nor Q in the equation of exchange is viewed as constant by monetarists.
  - *Changes in Q.* A reduction in the growth rate of the money supply may cause a reduction in aggregate output, Q. This effect could occur if people cut their purchases of goods and services because there is less money to spend. If that happens, the economy slows down. Hence, monetarism offers an explanation of how too little money can lead to a recession.
  - *Changes in V.* The velocity of money can change because of changes in people's need to hold money. Velocity is relatively stable from one year to the next, so that the effects of monetary policy are relatively predictable.

- To avoid the recession that could result from too little money, or the inflation that could result from too much money, **the monetarist policy recommendation is for the Fed to increase the money supply at a steady rate, equal to or slightly greater than the long-run growth in aggregate output.** Because the long-run growth of output tends to be about 2.5 to 3 percent, a steady annual monetary increase of about 3 percent or slightly higher is called for. **Monetarists recommend growth in the money supply that just matches the growth in long-run aggregate supply**, thereby avoiding the need for price level adjustments.

- The Fed is sometimes accused by monetarists of being too quick to increase or decrease the growth rate of the money supply. Monetarists claim that an activist policy by the Federal Reserve accentuates economic instability. To monitor the Fed, monetarists have established a *Shadow Open Market Committee*, a group of economists that examine monetary policy with a critical eye.

- Could the Fed ever adopt monetarism as the guiding principle of monetary policy? That is unlikely for there are some practical problems in implementing monetarism. The basic problem is that the Fed does not control the money supply, it only influences the quantity of money. The Fed only controls the monetary base, as explained in the previous chapter.

- When the Fed conducts open market operations or employs one of the other monetary policy tools to change the money supply, we can trace the outcome in the money market. An increase in the money supply is shown as a rightward shift in the money supply curve. The result is a lower interest rate.

- There are a number of possible difficulties that the Fed could face in designing an effective monetary policy. Five significant possibilities are
  - ***Large unpredictable shifts in the demand for money.***
  - ***Interest rate insensitivity among consumers and businesses.***
  - ***An unresponsive interest rate caused by a liquidity trap.*** A *liquidity trap* occurs when a demand curve for money becomes horizontal at some very low interest rate. Increases in the money supply won't push the interest rate down as when the demand curve for money is downward sloping. A liquidity trap occurs when consumers hold all increases in the money supply rather than buying bonds, which must occur in order for the interest rate to decrease. The public might hold off from buying bonds if they expected interest rates to increase significantly in the future.
  - ***Lags in the effects of monetary policy.*** Changes in the money supply affect the economy with, as Milton Friedman put it, a "long and variable lag."
  - ***Differential effects of monetary policy.*** Certain sectors of the economy, such as housing and the automotive sector are more interest rate sensitive than other sectors because purchases of these goods are typically financed with borrowed money. Thus, monetary policy affects these sectors of the economy more than other sectors.

14.4 The Federal Funds Rate and Market Interest Rates

- Monetary policy is more than just adjusting the money supply, since monetary policy can also operate through the instrument of short-term market interest rates.

- **A key interest rate is the federal funds rate, the interest rate on reserves banks lend to each other.** The federal funds rate is the price paid by banks that borrow reserves from other banks. The Fed does not directly set the federal funds rate, but can influence it by changing the quantity of bank reserves through the conduct of open market operations.

- When the federal funds rate changes because of Fed actions that manipulate the quantity of bank reserves, short-term market interest rates tend to adjust in the same direction. Thus, when the federal funds rate increases, short-term market interest rates tend to go up. When the federal funds rate decreases, short-term market interest rates tend to go down.

- Monetary policy that targets short-term interest rates can be tight (contractionary) or loose (expansionary), just as with monetary policy that works through the instrument of the money supply. A tight policy causes real interest rates in the economy to rise, with the goal of keeping inflation in check. If successful, then, a tight monetary policy would lead to nominal interest rates that are not much higher than the real rates.

- A loose monetary policy causes real short-term interest rates to fall, which leads to more lending by banks to consumers. Such a policy is usually advocated when the economy is weak and inflation is not a problem.

- **Monetary policy cannot lower interest rates in the long run, except through lower inflation.** Although the Fed could try to keep real rates low by expanding the money supply, the long-run result would likely be inflation that might cause nominal interest rates to soar as time passes.

StudyCheck6
Explain why the Fed would find it difficult to maintain low nominal interest rates.

14.5 How Independent Should A Central Bank Be?

- The Federal Reserve is unique among government agencies in being subject to relatively few explicit government directives. The Fed has a great deal of independence to conduct monetary policy as it pleases, without interference from Congress or the President or special interest groups.

- The fear which originally motivated Congress to insulate the Fed from politics is that political pressures could influence the Fed to pursue an expansionary monetary policy at the wrong moment—a policy that would ultimately lead to excessive inflation. Thus, if the Fed were subject to political pressure, decision-making could favor short-term popularity at the possible expense of long-term economic goals.

- One source of the Fed's independence from political pressure is the structure of the Board of Governors. The President of the United States appoints Governors to 14-year nonrenewable terms. Governors thus are given the freedom to make policy decisions without the worry of reappointment.

- By retaining independent control of its own purse strings, the Fed retains independence of action. The Fed is a banker's bank, and as such earns interest from the discount loans it makes to commercial banks. However, the major source of the Fed's earnings is interest from its holdings of Treasury securities – securities it may have purchased with newly-printed Federal Reserve Notes!

- Another source of Federal Reserve independence is found in the financial markets. The Fed's policy actions have the potential to disturb the stock and bond markets, providing substantial gains or inflicting massive losses on the owners of stocks, bonds, and other financial instruments. Financial market participants, called "bond market vigilantes" in the press, stand ready to bail out of investments when they perceive the Fed's actions will threaten the value of those investments. That threat of a sell-off of stocks or bonds influences the Fed to act responsibly, in the best long-term interests of the economy.

- Even homeowners help keep the Fed independent. Higher expected inflation causes increases in interest rates. The interest rates on adjustable rate home mortgages go up when other interest rates rise. Homeowners with that type of mortgage will see their monthly house payments pushed up by the upward surge in interest rates which accompanies expected inflation. Hence, this segment of the public has a vested interest in seeing that the Fed acts to keep inflation in check.

- Critics argue the Fed has too much power, and charge it with decision-making which favors its own self-interests and those of special interests, such as bankers.

- Monetarists view the Fed with suspicion. Many monetarists believe that market economies are inherently stable, and that fluctuations in economic activity occur because of unstable monetary policies.

StudyCheck 7
Do you think it would be possible for the Fed to lose its independence? Explain.

MONETARY POLICY AND PRICE STABILITY 397

FILL IN THE BLANKS

1. Many economists argue that _____ should be the Fed's primary goal.

2. Cyclical unemployment stems from spending that is insufficient to purchase the full-employment level of output at current prices. Thus, to cure a recession, either prices must _____ or the quantity of money available to be spent must _____.

3. An overwhelming amount of evidence shows _____ _____ to be the root cause of inflation.

4. The quantity of money affects aggregate demand. An increase in the money supply is associated with an _____ monetary policy, also called a *looser monetary policy* because the Fed is in effect loosening the purse strings to stimulate the economy with more money. An increase in the money supply shifts aggregate demand to the _____, and thus allows more aggregate output to be purchased at each possible price level. Conversely, a _____ monetary policy would have the effect of drying up liquidity and tightening the economy's purse strings, and is thus alternatively called a *tighter monetary policy*.

5. There are two **monetary policy targets** that the Fed can influence as part of monetary policy: the _____ _____ and short-term _____ _____.

6. The _____ for money is the quantities of money that people would prefer to hold at various nominal interest rates, *ceteris paribus*. It slopes downward because people will hold _____ money when the market interest rate, the price of money, is high.

7. Three motives make people willing to pay the price of holding money: _____ motive; the _____ motive; and the _____ motive.

8. The money market is characterized by demand and supply. The money supply curve is drawn as a _____ line. The intersection of demand and supply establishes the money market _____, where the quantity of money demanded equals the money supply.

9. The market interest rate will adjust to the equilibrium interest rate. A market interest rate that is above the equilibrium interest rate will _____ until the equilibrium interest rate is reached. Similarly, a market interest rate that is below the equilibrium interest rate will _____.

10. The quantity of money demanded is less than the quantity of money supplied when the market interest rate is above its equilibrium value, called an _____ _____ of money. When the quantity of money demanded is greater than the money supply, the situation is called an _____ _____ for money.

11. In recent years, observers speculate that the Fed has usually followed a _____ rule, by which it conducts monetary policy with the aim of keeping price increases among certain basic commodities, perhaps including gold, within a low target range.

12. The _____ ____ _____ was originally proposed in the nineteenth century as a means of explaining the link between money, prices, and output, as follows:
$$M \times V = P \times Q$$
In the equation, M stands for _____, V is _____, P is _____, and Q is _____.

13. The equation of exchange forms the basis for the quantity theory of money. The quantity theory assumes that V can be treated as a _____, and that Q is at its _____ level. These two assumptions leave only M and P, money and the price level to vary. Thus, the effect of a change in the quantity of money must be a _____ change in the price level.

14. _____ is a school of economic thought, associated with Nobel-winning economist Milton Friedman (1912–), that offers a modern version of the quantity theory.

15. To avoid the recession that could result from too little money, or the inflation that could result from too much money, the monetarist policy recommendation is for the Fed to increase the money supply at a _____ rate, equal to or slightly greater than the long-run growth in aggregate output. Monetarists recommend growth in the money supply that just matches the growth in _____-_____, thereby avoiding the need for price level adjustments.

16. An increase in the money supply is shown as a _____ shift in the money supply curve. The result is a _____ interest rate.

17. A _____ occurs when a demand curve for money becomes horizontal at some very low interest rate. Increases in the money supply won't push the interest rate down as when the demand curve for money is downward sloping.

18. Changes in the money supply affect the economy with, as Milton Friedman put it, a "_____ and _____ lag."

19. A key interest rate is the _____ _____ rate, the interest rate on reserves banks lend to each other. This interest rate is the price paid by banks that borrow reserves from other banks.

20. Monetary policy that targets short-term interest rates can be tight (contractionary) or loose (expansionary), just as with monetary policy that works through the instrument of the money supply. A _____ policy causes real interest rates in the economy to rise, with the goal of keeping inflation in check.

21. A _____ monetary policy causes real short-term interest rates to fall, which leads to more lending by banks to consumers. Such a policy is usually advocated when the economy is weak and inflation is not a problem.

22. Monetary policy cannot lower interest rates in the long run, except through lower _____. Although the Fed could try to keep real rates low by expanding the money supply, the long-run result would likely be _____ that might cause nominal interest rates to _____ as time passes.

E&A 23. One source of the Fed's _____ from political pressure is the structure of the Board of Governors. The President of the United States appoints Governors to 14-year _____ terms. Governors thus are given the freedom to make policy decisions without the worry of reappointment.

24. By retaining independent control of its own purse strings, the Fed retains independence of action. The Fed is a banker's bank, and as such earns interest from the discount loans it makes to commercial banks. However, the major source of the Fed's earnings is _____ from its holdings of Treasury securities – securities it may have purchased with newly-printed Federal Reserve Notes!

25. Monetarists view the Fed with suspicion. Many monetarists believe that market economies are inherently _____, and that fluctuations in economic activity occur because of _____ monetary policies.

TRUE/FALSE/EXPLAIN
If false, explain why in the space provided.

1. The Fed considers both inflation and unemployment when making monetary policy decisions.

2. An expansionary monetary policy is also termed a looser monetary policy.

3. Besides the money supply, monetary policy works through long-term interest rates.

4. The interest rate is the opportunity cost of holding money.

5. The speculative motive for holding money involves the use of money to purchase goods and services.

6. Money, bonds, and other investments are substitutes for each other.

7. The interest rate will adjust upward or downward to ensure that the quantity of money demanded and the quantity of money supplied are equal.

8. A price rule for monetary policy implies that the Fed concentrates on the unemployment rate when making monetary policy decisions.

9. The equation of exchange can be interpreted to state that total spending equals nominal GDP.

10. According to the quantity theory of money, aggregate output depends on the quantity of money.

11. According to the quantity theory, the only effect of an increase in the money supply is to increase employment.

12. Both the growth rate of the M2 money supply and the velocity of money have remained constant over many years.

13. Monetarism views an increase in the quantity of money as leading to increased aggregate spending, and hence increased real GDP.

14. Monetarists prefer an activist policy at the Fed.

15. In practice, the effects of changes in monetary policy are nearly instantaneous.

16. The existence of a liquidity trap makes monetary policy more effective.

17. The real interest rate is the sum of the nominal interest rate plus the inflation rate.

18. An open market sale of securities by the Fed increases bank reserves, decreases the federal funds rate, and decreases short-term interest rates in the marketplace.

19. The Fed is often urged to keep interest rates low.

20. Monetarists believe that the velocity of money fluctuates significantly over time, which explains why the inflation rate and rate of monetary growth often do not coincide.

402 CHAPTER 14

E&A 21. All things considered, the Fed has very little independence when it comes to conducting monetary policy.

22. Members of the Board of Governors, like Supreme Court justices, serve for life.

23. Income and other taxes provide most of the Fed's operating revenue.

24. "Bond market vigilantes" and other investors help put pressure on the Fed to make monetary policy decisions that are free of politics.

25. If you were a monetarist you would like to see the Fed given greater power.

MULTIPLE CHOICE
Circle the letter preceding the one best answer.

1. Evidence shows that inflation is caused by
   a. too little money in the economy.
   b. too much government spending
   c. businesses and labor unions.
   d. excessive growth in the money supply.

2. An increase in the money supply shifts
   a. aggregate demand to the right.
   b. aggregate demand to the left.
   c. aggregate supply to the right.
   d. aggregate supply to the left.

3. The Fed's two primary monetary policy targets are
   a. bank reserves and long-term interest rates.
   b. the monetary base and the discount rate.
   c. bank loans and consumer credit.
   d. the money supply and short-term interest rates.

4. The demand curve for money shows that
   a. people always hold the greatest amount of money they can get.
   b. it is never a good idea to hold money.
   c. money holdings decrease with a higher interest rate.
   d. money demand is a downward sloping curve with money holdings on the horizontal axis and the price level on the vertical axis.

5. An increase in the money supply is shown graphically as a
   a. leftward shift in the upward sloping money supply curve.
   b. rightward shift in the upward sloping money supply curve.
   c. rightward shift in the downward sloping money supply curve.
   d. rightward shift in the vertical money supply curve.

6. To expand the money supply, the Fed could do all of the following EXCEPT
   a. lower the discount rate.
   b. lower the reserve requirement.
   c. make more open market purchases of government securities.
   d. tighten regulation of bank lending.

7. An excess demand for money
   a. is impossible.
   b. occurs when the market interest rate is at equilibrium.
   c. occurs when the quantity of money demanded exceeds the quantity of money supplied at the current market interest rate.
   d. means that the price level is too high.

8. The equation of exchange is
   a. $MP = VQ$.
   b. $MV = PQ$.
   c. $PV = MQ$.
   d. the reciprocal of the percentage reserve requirement.

9. If the money supply is $4 trillion and nominal GDP is $3 trillion, the velocity of money is
   a. 4/3.
   b. 3/4.
   c. $12,000,000,000,000,000,000,000,000 (i.e., $12 trillion trillion).
   d. $1 trillion.

10. According to the quantity theory, the rate of inflation will tend toward
    a. zero.
    b. the rate of growth in the money supply.
    c. the inverse of the unemployment rate.
    d. its natural rate.

11. The results depicted in Multiple Choice Figure 1 would be most consistent with
    a. Keynesian theory.
    b. supply-side theory.
    c. the quantity theory.
    d. monetarist theory.

12. The economist most closely associated with monetarism is
    a. Adam Smith.
    b. John Maynard Keynes.
    c. Milton Friedman.
    d. John Kenneth Galbraith.

13. Monetarism focuses upon
    a. the need for secure property rights.
    b. the growth rate of the money supply.
    c. changes in the velocity of money over time.
    d. how technology has created new forms of money.

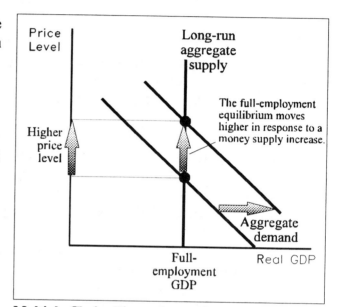

Multiple Choice Figure 1

14. A monetarist is most likely to advocate
    a. a slow, steady growth in the money supply.
    b. an increase in the money supply during recessions, but a decrease during prosperity.
    c. a decrease in the money supply during recessions, and an increase during prosperity.
    d. an exclusive reliance upon an activist monetary policy as a means by which the government can influence aggregate output and employment.

15. A difficulty in implementing monetarism is
    a. determining the best reserve requirement.
    b. maintaining sufficient reserves of gold.
    c. monitoring economic growth.
    d. measuring and controlling the quantity of money.

16. In Multiple Choice Figure 2, the vertical lines represent
    a. aggregate supply.
    b. aggregate demand.
    c. money supply.
    d. money demand.

17. In Multiple Choice Figure 2, the arrow labeled A represents a
    a. lower equilibrium market interest rate.
    b. lower inflation rate.
    c. lower money holdings.
    d. decrease in the natural rate of unemployment.

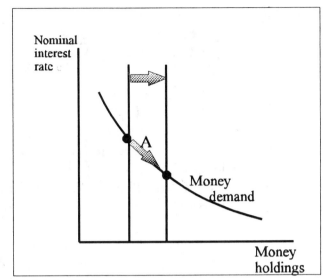

Multiple Choice Figure 2

18. The differential effects of monetary policy refers to the idea that
    a. monetary policy operates with a long and variable lag.
    b. the liquidity trap always sets in when monetary policy is used to stimulate the economy.
    c. monetary policy affects different parts of the economy more strongly than other parts.
    d. businesses and consumers are not sensitive to interest rate changes.

19. If nominal interest rates are 10 percent and the annual inflation rate is 12 percent, the real interest rate is
    a. 8 percent.
    b. 2 percent.
    c. 22 percent.
    d. -2 percent.

20. It is often suggested that the Fed should conduct its monetary policy so as to keep interest rates low. The major problem with this suggestion is that low nominal interest rates
    a. may be impossible to maintain over time, and attempting to do so could prove quite inflationary.
    b. could be maintained, but only at a substantial cost in terms of inflation.
    c. would discourage saving, which in turn would cut down on investment and potentially lead to a recession.
    d. would cut down on consumer interest income and thus potentially lead to a recession.

E&A 21. Federal Reserve independence is
a. good for the U.S. economy.
b. bad for the U.S. economy.
c. neither good nor bad for the U.S. economy.
d. harmful to businesses.

22. The Fed's major source of its income is from
a. fees charged when it clears checks for banks.
b. interest on the loans it makes to consumers.
c. interest from discount loans to banks.
d. interest from its ownership of Treasury securities.

23. Suppose the Fed were to abandon its independence and openly try to reelect a president of the United States by stimulating the economy through drastic increases in the money supply in the months before the presidential election. We would expect that
a. people would ignore the Fed's actions and focus on the candidates.
b. people would cheer the Fed on since increases in the money supply have no effect on the economy, but add to their wealth.
c. "bond market vigilantes" and other investors would bail out of investments likely to lose value because of higher expected inflation.
d. the unemployment rate would rise immediately.

24. Regarding members of the Board of Governors,
a. Congress selects members of the Board, often appointing people who contribute to their campaigns.
b. when a Democrat is president and there is an opening on the Board, a Republican must be appointed, and vice-versa.
c. each state is allowed one Governor, who is elected by popular vote.
d. sometimes a U.S. president will appointment or reappoint someone to the Board who is from the other political party.

25. According to the monetarists, the primary cause of economic instability (recessions and inflation) is
a. the Fed's steady increase in the money supply of about 3 percent per year.
b. unstable monetary policies by the Fed.
c. the U.S. Treasury.
d. the globalization of the economy.

GRASPING THE GRAPHS
Fill in each box with a concept that applies.

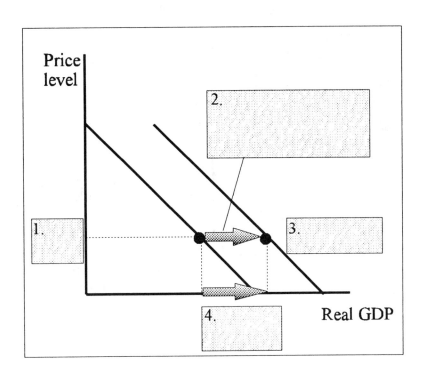

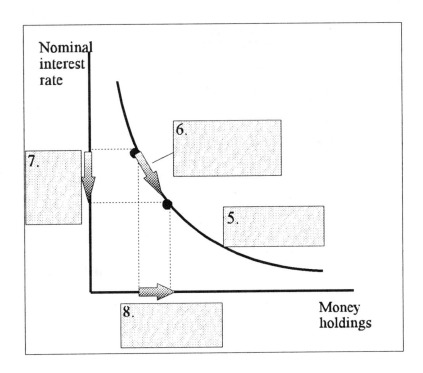

408 Chapter 14

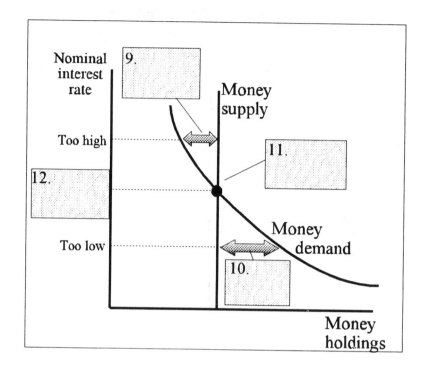

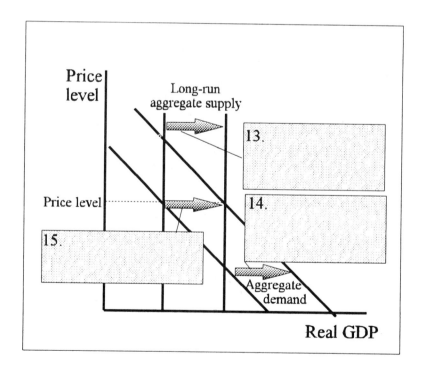

MONETARY POLICY AND PRICE STABILITY   409

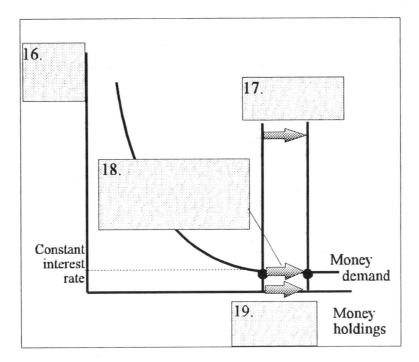

For additional practice in grasping this chapter's graphs, visit
http://www.prenhall.com/ayers and try *Smart Graph* 16 and 17,
along with *Active Graphs* 32, 33, 34, 35, and 36.

ANSWERS

STUDYCHECKS

1. When inflation occurs a tighter (contractionary) monetary policy is called for. Either a decrease in the money supply or higher short-term interest rates could be selected by the Fed as its target.

2. The graph should show the demand curve for money as downward sloping. The vertical axis should be labeled with the nominal interest rate and the horizontal axis with money holdings. A higher nominal interest rate would cause a movement up the curve, indicating that people would hold less money and seek out interest paying investments.

3. If someone will be purchasing more in the future they will increase their money holdings because of the transactions demand. If someone fears that event is likely to occur that will cause the need for more money, they will hold more money because of the precautionary motive (example: someone's car is acting up and will probably soon need a new transmission).

410 CHAPTER 14

If someone believes that interest rates will rise in the future, they will not invest in interest paying assets (such as bonds), but rather hold money until interest rates actually go up, at which point they will invest. This is the speculative motive at work.

4. When the interest rate is below equilibrium, there is an excess demand for money. People will offer their bonds and other investments for sale in order to try to satisfy the excess demand. The additional quantity of bonds offered for sale will only find buyers if they pay an interest rate higher than the current rate or offer a price that is discounted relative to the face value of the bond. As the interest rate rises, the excess demand for money decreases until it is eliminated at equilibrium.

5. Suppose that M = $100, V = 2, and Q = $10. Then, solving for P, the price level must be equal to 20. We have MV = PQ, or 100 (2) = 20 (10). Suppose that the money supply doubles to $200. Since V and Q must remain constant according to the quantity theory, we have 200 (2) = P (10). Solving for P we see that P equals 40. The price level doubled when the money supply doubled, as predicted by the quantity theory.

6. To lower nominal interest rates in the short run, the Fed would need an expansionary monetary policy. However, that would lead to inflation that would increase nominal interest rates over time. Conversely, if the Fed seeks to have low nominal rates in the long run, it must maintain a tight monetary policy to keep inflation at bay. Tight money increases real interest rates, thereby also increasing nominal rates in the short run.

7. Since the Fed was created by Congress, it would be possible for Congress to diminish Fed independence by changing the laws relating to the Fed. For example, Congress could make the Fed less independent by requiring it to turn over its interest income to Congress, and then having Congress provide the Fed's budget. Many other Congressional actions could reduce Fed independence. In fact, since Congress created the Fed, theoretically Congress could abolish it, and retain the powers of monetary policy for itself.

FILL IN THE BLANKS

1. price stability
2. fall, rise
3. excessive growth in money
4. expansionary, right, contractionary
5. money supply, interest rates
6. demand, less
7. transactions, precautionary, speculative
8. vertical, equilibrium
9. fall, rise

10. excess supply, excess demand
11. price
12. equation of exchange, the quantity of money, velocity, the price level, aggregate output
13. constant, maximum, proportional
14. Monetarism
15. steady, long-run aggregate supply
16. rightward, lower
17. liquidity trap
18. long, variable
19. federal funds
20. tight
21. loose
22. inflation, inflation, rise
23. independence, nonrenewable
24. interest
25. stable, unstable

TRUE/FALSE/EXPLAIN

1. True.
2. True.
3. False, monetary policy works through short-term interest rates.
4. True.
5. False, the speculative motive arises from a belief that interest rates will rise in the future. The transaction demand arises from purchasing.
6. True.
7. True.
8. False, a price rule means that the Fed pays a great deal of attention to prices, especially prices of basic commodities.
9. True.
10. False, aggregate output is independent of the quantity of money according to the quantity theory.
11. False, an increase in the money supply increases the price level according to the quantity theory.
12. False, the growth rate of M2 has been as low as 0 percent and as high as about 10 percent, while velocity increased during the 1990s.
13. False, more money leads to more aggregate spending and an increase in <u>nominal</u> GDP.
14. False, monetarists prefer that the Fed increase the money supply at a steady rate.
15. False, the effects of monetary policy occur with a lag.
16. False, the liquidity trap means that interest rates will be unresponsive to Fed actions to lower them.

17. True.
18. False, since bank reserves decrease, the federal funds rate increases, and interest rates increase.
19. True.
20. False, monetarists do acknowledge that velocity can change, but perceive changes in velocity as occurring slowly and predictably.
21. False, the Fed is considered to quite independent, even though the conduct of monetary policy occurs in a political atmosphere.
22. False, members of the Board of Governors serve 14-year terms.
23. False, the Fed's revenue comes from interest on bonds it owns, interest on discount loans, and fees it charges banks for its services.
24. True.
25. False, you would like to see the Fed stripped of its powers. You might even believe the Fed operates in its own interest rather than the public interest.

MULTIPLE CHOICE

1.	d	8.	b	15.	d	22.	d
2.	a	9.	b	16.	c	23.	c
3.	d	10.	b	17.	a	24.	d
4.	c	11.	d	18.	c	25.	b
5.	d	12.	c	19.	d		
6.	d	13.	b	20.	a		
7.	c	14.	a	21.	a		

GRASPING THE GRAPHS
Examples of correct answers

1. Same price level
2. More can be purchased at each price level.
3. Aggregate demand
4. More purchasing power
5. Money demand
6. Movement along money demand
7. Lower interest rate
8. More money holdings
9. Excess supply
10. Excess demand
11. Money market equilibrium

12. Equilibrium interest rate
13. Effect of economic growth
14. Monetarists aim for aggregate demand to increase only as much as long-run aggregate supply.
15. The result would be a constant price level, implying no inflation.
16. Nominal interest rate
17. Money supply
18. Liquidity trap in which the interest rate does not change
19. More money holdings

**Visit the Ayers/Collinge companion Website at http://www.prenhall.com/ayers
for further activities and exercises for this chapter.**

Part 6

THE GLOBAL ECONOMY

Chapter 15

INTO THE INTERNATIONAL MARKETPLACE

CHAPTER REVIEW

- International trade involves all of the elements of the economy within a country's borders—its *domestic* economy. In addition, international trade must also take into account foreign currencies and conflicting interests among countries.

15.1 Measuring International Transactions

- Countries trade with one another in order to increase their standards of living. Each country records the details of trade in its **balance of payments accounts**. The balance of payments accounts of the United States measure the economic interactions of the U.S. with other countries.

- The balance of payments accounts contain subaccounts that categorize the major types of international economic interactions. The two primary subaccounts are the current account and the capital account.

- A country **exports** goods and services when it sells them to another country. A country **imports** goods and services when it purchases them from another country. **The current account** measures the value of exports and imports for a specific period of time.

- The balance on the current account is the dollar value of exports minus the dollar value of imports.

- The current account divides up trade into categories of merchandise and services. The **balance of trade** refers to the merchandise portion only, meaning that it is the value of exported merchandise—tangible goods—minus the value of imported merchandise. The balance of trade is currently in deficit—the **trade deficit**—which means that the value of imported merchandise exceeds the value of exported merchandise.

- When it comes to services—intangible items—the United States exports more than it imports. The result is that the services component of the current account is in *surplus*. Because the trade deficit exceeds the services surplus, the current account overall is in deficit, which means that the value of all imports exceeds the value of all exports.

- The current account looks at flows of investment into and out of the country. Investments counted in the current account are primarily of two types: *direct investments and financial investments.*

- The balance on the U.S. capital account is the dollar value of capital inflows minus the dollar value of capital outflows. *Capital inflows* represent dollars that foreigners spend on investments in the United States. *Capital outflows* represent dollars that United States citizens and firms spend on investments abroad. Thus, when looking at the direction of dollar movements, capital inflows are similar to exports, and capital outflows are similar to imports.

- The following figure summarizes the balance of payments accounts.

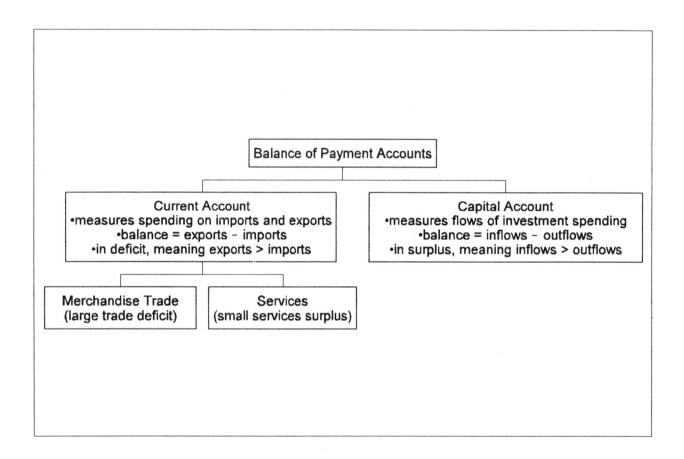

StudyCheck 1

The United States has a substantial current account deficit. Does this deficit imply anything about the capital and financial accounts? Explain.

15.2 The Impact of International Commerce

- The reason a country opens its doors to international trade, like the purpose of market trade within countries, is to get more value from the country's resources. However, while the economic pie grows because of trade, some of the slices get smaller.

- Opportunities in specific industries and types of occupations can change markedly because of international trade.

- The United States has an abundance of both physical and human capital relative to most, but not all, other countries. This means that the United States is likely to specialize in goods that are capital intensive. In other words, for the United States to gain from international trade, it exports goods that use a high proportion of capital in their production.

- Japan is in some respects more capital intensive than the United States, which explains why Japan exports so many electronic goods to this country. Over all, though, international trade causes the United States to specialize somewhat in capital-intensive goods. Exports thus increase the demand for different kinds of capital in the United States and increase the prices paid for capital.

- By increasing the return to human capital in the United States, international trade opens up attractive employment opportunities for those who have acquired skills and abilities. The return to a college education, a significant source of human capital, is higher than it would be without international trade. Conversely, job opportunities for low-skilled labor in the U.S. are harmed by international trade, as imports of labor-intensive goods lead to lower wages and fewer job openings in those industries.

- **International investment can substitute for trade.** Immigration can also substitute for trade by affecting trade patterns and the distribution of income within a country. Both capital investment and labor can move among countries, although there are usually some barriers to this migration.

- The barriers to capital movements arise from diverse sources. Investors often lack information about the risks involved in setting up shop in another country. Many of these risks are referred to as *political risks* because they involve instabilities associated with government.

- These kinds of political risks are in addition to general business risks associated with investing, and help slow down the flow of capital from one country to another. A further barrier to capital movements occurs when a government refuses to allow foreign investors into their country, or when government limits the amount of foreign investment.

- If a country has abundant capital relative to labor, it tends to have lower prices than other countries on capital-intensive goods. That country then tends to export goods that are produced with a relatively high proportion of capital and import goods that employ more labor. Likewise, labor-abundant countries tend to export goods that require a lot of labor to produce and import goods that require a lot of capital. Immigration provides countries that have relatively less labor an opportunity to increase their amount of labor.

StudyCheck 2

What would be the effect on international trade if all countries were to have identical ratios of capital to labor?

15.3 Exchange Rates

- Each country usually has its own currency. Different monies can be exchanged for each other in *currency markets,* also known as **foreign exchange markets**.

- The amount of one country's currency that trades for a unit of another country's currency is called an **exchange rate**.

INTO THE INTERNATIONAL MARKETPLACE   419

- Although global in nature, the basic operation of the currency market is easily understood using supply and demand analysis. Those on the demand side for yen include U.S. buyers of imported goods and services from Japan. They also include U.S. investors interested in such things as Japanese property, stocks, and bonds. Those supplying yen have the same sort of interests, except now the roles are reversed. They may be wanting U.S. goods or services, or U.S. investments. The exchange of currencies thus represents the exchange of goods, services, and investments—both buyers and sellers have a use for each other's currencies.

- As usual with supply and demand analysis, the horizontal axis represents the quantity of a good, and the vertical axis represents its price. Quantity here is the total amount of one currency, and price is its value per unit in terms of the other currency. That price is the exchange rate. In our example, we look at the quantity of yen and see its price in terms of dollars per yen. The market equilibrium exchange rate is associated with the intersection of demand and supply.

- At the market equilibrium exchange rate, the total quantity of yen offered for sale is just equal to the total quantity of yen purchased. Moreover, the total number of dollars being spent to obtain yen is just equal to the total number of dollars being received by those selling yen.

StudyCheck 3

How does international trade affect employment? Does it matter if there is a trade deficit? Explain, making reference to the role of the foreign exchange markets.

- Exchange rates can greatly affect the prices we see at our local stores. For example, imported products will seem cheaper if the dollar *strengthens*, meaning that it appreciates against many currencies. A stronger dollar buys more of other currencies, although just how much purchasing power is needed to make the dollar strong or how little to make it weak is a normative issue—a matter of subjective opinion. U.S. consumers and U.S. tourists abroad both like a strong dollar.

- Moreover, not only does a stronger dollar mean that the price of imports is lower to U.S. consumers, it also means that U.S. firms must keep their own prices lower to the extent that their products and imports are good substitutes among consumers.

- Although U.S. consumers benefit from a stronger dollar, U.S. producers of products that compete with imports and foreign tourists in the U.S. prefer to see the dollar weaken. A weak dollar means that U.S. goods and services seem cheap to foreigners, and foreign goods and services seem expensive to U.S. citizens.

- Some have argued that exchange rates will adjust until there is **purchasing power parity**, meaning that prices would be the same around the world for easily tradeable items. In reality, there are often too many costly details of trade for purchasing power parity to be a good guide. The most significant of these details are transportation and storage costs.

- Exchange rates do not remain constant. Currency **appreciation** occurs when a currency gets stronger. **Depreciation** occurs when the currency becomes weaker.

- The depreciation of the dollar against the yen from the early 1980s through the mid-1990s can be traced to an increase in U.S. demand for yen, which drove the dollar price of those yen higher. A dominant force behind the strong yen during this period was the demand by American importers for yen to buy the Japanese electronics and automobiles that they sold to U.S. consumers.

StudyCheck 4

Using a graph, show the effects on the exchange rate between the dollar and French franc of a major telecommunications advance in France that leads France to become a significant exporter to the United States of telecommunication services. Be sure to label both axes of your graph. (Hint: Place the quantity of French francs exchanged on the horizontal axis.)

StudyCheck 5

Suppose the U.S. government borrows more money, which in turn has the effect of increasing interest rates and the desirability of investing in the United States. On a supply and demand diagram for Japanese yen priced in terms of U.S. dollars, show the effect of this action on the exchange rate between the yen and the dollar. Label XR0 as the initial exchange rate, and XR1 as the new exchange rate. (Hint: Place the quantity of yen on the horizontal axis.)

- Governments sometimes try to influence the market exchange rates. The huge volume of global currency transactions overwhelms the efforts of any individual country. Countries have been slightly more effective when they work in synchrony. The most important of these joint efforts is conducted through a group of eight countries, called *the G8*, whose members include the United States, Britain, France, Germany, Japan, Italy, Canada and Russia. **The value of currencies exchanged worldwide in a single week exceeds the value of an entire year's worth of U.S. output.**

- In the period after World War II, governments from around the world adhered to the *Bretton Woods agreement*. The Bretton Woods agreement was a treaty signed in 1944 at Bretton Woods, New Hampshire, by most of the world's major trading countries. This agreement *pegged* the dollar to gold ($35/ounce) and all other currencies to the dollar, thereby implying *fixed exchange rates*. Governments agreed to take whatever actions would be necessary to maintain these rates. The system of fixed exchange rates was modified in stages and ultimately abandoned as unworkable. Since 1972 the system has been one of **floating exchange rates**, meaning that exchange rates have been allowed to adjust to whatever level the market dictates. However, **because governments still take actions intended to affect market exchange rates, the system is referred to as a *managed float* or *dirty float*.**

- Government inability to control exchange rates was highlighted by the precipitous depreciation of Asia's currencies as their values tumbled during the Asian currency crisis of 1998. By late July, 1998, for example, the Indonesian rupiah had dropped to 14,000 per dollar from 2,600 per dollar one year earlier. This plunge of the rupiah occurred in spite of efforts by the Indonesian government to prevent it. This abrupt depreciation of the rupiah dramatically increased the purchasing power of dollars in Indonesia and decreased the purchasing power of rupiah in the United States.

- Companies that import or export products do so in response to market prices, prices that depend centrally upon exchange rates. **Relatively higher prices at home than abroad lead to imports, while relatively lower prices at home than abroad cause exports.** The result of the prices in the free market is that countries export goods in which they have comparative advantages and import goods in which they do not.

- Recall from chapter 2 that comparative advantage occurs whenever the country can produce a good at a lower opportunity cost than could other countries. Looking at England in the following table, we see its comparative advantage is in the production of oil because the opportunity cost of oil is lower in England than in Japan. This means that Japan will export to England some of the computer chips it produces, while importing some of its oil from England.

Relative Prices within Countries in the Absence of Trade

Country	Price of a Computer Chip	Price of a Barrel of Oil	Opportunity Cost of a Barrel of Oil	Opportunity Cost of a Computer Chip
Japan	¥2,000	¥5,000	2.5 computer chips (¥5000/¥2000)	2/5 of a barrel of oil (¥2000/¥5000)
England	£3	£5	1.67 computer chips (£5/£3)	3/5 of a barrel of oil (£3/£5)

- Were the two countries to trade, the terms at which the countries could exchange oil for computer chips would settle somewhere between the two countries opportunity costs of oil for computer chips. For example, they might be 2 computer chips per barrel of oil. Equivalently, then, a computer chip would trade for ½ a barrel of oil. Currency exchange rates would adjust to make it so.

- The equilibrium exchange rate causes each country to export the good for which it has a comparative advantage and import the other good. In this way, both countries are better off by specializing and trading, meaning that their consumption possibilities would grow beyond their production possibilities. By trading, Japan obtains a barrel of oil in trade for 2 computer chips, which is less than the 2.5 computer chips a barrel of oil would cost in Japan. Trade allows England to obtain computer chips at the cost of ½ a barrel of oil rather than the cost of 3/5 of a barrel of oil that would prevail without trade.

15.4 Immigration and the Melting-Pot World

- Today immigrants account for about 8 percent of the U.S. population. The Immigration Act of 1965 opened the door to a new wave of mass immigration into the United States, totaling about 800,000 persons per year.

- Opposition to immigration arises from the following root causes:
    - Ethnic tensions arising prior to the assimilation of the newcomers into the existing culture;
    - A backlash stemming from concerns that immigration has high economic costs, such as in terms of subsidized education and social programs;
    - Concerns that immigration exposes the country to terrorist acts by those with interests hostile to America.

- The U.S. Census Bureau estimates that by the year 2050, the immigration rates established by the 1965 act will result in a U.S. population of up to 500 million people, which is about twice the population counted in the 1990 census.

- Immigration affects the economy in a variety of ways. Most controversially, immigration can change relative wages. Immigration of low-skilled workers can increase competition for low-skilled jobs and drive wages there down. Conversely, immigration of skilled workers can drive down wages that are available to other skilled workers. So immigration has the potential to either widen or reduce the wage gap between the skilled and unskilled.

- Immigrants also buy products and influence the buying habits of consumers in their new home country. Foreign products have often become popular after being introduced by immigrants.

- Another way that immigration can affect trade patterns is through the skills that immigrants bring to their new country. Also, opportunities for success in a country encourages particularly inventive and entrepreneurial immigrants. The entrepreneurship and development of technology arising from the efforts of these immigrants expands the country's production possibilities and in the process changes its patterns of trade.

- Whether or not a country allows easy immigration has a lot to do with the ownership of resources and the distribution of income within that country. For example, immigration can decrease the incomes and job opportunities for workers who find themselves in competition with the immigrants. Also, if immigrants can claim property rights or subsidies from longer-term citizens, the well-being of those citizens could easily fall, even as the country's output goes up. Thus, whether a country wants to allow easy immigration depends on its objective. If the country seeks to maximize the well-being of its longer-term citizens, it has to consider immigration's effects on those citizens' incomes and tax burdens, and might choose a relatively tight immigration policy.

- As a middle ground, many countries make special provisions for guest workers. *Guest workers* are temporary immigrants, granted limited rights to work and live in a country.

StudyCheck 6

Describe the manner in which the immigration of unskilled labor can substitute for the import of labor-intensive goods. What is a significant difference between the two alternatives?

FILL IN THE BLANKS

1. International trade involves all of the elements of the economy within a country's borders—its _____ economy. Each country records the details of trade in its _____ ___ _____ accounts.

2. The balance of payments accounts contain subaccounts that categorize the major types of international economic interactions. The two primary subaccounts are the _____ account and the _____ account.

3. A country _____ goods and services when it sells them to another country. A country _____ goods and services when it purchases them from another country. The _____ account measures the value of exports and imports for a specific period of time.

4. The balance on the current account is the dollar value of _____ minus the dollar value of _____. The current account divides up trade into categories of merchandise and services.

5. The _____ ____ _____ refers to the merchandise portion only, meaning that it is the value of exported merchandise—tangible goods—minus the value of imported merchandise. The _____ _____ is means that the value of imported merchandise exceeds the value of exported merchandise.

6. When it comes to services—intangible items—the United States exports more than it imports. The result is that the services component of the current account is in _____. Because the trade deficit exceeds the services surplus, the current account overall is in _____, which means that the value of imports exceeds the value of exports.

7. The current account looks at flows of investment into and out of the country. Investments counted in the current account are primarily of two types: _____ investments and _____ investments.

8. The balance on the U.S. capital account is the dollar value of capital inflows minus the dollar value of capital outflows. Capital _____ represent dollars that foreigners spend on investments in the United States. Capital _____ represent dollars that United States citizens and firms spend on investments abroad.

9. The United States has an abundance of both physical and human capital relative to most, but not all, other countries. This means that the United States is likely to specialize in goods that are _____ intensive.

10. The barriers to capital movements arise from diverse sources. Investors often lack information about the risks involved in setting up shop in another country. Many of these risks are referred to as _____ risks because they involve instabilities associated with government.

11. If a country has abundant capital relative to labor, it tends to have lower prices than other countries on _____-intensive goods. That country then tends to export goods that are produced with a relatively high proportion of _____ and import goods that employ more _____.

12. Each country usually has its own currency. Different monies can be exchanged for each other in currency markets, also known as _____ _____ markets. The amount of one country's currency that trades for a unit of another country's currency is called an _____ _____.

13. At the market equilibrium exchange rate, the total quantity of yen offered for sale is _____ to the total quantity of yen purchased. Moreover, the total number of dollars being spent to obtain yen is _____ to the total number of dollars being received by those selling yen.

14. Exchange rates can greatly affect the prices we see at our local stores. For example, imported products will seem cheaper if the dollar _____, meaning that it appreciates against many currencies. U.S. producers of products that compete with imports and foreign tourists in the U.S. prefer to see the dollar _____.

15. Some have argued that exchange rates will adjust until there is _____ _____ _____, meaning that prices would be the same around the world for easily tradeable items.

16. Exchange rates do not remain constant. Currency _____ occurs when a currency gets stronger. _____ occurs when the currency becomes weaker.

17. Governments sometimes try to influence the market exchange rates. The most important of these joint efforts is conducted through a group of eight countries, called the _____, whose members include the United States, Britain, France, Germany, Japan, Italy, Canada and Russia. The value of currencies exchanged worldwide in a single week exceeds the value of an entire _____ worth of U.S. output.

18. In the period after World War II, governments from around the world adhered to the _____ _____ agreement, which pegged the dollar to gold ($35/ounce) and

all other currencies to the dollar, thereby implying _____ exchange rates. Since 1972 the system has been one of _____ exchange rates, meaning that exchange rates have been allowed to adjust to whatever level the market dictates. However, because governments still take actions intended to affect market exchange rates, the system is referred to as a _____ float or a _____ _____.

19. Relatively higher prices at home than abroad lead to _____, while relatively lower prices at home than abroad cause _____. The result of the prices in the free market is that countries export goods in which they have comparative advantages and import goods in which they do not. In the following table, _____ has a comparative advantage in computer chip production and _____ has a comparative advantage in oil production.

Relative Prices within Countries in the Absence of Trade

Country	Price of a Computer Chip	Price of a Barrel of Oil	Opportunity Cost of a Barrel of Oil	Opportunity Cost of a Computer Chip
Japan	¥2,000	¥5,000	2.5 computer chips (¥5000/¥2000)	2/5 of a barrel of oil (¥2000/¥5000)
England	£3	£5	1.67 computer chips (£5/£3)	3/5 of a barrel of oil (£3/£5)

20. The equilibrium exchange rate causes each country to _____ the good for which it has a comparative advantage and _____ the other good. In this way, both countries are better off by specializing and trading, meaning that their consumption possibilities would grow beyond their _____ _____.

21. Today immigrants account for about ____ percent of the U.S. population. The _____ Act of 1965 opened the door to a new wave of mass immigration into the United States, totaling about 800,000 persons per year. The U.S. Census Bureau estimates that by the year 2050, the immigration rates established by the 1965 act will result in a U.S. population of up to 500 million people, which is about _____ the population counted in the 1990 census.

22. Immigration affects the economy in a variety of ways. Most controversially, immigration can change relative wages. Immigration of low-skilled workers can increase competition for low-skilled jobs and drive wages there _____. Conversely, immigration of skilled workers can drive _____ wages that are available to other skilled workers. So immigration has the potential to either widen or reduce the _____ gap between the skilled and unskilled.

23. Another way that immigration can affect trade patterns is through the skills that immigrants bring to their new country. Also, opportunities for success in a country encourages

particularly inventive and entrepreneurial immigrants. The entrepreneurship and development of technology arising from the efforts of these immigrants expands the country's _____ _____ and in the process changes its patterns of trade.

24. Whether or not a country allows easy immigration has a lot to do with the ownership of resources and the distribution of income within that country. For example, immigration can decrease the _____ and job opportunities for workers who find themselves in competition with the immigrants.

25. _____ workers are temporary immigrants, granted limited rights to work and live in a country.

TRUE/FALSE/EXPLAIN
If false, explain why in the space provided.

1. The current account and the capital account are the two main subaccounts of the balance of payments

2. Imported goods are entered into the balance of payments accounts as capital inflows.

3. When Japanese investors buy U.S. golf courses, their purchases show up in the capital account of the U.S. balance of payments accounts.

4. The persistent U.S. trade deficit in recent years must mean that the number of U.S. dollars that have left the country and have not returned has risen dramatically.

5. The services account has shown a surplus in recent years.

6. The larger is the U.S. trade deficit, the larger is the U.S. unemployment rate

7. The smaller and less diverse is a country, the more important is international trade.

8. Imports lead to job losses in specific industries, but there is no reason to believe that imports cause job losses in the aggregate.

9. International trade increases the return to human capital in the U.S.

10. An appreciation in the dollar means that consumers pay less for imports.

11. U.S. producers prefer a stronger dollar.

12. When a currency strengthens, it appreciates.

13. In foreign exchange markets, a managed float refers to an issuance of government bonds payable in the currency of another country.

14. U.S. manufacturers seeking to attract consumers away from rival foreign imports will have more success if the dollar strengthens against other currencies.

15. Exchange rates among the world's currencies are currently set in accordance with the Bretton Woods Agreement.

16. Relatively higher prices at home than abroad cause a country to import a good.

430 CHAPTER 15

17. International trade forces banks around the world to pay their depositors the same interest rates, no matter the currency in which interest is paid.

18. If the inauguration of international trade causes the price of widgets in a country to rise from 1 peso apiece to 2 pesos apiece, the most likely reason is that the country is exporting widgets.

19. If the start of international trade causes the price of widgets in a country to rise from 1 peso apiece to 2 pesos apiece, the country can be presumed to have a comparative advantage in the production of widgets.

20. Some countries have comparative advantages in all of the goods they consume.

21. The Immigration Act of 1965 reduced the number of immigrants to the U.S.

22. If immigrants bring new skills and technology to a country, they can expand that country's production possibilities.

23. The wage gap between skilled and unskilled labor can be increased or decreased by immigration.

24. No matter what a country's goals are, a tight immigration policy that limits the number of immigrants can never be justified.

25. The Bracero program is an example of allowing guest workers to enter the country.

MULTIPLE CHOICE
Circle the letter preceding the one best answer.

1. Which of the following is not included in the balance of payments accounts?
   a. Imports and exports of goods.
   b. Imports and exports of services.
   c. Immigration.
   d. Gifts and foreign aid.

2. If the services account is in surplus, this means that
   a. the value of imports and exports of services are equal.
   b. the value of imports of services is less than the value of the exports of services.
   c. the value of imports of services is more than the value of the exports of services.
   d. consumers gain more than producers lose.

3. A capital outflow in the U.S. balance of payments accounts occurs when
   a. Americans purchase imported goods.
   b. Americans purchase imported services.
   c. Americans invest in other countries.
   d. citizens of other countries invest in the U.S.

4. If capital outflows exceed capital inflows, the balance on the capital account will be
   a. positive.
   b. negative.
   c. either positive or negative depending upon the balance of trade.
   d. zero.

5. U.S. exports tend to be
   a. labor intensive.
   b. capital intensive.
   c. a combination of capital and labor intensive in equal proportions.
   d. not intensive in either capital or labor.

6. Regarding capital and labor,
   a. they cannot move from one country to another.
   b. they can move freely from one country to another.
   c. they can move from one country to another, with some barriers to their movement.
   d. labor can move, but capital cannot.

7. The takeover of American property by the Cuban government in the early 1960s is an example of
    a. currency appreciation.
    b. currency depreciation.
    c. purchasing power parity.
    d. political risk.

8. If a country has abundant capital relative to labor, it is likely to
    a. import goods that are capital-intensive and export goods that are labor-intensive.
    b. export goods that are capital-intensive and import goods that are labor-intensive.
    c. export more goods than it imports.
    d. import more goods than it exports.

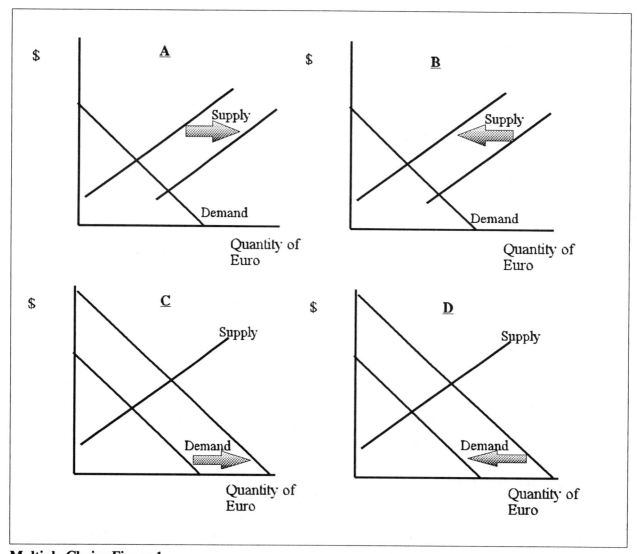

Multiple Choice Figure 1

9. In Multiple Choice Figure 1, appreciation of the dollar would occur following the supply and demand shifts shown in graphs
   a. A and B.
   b. A and C.
   c. A and D.
   d. B and C.

10. In Multiple Choice Figure 1, appreciation of the euro would occur following the supply and demand shifts shown in graphs
    a. A and B.
    b. A and C.
    c. A and D.
    d. B and C.

11. In Multiple Choice Figure 1, depreciation of the dollar would occur following the supply and demand shifts shown in graphs
    a. A and B.
    b. A and C.
    c. A and D.
    d. B and C.

12. In Multiple Choice Figure 1, depreciation of the euro would occur following the supply and demand shifts shown in graphs
    a. A and B.
    b. A and C.
    c. A and D.
    d. B and C.

13. Suppose that, ceteris paribus, European investors decide that investment in the United States is safer than it used to be. Which of the graphs in Multiple Choice Figure 1 is the most likely result of this decision?
    a. A
    b. B
    c. C
    d. D

14. Suppose that, ceteris paribus, American investors decide that investment in Europe is safer than it used to be. Which of the graphs in Multiple Choice Figure 1 is the most likely result of this decision?
    a. A
    b. B
    c. C
    d. D

434 CHAPTER 15

15. Suppose that, in response to a "buy American" advertising campaign, U.S. consumers become less inclined to buy goods made in Europe. Which of the graphs in Multiple Choice Figure 1 is the most likely result of this decision?
    a. A
    b. B
    c. C
    d. D

16. Suppose that Europeans decide that travel to the United States is less pleasant than it used to be. Which of the graphs in Multiple Choice Figure 1 is the most likely result of this change?
    a. A
    b. B
    c. C
    d. D

17. Suppose the initial exchange rate between U.S. dollars and the Japanese yen is one dollar per 100 yen. If the Japanese demand for U.S. output increases, the dollar would _____ and exchange for ____ than 100 yen.
    a. appreciate; more
    b. appreciate; less
    c. depreciate; more
    d. depreciate; less

18. The Asian currency crisis of 1998 provided an example of
    a. government control of exchange rates.
    b. the crisis that can occur when a country's currency appreciates.
    c. the crisis that can occur when a country's currency depreciates.
    d. the crisis that can occur when a country decides to stop all international trade with other countries.

19. Under a managed float, government
    a. sets an exchange rate directly, thereby eliminating the currency market.
    b. backs its currency with gold, thus limiting the fluctuations that occur in the price of its currency.
    c. does not intervene in free currency markets, with the result that exchange rates often fluctuate dramatically because of speculators and international capital movements.
    d. intervenes in the foreign exchange market by buying and selling currencies.

20. Suppose that fish and fowl are the only two tradeable goods. In the absence of trade, suppose that fish sold for 5,000 yen in Japan and for 5 pounds in England. Likewise, in the absence of trade, fowl sold for 3,000 yen in Japan and 2 pounds in England. We can conclude
   a. nothing about the comparative advantages of the countries.
   b. that England has a comparative advantage in the production of fowl and Japan has a comparative advantage in the production of fish
   c. that England has a comparative advantage in the production of fish and Japan has a comparative advantage in the production of fowl.
   d. that England has a comparative advantage in the production of both goods.

E&A 21. Immigrants make up about _____ percent of the U.S. population.
   a. 2
   b. 8
   c. 22
   d. 33

22. If immigration into the U.S. continues at its current pace it will take about ____ years for the U.S. population to be double what it was in 1990.
   a. 15
   b. 25
   c. 50
   d. 100

23. Allowing low-skill workers to immigrate into the U.S. would be expected to
   a. lead to no change in the wage gap between the skilled and unskilled.
   b. widen the wage gap between the skilled and unskilled.
   c. diminish the wage gap between the skilled and unskilled.
   d. change the wage gap between the skilled and unskilled in unpredictable ways.

24. Providing subsidies to immigrants
   a. always makes the current residents of a country better off since the immigrants will add to the country's production.
   b. will have no effect on the well being of current residents since the government will be paying the subsidies in question.
   c. could make current residents worse off, even if the country's production rises due to immigration.
   d. could increase the tax burden on current residents, but the new skills and entrepreneurial spirit of immigrants guarantee that the higher taxes will be more than offset.

436 CHAPTER 15

25. Guest workers are
   a. permanent immigrants.
   b. temporary immigrants.
   c. working illegally.
   d. students in a country other than the country where they have citizenship.

GRASPING THE GRAPHS
Fill in the boxes with a concept that applies.

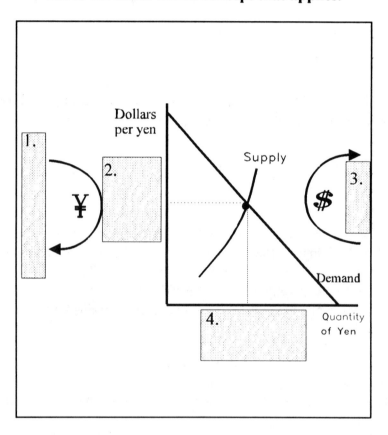

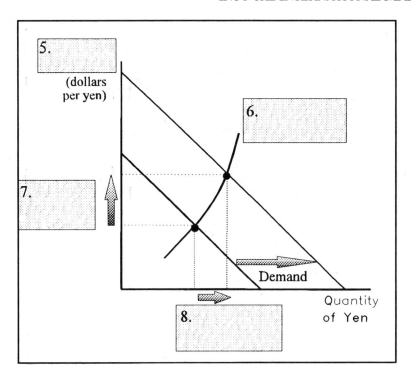

For additional practice in grasping this chapter's graphs, visit
http://www.prenhall.com/ayers and try *Active Graphs* 65, 66, and 67.

ANSWERS

STUDYCHECKS

1. Yes, to compensate for the current account deficit, there must be a surplus in the capital and financial accounts. The result is a net inflow of foreign investment spending. Overall, by definition, the balance of payments must be zero.

2. If migration resulted in all countries having identical ratios of capital to labor, world trade would shrink considerably. This is because countries with abundant capital tend to export goods that are capital-intensive, while countries with abundant labor tend to export labor-intensive goods.

3. International trade changes the distribution of jobs in a country. However, there is no reason to expect any effect on employment in total, even if the country runs a substantial trade deficit. The reason for this result can be found in the foreign exchange markets. A currency

438   CHAPTER 15

is primarily of value in the country that issues it. Thus, when currencies enter the foreign exchange market, they ordinarily bounce back to their respective countries in the form of payments for exports, investments, or in other ways. Since a country's central bank can also replace any currency that does stay abroad, foreign trade and investment is unlikely to affect aggregate spending and employment in the home country. However, foreign trade and investment do lead to more of some jobs and fewer of others.

4. See StudyCheck 4 Figure. The dollar depreciates and the franc appreciates as U.S. telecommunication customers increase their demands for French products.

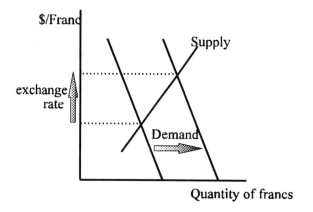

StudyCheck 4 Figure

5. See StudyCheck 5 Figure. The dollar appreciates and the yen depreciates as Japanese investors supply more yen in exchange for dollars to invest.

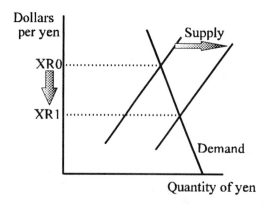

StudyCheck 5 Figure

6. Immigration of unskilled labor lowers wage rates and thus promotes the development of labor-intensive industries within the country. This means the country need not import as many of those goods: it has substituted domestic production for imports. However, not only do the immigrants increase domestic production of labor-intensive goods, they also increase population. More people means more to share in the consumption of both private-sector and public-sector goods and services. Because the immigrants in question earn income through the sale of unskilled labor services, their incomes are low. Thus, on average, they contribute less tax revenue and consume more services than the average citizen.

FILL IN THE BLANKS

1. domestic, balance of payments
2. current, capital
3. exports, imports, current account
4. exports, imports
5. balance of trade, trade deficit
6. surplus, deficit
7. direct, financial
8. inflows, outflows
9. capital
10. political
11. capital, capital, labor
12. foreign exchange, exchange rate
13. equal, equal
14. strengthens, weaken
15. purchasing power parity
16. appreciation, Depreciation
17. G8, year's
18. Bretton Woods, fixed, floating, managed, dirty
19. imports, exports, Japan, England
20. export, import, production possibilities
21. 8, Immigration, twice
22. down, down, wage
23. production possibilities
24. incomes
25. Guest

TRUE/FALSE/EXPLAIN

1. True.
2. False, imports represented negative entry in the current account.
3. True.
4. False, countervailing flows of dollars show up elsewhere in the current account, in the capital account, and in the statistical discrepancy.
5. True.
6. False, the record trade deficits of the 1980s and 1990s were associated with very low U.S. unemployment.
7. True.
8. True.
9. True.
10. True.
11. False, producers prefer a weaker dollar because it makes their exports cheaper and their competitors' imports more expensive.
12. True.
13. False, a managed float occurs when governments attempt to influence market exchange rates.
14. False, a stronger dollar makes imports less expensive and consumers more likely to buy them.
15. False, supply and demand in the marketplace determine exchange rates.
16. True.
17. False, banks in countries with high inflation or high risk will have to pay more to attract deposits.
18. True.
19. True.
20. False, since comparative advantage is defined terms of opportunity costs, it is not possible for country to have comparative advantages and all the goods that it consumes.
21. False, the Immigration Act of 1965 increased U.S. immigration.
22. True.
23. True.
24. False, a tight immigration policy can be justified if current residents are made worse off by immigration.
25. True.

MULTIPLE CHOICE

1. c
2. c
3. c
4. b
5. b
6. c
7. d
8. b
9. c
10. d
11. d
12. c
13. a
14. c
15. d
16. b
17. a
18. c
19. d
20. b
21. b
22. c
23. b
24. c
25. b

GRASPING THE GRAPHS
Examples of correct answers

1. Japan
2. Equilibrium exchange rate
3. USA
4. Equilibrium quantity of yen
5. Exchange rate
6. Supply of yen
7. Dollar depreciates, yen appreciates
8. Larger quantity of yen exchanged

Visit the Ayers/Collinge companion Website at http://www.prenhall.com/ayers for further activities and exercises for this chapter.

Chapter 16

POLICY TOWARD TRADE

CHAPTER REVIEW

16.1 Assessing Gains from Trade

- International trade occurs in response to differences between the price of a good in the country's own market—its domestic market—and the price that the good sells for in the rest of the world—the *world price*. When a country opens its doors to international trade, the price in the domestic market will come to equal that in the world market. If that means that the domestic price rises to meet the higher world price, then the country exports the good. If the world price causes the domestic price to drop, then the country imports the good.

- Before free trade, the country's prices would have been based solely on its own domestic supply and demand curves. However, goods and services that are widely traded among countries have a *world price*, which is the price that the good trades for in the global marketplace.

- The world price of a good is determined by supply and demand for the good from all trading countries. **Free trade implies that a country's producers must accept world market prices, which would entail a higher price for some goods and a lower price for others.**

- **Imports allow domestic consumers to pay a lower price for goods.** They benefit from a lower price per unit for goods that they buy. **They also gain by consuming more of the good**, supplementing the lower quantity supplied by domestic producers with imports from other countries. The gains to consumers are measured by the increase in consumer surplus, defined as the difference between demand and price.

- The price drop from imports causes producers to lose, however. In general, producer surplus is defined as the difference between price and supply. After the lower price that results from international trade, producer surplus drops.

- **The gains to consumers from imports more than offset the losses to producers, which reveals that the country as a whole is better off allowing imports.**

StudyCheck 1
Graph a situation in which the world price leads to imports. Label the domestic quantity demanded, domestic quantity supplied, and the amount imported. Indicate the amount that consumers gain or lose. Also indicate the amount that producers gain or lose.

- Suppose the world price is above the domestic price. In this case, the price difference causes the domestic quantity supplied to be greater than the domestic quantity demanded. This difference between quantity supplied and the quantity demanded results in an excess quantity of the product. This excess quantity is exported.

- **In the case of exports, producers win and consumers lose.** Producers win because they sell more at a higher price. Their gain is measured by the increase in producer surplus. Consumers lose because they must pay the higher world price, and thus consume less. Their consumer surplus drops. Because producer surplus increases by more than consumer surplus shrinks, producers gain more than consumers lose. So, on balance, **the country as a whole gains by allowing exports.** In short, both imports and exports lead to more gains than losses.

StudyCheck 2

Graph a situation in which the world price leads to exports. Label the domestic quantity demanded, domestic quantity supplied, and the amount exported. Indicate the amount that consumers gain or lose. Also indicate the amount that producers gain or lose.

16.2 Trade Agreements

- Countries must choose how wide to open their doors to international trade. An **open economy** is a country that erects no barriers to international trade and investment. In contrast, a *closed economy* shuts itself off from foreign investment and trade.

- Countries design their trade policies with an eye toward their own self interests. Since governments are by nature political, trade strategies usually contain a mix of political and economic objectives. However, most countries recognize that their interests are usually best served by freeing up trade with other countries. In a misguided fight against the high unemployment of the Great Depression of the 1930s, the U.S. and other countries engaged in a *trade war*, a situation in which countries punish each other and themselves through retaliatory trade restrictions.

- Most countries have signed the **General Agreement on Tariffs and Trade (GATT)** that aims to avoid trade wars and promote free trade. The GATT was initially signed in 1947 by the 23 major trading countries of the world at that time. Over the intervening years, the agreement has been updated and membership has grown to 110 countries.

- Since 1995, the GATT has been administered by the **World Trade Organization,** an arm of the GATT created to settle trade disputes among GATT members and monitor compliance with provisions of the GATT.

- The initial impetus for the GATT agreement was the prohibitively high **tariffs**—taxes on imports— imposed by the United States and some other countries in the decade prior to World War II. Most significantly, the **Smoot-Hawley Act** was passed by the U.S. Congress in 1930 as a means to fight the unemployment of the Great Depression. The Act raised import tariffs to an average rate of 52 percent on more than 20,000 products, a level that was so prohibitively high that imports nearly ceased. Such *beggar-thy-neighbor* protectionist policies didn't work for the U.S. or anybody else.

- The GATT required significant tariff reductions. It has been strengthened over the years through rounds of trade negotiations that have achieved further reductions in tariffs. The negotiations have also placed restrictions on **quotas**, which limit the quantity of imports of products a country allows, and on other **nontariff barriers**, which is a catch-all category for the variety of other actions a country can take to restrict trade. Most recently, the *Uruguay round* of negotiations took eight years of often contentious bargaining before being ratified by the United States and other countries in late 1994. It established the World Trade Organization and dealt with various thorny issues, such as tariffs, agricultural subsidies, services, and intellectual property.

- In addition to joining the GATT, most countries have also gone the route of forming regional **trading blocs**, agreements that lower trade barriers among member countries. For example, the European Economic Community is considered a trading bloc, because it has lower trade barriers among its member countries than to the rest of the world. By signing the **North American Free Trade Agreement,** commonly known as **NAFTA**, the United States, Canada, and Mexico also formed a trading bloc. The *Mercosur* is primarily a South American trading bloc.

- To the extent that regional trading blocs reduce tariffs and other trade restrictions, the trading blocs promote trade among their members. This trade can come from two sources. First is the **trade creation effect,** which involves an increase in world trade. The trade creation effect is efficient, since it allows countries to specialize according to comparative advantage.

- The second is the **trade diversion effect,** which represents trade that would have occurred with countries outside the trading bloc, but that is diverted to countries within a trading bloc in response to lower tariff rates. Trade diversion is inefficient, since it causes trade to respond to price signals from government—relative tariff rates—rather than to comparative advantage.

POLICY TOWARD TRADE 447

- Economists generally support regional trading blocs as a step toward free trade. However, even supporters of regional agreements have reservations about trade-diversion effects.

16.3 Trade Policy Options

- Counter to the spirit of the GATT and regional trading blocs, all major countries have some restrictions on trade. Policies that accomplish this goal are termed *protectionist,* even though these policies usually harm rather than protect the economy as a whole.

- Protectionist policies come in two basic forms: tariffs and nontariff barriers. Nontariff barriers can be either quotas—quantity restrictions on imports—or any of a variety of other actions that make importing more difficult.

- A tariff is a tax on an imported product. Demand for an imported product tells the quantities of the product consumers would purchase from foreign sources at each possible price. This demand is sometimes called *residual demand,* since it represents demand that is left over after consumers have bought from domestic suppliers. **Tariffs increase the cost of selling imported products.**

- By raising barriers to the entry of foreign products, **tariffs can be viewed as a form of price support for domestic producers.** The higher price of imports causes the demand curve to shift to the right for domestic products that are close substitutes.

- Tariffs are said to be *transparent,* meaning that their effects on prices are clear for all to see. The United States has an extensive array of tariffs, most of which are currently below 6 percent and falling. Most other major trading countries also have similar tariffs. With some exceptions, tariff rates are kept low by the GATT.

- Import quotas are an alternative to import tariffs and can accomplish the same goals as a tariff. Unlike an import tariff, an import quota restricts the quantity of imports directly and thus cuts off supply from abroad at the quota quantity.

448   CHAPTER 16

StudyCheck 3

Graph the effects of an import quota, indicating the quantity that is allowed to be imported, and the amount by which the domestic price would rise in response to the quota.

- As an alternative to tariffs and import quotas, the United States and some other countries have chosen to negotiate **voluntary export restraints,** in which individual exporting countries agree to limit the quantities they export. The alternative would be for the United States or other importing countries to impose import quotas.

- Exporting countries can charge higher prices per unit under a voluntary export restraint than they could if they face import quotas. Exporting countries charge more because they are not competing against each other—they each have their preassigned export restraints and are not allowed to fill those of other exporting countries.

- Quotas and voluntary export restraints are examples of nontariff barriers to trade, which include all ways other than tariffs that countries make importing difficult. Most nontariff barriers do not restrict imports explicitly; their effects are even less transparent than quotas. For example, paperwork and red tape delays can inhibit trade.

16.4 The Free Trade Debate

- If the arguments for and against free trade were to be counted, free trade would come up very short. However, the number of objections is not important. It is their validity that matters.

POLICY TOWARD TRADE 449

The objections to free trade commonly have limited applicability or are based on questionable logic.

- If imports or exports seriously threaten national defense, it makes sense to restrict them. However, translating national defense interests into policy requires judgments and debate. The judgments are often difficult and the source of debate.

StudyCheck 4

Why is it difficult to determine when international trade should be restricted for reasons of national defense? Provide an example where the choice is unclear.

- The United States sometimes uses *trade sanctions*, which restrict trade with countries such as Cuba and Iraq that have policies it opposes. Note that Cuba's Fidel Castro and Iraq's Saddam Hussein have had remarkable staying power, even as the trade sanctions contributed to the poverty of their economies. Despite their lack of effectiveness, trade sanctions are often popular with the public.

- Some U.S. industries cannot produce products as cheaply as products from abroad, perhaps because foreign producers face weak standards of behavior. For example, they might not need to do as much to protect the environment and the health and safety of their workers. Should the United States attempt to estimate the extra costs of complying with U.S. standards and then add that cost to imports by imposing an appropriate set of tariffs? Some critics of current trade policy suggest that this approach is the only way to achieve a *level playing field*.

- **Dumping** is defined as the selling of a good for less than its cost of production. Countries dump for many reasons. For example, the company might have overestimated demand for

450　Chapter 16

its product and finds itself stuck with too much—a clearance sale, so to speak. Alternatively, a company may be selling output at a price that covers wages, materials, and other operating expenses of production, but does not cover the cost of its capital and other costs that it must pay whether it produces or not. However, dumping is illegal across countries according to the GATT.

- The United States presumes dumping whenever a foreign company charges less in the United States than it does at home, irrespective of its costs. The GATT and U.S. law permit anti-dumping tariffs when dumping harms a domestic industry.

- Consumers gain from the low prices that result from dumping. The only strong economic argument in favor of restricting dumping occurs in the special case of strategic dumping. **Strategic dumping** is dumping that aims to drive the competition out of business so that the firms doing the dumping can monopolize output and drive prices up in the future. However, the prospects for successful strategic dumping are highly questionable in most industries.

- Developing countries often try to nurture new industries they hope will one day become a source of export earnings. These **infant industries** are thought to need protection in the rough world marketplace. The infant industry argument claims that government must first identify promising industries and then erect import barriers to protect them. When the infants grow strong enough to fend for themselves, government should remove the barriers.

- The infant industry argument is unconvincing if markets function efficiently. In the free marketplace, *venture capitalists* and other private investors will often support firms through many years of losses. They will do so if they expect that the firms will eventually become profitable and reward their patience. Unfortunately, there is much less assurance that government will pick industries that are likely to survive on their own. Governments often use political considerations to select so-called infant industries. By requiring government subsidies to stay afloat, and by charging prices above prices in the rest of the world, such industries have proven to be expensive for governments and consumers alike.

E&A 16.5 Energy Security—A Question of Oil Imports

- There are many possibilities for developing *alternative fuels*, so-called because they provide an alternative to the traditional fossil fuels of coal, natural gas and crude oil. These alternative fuels have one thing in common—they all cost more than the oil and other fossil fuels that they would replace. For that reason, without government assistance, the marketplace has not financed the development and production of such alternative fuels as ethanol, wind power, and solar power.

- The price of oil in the world market has fluctuated from under $20 per barrel to over $30 per barrel in the last few years. However, the cost of importing that oil into the United States might be significantly higher. There are costs that the importers do not currently pay that perhaps the country as a whole does pay. These are the costs having to do with energy freedom.

- The U.S. economy consumes tremendous amounts of petroleum, about 777 million gallons per day as of January, 2002. The U.S. imports 55 - 60 percent of the oil it uses, with imports exceeding 50 percent of the total for the first time in 1994. Because the oil market is global, a disruption in oil exports from the Middle East would bring Europeans and other countries into competition for oil that would otherwise go to the United States. By the same token, the U.S. presence in world oil market increases petroleum prices and the wealth of oil exporters. This situation means that:
  - The U.S. is vulnerable to political instability in the Middle East and in other oil-exporting countries.
  - The U.S. is a source of income to Middle Eastern countries with interests hostile to those of the United States.

- These *external costs* of oil imports are not reflected in the price paid by importers. To "internalize" them, the United States could levy an *oil import fee*, an common name for an import tariff when applied to oil.

- An oil import fee would raise the price of imported oil and encourage the development of alternative fuels. U.S. producers would produce more, and consumers consume less.

- If the U.S. raises the price of imported oil, U.S. producers will substitute domestic oil, which increases the price of domestic oil relative to oil available on the world market. The higher price would attract resources from elsewhere in the economy to increase production from existing U.S. oilfields, as well as to increase the search for new supplies. Likewise, some existing industries that consume large amounts of oil would shrink or leave the country. For example, a higher oil price in the U.S. relative to other countries would probably cause petrochemical production to be moved abroad.

- Since oil is a nonrenewable resource, opponents of oil import fees argue that such a fee would "drain America first." Down the road, as U.S. wells are pumped dry more quickly, the U.S. might be forced to rely even more heavily on foreign supplies. In that view, oil import fees might help in the present, but would make matters worse over time. The economy would grow faster and stronger with cheaper energy and be better positioned to weather energy disruptions if they ever do materialize.

- Also, higher oil prices could prompt the substitution of coal and nuclear power, both of which can harm the environment. Oil production itself can cause significant environmental damage. For example, the General Accounting Office estimated in July, 2002, that oil companies pumping oil from the Alaska's North Slope oil fields will face about $6 billion worth of environmental cleanup costs when their wells run dry. Since the opening of the Trans-Alaska pipeline in 1977, oil companies have pumped more than 13 billion barrels of oil and provided about 20 percent of the oil produced in the United States. The prospect of an additional environmental damages to the Alaska National Wildlife Refuge caused to the U.S. Congress to reject President Bush's proposal to allow oil exploration in that area.

- The subject of oil import fees is obviously contentious, with the topic discussed off and on for decades. While the U.S. does not have an oil import fee, it does have another policy that gives it a measure of protection from the uncertainties of oil politics. Specifically, the U.S. maintains a *Strategic Petroleum Reserve* in the form of a huge quantity of oil that the U.S. government has been stashing away each year. That reserve was tapped when, in the face of oil prices that had doubled to more than $30 per barrel in 2000, President Clinton ordered a limited sale from that reserve. Whether for this reason or other reasons, the price did drop back after that action.

StudyCheck 5

Explain the effects of an oil import fee on domestic production and consumption, as well as the amount imported. Why might the fee increase the use of alternative fuels? How might these alternative fuels be more environmentally damaging than the oil they replace?

FILL IN THE BLANKS

1. International trade occurs in response to differences between the price of a good in the country's own market—its _____ market—and the price that the good sells for in the rest of the world—the world price. When a country opens its doors to international trade, the price in the domestic market will come to _____ that in the world market. If that means that the domestic price rises to meet the higher world price, then the country _____ the good. If the world price causes the domestic price to drop, then the country _____ the good.

2. Imports allow domestic consumers to pay a _____ price for goods. The gains to consumers are measured by the increase in _____ _____, defined as the difference between demand and price. The price _____ from imports causes producers to lose, however. In general, producer surplus is defined as the difference between price and supply. After the lower price that results from international trade, however, producer surplus _____. The gains to consumers from imports more than offset the losses to producers, which reveals that the country as a whole is better off allowing imports.

3. Suppose the world price is above the domestic price. In this case, the price difference causes the domestic quantity supplied to be _____ than the domestic quantity demanded. This difference between quantity supplied and the quantity demanded results in an _____ quantity of the product, which is then _____.

4. In the case of exports, producers win and consumers lose. Producers win because they sell more at a higher price. Their gain is measured by the _____ in producer surplus. Consumers lose because they must pay the higher world price, and thus consume less. Their consumer surplus drops _____. Because producer surplus increases by more than consumer surplus shrinks, producers gain more than consumers lose. So, on balance, the country as a whole gains by allowing exports. In short, both imports and exports lead to more gains than losses.

5. Countries must choose how wide to open their doors to international trade. An _____ economy is a country that erects no barriers to international trade and investment. In contrast, a _____ economy shuts itself off from foreign investment and trade.

6. Most countries have signed the _____ _____ _____ _____ _____ _____ (GATT) that aims to avoid trade wars and promote free trade. Since 1995, the GATT has been administered by the _____ _____ _____, an arm of the GATT created to settle trade disputes among GATT members and monitor compliance with provisions of the GATT.

7. The initial impetus for the GATT agreement was the prohibitively high tariffs—taxes on imports— imposed by the United States and some other countries in the decade prior to World War II. Most significantly, the _____-_____ Act was passed by the U.S. Congress in 1930 as a means to fight the unemployment of the Great Depression. The Act raised import tariffs to an average rate of 52 percent on more than 20,000 products. Such _____-thy-neighbor protectionist policies didn't work for the U.S. or anybody else.

8. The GATT required significant tariff _____. Most recently, the _____ round of negotiations took eight years of often contentious bargaining before being ratified by the United States and other countries in late 1994.

9. In addition to joining the GATT, most countries have also gone the route of forming _____ _____ _____, agreements that lower trade barriers among member countries. Examples include the European Economic Community and the North American Free Trade Agreement.

10. To the extent that regional trading blocs reduce tariffs and other trade restrictions, the trading blocs promote trade among their members. This trade can come from two sources. First is the _____ _____ effect, which involves an increase in world trade. This effect is efficient, since it allows countries to specialize according to comparative advantage.

11. The second is the _____ _____ effect, which represents trade that would have occurred with countries outside the trading bloc, but that is diverted to countries within a trading bloc in response to lower tariff rates. This effect is inefficient, since it causes trade to respond to price signals from government—relative tariff rates—rather than to comparative advantage.

12. Protectionist policies come in two basic forms: _____ and _____ barriers. Nontariff barriers can be either quotas—quantity restrictions on imports—or any of a variety of other actions that make importing more difficult.

13. A _____ is a tax on an imported product. Demand for an imported product tells the quantities of the product consumers would purchase from foreign sources at each possible price. This demand is sometimes called _____ demand, since it represents demand that is left over after consumers have bought from domestic suppliers.

14. Tariffs are said to be _____, meaning that their effects on prices are clear for all to see. The United States has an extensive array of tariffs, most of which are currently below ____ percent and falling.

15. Import _____ are an alternative to import tariffs and can accomplish the same goals as a tariff by restricting the quantity of imports directly.

16. As an alternative to tariffs and import quotas, the United States and some other countries have chosen to negotiate _____ _____ _____, in which individual exporting countries agree to limit the quantities they export.

17. Exporting countries can charge _____ prices per unit under a voluntary export restraint than they could if they face import quotas. Exporting countries charge more because they are not competing against each other—they each have their preassigned export restraints and are not allowed to fill those of other exporting countries.

18. Quotas and voluntary export restraints are examples of _____ _____ to trade, which include all ways other than tariffs that countries make importing difficult.

19. _____ is defined as the selling of a good for less than its cost of production. _____ _____ aims to drive the competition out of business so that the firms doing the dumping can monopolize output and drive prices up in the future.

20. Developing countries often try to nurture new industries they hope will one day become a source of export earnings. These _____ industries are thought to need protection in the rough world marketplace.

21. There are many possibilities for developing alternative fuels, so-called because they provide an alternative to the traditional fossil fuels of coal, natural gas and crude oil. These alternative fuels have one thing in common—they all cost _____ than the oil and other fossil fuels that they would replace. For that reason, without _____ assistance, the marketplace has not financed the development and production of such alternative fuels as ethanol, wind power, and solar power.

22. The price of oil in the world market has fluctuated from under _____ per barrel to over _____ per barrel in the last few years.

23. The U.S. economy consumes tremendous amounts of petroleum, about 777 million gallons per day as of January, 2002. The U.S. imports _____ to _____ percent of the oil it uses, with imports exceeding 50 percent of the total for the first time in 1994.

24. The _____ costs of oil imports are not reflected in the price paid by importers. To "internalize" them, the United States could levy an _____ _____ fee, an common name for an import tariff when applied to oil. Such a fee would raise _____ the price of imported oil and encourage the development of alternative fuels. U.S. producers would produce _____, and consumers consume _____. If the U.S. raises the price of imported oil, U.S. producers will substitute domestic oil, which _____ the price of domestic oil relative to oil available on the world market.

25. While the U.S. does not have an oil import fee, it does have another policy that gives it a measure of protection from the uncertainties of oil politics. Specifically, the U.S. maintains a _____ _____ _____ in the form of a huge quantity of oil that the U.S. government has been stashing away each year.

TRUE/FALSE/EXPLAIN
If false, explain why in the space provided.

1. Free trade refers to when a country uses quotas rather than tariffs as a way to restrict imports.

2. When a country imposes an import tariff or other trade restriction, the gains to the country's producers will normally exceed the loss to the country's consumers.

3. When a tariff is imposed on imports of gizmos, both the country's gizmo producers and the government treasury will benefit.

4. Imposing a tariff on the import of a good will raise its price in the domestic market, unless the good is also produced and sold domestically.

5. Tariffs bring in government revenues, but have no effect on the quantity of goods imported.

6. A quota can be set to have the same effect as a tariff in terms of the quantity of a product allowed into the country and the prices paid by consumers.

7. A sugar import quota benefits producers of corn-based sweeteners.

8. The United States restricts the import of sugar through a set of country-by-country quotas.

9. Other countries would prefer that the United States negotiate import quotas rather than voluntary export restraints.

10. Both voluntary export restraints and import quotas drive up prices to U.S. consumers.

11. When other countries voluntarily limit their exports to the United States, the United States pays less per unit for those exports.

12. Economists usually call for greater restrictions on imports than politicians will agree to.

13. The General Agreement on Tariffs and Trade (GATT) is a pact among countries who seek to protect their domestic industries against foreign competition through the maintenance of high tariff barriers.

14. The United States belongs to a regional trading bloc, entitled the NAFTA.

15. In the absence of government protection, private investors are likely to support infant industries that promise to mature into profitable companies in the future.

16. It is often difficult to determine in practice the extent to which imports or exports truly threaten national defense.

458 CHAPTER 16

17. The only time it makes economic sense for government to restrict imports is in the case of infant industries.

18. At least temporarily, dumping by foreign companies results in lower prices for U.S. consumers.

19. Strategic dumping refers to when a country's producers use unprofitably low prices as a way to drive producers in other countries out of business, after which prices would be set much higher.

20. Prospects for successful strategic dumping are common in most industries.

E&A 21. Alternative fuels have typically cost more than the coal, natural gas, or crude oil that they are intended to replace.

22. One reason for government to subsidize alternative fuels is to promote energy security.

23. Oil imported into the United States comes almost exclusively from countries of the Middle East.

24. External costs of oil imports could be internalized by an oil import fee.

25. Opponents of an oil import fee argue that such a fee would "drain America first."

MULTIPLE CHOICE
Circle the letter preceding the one best answer.

1. In Multiple Choice Figure 1, the point labeled G represents the
   a. domestic quantity produced when international trade is allowed.
   b. domestic quantity consumed when international trade is allowed.
   c. domestic quantity both produced and consumed when international trade is not allowed.
   d. quantity of imports when international trade is allowed.

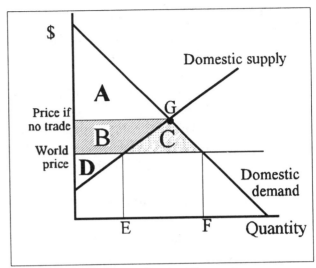

Multiple Choice Figure 1

2. In Multiple Choice Figure 1, the amount of social surplus in the absence of international trade is given by the areas
   a. A + B + C.
   b. A + B + C + D.
   c. A + B + D.
   d. A + B + D – C.

3. In Multiple Choice Figure 1, point E represents the quantity _____ and point F represents the quantity _____ when international trade is allowed.
   a. produced domestically; consumed domestically
   b. consumed domestically; produced domestically
   c. imported; exported
   d. consumed domestically; exported

4. In Multiple Choice Figure 1, the distance between point E and point F represents the quantity that is
   a. imported.
   b. exported.
   c. produced domestically.
   d. consumed domestically.

5. In Multiple Choice Figure 2, the point labeled G represents the
   a. domestic quantity produced when international trade is allowed.
   b. domestic quantity consumed when international trade is allowed.
   c. domestic quantity both produced and consumed when international trade is not allowed.
   d. quantity of imports when international trade is allowed.

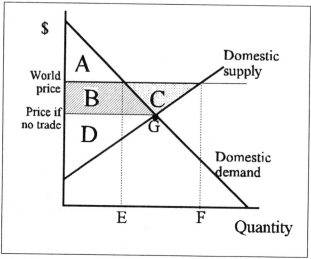

Multiple Choice Figure 2

6. In Multiple Choice Figure 2, the amount of social surplus in the presence of international trade is given by the areas
   a. A + B + C.
   b. A + B + C + D.
   c. A + B + D.
   d. A + B + D − C.

7. In Multiple Choice Figure 2, point E represents the quantity _____ and point F represents the quantity _____ when international trade is allowed.
   a. produced domestically; consumed domestically
   b. consumed domestically; produced domestically
   c. imported; exported
   d. consumed domestically; exported

8. In Multiple Choice Figure 2, the distance between point E and point F represents the quantity that is
   a. imported.
   b. exported.
   c. produced domestically.
   d. consumed domestically.

9. If the United States imposes a tariff on the import of tin, which of the following groups will lose?
   a. U.S. tin producers.
   b. The U.S. Treasury.
   c. U.S. producers of substitutes for tin.
   d. The U.S. economy as a whole.

10. As a general rule, a country gains the most when it
    a. restricts neither imports nor exports.
    b. prohibits all foreign trade.
    c. restricts imports but not exports.
    d. restricts exports but not imports.

11. One reason for the enactment of tariffs into law is that they
    a. result in net job creation in the countries that enact them.
    b. reflect the overwhelming belief among economists that free trade is harmful.
    c. act as a price support for domestic producers.
    d. encourage consumers to purchase imported goods.

12. Which of the following has the effect of increasing the price that foreigners receive for exporting their products to the United States?
    a. A voluntary export restraint.
    b. An import quota.
    c. A tariff.
    d. Nontariff barriers.

13. If the United States gives other countries a choice between voluntary export restraints or the U.S. imposition of import quotas, the other countries are likely to choose
    a. import quotas, because this allows them to compete with other countries to fill those quotas.
    b. import quotas, because this allows them to charge higher prices.
    c. voluntary export restraints, because that would allow them to charge higher prices.
    d. voluntary export restraints, because they are voluntary.

14. The U.S. requirement that Mexican bricks imported into the United States be stamped "Made in Mexico" is an example of a
    a. tariff.
    b. quota.
    c. subsidy.
    d. nontariff barrier.

15. The General Agreement on Tariffs and Trade is administered by the
    a. president of the United States.
    b. U.S. Department of Commerce.
    c. United Nations.
    d. World Trade Organization.

462 CHAPTER 16

16. Which of the following forms a trading bloc?
    a. The United States.
    b. The United Nations.
    c. The World Trade Organization.
    d. The North American Free Trade Agreement.

17. A favorable effect of a trading bloc is
    a. trade diversion.
    b. trade creation.
    c. devaluation of the currency.
    d. the regional effect.

18. Regarding the numerous arguments against free trade,
    a. a number of them are so convincing that it is clear that the United States should restrict trade.
    b. free trade is widely recognized as inefficient, so that additional arguments against free trade are unnecessary.
    c. most of them apply to a country's exports, but not to its imports.
    d. they are mostly based on questionable assumptions or have limited applicability.

19. If the United States were to impose a fee on the import of shoes, it would be likely to do all of the following EXCEPT
    a. violate GATT.
    b. benefit U.S. shoe producers.
    c. provide government revenues.
    d. provide benefits to the United States greater than costs to the United States.

20. In his 1999 State of the Union Address, President Clinton warned the Japanese against dumping steel in the U.S. market. If the Japanese had been doing this, then
    a. U.S. producers of steel lost more than U.S. consumers of steel gained while the dumping occurred.
    b. the Japanese priced their steel sold in the United States below the price for which it was sold in Japan, and possibly below cost.
    c. the United States need for steelmaking capacity during wartime clearly required that retaliatory action be taken until this dumping stopped.
    d. the quality of products made with dumped Japanese steel cannot be relied upon.

21. Which of the following would be an advantage to the United States of imposing a fee on imported oil?
    a. U.S. consumers would paying lower prices for gasoline.
    b. U.S. fuel-using industries would see their costs go down relative to similar industries in other countries.
    c. the U.S. environment would be better protected.
    d. the United States would have less reason to try to influence political events in oil-producing countries.

22. An oil import fee would cause U.S. oil production to _____ and U.S. oil consumption to _____.
    a. increase; increase
    b. increase; decrease
    c. decrease; increase
    d. decrease; decrease

23. If the United States raises the price of imported oil,
    a. there would be no effect on the amount of oil pumped from existing fields.
    b. less effort would be put into finding new U.S. oilfields or other sources of energy supply.
    c. some existing industries that consume large amounts of oil would shrink or leave the country.
    d. demand would decrease for coal and nuclear power.

24. Since the opening of the Trans Alaskan pipeline, oil from Alaska has accounted for about ___ percent of total oil production in the United States.
    a. 10
    b. 20
    c. 50
    d. 75

25. The strategic petroleum reserve is a
    a. huge quantity of oil the U.S. government has been stashing away in order to offset potential disruptions in the supply of oil from other countries.
    b. military force that can be deployed at short notice in order to protect the world's oilfields.
    c. military force that is composed of Army reservists who are called to active-duty in order to protect America's oilfields in a time of crisis.
    d. very large oilfield that is found under the Alaskan National Wildlife Refuge, and which the U.S. government has set aside for use only in time of national emergency.

GRASPING THE GRAPHS
Fill in each box with a concept that applies.

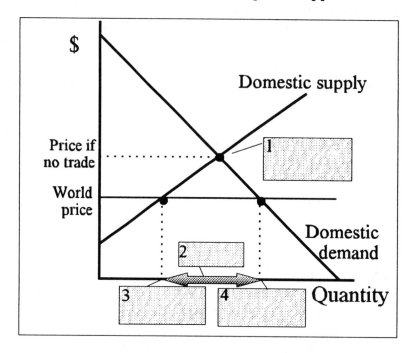

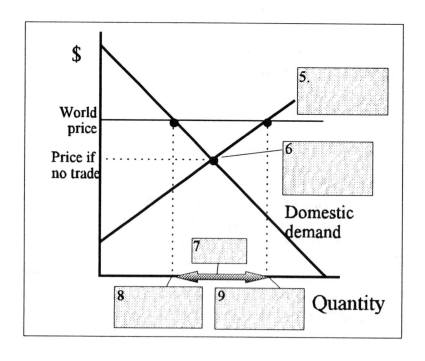

POLICY TOWARD TRADE 465

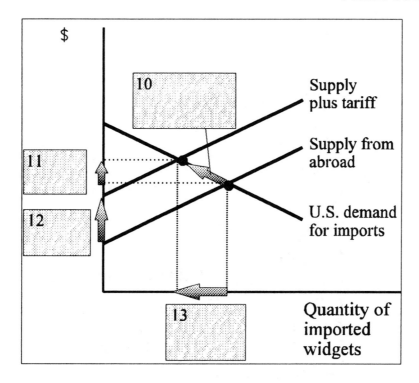

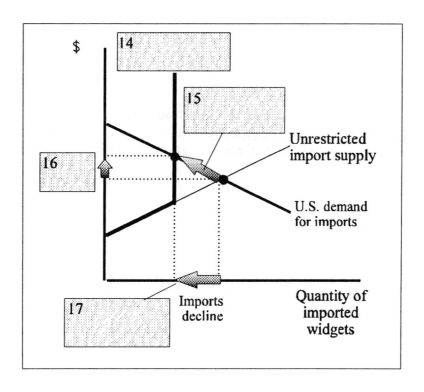

466 CHAPTER 16

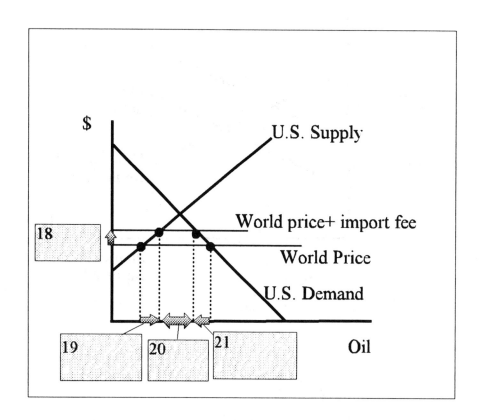

**For additional practice in grasping this chapter's graphs, visit
http://www.prenhall.com/ayers and try *Smart Graph* 35,
along with *Active Graphs* 68 and 69.**

ANSWERS

STUDYCHECKS

1. See StudyCheck 1 Figure. Consumer surplus rises from area A to areas A + B + C, while producer surplus drops from areas B + D down to area D. Since the gains to consumers exceed the loss to producers, the country on balance is better off.

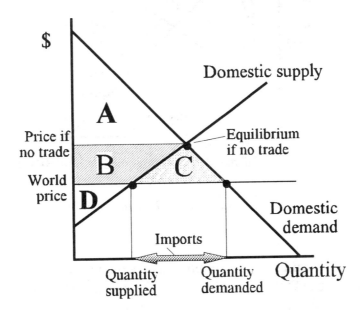

StudyCheck 1 Figure

468 CHAPTER 16

2. See StudyCheck 2 Figure. The country's consumers see their consumer surplus drop from areas A + B to only area A. However, producer surplus rises from area D to area B + C + D, meaning that on balance, the country is better off.

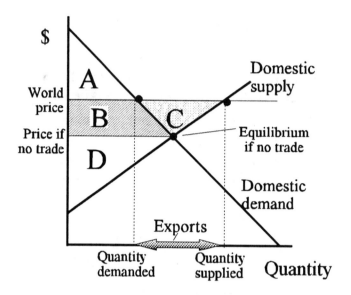

StudyCheck 2 Figure

3. See StudyCheck 3 Figure. Like an import tariff, a quota also reduces the quantity of imports and increases price in the domestic market. The quota truncates supply from abroad at the maximum allowable import quantity, thus causing import supply to become vertical at that point.

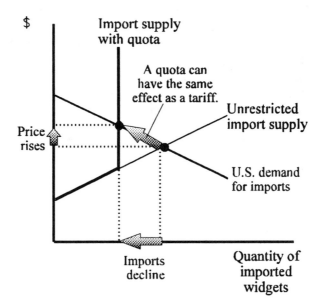

StudyCheck 3 Figure

4. Exports or imports that can be used militarily also have valuable civilian uses. In addition, the United States may be incapable of preventing world trade in these items. U.S. export or import restrictions may merely serve to transfer production from the United States to other countries. For example, if the United States prohibits the export of high-powered computers, new computer research and production efforts will tend to migrate to other countries. This occurrence would be unfortunate for the United States because it would both harm that industry and cause the United States to forgo some of the important external benefits to the rest of the U.S. economy from high-tech industries.

5. By raising the price of imported oil, an oil import fee would reduce oil imports and increase the U.S. price of oil to match the price of the imports. The higher price might prompt additional domestic oil production or discoveries. It might also trigger the development of alternative fuels, such as coal or nuclear power, both of which present significant environmental hazards.

FILL IN THE BLANKS

1. domestic, equal, exports, imports
2. lower, consumer surplus, decrease, decreases
3. greater, excess, exported

4. increase, decreases
5. open, closed
6. General Agreement on Tariffs and Trade, World Trade Organization
7. Smoot-Hawley, beggar
8. reductions, Uruguay
9. regional trading blocs
10. trade creation
11. trade diversion
12. tariffs, nontariff
13. tariff, residual
14. transparent, six
15. quotas
16. voluntary export restraints
17. higher
18. nontariff barriers
19. Dumping, Strategic dumping
20. infant
21. more, government
22. $20, $30
23. 55, 60
24. external, oil import, raise, more, less, increases
25. Strategic Petroleum Reserve

TRUE/FALSE/EXPLAIN

1. False, free trade refers to when a country does not restrict imports or exports at all.
2. False, import restrictions lead to losses to consumers that are greater than the gains to producers.
3. True.
4. False, a tariff will increase the price of a good in the domestic market whether or not the good is produced and sold domestically.
5. False, although tariffs do bring in government revenues, they also decrease the quantity of goods imported.
6. True.
7. True.
8. True.
9. False, voluntary export restraints allow other countries to sell to the United States at higher prices.
10. True.
11. False, the United States winds up paying more per unit to import the exports of those countries.

12. False, economists usually come down the side of free trade, even though there are often strong political pressures to restrict it.
13. False, the GATT is a pact among countries that promotes freer trade.
14. True.
15. True.
16. True.
17. False, it is not clear that infant industries make for a good argument for protectionist trade policy, while it is clear that some other arguments are at times valid, such as the national defense argument.
18. True.
19. True.
20. False, it is very difficult to drive all of your competitors out of business and prevent them from coming back in once you raise prices.
21. True.
22. True.
23. False, the Middle East provides about a quarter of the oil imported into the United States.
24. True.
25. True.

MULTIPLE CHOICE

1.	c	8.	b	15.	d	22.	b
2.	c	9.	d	16.	d	23.	c
3.	a	10.	a	17.	b	24.	b
4.	a	11.	c	18.	d	25.	a
5.	c	12.	a	19.	d		
6.	b	13.	c	20.	b		
7.	b	14.	d	21.	d		

GRASPING THE GRAPHS
Examples of correct answers

1. Equilibrium before international trade
2. Imports
3. Domestic quantity produced
4. Domestic quantity consumed
5. Domestic supply
6. Equilibrium before international trade

CHAPTER 16

7. Exports
8. Domestic quantity consumed
9. Domestic quantity produced
10. Change in equilibrium
11. Higher price
12. Tariff
13. Lower quantity
14. Supply with quota
15. Change in equilibrium
16. Higher price
17. Quantity of imports
18. Higher price
19. Increased domestic production
20. Reduced domestic consumption
21. Imports after fee

**Visit the Ayers/Collinge companion Website at http://www.prenhall.com/ayers
for further activities and exercises for this chapter.**

Chapter 17

ECONOMIC DEVELOPMENT

CHAPTER REVIEW

17.1 Developing Economies and Poverty

- Two-thirds of the world's countries are **less developed countries (LDCs)**, also sometimes called developing countries. The quality of life in these countries severely lags behind the other one-third of countries, the richer, industrialized, developed nations.

- Included within the group of LDCs are a special group of countries called the *transition economies*. These are the formerly communist countries, including Russia, China, and others. They are called transition economies because they have been moving from reliance upon government central planning to the free market.

- As a field in economics, **economic development** studies why entire countries remain mired deep in poverty, while other countries prosper. The data that describes a country's economic development are called *indicators*. A country is better off when its development indicators improve over time. The indicators examined in economic development studies vary.

- **Per capita income is probably the indicator referred to most frequently, but often a set of indicators is needed to assess the level of development in a country.**

StudyCheck 1
Why is per-capita income a good indicator for countries? What other examples of development indicators can you think of?

---

474   CHAPTER 17

- The LDCs vary in their climate, natural resources, land area, population, and other characteristics. For this reason, there are significant differences in the problems they face. While the LDCs differ, they do share several problems in common:
    - *Poverty.* Per capita income is low in the LDCs.
    - *Deficiencies in infrastructure. Infrastructure* includes roads, bridges, dams, schools, airports, hospitals, water treatment facilities, sanitation facilities, and other capital that promotes prosperity and well-being. These investments are largely absent in the LDCs.
    - *Low life expectancy.* Disease and lack of medical care contribute to health problems and high death rates among the populations of LDCs.
    - *High population growth.* Overpopulation creates lack of opportunity and the need to feed large numbers of people. The result is sometimes malnutrition and even starvation.
    - The extreme poverty of the LDCs has enormous consequences for the people living in those countries, including the prospect of an early death.

- To the impoverished worker who toils in the countryside without electricity, indoor plumbing, and safe drinking water, the hope of a better life is often associated with migration to a big city. That would be the capital city of Nairobi to the more than 30 million people living in Kenya, the African country about twice the size of Nevada. Consider life in Kenya in order to make several important points about development.

- According to the U.S. Central Intelligence Agency (CIA), 75 percent of the population of Kenya can read and write, but 50 percent are unemployed. The chief occupation of the people is farming, an occupation that provides a living for 75 to 80 percent of them. Because of Kenya's bountiful wildlife, tourism is a major industry. Small-scale manufacturing is also significant. A significant portion of Kenya's manufactured goods are exported to other countries.

- Although the country's birth rate is high, so is its death rate, due to the prevalence of HIV/AIDS. The population is growing at better than 1 percent a year. The per capita GDP of $1,500 is high for Africa.

- As true of other LDCs, Kenya mixes agriculture and urbanization. To understand this trait of LDCs, consider **Rostow's stages of economic development** model. In 1960, American economic historian Walter W. Rostow suggested that countries pass through five stages in their development.
    - *Stage 1: Traditional society.* The first stage in Rostow's model, traditional society, describes a country where subsistence agriculture dominates economic activity.
    - *Stage 2: Preconditions for takeoff.* In the second stage, agricultural production rises so as to permit people to trade excess production. Transportation is needed to take crops to distant markets, so that investment in transportation is a key in moving to stage 2.

- - *Stage 3: Takeoff.* In the third stage, large numbers of farmers leave agriculture to take jobs in industry. Thus, the country begins the process of urbanization, but remains focused on agriculture and just a few manufacturing industries. Again, more investment is needed, this time to create a manufacturing sector.
  - *Stage 4: Drive to maturity.* In the fourth stage, there is economic diversification, with many different goods and services produced.
  - *Stage 5: High mass consumption.* In the final stage, the production of consumer goods and services dominates economic activity.

- Clearly, stage 5 describes the United States and other high income countries. Kenya, like many LDCs, combines stages. While Rostow's model can help us by picturing economic development as occurring in a sequence of steps, development does not necessarily occur in the way specified by the model. Furthermore, the model does not identify the causes of movements from one stage to the next. The model is criticized by economists for these reasons, but it is still useful for emphasizing the role of investment in development.

- The stated mission of the *United Nations (UN)* is to promote world peace and prosperity through international cooperation. Consider the eight economic development goals set by the United Nations:

  Goal 1. Eradicate extreme poverty and hunger.
  Goal 2. Achieve universal primary education.
  Goal 3. Promote gender equality and empower women.
  Goal 4. Reduce child mortality.
  Goal 5. Improve maternal health.
  Goal 6. Combat HIV/AIDS, malaria, and other diseases.
  Goal 7. Ensure environmental sustainability.
  Goal 8. Develop a global partnership for development.

- The U. N. plans to apply its resources so as to achieve these goals by 2015. The goals are associated with *targets,* specific results that when achieved will mean each goal has been met.

- Regarding the effort to combat HIV/AIDS, the sixth goal, the developing world is home to 95 percent of all HIV/AIDS sufferers. The World Health Organization (WHO) predicts that seventy million people will die in the next 20 years unless drastic action or a major breakthrough occurs in the treatment of HIV/AIDS. One estimate has it that AIDS has killed more people than all wars and natural disasters throughout history and that forty million children have already lost one or both parents to AIDS.

- One reason that AIDS claims so many lives in the LDCs revolves around missing infrastructure. Without transportation facilities, life-prolonging medicines cannot reach those who need them. Without medical personnel, the sick cannot be properly cared for. Without education, AIDS is more likely to spread. In the LDCs, investments in infrastructure such as roads, hospitals, and schools will complement treatment with drugs in the fight against AIDS.

476   CHAPTER 17

- To track development progress, the UN refers to its world indicators. Grouping them, the indicators measure just two characteristics. One is infrastructure. The sanitation, water, computer, and telephone statistics shed light on access to capital, which makes people more productive. Note that the rural population has less access than the urban population. The indicators that relate to infants and children's health, on the other hand, reveal the effects of poverty.

17.2 Population Growth

- The world has seen its population grow rapidly, from just under 3 billion in 1960 to over 6 billion today. Population has exploded over the last three-and-a-half centuries, and is projected to keep increasing. Part of the reason for this growth is that advances in medicine and hygiene have lowered death rates, thereby increasing longevity. Birthrates have also been high, however, especially among the segments of the population least able to afford raising children.

- Economics was once called **the dismal science**. The term dates to the early nineteenth century. At that time, Thomas Robert Malthus popularized the notion that economics could only hope to delay the day of reckoning, in which the world's population finds itself at the brink of starvation. According to this Malthusian view, starvation is the only force that can keep population in check. While economics can temporarily improve the world, the inevitability of population growth and the limits of the earth's capacity to produce must inevitably reduce us all to no more than a subsistence existence.

- Technological change has enabled the world to get much more output for its resources than ever imagined by Malthus.

- There is still room for concern. If the world continues to experience the same population growth rate that it has over the course of the twentieth century, it must ultimately fill every nook and cranny with people. There would be no room to produce the food to feed them. Since population grows geometrically, it doubles according to *the rule of seventy-two*, which states that doubling time equals 72 divided by the rate of growth. For example, at a growth rate of 1.5 percent, a country's population would double every 48 years.

- Economic incentives can put a brake on population growth. Specifically, **as countries become wealthier, the opportunity cost of people's time rises.** Because children take time, people choose to have fewer of them. This is especially true in countries that provide reliable retirement benefits for the elderly. Fertility refers to the number of children born per woman. The fertility rate reflects both economic incentives and traditions such as attitudes toward family size.

- Unless we face the full costs and benefits of our actions, we cannot be expected to make efficient choices. One group that frequently does not bear all the costs of its decisions is

ECONOMIC DEVELOPMENT 477

parents. For example, efficiency would suggest that parents should pay all costs of rearing children, including costs of food, shelter, and education. However, equity suggests that children should have comparable opportunities.

- To the extent that the costs of rearing children are paid by others, parents face a marginal cost of rearing children that does not reflect the full cost of those children to society. The result is that government subsidies tend to increase population growth rates.

- In some cases, couples may choose to have children they don't want—*unwanted children*—in order to receive extra government aid or tax write-offs. These are children that the parents would prefer not to have, except for the extra income they cause.

17.3 Prices and Property Rights
- For countries to develop, they need capital, which requires investment from private sources or government. Consider private investment. In deciding what projects to fund, banks, private investors, and multinational firms look at market prices and the security of property rights. In other words, the investors follow **price signals** to guide them in the direction of the greatest profits.

- **Because of the central importance of prices in guiding consumption and investment spending, the market economy is often called the** *price system* **so as to emphasize the importance of the many price signals throughout the world economy.**

- Prices responds to scarcity. Other things equal, the scarcer the resources, the higher are their prices. Higher prices make it profitable to find or develop substitutes, which would not be economical at lower prices. Well before any resource gets used up, its increasing scarcity drives its price higher. When the price of a nonrenewable resource rises, the market is motivated to explore for more and to develop substitutes.

- In the 1970s, the high price of oil resulted in major new finds in Mexico, Alaska, the North Sea, and elsewhere. Today, oil rigs can be found in many LDCs, as the search for oil has spread to the far corners of the globe. Substitutes include technology to give motor vehicles more miles per gallon and insulation to reduce the energy costs of homes, as well as fuel alternatives to oil, coal, and natural gas.

- There are many other examples of prices preventing resource shortages. As prices have risen, technology has responded. The rising price of copper spurred new technologies, such as fiber optics, that greatly reduced the world's need for copper.

> **StudyCheck 2**
> How does the price system prevents an economy from running out of the central resources?

- In the realm of food, too, technology has so far been very successful at increasing yields per acre more rapidly than necessary to meet the needs of growing populations. The hunger spots in the world today have much less to do with agricultural technology than with political instability that interrupt the production and distribution of food.

- For example, in the 1800s, an energy crisis was brought about by a scarcity of whale oil, which at the time was used in reading lamps. The scarcity was prompted by tight supplies and high prices, as whaling ships decimated the population of the world's whales in response to growing demand. The price system dangled the lure of profit to successful innovators who could find new energy sources. This incentive eventually brought about the age of petroleum.

- Many developing countries' exports are heavily weighted toward the export of natural resources. The problem for these countries occurs when the prices of *commodities*, including natural resources such as copper, tin, and precious metals, and agricultural commodities such as rice, bananas, and cocoa, are not high enough to sustain development. The **Prebisch-Singer thesis**, which was advanced in the 1950s, states that developing countries will be trapped in poverty because the price of their exports will be driven down by increasing commodity supplies, as the price system responds. This can lead to **immiserizing growth**, where increasing supplies of commodities exported by the LDCs causes prices to drop so far that these countries end up worse off because of trade.

- Although low commodity and agricultural prices are a problem for the LDCs that export these goods, the Prebisch-Singer thesis is not generally accepted by economists as an explanation for the ills of these countries.

- A key ingredient of the market economy, one lacking in many less developed countries, is the ingredient of secure **property rights**, meaning rights of ownership. Investors need to know that they will be able to retain the fruits of their investments, or they will not invest. They

ECONOMIC DEVELOPMENT 479

must not fear that government action in the future will prevent them from reaping the rewards that they envision when they make their investments in the present.

- New investments would be deterred if there's a fear of regulatory *takings,* in which government reduces the value of property by restricting the manner in which can be used. In extreme cases, investors might fear government expropriation, such as the expropriation of oil wells that occurred in Colombia and other countries in the 1960s and 1970s. Investors must also be confident that government regulations will be enforced evenhandedly, and not skewed by bribery or favoritism. Civil unrest and terrorism are also problems that can reduce the attractiveness of investments.

- Most of the high-growth countries have in common a significant role for the price system and property rights. Virtues such as integrity, industriousness, generosity, and respect for others also promotes a high growth rate and economic development.

- Besides poverty, the LDCs have conflict in common. A study of the 75 countries that have U.S. AID missions showed that between 1996 and 2001, two-thirds of them had major conflicts. There is nothing more destructive to standards of living than warfare. Economics is central to many of the world's conflicts, which often concern the ownership of property. Conflict over property can range from boundary disputes to the control of entire countries.

StudyCheck 3
Explain and give an example of how disputes over property can lead to warfare.

17.4 Foreign Aid: The IMF and the World Bank
- When one country helps another country, the mechanism is often *foreign aid*, comprised of donated money or products. Countries provide foreign aid on their own and through membership in the two most important organizations that channel resources to the poorer countries: the **World Bank** and the **International Monetary Fund**, commonly called by its initials as the **IMF**.

- The United States plays a major role in foreign aid. For example, as reported by the White House in 2002, the United States is:
  - The top importer of goods from developing countries, importing $450 billion in 2000, eight times greater than all Official Development Assistance (ODA) to developing countries from all donors.
  - The top source of private capital to developing countries, averaging $36 billion annually between 1997 and 2000.
  - The world leader in charitable donations to developing countries -- $4 billion in 2000.
  - One of the top two providers of Official Development Assistance (ODA). In 2000, the United States provided $10 billion in ODA. This ODA is expected to increase substantially from 2001 to 2003 in key sectors:
    - HIV/AIDS - 54 percent.
    - Basic Education - 50 percent.
    - Trade and Investment - 38 percent.
    - Agriculture - 38 percent

- The United States is also spending $1 billion per month for the war on terrorism and has contributed $976 million to international peacekeeping in 2001.

- USAID's core Development Assistance account is expected to increase 22 percent overall from 2001 to 2003. The greatest share goes to promote economic growth and agricultural development, since agriculture is especially important in LDCs that have difficulty raising enough food to feed themselves. Such aid might take the form of teaching farmers new technologies and techniques that promise to increase crop yields.

- One of the problems poor nations face is a crushing debt load. Banks in the developed countries have loaned billions of dollars to the governments of LDCs to finance infrastructure. Unfortunately for many LDCs, their economies do not generate enough tax dollars to repay the money owed.

- To provide debt relief to the world's poorest and most heavily indebted countries, the United States and other countries help to pay for the debt initiative for Heavily Indebted Poor Countries (HIPC). This program was established by the IMF and the World Bank, the two most important multinational agencies involved in foreign assistance.

- The IMF is a fund that can be drawn on by member countries needing temporary financing to deal with monetary and financial problems. The IMF was established in 1944 with the goal of ensuring a stable world monetary and financial system. According to its Articles of Agreement, the purposes of the IMF are to:
  - Promote international monetary cooperation.
  - Facilitate the expansion of international trade.
  - Encourage exchange rate stability.

- - Further the establishment of a *multilateral* (multi-country) payments system.
  - Provide resources to member countries experiencing balance of payments problems.
  - Money to finance IMF operations comes from membership fees, called quotas, that are proportional to the size and economic strength of its 184 member countries. The United States has the largest quota, amounting to 17.6 percent of IMF funding. All member countries, rich and poor alike, have access to IMF resources.

- The main activities of the IMF include surveillance, financial assistance, and technical assistance.

- *Surveillance.* This procedure involves a policy discussion between the IMF and a member country. An annual IMF appraisal of each member country's exchange rate policies is part of the process. Surveillance is intended to see that a country's economic policies furnish a strong foundation for stable exchange rates, which the IMF believes is a key to world prosperity. Global surveillance is also carried out, such as in 2001 when the IMF pointed out in a *World Economic Outlook* report the need for countries to stimulate aggregate demand in the face of weakening global growth.

- *Financial assistance.* As of February, 2002, the IMF had about $77 billion in credits and loans outstanding to 88 countries. This assistance is provided to countries that have balance of payments problems. The purpose of this assistance is to encourage reforms in the policies of countries receiving the assistance. Some of this assistance is in the form of debt relief provided through the HIPC initiative, mentioned above. IMF loans are intended to support reforms aimed at eliminating the root causes of a country's problems.

- *Technical assistance.* Poor countries are often ill-equipped to develop their own fiscal and monetary policies because the human capital necessary to develop sound policies is not available domestically. Thus, the IMF provides help so that countries can design policies that strengthen their economies. For example, the IMF assisted Russia and other transition economies in setting up central banking and treasury systems. Part of the technical assistance offered is in the area of statistics. For a country to be able to implement and monitor effective policies, there must be statistics on unemployment, inflation, GDP, and other key macro variables. Countries that lack expertise in this area can tap into the IMF's expertise.

- Through the provision of surveillance, financial assistance, and technical assistance, the IMF aims to tie member countries more closely into the world economy, and advise members on how to deal with problems that arise from their trade and financial interactions with other countries.

- Sometimes these problems call for IMF financial assistance, which the IMF offers under the condition that the countries undertake economic reforms that are in accord with IMF advice. The reforms can be painful, which leads some countries to complain about IMF arm-twisting.

- They might even complain of IMF *imperialism,* saying that the IMF seeks to force the values of Western economies upon countries around the world. The IMF has responded to this criticism by reforms intended to make IMF loan conditions less burdensome.

- The IMF is known for the massive loans that it extended to Mexico during the 1994-95 peso crisis; to the countries of Asia during the 1997-98 Asian financial crisis; and to Russia in 1998 as that country struggled through multiple economic and social crises. The purpose of these loans was to allow these countries to pay their debts to other countries, while reforming their economic and financial systems. When the IMF compiled a ranking of its largest borrowers between the years 1947 and 2000, Mexico, Korea, and Russia were the top three recipients of IMF loans.

- Critics of IMF lending practices term many IMF loans "bailouts" that will lead to more bailouts in the future, because countries' lenders will not be as careful when they realize the IMF will step in with money when the countries get into trouble. Careless lending practices can impede economic development and sound growth because money will go into projects that are unsound and should not be undertaken. The IMF has publicly recognized the *moral hazard* in making unlimited loans—that countries will be prompted to follow unsound policies that will lead to future crises, and that lenders will be encouraged to make unsound loans if they believe that the IMF will see that they are repaid in the event of default by borrowing countries.

- The World Bank does what most people expect banks to do, loan money. **World Bank loans to less-developed member countries are intended to further their economic development.** Since its creation more than 50 years ago, the World Bank has loaned more than $400 billion. The similarities between the World Bank and the IMF include that they are both headquartered in Washington, D.C., that they are both owned by the governments of member countries, that virtually every country is a member of both institutions, and that they were both started in July 1944.

- Consider the characteristics of the World Bank's loans in more detail:
    - World Bank loans, which only go to developing countries, must be repaid. Unlike aid programs, the World Bank does not provide grants, which are gifts of money. The money for the Bank's loans comes partly from government grants and partly from borrowings from the private sector and governments.
    - Lending is of two types. The first is lending to countries that are able to pay near-market interest on the loans they receive. The second involves loans to countries that cannot afford to pay interest. These loans are called credits and are provided through a World Bank affiliate, the International Development Association, for terms of 35 to 40 years. Although interest is not charged, the credits must be repaid. Such credits only go to the very poorest countries and average about $6 billion per year.
    - The World Bank can only lend to member governments or under a member government's guarantee.

ECONOMIC DEVELOPMENT 483

- To ensure that money is well-invested, the Bank evaluates projects and only lends when a project is expected to earn at least a 10 percent rate of economic return.

- A top priority of the World Bank is to stimulate development of the private sector, although direct loans to the private sector are prohibited. The Bank seeks to encourage the private sector by promoting stable, honest government economic policies that focus on expanding the significance of markets. Although the Bank cannot make loans to the private sector, an affiliate called the International Finance Corporation exists for that purpose. It also aids governments in privatizing formerly government-owned businesses.

- The World Bank's focus on the private sector is a relatively recent development. From its inception through the 1970s, the Bank tended toward policies that emphasized expanding the government sector in developing countries. It was thought that large-scale government projects were the key to bringing about prosperity, including promoting government-owned industries. However, the Bank changed its policies in response to the successes of the U.S. economy and the failure of central planning in the communist countries in the 1980s, along with the successes of market economies in Hong Kong, Malaysia, and other places.

17.5 Russia—A Rough Transition to the Price System

- For much of the last century, the former Soviet Union tried to substitute its form of communism for the price system of the free marketplace. The market economy of modern Russia was itself substituted for the communist economy of the USSR after the overthrow of communism in 1991.

- Russia is only today starting to realize the potential of its relatively new market economy. During the early years of the transition to a market-oriented system, output fell and unemployment increased.

- Unlike capitalist countries, the former Communist countries of Eastern Europe and the Soviet Union had no competitive market prices to ensure an efficient allocation of resources. Prices were set for purposes of equity and political expediency, not for efficiency. Soviet planners tried to match resources to outputs and outputs to needs, but faced a difficult problem. To allocate efficiently, planners must know how much value consumers place on alternative outputs. They also must compute the opportunity costs of inputs. In contrast, free markets reveal this information automatically; it is implicit in market prices.

- To acquire the information they need, the Soviet planners estimated *shadow prices*, which are what the market prices would have been if there had been free markets. Although the planners resorted to complex mathematical models, the estimated shadow prices were still only rough approximations to true market prices. When planners imposed incorrectly estimated prices, people and businesses were led to many wrong decisions about what and how to produce. The result was both surpluses and shortages.

- Even if the shadow prices were accurate, they would not have been the prices people actually pay. Bread was priced very cheaply for political reasons, and customers bought it in much larger quantities than they would have if bread prices reflected the costs of the foodstuffs, labor, and other items used in producing that bread. Still, for political reasons, government attempted to turn out as much of this necessity as consumers would choose to buy.

- Politically set prices had one interesting positive effect. They forced Russian authorities to exercise monetary restraint. Too many rubles would just add more purchasing power, which consumers would spend on underpriced goods. The Soviet Union did not have the wherewithal to produce enough of these goods as it was. The only way to prevent even greater shortages was to keep additional money from circulating in the economy. Thus, in the former Soviet Union, price inflation was kept low because government set the prices, and monetary growth was restrained in order to allow the policy of low prices to work. In contrast, when markets are free, the process is reversed. Monetary restraint must be exercised to keep inflation from taking hold in the marketplace.

StudyCheck 4
Explain the role of prices in the former Soviet Union. Include in your explanation a discussion of shadow prices and subsidies.

- The arms buildup of the 1980s hastened the decline of the Soviet economy and prompted an overthrow of the central planners. First, there was Mikhail Gorbachev, would-be reformer of the communist system. Then came Boris Yeltsin, a free-market revolutionary who extricated Russia from the splinters of the Soviet Union. Many thought that, with markets freed from the central planners, living standards would quickly rise. The statistics said otherwise.

- Russia embraced capitalist ideas, but at first failed to impose a key ingredient necessary for the success of free markets. That ingredient is certainty over property rights. If individuals and businesses have no confidence that they will be able to keep the fruits of their labors and investments, the profit motive is lost. We all want to profit, but only if we can keep or spend those profits for our own sakes. Few would seek profit in order to turn it over to the government. Unfortunately, in modern Russia, that has been a danger.

- After the downfall of the Soviet Union, Russia experienced a problem of too many governments claiming jurisdiction over the same economic activity. For example, while it has been possible to buy land in Russia, it has also been nearly impossible to obtain a clear title to it. One government would grant the title, while another government would lie in wait to claim the land as its own somewhere down the line.

- With all the governments came a host of taxes. To some extent, all taxes represent an expropriation of private property. Post-Soviet taxes sometimes carried this expropriation to an absurd extreme. Specifically, when taxes from the various jurisdictions were added together, they would often sum to over 100 percent. This means that, for every dollar of profit a business would make, it would owe more than a dollar to the government.

- It would seem that no business would voluntarily choose to operate under these conditions. Yet business did go on in Russia. The reason is at least threefold. First, many profits are hidden from the tax collector, either through bribery or techniques of accounting. Second, and related to the first, there has been and continues to be a thriving underground economy that is not reported to authorities. Third, business looked to the future, a feature that is already unfolding in the form of greater clarification as to property ownership and taxation. The result of these early problems of transition is that Russia has since seen rapid economic growth.

- Much of the underground economy in Russia is ruled by organized crime. There are thought to be hundreds of criminal organizations in modern Russia. Oftentimes, their leaders are former officials of the communist government, officials with connections to networks of "enforcers." In a way, these former officials are entrepreneurs. They provide a service for which there is a strong demand. That service is the protection of property rights. For a price, the local crime boss will protect your property from other criminals. Through his connections, he can also offer some protection from excessive government regulation and taxation. It is thus not surprising to find that statistics from the Russian government show that the transition to free markets caused the Russian economy to shrink.

- When economic activity is not reported, government can collect no taxes on it directly. There is a way in which it can be taxed indirectly, however. That way is through inflation. Authorities in Russia's central bank printed money freely, allowing government to spend without collecting taxes. Instead, the tax was inflation that eroded purchasing power in the legitimate and underground economies alike.

- Russia has undergone a dramatic upheaval, in which the old order of communism was thrown out to make way for the new order of capitalism. However, capitalistic free markets cannot function without the ownership of private property. There has been movement in this direction, such as Russia's adoption of a supply-side tax policy that attempts to secure property rights and avoid prohibitively high tax rates. We can expect the underground economy to diminish in importance because of those tax changes.

StudyCheck 5
Citizens of the former Soviet Union were unhappy with the slow pace of economic development after its breakup. What role did property rights play? How did criminals both hurt and help this process?

FILL IN THE BLANKS

1. Two-thirds of the world's countries are _____-_____ countries (LDCs). Included within the group of LDCs are a special group of countries called the _____ economies. These are the formerly communist countries, including Russia, China, and others.

2. The data that describes a country's economic development are called _____ indicators.

3. _____ includes roads, bridges, dams, schools, airports, hospitals, water treatment facilities, sanitation facilities, and other capital that promotes prosperity and well-being. These investments are largely absent in the LDCs.

4. In 1960, American economic historian Walter W. Rostow suggested that countries pass through five stages in their development.
   - Stage 1: _____ _____.
   - Stage 2: _____ _____ _____.
   - Stage 3: _____.
   - Stage 4: _____ _____ _____.
   - Stage 5: _____ _____ _____.

5. Clearly, stage ____ describes the United States and other high income countries

6. The UN's development goals are associated with _____, specific results that when achieved will mean each goal has been met. Regarding the effort to combat HIV/AIDS, the sixth goal, the developing world is home to ____ percent of all HIV/AIDS sufferers.

7. To track development progress, the UN refers to its world indicators. Grouping them, the indicators measure just two characteristics. One is _____. The sanitation, water, computer, and telephone statistics shed light on access to capital, which makes people more productive. Note that the rural population has less access than the urban population. The indicators that relate to infants and children's health, on the other hand, reveal the effects of _____.

8. The world has seen its population grow rapidly, from just under 3 billion in 1960 to over ____ billion today.

9. Economics was once called the _____ _____. The term dates to the early nineteenth century. At that time, Thomas Robert Malthus popularized the notion that economics could only hope to delay the day of reckoning, in which the world's population finds itself at the brink of starvation. _____ _____ has enabled the world to get much more output for its resources than ever imagined by Malthus.

10. Since population grows geometrically, it doubles according to the _____ _____-_____ which states that doubling time equals 72 divided by the rate of growth.

11. Economic incentives can put a brake on population growth. Specifically, as countries become wealthier, the opportunity cost of people's time _____. Because children take time, people choose to have _____ of them. _____ refers to the number of children born per woman.

12. Unless we face the full costs and benefits of our actions, we cannot be expected to make _____ choices. One group that frequently does not bear all the costs of its decisions is parents. To the extent that the costs of rearing children are paid by others, parents face a _____ _____ of rearing children that does not reflect the full cost of those children to society. The result is that government subsidies tend to _____ population growth rates.

13. For countries to develop, they need capital, which requires investment from private sources or government. Consider private investment. In deciding what projects to fund, banks, private investors, and multinational firms look at market prices and the security of property rights. In other words, the investors follow _____ signals to guide them in the direction of the greatest profits.

14. Because of the central importance of prices in guiding consumption and investment spending, the market economy is often called the _____ _____ so as to emphasize the importance of the many price signals throughout the world economy. Prices respond to scarcity. Other things equal, the scarcer are resources, the _____ are their prices. Higher prices make it profitable to find or develop _____.

15. Many developing countries' exports are heavily weighted toward the export of natural resources. The problem for these countries occurs when the prices of _____, including natural resources such as copper, tin, and precious metals, rice, bananas, and cocoa, are not high enough to sustain development. The _____-_____ thesis, which was advanced in the 1950s, states that developing countries will be trapped in poverty because the price of their exports will be driven down by increasing commodity supplies, as the price system responds. This can lead to _____ growth, where increasing supplies of commodities exported by the LDCs causes prices to drop so far that these countries end up worse off because of trade.

16. A key ingredient of the market economy, one lacking in many less developed countries, is the ingredient of secure _____ _____, meaning rights of ownership. New investments would be deterred if there's a fear of regulatory _____, in which government reduces the value of property by restricting the manner in which can be used.

17. A study of the 75 countries that have U.S. AID missions showed that between 1996 and 2001, _____ of them had major conflicts. To provide debt relief to the world's poorest and most heavily indebted countries, the United States and other countries help to pay for the debt initiative for _____ _____ _____ _____ (HIPC). This program was established by the IMF and the World Bank, the two most important multinational agencies involved in foreign assistance.

18. The IMF is a fund that can be drawn on by member countries needing temporary financing to deal with monetary and financial problems. The IMF was established in _____ with the goal of ensuring a stable world monetary and financial system. Money to finance IMF operations comes from membership fees, called _____, that are proportional to the size and economic strength of its 184 member countries. The _____ _____ has the largest quota, amounting to 17.6 percent of IMF funding. The main activities of the IMF include _____ _____ _____, and technical assistance. The IMF has publicly recognized the _____ _____ in making unlimited loans—that countries will be prompted to follow unsound policies that will lead to future crises, and that lenders will be encouraged to make unsound loans if they believe that the IMF will see that they are repaid in the event of default by borrowing countries.

19. The World Bank loans money. World Bank loans, which only go to developing countries, must be repaid. Unlike aid programs, the World Bank does not provide _____, which are gifts of money. Lending is of two types. The first is lending to countries that are able to pay near-market interest on the loans they receive. The second involves loans to countries that cannot afford to pay interest. These loans are called _____ and are provided through a World Bank affiliate, the International Development Association, for terms of 35 to 40 years. The World Bank can only lend to member governments or under a member government's guarantee.

20. To ensure that money is well-invested, the World Bank evaluates projects and only lends when a project is expected to earn at least a _____ percent rate of economic return. A top priority of the World Bank is to stimulate development of the _____ sector. Direct loans to the private sector are prohibited. From its inception through the 1970s, the Bank tended toward policies that emphasized expanding the _____ sector in developing countries.

E&A 21. Russia is only today starting to realize the potential of its relatively new market economy. During the early years of the transition to a market-oriented system, output _____ and unemployment _____.

22. Unlike capitalist countries, the former Communist countries of Eastern Europe and the Soviet Union had no competitive market prices to ensure an _____ allocation of resources. Prices were set for purposes of equity and political expediency, not for efficiency. Soviet planners tried to match resources to outputs and outputs to needs, but faced a difficult

problem. To allocate efficiently, planners must know how much value consumers place on alternative outputs. They also must compute the opportunity costs of inputs. In contrast, free markets reveal this information automatically; it is implicit in market prices. To acquire the information they need, the Soviet planners estimated _____ prices, which are what the market prices would have been if there had been free markets. The result was both _____ and _____. Bread was priced very cheaply for _____ reasons, and customers bought it in much larger quantities than they would have if bread prices reflected the costs of the foodstuffs, labor, and other items used in producing that bread.

23. Politically set prices had one interesting positive effect. They forced Russian authorities to exercise _____ restraint. Too many rubles would just add more purchasing power, which consumers would spend on underpriced goods.

24. Russia embraced capitalist ideas, but at first failed to impose a key ingredient necessary for the success of free markets. That ingredient is certainty over _____ rights. If individuals and businesses have no confidence that they will be able to keep the fruits of their labors and investments, the profit motive is lost.

25. To some extent, all taxes represent an expropriation of private property. Post-Soviet taxes sometimes carried this expropriation to an absurd extreme. Specifically, when taxes from the various jurisdictions were added together, they would often sum to over _____ percent. This means that, for every dollar of profit a business would make, it would owe more than a dollar to the government. When economic activity is not reported, government can collect no taxes on it directly. There is a way in which it can be taxed indirectly, however. That way is through _____. Authorities in Russia's central bank printed money freely, allowing government to spend without collecting taxes.

TRUE/FALSE/EXPLAIN
If false, explain why in the space provided.

1. The transition economies include the entire group of less-developed countries.

2. A country's per-capita income is a good development indicator.

3. Low population growth is a problem that plagues the less-developed countries of the world.

4. The infrastructure of a country includes such things as its inflation rate, GDP, and other economic statistics.

5. Per-capita gross national income is as little as a few hundred dollars a year in the poorest countries of the world.

6. In countries with the lowest life expectancy, the life expectancy at birth is about 50 years.

7. Less than half the population in low income countries have access to improved sanitation.

8. Stage 1 of Rostow's stages of economic development model is the "preconditions for takeoff stage," in which agricultural surpluses are accumulated.

9. The eight development goals of the United Nations include expanding the role of agriculture in less-developed countries so that these countries can feed themselves.

10. World population in the year 2002 was approximately 9 billion people.

11. Malthus characterization of economics as the dismal science arises because of his prediction that prices and interest rates will always rise.

12. According to the rule of 72, if population growth were 3 percent a year, then it would take 15 years for a country's population to double.

13. Because greater wealth increases the opportunity cost of time devoted to raising children, people in wealthier countries face the incentive to have fewer children.

14. The average number of children born per woman in most less-developed nations is greater than 10.

15. A government subsidy that goes toward child rearing shifts the marginal cost to parents downward, thus increasing the population.

16. If the marginal cost of an additional child is negative, parents will choose not to have that child.

17. The Prebisch-Singer thesis states that the less-developed countries will grow rich because of opportunities afforded by exporting their goods to the developed nations

18. Immiserizing growth would be associated with improvements in standards of living in less-developed countries.

19. During the 1990 to 2000 period, most of the less developed nations experienced negative growth rates.

20. Most U.S. foreign aid takes the form of humanitarian assistance.

21. Shadow prices are estimates of market prices that were used by Soviet planners.

22. The root cause of the collapse of the Soviet government was the high inflation created by too much money in the Soviet economy.

23. Immediately upon embracing free market ideas, Russia established a strong system of property rights.

24. One economic problem that Russia has avoided in transitioning to a market economy is the problem of an underground economy.

25. During the first 10 years of its transition away from central planning, Russia succeeded in keeping its unemployment rate below 10 percent every year.

MULTIPLE CHOICE
Circle the letter preceding the one best answer.

1. The so-called transition economies include
   a. Russia and China.
   b. the U.S. and Great Britain.
   c. Mexico and Canada.
   d. most countries in Asia, including Japan and Korea.

2. Which is not generally a problem for the LDCs?
   a. Poverty
   b. Deficiencies in infrastructure.
   c. High population growth.
   d. Long life expectancies that threaten to bankrupt their Social Security programs.

3. Which of the following amounts comes closest to annual per-capita gross national income in the United States?
   a. $17,000
   b. $27,000
   c. $34,000
   d. $46,000

4. In low income countries the infant mortality rate is about _____ times the infant mortality rate in the United States.
   a. 2
   b. 4
   c. 10
   d. 20

5. In the U.S., life expectancy at birth is about _____ more years than life expectancy at birth in typical low income countries.
   a. 40
   b. 20
   c. 10
   d. 5

6. When a country moves from stage 2 to stage 3 in Rostow's model of economic development, that country moves to
   a. preconditions for takeoff.
   b. takeoff.
   c. the drive to maturity.
   d. the stage of high mass consumption.

7. Regarding Rostow's model of economic development, economists
   a. accept the model without reservation.
   b. completely reject the model as incorrect.
   c. criticize the model, but find it useful nonetheless.
   d. believe the model applies to countries in transition, but not to any other LDCs.

8. Which is not a development goal of the United Nations?
   a. Eradicate poverty and hunger.
   b. Achieve universal primary education.
   c. Encourage marriage and discourage divorce.
   d. Combat HIV and other diseases.

9. When it comes to world access to improved drinking water in urban areas, the United Nations concludes that
   a. only about one-third of urban residents have such access.
   b. about half of the urban population drinks from improved sources.
   c. approximately two-thirds of urban dwellers have access to improved drinking water.
   d. improved drinking water sources are available to about 95 percent of the urban population.

10. Regarding population growth between now and the year 2020, it is estimated by the U.S. Census Bureau that
    a. the earth's population will increase.
    b. the earth's population will remain approximately constant because of advances in birth control.
    c. wars will cause the population of the planet to decrease.
    d. the female population will grow, but the male population will shrink.

11. Thomas Robert Malthus predicted in the nineteenth century that
    a. war would soon be abolished by international law, thus ushering in a new era of prosperity.
    b. people in the 20th century would eat quite well because of supermarkets, improved farming techniques, and new kinds of food.
    c. birth control would keep population in check.
    d. mass starvation would characterize the future.

12. Typically, in the wealthier nations the number of children born per woman is
    a. about three.
    b. four or more.
    c. around one and one-half to two.
    d. just about zero.

13. Because of government subsidies such as free schooling,
    a. fewer children are born into poverty.
    b. the number of children born into poverty does not change.
    c. more children are born into poverty.
    d. all children have equal opportunities in life.

14. The demand curve for children is graphed as a
    a. upward sloping line.
    b. downward sloping line.
    c. vertical line.
    d. horizontal line.

15. If government subsidies are large enough to shift the marginal cost of raising children to below zero, then we can conclude that
    a. parents will pay the entire cost of educating their children.
    b. people will choose to have no children.
    c. population will grow faster than if the marginal cost were above zero.
    d. population will grow slower than if the marginal cost were above zero.

496 CHAPTER 17

16. Regarding foreign aid, the opinion of the majority of Americans is that
    a. the U.S. should give no foreign aid since it is a waste of taxpayer dollars.
    b. foreign aid is supported in principle, but the country spends too much on foreign aid, and the amount should be cut.
    c. the country spends far too little on foreign aid, and the amount should be drastically increased.
    d. foreign aid should go toward arming America's friends, while food aid should be cut way back.

17. IMF surveillance refers to
    a. the IMF's efforts to track terrorists.
    b. IMF monitoring of a member country's economy, along with policy discussion with that country.
    c. refusing to lend to a particular country.
    d. the fees the IMF charges its members.

18. The IMF provides financial assistance to countries primarily in order to
    a. ensure their military strength.
    b. help them deal with balance of payments problems.
    c. pay for bridges, roads, dams, and the like.
    d. develop oil and other natural resources.

19. When the moral hazard associated with IMF loans is brought up, people are referring to
    a. the excessively high interest rate on those loans.
    b. the purposes of the loans, which some people consider to be immoral.
    c. the fact that the IMF will not lend to countries where its officials find their lives threatened by terrorists.
    d. the notion that IMF loans bailout countries in trouble, encouraging them to get in trouble again in the future.

20. The World Bank seeks to
    a. increase the size of government in LDCs, since these countries tend to lack a sufficient amount of government.
    b. provide gifts of money to poor countries.
    c. loan money to private sector firms.
    d. provide funding for projects that are expected to earn at least a 10 percent rate of economic return.

21. For several years in the mid-1990s, Russia saw its aggregate output
    a. remain constant.
    b. increase significantly due to free market reforms.
    c. decrease.
    d. increase one year and then decrease the next.

22. In the Soviet Union, shadow prices were set
    a. by the free market.
    b. by government planners who estimated free market prices.
    c. by government planners who sought to set prices as different from market prices as possible.
    d. with the goal of making actual prices that people paid equal to the shadow prices.

23. The Soviet Union's monetary policy could best be characterized as
    a. inflationary.
    b. showing restraint.
    c. irrational.
    d. nonexistent.

24. Because post-communist Russia initially had too many governments,
    a. property rights were clearly defined.
    b. taxes had to abolished.
    c. taxes were not abolished, but were kept very low.
    d. many taxes were imposed.

25. The supply-side tax policy that was adopted in Russia prompts economists to conclude that the underground economy will
    a. disappear.
    b. diminish in size.
    c. grow slightly.
    d. grow dramatically

GRASPING THE GRAPHS
Fill in each box with a concept that applies.

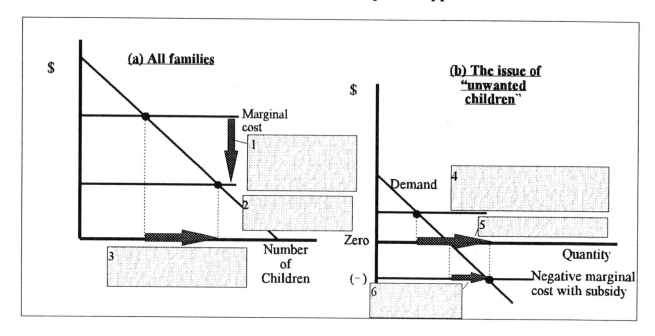

For additional practice in grasping this chapter's graphs, visit
http://www.prenhall.com/ayers and try *Active Graph 70*.

ANSWERS

STUDYCHECKS

1. Per-capita income, income per person, allows us to gauge the purchasing power of people in different countries. Their incomes help us understand how much in the way of goods and services they might be able to consume. More direct indicators of living standards are numerous, ranging from the number of doctors per 1,000 people to the number of calories consumed daily by the average person. Such direct indicators help us understand the living conditions of people in other countries.

2. The price system works automatically to allocate resources efficiently. As resources grow scarcer, higher prices provide incentives for conservation and for the development of substitutes.

3. Wars can break out because of disputes relating to common property and territorial boundaries. For example, the Gulf War started from a dispute over the ownership of Kuwaiti oil fields.

4. Prices in the Soviet Union were set for reasons of equity and political expediency, rather than for reasons of efficiency. Estimates of market prices, so-called shadow prices, were used to allocate resources. Inaccurate estimates routinely led to inefficient decisions. Resources were also wasted as government held down the prices of necessities, such as the price of bread. Low prices forced monetary restraint and a nonconvertible ruble. Holding prices down at home meant that Soviet authorities would not allow foreigners to buy rubles with their own currencies. Thus, foreign commerce was ordinarily conducted with inefficient barter trades.

5. Capitalism requires private property. However, in post-Soviet Russia, the existence of high taxes, numerous governments with unclear jurisdictions, and hundreds of criminal gangs put property rights in jeopardy. Thus, investment lagged and the economy grew more sluggishly than it otherwise would have. In one sense, the criminal gangs aided in securing property rights. Specifically, for a fee or cut of profits, criminal gangs would often promise protection from rival gangs and influence with government authorities.

FILL IN THE BLANKS

1. less-developed, transition
2. indicators
3. Infrastructure
4. Traditional society, Preconditions for takeoff, Takeoff, Drive to maturity, High mass consumption
5. 5
6. targets
7. infrastructure, poverty
8. 6
9. dismal science, Technological change
10. rule of seventy-two
11. rises, fewer, Fertility
12. efficient, marginal cost, increase
13. price
14. price system, higher, substitutes
15. commodities, Prebisch-Singer, immiserizing
16. property rights, takings
17. two-thirds, Heavily Indebted Poor Countries
18. 1944, quotas, United States, surveillance, financial assistance, moral hazard
19. grants, credits

500 CHAPTER 17

20. 10, private, government
21. fell, increased
22. efficient, shadow, surpluses, shortages, political
23. monetary
24. property
25. 100, inflation

TRUE/FALSE/EXPLAIN

1. False, The transition economies are the formerly communist countries such as Russia and the countries of Eastern Europe, and China.
2. True.
3. False, the problem is one of high population growth.
4. False, infrastructure is capital such as roads and schools.
5. True.
6. False, life expectancy in some countries is even less than 50.
7. True.
8. False, stage 1 is traditional society.
9. False.
10. False, world population was about 6 billion.
11. False, economics as the dismal science refers to Malthus' prediction of mass starvation.
12. False, it would take 24 years to double.
13. True.
14. False, the average number is typically less than 10 even in countries where fertility rates are high.
15. True.
16. False, a negative marginal cost promotes greater population growth.
17. False, the Prebisch-Singer thesis predicts that LDCs will export commodities, but remain mired in poverty.
18. False, immiserizing growth does not increase living standards.
19. False, but a few countries did experience negative growth during that period.
20. True.
21. True.
22. False, inflation was kept low because of monetary restraint, but the communist system collapsed for many other reasons, including the effects of the arms race of the 1980s
23. False, property rights were initially unclear.
24. False, the underground economy in Russia is quite large.
25. False, unemployment reached over 13 percent at one point.

MULTIPLE CHOICE

1. a
2. d
3. c
4. c
5. b
6. b
7. c
8. c
9. d
10. a
11. d
12. c
13. c
14. b
15. c
16. b
17. b
18. b
19. d
20. d
21. c
22. b
23. b
24. d
25. b

GRASPING THE GRAPHS
Examples of correct answers

1. Subsidies shift down the marginal cost to parents.
2. Demand = marginal benefit to parents.
3. Subsidies increased population growth.
4. Unsubsidized marginal cost
5. Population growth
6. "Unwanted children"

Visit the Ayers/Collinge companion Website at http://www.prenhall.com/ayers for further activities and exercises for this chapter.